SCHOLARS OF BYZANTIUM

SCHOLARS OF BYZANTIUM

N.G. Wilson

The Johns Hopkins University Press

Baltimore, Maryland

First published in Great Britain in 1983 by
Gerald Duckworth & Co. Ltd.
The Old Piano Factory
43 Gloucester Crescent, London NW1

First published in the United States of America in 1983 by
The Johns Hopkins University Press,
Baltimore, Maryland 21218

Library of Congress Cataloging in Publication Data

Wilson, Nigel Guy.
 Scholars of Byzantium.

 Includes bibliographical references and index.
 1. Classical philology – Study and teaching –
Byzantine Empire. 2. Byzantine Empire – Civilization.
I. Title.
PA78.B97W54 1983   001.2′09495   83-195
ISBN 0-8018-3052-4

Photoset in North Wales by
Derek Doyle & Associates, Mold, Clwyd,
and printed in Great Britain by
Unwin Brothers Limited, Woking

Contents

Preface   ix
Abbreviations   x

1. Introduction

(i)   Literary culture in Byzantium   1
(ii)   Atticism   4
(iii) The ancient authors and the Christians   8
(iv)   Censorship   12
(v)   The ancient authors as school texts   18

2. The Schools of Late Antiquity

(i)   Antioch   28
(ii)   Gaza   30
(iii) Scholia   33
(iv)   Athens   36
(v)   Alexandria   42
(vi)   Constantinople   49

3. Dark Ages and Iconoclasm

(i)   Interlude   61
(ii)   Two changes in production: paper and a new script   63
(iii) Fresh signs of activity   68

4. A New Start

(i)   Leo the Philosopher   79
(ii)   The evidence of manuscripts from *c*. 800 to *c*. 875   85

5. Photius

(i)   Introduction   89
(ii)   The *Lexicon*   90
(iii) The *Bibliotheca*   93
(iv)   The letters   111
(v)   The *Amphilochia*   114

6. Arethas

(i)   The extant manuscripts   120
(ii) Other texts   126
(iii) Arethas as a reader   130

7. From Arethas' Contemporaries to the End of the Tenth Century

(i)   The activity of copyists   136
(ii) Education and patronage   140
(iii) The *Suda*   145

8. The Eleventh Century

(i)   Introduction: the schools   148
(ii) John Mauropous   151
(iii) John Italos   153
(iv) Michael Psellos   156
(v)   Some critical essays on Christian authors   166
(vi) Response to the classics of pagan literature   172
(vii) The epitome of Dio Cassius   179

9. From Alexius Comnenus to the Fourth Crusade

(i)   The early years   180
(ii) Gregory of Corinth   184
(iii) The brothers Tzetzes   190
(iv) Eustathius   196
(v)   Michael Choniates   204
(vi) A mysterious partnership   206

10. Greek in Italy and Sicily

(i)   From late antiquity to the eleventh century   209
(ii) The twelfth century   212
(iii) An essay on a Greek novel   216

11. Disaster and Recovery

(i)   Nicaea   218
(ii) Gregory of Cyprus   223
(iii) Other evidence   225
(iv) A second glance westwards   226

12.   The Palaeologan Revival

(i)   Introduction   229
(ii)   Maximus Planudes   230
(iii) Some lesser contemporaries   241
(iv)   Other students of Greek poetry   244
(v)   Demetrius Triclinius   249
(vi)   Theodorus Metochites   256

13.   The Epigoni   265

Epilogue   273

Index   277

Preface

The style and arrangement of this book require a word of explanation. In the first place, since it describes a cultural process lasting for a millennium it may be thought to err on the side of brevity. A longer book could certainly have been written, but having collected material for nearly twenty years I knew that many more years would be needed for an exhaustive account, and decided that there was something to be said for a relatively brief synoptic treatment. The result will be more readable, and in view of the conclusions reached while writing it I do not think it very likely that a delayed longer version would have led to substantially different estimates of the value to be attached to the operations of Byzantine philologists. Secondly, the material in each chapter except the last, where the changing nature of the story to be told seemed to remove the need, has been divided into short sections. This is the method adopted in *Scribes and Scholars* (ed. 2, Oxford 1974), which seems to have found favour with readers, and I hope that its repetition here in a longer book will not lend too staccato a character to the narrative.

My account depends on two types of evidence, the writings of known scholars and manuscripts transcribed for readers who usually remained anonymous. In order to emphasise the importance of the manuscripts as primary sources I give their shelf-marks in the main body of the text. A number of very minor scholarly productions receive no mention. Their exclusion is conscious, but I do not flatter myself that my decisions will seem correct in all cases to all readers. I am aware that I have not analysed the work of the lexicographers, many of whom are anonymous, and it may be thought that they receive less attention than is their due. For this shortcoming I offer the partial defence that progress in the preparation of editions of the lexica has been very slow, so that it is far from easy to give even a moderately reliable sketch of the position.

I have been rather sparing with bibliographical references, believing that completeness in this regard is an academic habit greatly overvalued at present. (Up-to-date information of this kind is in any case available in Professor Hunger's excellent reference work *Die hochsprachliche profane Literatur der Byzantiner*.) Standard editions of texts are generally taken for granted. I have also saved space by not citing the catalogues which describe the manuscripts referred to. This has one admitted drawback; where my information differs in some way from what is published elsewhere, the reader must infer that I have examined the manuscript in question and silently corrected statements which no longer seem satisfactory in the light of modern knowledge.

It is a pleasant duty to thank the publisher for his enthusiastic support and rapid production of the book.

N.G.W.

Abbreviations

Abh	Abhandlungen
AJP	American Journal of Philology
AnalBoll	Analecta Bollandiana
BICS	Bulletin of the Institute of Classical Studies
BngrJ	Byzantinische-neugriechische Jahrbücher
ByzModGrStud	Byzantine and Modern Greek Studies
BZ	Byzantinische Zeitschrift
CAG	Commentaria in Aristotelem graeca
CatMssAlchGrecs	Catalogues des manuscrits alchimiques grecs
CP	Classical Philology
CQ	Classical Quarterly
CR	Classical Review
DOP	Dumbarton Oaks Papers
EEBS	Epeteris Hetaireias Byzantinon Spoudon
EC	Echos d'Orient
GGA	Göttingische Gelehrte Anzeigen
GRBS	Greek, Roman and Byzantine Studies
HSCP	Harvard Studies in Classical Philology
JHS	Journal of Hellenic Studies
JOB	Jahrbuch der Oesterreichischen Byzantinistik
JOBG	Jahrbuch der Oesterreichischen Byzantinischen Gesellschaft
NGG	Nachrichten der Gesellschaft der Wissenschaften in Göttingen
OrChrPer	Orientalia Christiana Periodica
ParPass	La Parola del Passato
PBSR	Papers of the British School at Rome
PCPS	Proceedings of the Cambridge Philological Society
PG	Patrologia graeca
PhW	Philologische Wochenschrift
RE	Realenzyklopädie
REB	Revue des études byzantines
REG	Revue des études grecques
RevHistTextes	Revue d'histoire des textes
RFIC	Rivista di filologia e d'istruzione classica
RhMus	Rheinisches Museum
SB	Sitzungsberichte
SCO	Studi classici e orientali
SIFC	Studi italiani di filologia classica
StudBizNeoell	Rivista di studi bizantini e neoellenici
TAPA	Transactions of the American Philological Association
VizVrem	Vizantiskij Vremennik
ZPE	Zeitschrift für Papyrologie und Epigraphik

1

Introduction

(i) Literary culture in Byzantium

This book is intended to give an account of what happened to Greek
literature from the end of the ancient world until the time of its
reappearance in western Europe during the Renaissance. The Byzantine
empire is usually, and for this purpose rightly, regarded as being
responsible for the preservation of a cultural inheritance. My object is to
explain why the Byzantines thought it worth while to act as they did and
how they set about their task. In order to do that it is necessary to begin
with an explanation of the importance they attached to literacy and
culture. But though most of the book will be concerned with scholarship in
the narrow definition of that term as the serious study of literary texts, it
would be a mistake to treat the writings of ancient Greece as if they
appealed to later ages for literary reasons only, and I have made an effort
not to leave out of account the philosophical and scientific writings of
antiquity. The latter, though often appealing only to a tiny group of
professional specialists, were nevertheless of great importance to them as
either the best or at least a by no means negligible source of practical
information.

The Byzantine empire is often thought of as an age of decline. Such a
view does not do justice to its distinctive qualities as the home of a new
style of art and as a civilising influence in eastern Europe. But there is a
sense in which it was obviously inferior to the empire that had once
controlled the whole Mediterranean area. In economic terms it was not
able to provide for the inhabitants of its towns and villages the standard of
living and amenities that had been enjoyed by the vast majority of the
citizens of the Roman empire. We may infer that one of the direct
consequences of the decline in standards was a reduction in the number of
people able to acquire an education. Although there is some evidence,
principally from lives of saints, that elementary education was widely
available, the impression must remain that literacy was less widespread
and the average level of culture less high than had been the case in the
ancient world.[1] It is hard to imagine, for instance, a Byzantine province

---

[1] Contrast the pictures given by R. Browning, 'Literacy in the Byzantine world', *Byz
ModGrStud* 4 (1978) 39-54 and F.D. Harvey, 'Literacy in the Athenian democracy', *REG* 79
(1966) 585-635.

producing evidence of readers with such diverse and learned interests as those proved by the finds of papyri from the country districts of Greco-Roman Egypt. From the reduced economic circumstances of the Byzantine empire it would be tempting to infer that the prospects for the survival of ancient Greek literature were poor, and that there would be little chance of it being the object of scholarly study. Certainly a great deal was lost, and it is impossible to deny that the Byzantines failed to save many texts that had come down to them. Publishing and the book trade in general were so much less well organised than they had been in antiquity that the use of these terms in a Byzantine context is scarcely legitimate. Photius in the ninth century, to name only the most obvious example, read many texts that ceased to be copied soon after. But although some blame must attach to the Byzantines, care should be taken not to allocate them too large a share of the responsibility. At least some of the texts read by Photius will have been lost in 1204 when Constantinople was destroyed by the Fourth Crusade, and there were almost certainly many other books that Photius had not been able to read because even the resources of the richer society of antiquity had failed to guarantee production in sufficient numbers of copies for them to survive the hazards of war and accidental destruction.

In view of their limited resources the Byzantines made a creditable effort to preserve a high standard of literary culture. As will become clear, they achieved what may be their greatest success at a time of economic and political decline in the late thirteenth and early fourteenth centuries. But at all times they maintained, even if only in a small section of their society, an intense interest in literature. One might suggest that though their cultural activities were confined to the few by economic circumstances, the intensity of activity was greater than at almost any time in antiquity itself. The Byzantines struggled against great odds to uphold their ideals, and these can be seen in various distinctive features of their society. The government required of its chief functionaries a good grounding in classical literature, and they attempted to display their culture in the documents drafted for public circulation by the excellence of their prose style and sometimes even by literary allusions. The government's expectations of candidates for employment in the top ranks of the civil service are made clear by an order of the emperor Constantius and his junior colleague Julian in 360 (*Theodosian Code* 14.1.1): 'No person shall obtain a post of the first rank unless it shall be proved that he excels in long practice of liberal studies, and that he is so polished in literary matters that words flow from his pen faultlessly.' Although this order may soon have been forgotten and does not appear to have been renewed by later emperors, in practice successive governments behaved as if it were still in force. The church authorities did the same. Bureaucrats were expected to achieve a very high standard of prose style in the documents that they drafted. On occasion they allowed their authorship to be known, and so it comes about that the collected works of an eminent man of letters may include the text of an imperial edict. There is one such (although it

may be a draft rather than an actual text, as it diverges in technical details
from the usual form) in the minor writings of Michael Psellos; it is a letter
sent by the emperor Michael VII Dukas Parapinakes in 1074 to Robert
Guiscard arranging a treaty on the occasion of the marriage between the
emperor's son Constantine and Robert's daughter Helen.[2] Psellos'
contemporary John Mauropous also included one in his collected works
(preserved in Vat. gr. 676); it is a draft, since certain figures are left
unspecified, of the famous decree of the emperor Constantine IX
Monomachus setting up the faculty of law *c.* 1045.[3] Documents of this
kind could be highly regarded as literary products because of the
importance generally attached to the preamble, in which it was common
for the author to expound some part of the official orthodoxy about the
emperor as the representative of God on earth. The circulation of these
documents was an important part of the government's propaganda
machine,[4] and the value of the preambles can also be detected in the fact
that there exist a number of collections of formulae put together either for
the benefit of newly appointed administrators or, perhaps more probably,
for use in secondary schools as part of the regular course in rhetoric
(Oxford, Barocci 131 and Heidelberg, Pal. gr. 356).

The enthusiasm of the administrators for a display of literary knowledge
could sometimes be overdone. A striking example occurs in a letter from
the emperor Alexios III to the republic of Genoa in 1199.[5] What could be
more inappropriate, in a letter addressed to a western city state, where the
knowledge of Greek was practically non-existent and all understanding of
ancient Greece was filtered through a limited number of Latin classics,
than to begin by saying: 'The dicta and sayings of the wise men of pagan
antiquity are not false but hit the mark regularly; for example their wise
poet Hesiod declared that a whole city reaps the benefit of an evil man',
which is a reference to a famous line in Hesiod's *Works and Days* (240)?
This is not the only example of literary knowledge being applied to the
tasks of diplomacy. A more striking case occurs in the career of Leo
Choerosphactes, who served as an envoy to the Bulgarians and the Arabs.
The first fourteen of his surviving letters, known from a single manuscript
(Patmos 178) as is often the case with works of Byzantine secular
literature, are his correspondence with the Bulgarian ruler Symeon. They
throw into sharp relief the combination of literacy and cunning with which
the Byzantines tackled political business. On his first mission in 896 Leo's
task was to secure the release of Byzantine prisoners of war. The
Bulgarian, knowing that the Byzantine emperor had been able to predict

[2] Ed. E. Kurtz & F. Drexl, *Michaelis Pselli scripta minora* I (Milan 1936) 329-34 (= F.
Dölger, *Regesten der Kaiserurkunden des oströmischen Reiches von 565-1453* (Munich
1924-65) no. 1003).

[3] Ed. A. Salač (Prague 1954) (=Dölger, *Regesten*, no. 863).

[4] H. Hunger, *Prooimion: Elemente der byzantinischen Kaiseridee in den Arengen der
Urkunden* (Vienna 1964) and R. Browning, *Notes on Byzantine Prooimia* (Vienna 1966).
They do not mention the quotation from Hesiod discussed below.

[5] Ed. F. Miklosich & J. Müller, *Acta et diplomata graeca medii aevi* (Vienna 1860-90)
vol. iii, 46-7 (= Dölger, *Regesten*, no. 1649).

an eclipse of the sun, challenged his envoy to predict whether the prisoners would be released. Faced with the delicate task of reading the thoughts of the enemy Leo rose to the occasion by drafting a letter[6] which included a complicated and ambiguous sentence on the point at issue. The ambiguity was created by an artificial order of words involving a negative and the fact, which becomes clear from the following letters, that the text, though a formal communication to a head of state, was not punctuated. The absence of punctuation is perhaps less surprising than it seems, since ninth-century manuscripts that have come down to us are not by any means fully punctuated. Symeon read the text in what he thought was the obvious way, declared that it failed to represent his thoughts, and declined to release the prisoners, while claiming that he had been willing to do so if the envoy had been able to read his thoughts correctly (letter 3). Leo replied (letter 4) by giving the Bulgarian a lesson in interpretation and punctuation, saying that his secretaries were not competent in the latter art. Symeon responded by a curt note (letter 5): 'I did not make a promise about the prisoners; I did not say anything to you; I will not send them back to you'. Leo was not defeated, but taking advantage of the absence of punctuation once again he managed to twist the meaning of the Bulgarian's letter as follows (letter 6): 'I did not fail to make you a promise about the prisoners [using two negatives to make a positive statement, as can be done in Greek]; I spoke to you about it; what is there that I shall not send back to you?' (transferring the indefinite pronoun 'anything' to the following clause and making it interrogative). Not content with this ingenious performance he followed it with another (letter 7), in which he tried to make out that the first clause of Symeon's note was to be taken as ironical. Despite the flimsiness of the arguments, which might well have been taken amiss and led to still cooler relations, the Bulgarian eventually agreed to the Byzantine request, for reasons which are not entirely clear.

(ii) Atticism

Popular belief has it that in ancient China the would-be administrator was examined by being shut in a room and told to write down everything that he knew. The same imaginary candidate in Byzantium would have been asked instead to write a piece of prose, in which he would not be required to show knowledge of anything except the Bible and classical texts that he had read at school, but whatever he wrote would have been subjected to close scrutiny to see if it conformed to the rules of the ideal Attic prose, the language of Athens in the fifth and fourth centuries B.C. The convention that formal prose must be couched in this archaic idiom went back to the early days of the Roman empire. At that date it probably indicated a conscious desire on the part of educated Greeks who regretted the reduced state of their country to restore dignity and self-respect by nostalgic imitation of the language that had been written in the days of their great

---

[6] No. 2 in the edition of G. Kolias (Athens 1939).

ancestors of classical Athens under Pericles and Demosthenes. It became the accepted fashion to neglect the spoken language, and instead to follow the style, syntax, and vocabulary of authors who had lived five hundred years earlier. Greek had not altered in those five hundred years as much as most other languages have in a comparable period, but the papyri recovered from Egypt and the books of the New Testament show that there had been simplifications in syntax and changes in vocabulary. The new fashion of Atticism, as it is conveniently termed, may well have surprised its unknown inventors by the welcome it received, and instead of being the passing vogue of a single generation it took root to such an extent that it lasted until the end of the Byzantine period and might be said, thanks to the efforts of Adamantios Korais (1743-1833) to purify the language, to have continued in a modified form up to modern times. This highly artificial idiom was even made the basis of the language spoken in the limited circle of the imperial court in the last days of Byzantium, if we can trust the testimony of the Italian Filelfo (1398-1481), who had lived in Constantinople during the years 1420-7.[1]

Imitation of a language that had never been less than half a millennium out of date was not entirely simple, and it was not long before means were devised to help the student who had to master it. The literature of the fifth and fourth centuries B.C. continued to be studied as intensively as before in schools, and lists of Attic words and expressions began to be compiled, as it was no longer possible for the self-respecting writer to permit himself the usages found in Hellenistic or more recent authors. A large number of lexicographical guides were composed for the aspiring writer. Several of them are still extant. Two of the earliest are by Pollux, who dedicated his bulky compilation to the future emperor Commodus between 166 and 176, and Phrynichus, a contemporary of Pollux, who, besides a much larger work now lost, put together a list of about four hundred expressions to be avoided by the careful author. Later, in the Byzantine period itself, similar compilations, some of them substantial, were still frequently produced. The last of any note is due to a fourteenth-century schoolmaster in Thessalonica, Thomas Magister.

The difficulties of accurate imitation are obvious, and whereas in its early days the fashion produced some writing of passable quality in such authors as Lucian (c. 120-after 180), almost all later Atticist writing needs only the most elementary analysis to show how superficial the imitation really is. What is more, the Byzantines themselves could not always follow easily texts composed in such a highly artificial language. The patriarch Nicephorus' *History* was couched in a style that caused one reader to gloss a number of the difficult words with more intelligible alternatives, and the biography of Nicephorus by Ignatius has many such glosses in the principal manuscript copy (Vat. gr. 1809).[2] Other factors might also have

[1] Filelfo, Letter in Book 9, dated Milan XV Kal. Mart. 1451, addressed to 'Sphortiae Secundo'.

[2] *Nicephori archiepiscopi Constantinopolitani opuscula historica*, ed. C. de Boor (Leipzig 1880) xvii f.

been expected to work against the continuation of the Atticist rules. If we are right in thinking that the achievements of classical Athens were the original inspiration, that motive could have disappeared in the time of the later Roman empire. The inhabitants of the eastern half of the empire called themselves Romans (*Rhomaioi*), they lived under Roman emperors, despite the division of the empire into two increasingly independent halves, and Rome rather than Athens was the source of their legal system and institutions. More important, but not as significant in its results as would be expected, was the adoption of Christianity as the official religion of the empire. As paganism gradually died out in the fourth and fifth centuries a reasonable man would have forecast that its literary classics would cease to dominate the school curriculum and consequently no longer serve as the criteria of good prose writing. The Bible was now well known to everyone; why should its language not become acceptable for all literary purposes? In fact it did become acceptable to some extent, as Christian writers permitted themselves a certain admixture of vocabulary culled from the New Testament and Septuagint. But despite that the majority never gave up the fiction that they were writing in imitation of Attic models. The texts that served as the models continued to be read in the schools. The effect of this unswerving dependence on, and general admiration of, ancient masters was precisely what would be expected. No writer had freedom to express himself in an individual style if he followed the rules strictly. The rhetorician Phoebammon asserted, but without citing any example in support of his case, that imitation could be reconciled with individual character.[3] The fact remains that few writers achieved more than a mediocre result. Byzantine literature remains as a whole unknown to the educated public of today because it is thought to contain no texts that will stand the test of being translated into a modern language for general circulation. In an eloquent passage about the decay of taste in Byzantium Gibbon remarked: 'Not a single composition of history, philosophy, or literature, has been saved from oblivion by the intrinsic beauties of style or sentiment, of original fancy, or even of successful imitation.'[4] One does not need to be an extravagant apologist to maintain that Gibbon exaggerated, and that the memoirs of Michael Psellos and the history written by Anna Comnena achieve a merit, despite their self-imposed stylistic handicap, that entitles them to the attention of a modern audience.

The great drawback for modern interpreters of Atticist texts is that the Byzantines' devotion to their models often led to obscurity of expression. Purists held that modern institutions had to be described in terms used by the classical authors. Foreign invaders from the north or east could therefore only be introduced into a formal historical narrative as Scythians or Mysians (a mistake for Moesians) or Persians, those nations being the invaders that the ancients had had to face from the areas in

---

[3] Ed. H. Rabe, *Prolegomenon sylloge* (Leipzig 1927) 382.1 ff.
[4] *Decline and Fall of the Roman Empire*, chapter 53, ed. J.B. Bury, vol. vi, 107.

question. Similarly with the terms, mostly Latin in origin, used to describe the running of the Byzantine state. In practice writers sometimes relaxed the rule or added a parenthesis in which the offending modern word was allowed to appear, so removing the ambiguity. But it is not always immediately clear what an author implies by this practice. The historian Procopius uses the technique of the explanatory parenthesis quite frequently, not only for the language of government but for references to Christianity. His apparent objectivity, implying a certain distance in the relation between himself and the church, has often been taken to show that his personal beliefs were agnostic. When the expressions in question are seen in the context of Atticist practice it becomes clear that there is no positive reason whatever for thinking Procopius anything other than an orthodox believer. It would of course have been convenient for a heretic or agnostic to use Atticist formulae; but no writer would have been suspected by the church authorities on that account. The same mistake has been made with regard to Procopius' younger contemporary Agathias, who continued his history.[5]

The Atticist writers held the field almost unchallenged. Only occasionally was a protest made against the conventions. The emperor Constantine Porphyrogenitus (907-59) announced in the preface to his *Book of Ceremonies* that he would use the simple style of ordinary speech, and his writings are not strictly Atticist. Another writer of similar outlook is the author of a treatise on siege machinery who has been thought to be one of the compilers of the encyclopaedia commissioned by the same emperor. After remarking that some of the technical terms found in the ancient texts are no longer current he asks that captious critics of phraseology, who look for an Attic composition and other stylistic merits, should not correct him for his ordinary and humble language, since clarity is the first requirement in all books about siege technique.[6] Quite unexpectedly he follows this request with a reference to Porphyry's *Life of Plotinus* (8) in which the biographer explains how his master when drafting his own writings attached no importance to calligraphy, word-division and orthography, but concentrated on the content. The quotation is recherché, and our anonymous author is far from writing the language of the man in the street. His protest is mild, and he had few sympathisers. But there is a small minority who avoid the temptation to archaise, and there is another hint of resistance to the prevailing fashion in the existence of a paraphrase of an Atticist work in a more popular style: the history by Nicetas Choniates (*c.* 1150-1213) exists in a fourteenth-century version which cannot be properly described as spoken Greek of the time but clearly represents an attempt to simplify the obscure and learned

---

[5] On the historians see Averil Cameron, *Agathias* (Oxford 1970) 75ff; for the more general question C. Mango, *Byzantine Literature as a Distorting Mirror* (Inaugural Lecture) (Oxford 1975).

[6] Ed. R. Schneider, *Abh. Göttingen* 11 (1908) part 1, p. 8 (= 200.14 ff); see also pp. 84-5 for the question of authorship.

language of an affected author. Yet the manuscripts of the paraphrase do not outnumber those of the genuine text.[7]

(iii)   The ancient authors and the Christians

The classical texts of pagan antiquity could not have kept their position in the school curriculum if there had been a concerted campaign by the church authorities to remove them. The curriculum did not in fact remain completely unchanged: study of the Psalms appears to have become part of it. It was, however, still fundamentally a collection of pagan books. Isolated expressions of hostility towards an alien and out-of-date culture are not hard to find in the church fathers. One striking example comes from the hymns of Romanos in the first half of the sixth century. Several classical authors are singled out for abuse. They include Homer, Plato, Demosthenes and Aratus. A series of untranslatable puns is used to cast scorn on the pagans, and it has been suggested that the attack is to be associated with the closure of the philosophical school in Athens by Justinian in 529. 'Why do the pagans delude themselves with Aratus the thrice-accursed (τὸν τρισκατάρατον)? Why do they wander aimlessly in the direction of Plato (πλανῶνται πρὸς Πλάτωνα)? Why do they love Demosthenes the weak (τὸν ἀσθενῆ)? Why do they not realise that Homer is an empty dream (ὄνειρον ἀργόν)?' Homer, Plato and Demosthenes were central school authors; so too in all probability was Aratus (c. 315-c. 240 B.C.), whose poem of a thousand hexameters on the constellations and the signs indicating good and bad weather was certainly very widely read at all times and was probably used as an elementary introduction to astronomy. Romanos continues: 'Why are they always talking of Pythagoras, who has been deservedly silenced?' There were no genuine works of Pythagoras, but perhaps Romanos is thinking of a forgery called the *Golden Verses*. Alternatively the attack on Pythagoras may have been provoked by his doctrine of the transmigration of souls, which elsewhere serves as a ground for abuse of the Manichaean heretics. It has also been noted that Pythagoras, along with Plato, is a target of Justinian's criticism. Romanos even makes cheap gibes at Galen and Hippocrates, asking them to compare their art with the miracles of healing performed in the Bible.[1]

While Romanos may have represented and reinforced the attitude of the man in the street, many highly placed members of the church fortunately took a more balanced view of the proper relation between the two cultures. The usual compromise position was that one should not refuse to exploit anything of value that could be found in the pagan authors. An influential exponent of this view in the first half of the eighth century was St. John Damascene. 'If we could glean something of value from the pagans, it is not one of the things forbidden to us. Let us be like honest bankers, piling

---

[7] H.G. Beck in *Byzantine Books and Bookmen, a Dumbarton Oaks colloquium* (Washington 1975) 54.

[1] P. Maas, *BZ* 15 (1906) 1-43, esp. 20-2 (= *Kleine Schriften* (Munich 1973) 288-306, esp. 308-9).

up genuine and pure currency, and rejecting the counterfeit. Let us accept their most noble writings, while casting their ridiculous gods and foreign myths to the dogs; for we can derive great strength from them.'[2] Elsewhere John cites Didymus the Blind (313-398), professor of exegesis in Alexandria, for a similar attitude of acquiescence in the study of grammar, rhetoric and philosophy because of the benefit that they bring in the skills of reading, forceful expression and convincing argument. There is an unspoken implication that pagan texts will be used for this purpose, and by a metaphor which may be thought a trifle less than felicitous grammar is compared to another man's wife.[3] As an Alexandrian Didymus had an illustrious predecessor who could be cited in case of need as a precedent for such views. Origen (*c*. 185-*c*. 255) had run a school in which the reading of classical literature was encouraged, with particular emphasis on the philosophers. The only exception was that authors who denied the existence of a deity or divine providence were to be avoided.[4] In passing it may be worth adding that Origen was notable for his adoption of one of the techniques of pagan scholarship: the system of critical signs which had been developed at Alexandria in the Hellenistic period by Zenodotus, Aristophanes of Byzantium and Aristarchus, and which gave helpful information to the scholarly reader somewhat akin to that nowadays given in the apparatus criticus of a learned edition, was taken over by Origen for his work on the text of the Old Testament. But probably the most influential of all the fathers who explicitly recommended a certain degree of acquaintance with the classics was St. Basil (330-379). His short essay on the subject addressed to his nephews was regularly transmitted with the corpus of his homilies, and though it has often been interpreted as offering no more than a grudging admission of the value of studying the ancient classics, even that view of his essay is sufficient to justify laying emphasis on it in the present context. In fact Basil does make it quite clear that there are valuable moral lessons to be learned from an attentive reading of pagan authors, and after giving some examples he begins his last chapter with a sentence that depends for its interpretation on the question whether Basil understood correctly one of the more subtle features of classical Attic, which on the whole he handled fairly competently, the use of a particle (πον). His text runs, if translated according to the rules of classical Attic: 'but these lessons, I imagine, we shall be able to learn more completely in our own literature too.' The expression of diffidence, which may not be more than a polite academic mannerism, is not the statement of a man who concedes unwillingly that there is some value in ancient literature.[5]

Statements of principle do not always match reality. A better proof of the tolerance extended to the classics is to be sought in the conduct of individuals. The books read by the average schoolchild did not change

---

[2] *De fide orthodoxa*, *PG* 94.1177B (p. 210 in the ed. of B. Kotter (Berlin 1973)).
[3] *PG* 96.344AB.
[4] St. Gregory Thaumaturgus, *PG* 10.1088A, 1093A.
[5] *St. Basil on the Value of Greek Literature*, ed. N.G. Wilson (London 1975) 10.

much when the master became a Christian instead of a pagan. Only once, so far as is known, and then in exceptional circumstances which we shall have occasion to notice again, was there a deliberate attempt to substitute Christian books for pagan. Julian's persecution of the Christians in 362 led to a reaction, and Apollinaris (*c.* 310-*c.* 390), collaborating with his father, tried to draw up an entirely Christian curriculum.[6] Homer was replaced by a paraphrase of the Psalms in hexameters of pseudo-Homeric style, and the historical books of the Bible were converted into the iambic verse of Greek tragedy. There is some evidence that hexameter paraphrases had been attempted before on a small scale.[7] What is more curious is the report that Apollinaris recast the Gospels and Epistles in the form of Platonic dialogues. The implication would appear to be that notwithstanding his religious scruples he felt the need to maintain the tradition of Atticist style, or that he was determined to make the New Testament attractive to pagans who thought it stylistically beneath their notice. The second interpretation may receive some indirect confirmation from St. Jerome's famous remark about St. Luke's style being superior to that of the other evangelists because he was a doctor and writing for the Greeks.[8] But Apollinaris' revolt against educational practices soon gave way to a more traditional inertia. The threat from paganism receded when Julian was killed in Persia. A paraphrase of the Psalms, whose authenticity is not generally accepted, still exists, and the other works have been lost. Apollinaris was forgotten, his disappearance perhaps assisted by a lapse into heresy. The fact remains that the Christians did not have a literature capable of providing a full syllabus of texts to replace the conventional pattern of education. Julian struck a shrewd blow by forbidding Christians to teach the classics. Christian parents would have to see their children taught by unbelievers or receive very little education. Many realised that there was something to be lost by abandoning the texts that had educated Greeks for hundreds of years. The Greek philosophers themselves provided much of the material required in order to refute the follies of pagan religion or the objectionable views of immoral groups such as the Epicureans. It was not felt to be necessary to censor the texts where they conflicted openly with Christian thought or the more prudish tastes encouraged by the new religion. In some difficult cases the device of allegorical interpretation could be brought into use. Not that this was a novelty: it seems to have been developed originally by a certain Theagenes of Rhegion as far back as the sixth century B.C. in order to avoid a literal interpretation of passages in Homer which gave an unflattering picture of the gods. The method was not just a passing fashion, but was taken up later by the Stoics, and there still exists a short pamphlet under the name of Heraclitus which explains the allegorical significance of many passages

[6] Socrates, *Hist. eccl.* 3. 6. Sozomen, *Hist. eccl.* 5.18 gives a slightly different and less plausible account.
[7] K. Thraede, *Reallexikon für Antike und Christentum* s.v. Epos, 5 (1962) 999. Scepticism about the truth of the story seems unnecessary.
[8] Letter 19.38.

of Homer. As the Christians themselves were adepts at explaining their own books in the same way, they could readily understand it as a means of making pagan texts acceptable.

As long as paganism retained some appeal to the educated classes, pagans and Christians were often to be found working together on good terms. A Christian professor of rhetoric would not exclude a pagan from his classes. In the fourth century at Athens Prohaeresius lectured to and was admired by his pagan student Eunapius. Nor did the member of the church avoid pagan instructors: St. Gregory of Nazianzus went not only to Prohaeresius but also to the pagan Himerius. St. Basil studied with Libanius, the leading professor of rhetoric of his day and well known as a pagan, and the surviving correspondence of the two men, often suspected of being a forgery, is now thought to be for the most part authentic.[9] St. Gregory of Nyssa, on receiving a request from Stageirius, who was probably a pagan teaching at Caesarea in Cappadocia, for timber to roof his house, replied wittily with literary allusions which would be a still more impressive display of classical culture if his correspondent were a fellow Christian. He takes up the use of a very rare word applied to him by Stageirius and suggests, wrongly so far as we are able to tell, that it was culled from Plato; but then he says that he will give the timber required in the form of beams 'which in the language of your favourite poet Homer cast long shadows; and since you make much of the Persian Wars in your studies, I will give you as many as the number of soldiers that fought at Thermopylae'.[10] Rather later, in the school at Gaza in the late fifth and early sixth century, both the literatures were studied together. At much the same time we find a good example of the value that Christians attached to a traditional education. Zacharias Scholasticus postponed the start of his study of law for a year in order to improve his knowledge of literature, and it is specifically stated that his motive was to demonstrate to pagans that Christians could achieve an equally high standard in the field that pagans tended to regard as their own preserve.[11] Even more telling is an episode in the doctrinal controversy between St. Gregory of Nyssa and Eunomius in the late fourth century. Gregory sent a draft of his polemic to two pupils of Libanius, asking them to bring it to the attention of their master, and Gregory clearly thinks it important to obtain the famous critic's approval of his style, even though the work is addressed exclusively to a Christian audience.[12] Finally we may note that the most famous of all the Greek fathers, St. John Chrysostom, is reported by one of the church historians to have been a student of Libanius. The report is backed up by the inference that certain passages in one of the saint's early works are best

[9] P. Maas, *SB Berlin* 1912, 1117-9 (the second part of a paper inexplicably omitted from his *Kleine Schriften*). Cf. also Greg. Nyss. *ep.* 13.

[10] P. Maas, ibid. 993.

[11] *Vie de Sévère*, ed. M.A. Kugener, *Patrologia Orientalis* 2 (Paris 1907) 46.

[12] Letter 15, ed. G. Pasquali, and cf. P. Maas, *BZ* 26 (1926) 380.

explained if they can be treated as deriving from Libanius.[13]

(iv) Censorship

Despite the tolerant and indeed often respectful attitude of the Christians towards pagan culture under the late Roman empire it has sometimes been suggested, and the idea is intrinsically plausible, that a form of censorship operated in the middle ages, to the detriment of pagan authors whose ideas were unacceptable to the ecclesiastical authorities. Such a censorship rarely if ever existed, and more than one pagan whose views gave offence to the church nevertheless survived. Even the apostate Julian, a regular target of pious abuse, withstood the attacks, one of which is recorded in a manuscript now in Vienna (hist. gr. 45): 'at this point in the book there were thirteen leaves containing works by the apostate Julian; the abbot of the monastery of St. John the Baptist read them and realised that they were dangerous, so he threw them into the sea.'[1] A copyist who had to transcribe Julian's oration on the sun noted that it was full of Greek impiety and nonsense, but also full of rhetoric and artistic forcefulness (Marc. gr. 436).[2] The doubts and difficulties of such readers did not cause these controversial writings to disappear, and the letters in particular continued to be read fairly widely, since they formed part of various collections that circulated as models of prose style. Another writer capable of moving the Byzantines to anger was Lucian, whose occasional scornful comments on the early Christians earned him equally scornful epithets from the orthodox reader. The ancient and medieval commentaries on his essays are found to contain no less than thirty-nine terms of abuse directed against him.[3] Yet the essays remained firm favourites with Byzantine readers of all periods. The idea that the church at an early stage of its history determined to censor or destroy classical poetry, which can be traced back to the Venetian humanist Pietro Alcionio (1486-1527), is also unfounded. Many papyri have now been found which belong to the fourth century or later and contain classical poetry. Greek tragedy, Aristophanes, Callimachus and even Sappho were still being copied in Egypt in the sixth and seventh centuries,[4] by which time the church might have been expected to enforce an illiberal policy if it had one. There is no reason to think that these papyri are fragments of books surreptitiously copied by a few remaining crypto-pagans, and the subsequent disappearance of some

---

[13] Socrates, *Hist. eccl.* 4.26, 6.3. C. Fabricius, *Zu den Jugendschriften des Johannes Chrysostomus* (Lund 1962) 22 n.1, 119-21. See further in general I. Ševčenko in K. Weitzmann (ed.), *Age of spirituality: a symposium* (New York 1980) 53-73.

[1] C. Van der Vorst & H. Delehaye, *Catalogus codicum hagiographicorum graecorum Germaniae Belgi Angliae (Subsidia Hagiographica* 13) (Brussels 1913) 55-6.

[2] J. Bidez, *La tradition manuscrite et les éditions des discours de l'empereur Julien* (Gent-Paris 1929) 68.

[3] H. Rabe, *Scholia in Lucianum* (Leipzig 1906) 336.

[4] Aristophanes is represented by a Louvre papyrus of the *Birds* and P. Strasb. 621 of the *Clouds*; Callimachus by P. Oxy. 2258; Sappho by P. Berol. 5006; Sophocles by P. Ant. 72; Euripides by P. Berol. 5005 of the *Helen* and several others.

authors must be ascribed to other factors, such as the loss of a place in the school curriculum or the reduction of the number of texts surviving in an age of civil war or foreign invasion.

There was, however, one classical author capable of leading his admirers into difficulty. Plato's views on certain issues were in conflict with those of the Church, and even such a great student of the Bible as Origen was condemned on account of his undue adherence to Platonic doctrine, as a result of which a good many of his writings, though perhaps never burned or formally forbidden, have not come down to us. Some Neoplatonists found it necessary or tactful to come to an agreement with the church whereby they were able to continue teaching in return for an undertaking to tone down the anti-Christian element in their philosophical system. In the middle Byzantine period there was a famous episode involving the study of Plato. John Italos, a pupil of the powerful intellectual and statesman Michael Psellos, who had succeeded his master in the post of professor of philosophy, became so enthusiastic a supporter of Plato's philosophy that orthodox churchmen were alarmed, and in due course a formal condemnation was issued in 1082. The unfortunate John Italos disappears from view, but the works of Plato were not heaped on a ceremonial bonfire, nor have the philosophical essays of Italos disappeared without trace. Instead anathemas were pronounced, and ordered to be included in the liturgy for Orthodoxy Sunday, the first in Lent, against those who believe in pagan ideas about the soul and the creation of the world, also those who accept the Platonic theory of ideas and those who study pagan literature for any purposes not purely educational.[5] The notion of education implicit in this saving clause is typical of Byzantium; the literary study of the ancient authors does not commit one to acceptance of their views, nor does the falsehood of their views on many questions disqualify them from being suitable material for a school syllabus.

One other episode from the eleventh century needs to be mentioned here. In his denunciation of the patriarch Michael Cerularius, given in 1058 or 1059, Psellos refers briefly and obscurely to an order requiring that the works of Porphyry (232/3-c.305) should be burned. Psellos alleges that the patriarch rescued half-burnt copies and introduced notions from them into his own writings, so becoming a second Porphyry and deserving the same treatment. While the third-century philosopher's introduction to Aristotle's *Categories* had an unassailable position as a school textbook, not all that he wrote was so acceptable. He had attacked Christianity and written extensively on Platonism. Psellos suggests that an essay on demonology may have been the immediate cause of offence.[6]

Although there is no sign that texts of Plato ceased to be copied, it may be significant that a writer called Isaac Sebastocrator, who may be the brother of the emperor Alexius I Comnenus (1081-1118) and in that case

---

[5] The text is edited and discussed by J. Gouillard, *Travaux et mémoires* 2 (1967); see especially 57-61 (lines 214 ff, 218 ff) and 188-94.

[6] E. Kurtz & F. Drexl, *Michaelis Pselli scripta minora* I (Milan 1936) 267.

was perhaps writing while the condemnation of Italos was still
remembered by many people, evidently felt the need to take precautions
in drafting his work on the nature of evil. He deals with a large number of
arguments drawn from Plato and the late Neoplatonist Proclus (412-
485), but it has been observed that he avoids using material from Proclus
which is Neoplatonic and cannot be reconciled with Christian thinking,
while he contrives not to mention Plato by name, citing instead as his
source whenever possible pseudo-Dionysius the Areopagite.[7]

In matters of doctrine the church naturally did exercise control, and in
the twelfth century it is possible to see three instances of that control
being imposed firmly. The first occurred in 1117 and involved Eustratius,
the metropolitan of Nicea, who had been implicated in the affair of Italos
in 1082 when he was no more than a deacon, but had managed to
extricate himself. As metropolitan he found himself conducting some
delicate negotiations with the Armenians over their view of the human
nature of Christ, in which certain works of St. Cyril of Alexandria had
been useful to him. Some heretical propositions outlined in these works
began to circulate, and the orthodox were disturbed. An order was issued
that the texts of Cyril should be surrendered and all the copies handed in
to the patriarchate within thirty days to be burnt. But Eustratius
survived this episode, and his commentaries on Aristotle's *Nicomachean
Ethics* and *Analytica posteriora* have come down to us. In 1140 it came to
the notice of the patriarch that a monk had composed some heretical
writings which were beginning to circulate; after a search three copies
were obtained by the authorities and burnt. And in 1157 a certain
Soterichos Panteugenos got himself into trouble, perhaps by a false
interpretation of St. John 17:19, from Jesus' prayer for the church, 'And
for their sake I consecrate myself, that they also may be consecrated in
truth.' He was declared by a synod to be unfit to hold any position in the
church. But it is noticeable that there is no known case of an attempt to
burn copies of pagan authors, and this treatment seems to have been
reserved by the church authorities for the works of heretics.[8] There are
only two or three occasions which appear to constitute exceptions to the
rule. The first occurred in the reign of the emperor Jovianus (363-4),
when a temple in Antioch built by Hadrian in honour of Trajan and
recently converted by Julian the apostate into a library was deliberately
burnt. Our source for this information is an obscure and not necessarily
reliable article on Jovianus in the Suda lexicon (I 401), but it should
perhaps be accepted as essentially correct, since a desire for revenge after
the events of Julian's reign might be expected to lead to acts of
extremism. A second and less certain instance arises out of the report of
the untrustworthy chronicler Malalas who says that late in Justinian's

---

[7] See H. Boese, *Procli tria opuscula* (Berlin 1960) xxii-xxiii and J.J. Rizzo, *Isaac
Sebastocrator περὶ τῆς τῶν κακῶν ὑποστάσεως (De malorum subsistentia)* (Meisenheim
am Glan 1971) ix.xi..

[8] The ecclesiastical documents in question are nos. 1003, 1007 and 1041 in V. Grumel,
Regestes des actes du patriarcat de Constantinople, fasc. 3 (Istanbul 1947).

reign some pagans were arrested and their books burnt.[9] The third case barely falls within the chronological limits of the present study: *c.* 1460 the major work of the Platonist philosopher George Gemistos Plethon (1355-1452), the *Laws*, was burnt by the patriarch Gennadios (George) Scholarios to whom it had been sent for inspection, on the ground that it was an attempt to restore the pagan religion of classical antiquity. Here it is the alleged attempt to set up a rival faith, not the interest in the ancient world as such, that led to the destruction of the book. A certain amount of it still survives, having been copied as excerpts by friends of the author before the master copy was sent to the patriarch.

A consistent policy of destruction of every text that failed to meet the requirement of impeccable orthodoxy cannot be traced in Byzantium. The church may have realised that it would in any case be difficult to enforce. It did take one measure to discourage the spread of unsound theology: texts that met with official disapproval appear to have been kept in a special chest in the patriarchate and released only to suitable persons. The special chest is recorded by patriarch Germanos I (d. 733).[10] The lack of evidence about many features of Byzantine life is so severe that its occurrence in this sole source may be due to chance, and there is a hint of the same method of limiting access to undesirable literature in the sixth-century writer Leontius of Byzantium.[11] He wanted to read Theodore of Mopsuestia, a biblical commentator of the so-called school of Antioch (*c.* 350-428), and remarks: 'We have only just been able, with great trouble and innumerable ingenious devices, to find his book against the incarnation of Christ, because they are very cautious in their manner of releasing it to the uninitiated.' The persons in question are not identified, but it is hard to avoid the inference that Leontius had gone to the patriarch's office and been refused access, at least initially, to the supposedly dangerous writings of Theodore. Leontius goes on to invite the reader, if he has leisure and inclination, to look over Theodore's other books, as they too may contain statements on the same topic.

Censorship can be exercised in other ways. Books may be allowed to circulate in versions that their authors would not have approved of. In 1573 Pope Gregory XIII authorised a new edition of Boccaccio's *Decameron* revised according to the principles laid down by the Council of Trent: the Italian monk and abbot of I.4 were transmuted into a student of Paris and his master, and there were other such substitutions, besides some omissions. This publication contrasts interestingly with the reform of the Julian calendar approved by the same Pope nine years later. In 1818 Thomas Bowdler anticipated the attitudes that became characteristic of Victorian England by publishing an edition of Shakespeare in which 'those words and expressions are omitted which cannot with propriety be read aloud in a family'. He also dealt with

[9] Malalas 491.18-20, referring to 559 or 562; cf. H. Stein, *Histoire du Bas-Empire* (Paris 1949-59) 799-800.

[10] *PG* 98.53A.

[11] *PG* 86.1384.

Gibbon's *Decline and Fall of the Roman Empire* in the same way. Classical literature contains many passages that would not, at least until very recently, have been thought acceptable in texts that were a regular part of a school syllabus, and it would not be surprising if there were signs of tampering with them, either at the instigation of high authority or because individuals took it upon themselves to remove or tone down the offending passages. One obvious target for such operations would be Aristophanes, but so far no manuscript of his plays has been reported as offering a text that has been subjected to alterations of this kind. It is theoretically possible that a number of late manuscripts of classical authors, copied in the fourteenth century or later and not yet investigated in detail, will reveal bowdlerised texts, but the number that have come to light hitherto is so small that we are entitled to say that there was very little attempt to remove obscene or objectionable language. One interesting isolated case is the chapter of Herodotus which reports the custom of sacred prostitution in Babylon (1.199). It is missing from a group of four manuscripts, three of which are late enough to have been influenced by the work of Maximus Planudes, of whom there will be more to say in a moment (Vat. gr. 123, Emmanuel College Cambridge 30 and Vienna, hist. gr. 85). But the fourth member of the group is of the late tenth or early eleventh century (Vat. gr. 2369), and lacks the text of 1.197.1-205.2. According to C. Hude in the preface to his edition[12] two folios have fallen out, and if that is correct there will have been ample room for them to include the chapter in question. In that case the omission might be due to Planudes, but on a closer investigation of the manuscript it turns out that only one folio has fallen out. The quires were regularly constituted of eight leaves and one of them has lost its last leaf, which would have accommodated the text exactly on the assumption that chapter 199 was already missing, whereas the supposition of a second lost folio cannot be reconciled with these calculations. Consequently we are unable to say exactly when the chapter was censored.

A similar uncertainty concerns a passage of the speech against Neaira in the corpus of Demosthenes' orations which is not regarded as genuine.[13] The manuscripts of Demosthenes omit an expression describing the courtesan's sexual deviations, but the rhetorician Hermogenes cites it as an example of language too vulgar to be tolerated (*De ideis* II p. 325 Rabe). Ancient critics had for centuries used, often with very slender support, the argument that an improper word or passage was unworthy of the author and should not be accepted as genuine. They did not, however, delete such passages from the text, contenting themselves by marking the offending passage with a special sign in the margin. But at some stage the phrase about Neaira did disappear. It was still read by Procopius, who borrowed it in his *Secret History* (9.18) for his account of the conduct of the empress Theodora.

---

[12] Ed. 3 (Oxford 1927) vi. See also *Antike und Abendland* 16 (1970) 73.
[13] R. Kassel, *RhMus* 116 (1973) 104-5.

Gibbon, who thought it proper to leave this passage 'in the obscurity of a learned language',[14] nevertheless paraphrased the implication of the objectionable words by the remark: 'She wished for a fourth altar on which she might pour libations to the god of love.' This example of apparent censorship in the tradition of the Demosthenic corpus is a famous but isolated case, and though we have included it here it is only proper to conclude by noting that there is at least a chance that Procopius knew the phrase from his study of Hermogenes, a prescribed school author, rather than direct acquaintance with Demosthenes, and that Hermogenes himself committed an error in attributing the phrase to the Neaira speech. In addition, if the attribution is accepted as valid, it is still uncertain whether the deletion had already taken place in manuscripts other than those known to Procopius or is due to prudish scribes of a later date who noted Hermogenes' comment and took the additional step of removing the words from the text.

In view of what has been said above about the church's objections to some features of Plato's thought it is not surprising to find that his text was sometimes adjusted. One passage of the *Phaedo* is especially famous. Where Plato had said (114c3) that the souls of those who have purified themselves sufficiently through philosophy live for ever without being reincarnated (ἄνευ σωμάτων), the church historian Eusebius (*c.* 260-340), wishing to adjust Plato's statement to coincide with the Christian doctrine of resurrection, altered the text so as to make Plato say that the souls live 'without trouble' (ἄνευ καμάτων).[15]

But on the whole texts were treated with respect. The one significant exception is provided by Maximus Planudes (1255-1305), who tells us that in preparing a new edition of the *Greek Anthology* he decided to omit a number of erotic poems as obscene. A note to this effect can be read in his autograph (Marc. gr. 481, dated 1299). If he interfered with a text which did not by any means certainly belong to those that he read in class with his pupils, one may reasonably ask whether there is any sign of his altering others with a similar intention. Some suspicion attaches to him on account of his translations of Ovid into Greek. His version of the *Heroides* is admittedly free from deliberate alteration. But there is also a version of Ovid's love poems, known to us only in the form of excerpts, and although it is not specifically attributed to Planudes by the manuscript (Naples II C 32), it is very difficult to imagine anyone apart from Planudes or one of his pupils as the author of it, because a knowledge of Latin was extremely rare, in practice confined to a tiny group of lawyers and interpreters who would almost certainly have found Ovid bizarre and frivolous. The version of the amatory poems is full of

---

[14] Colin Haycraft kindly points out to me that though this phrase is usually cited (for instance in the last two editions of the *Oxford Dictionary of Quotations*) as 'the decent obscurity of a learned language', 'decent' is not in Gibbon's text either in his description of Theodora or in his autobiography (p. 193 in Bonnard's edition).

[15] *Praep. Evang.* 13.16.10. See also P. Canivet, *Histoire d'une entreprise apologétique au Ve siècle* (Paris 1958) 147 ff, for a number of other, mostly less drastic, examples.

petty bowdlerisation. Here are some renderings: *amor, τόδε τὸ πρᾶγμα* :
Venus, τὸ ἔργον: *puella, ὁ φίλος*: *puellae, οἱ ἄνθρωποι*: *cultissima
femina, τὸ πλῆθος* . One would like to think that Planudes, whose other
activities were far from contemptible, did not descend to censorship of
this type, and it is possible that the alterations should be put down to the
unidentified excerptor.[16]

The final example is rather different, and concerns three of the essays
in Plutarch's *Moralia*. There is a small group of manuscripts which
presents a text that has been tampered with, and as all the manuscripts
in question are late enough to be subject to the influence of Planudes and
his circle it is tempting to suspect that he has been at work here too.
However, his other work on Plutarch, which was very extensive, does not
show any sign of such activity, and it is better to direct our suspicions at
some unidentified pupil once again. The nature of the alterations is not
so simple in this case. Although there are a certain number made for the
usual purpose of toning down a text that seemed objectionable, others
have the effect of adjusting the phrasing so that it conforms to the rules
for the rhythm in the final syllables of a clause. Byzantine writers, who
were operating with a language that had a well marked stress, liked to
end a clause if possible in such a way that there was an even number of
unstressed syllables between the last two stressed syllables. It is rather
strange that this rule, which had come into fashion in the fourth century
in the writings of the sophist Himerius (310-390) and remained valid
throughout the period, did not lead more often to alteration of Greek
prose texts, but this is the sole example so far reported. It can be taken as
a striking proof that the Byzantines very rarely had the courage to make
what they might have seen as improvements in the text of the classics.[17]

(v)   The ancient authors as school texts

It is now time to attempt to describe the school curriculum of late
antiquity and the middle ages. In the absence of writings by educational
theorists which deal with this topic – there is no Greek text analogous to
Cassiodorus' *Institutiones* – we are forced to make inferences from
passing remarks by various authors and from the relative frequency with
which texts appear in the surviving copies. The argument from frequency
is based on the assumption that certainly in the middle ages and
probably in antiquity economic resources did not permit mass
production of texts that were not in regular use in the schools. For most
of antiquity the four central authors were Homer, with a strong
preference for the *Iliad* over the *Odyssey*, Euripides, Menander and
Demosthenes. A survey of the papyri recovered from Egypt (the small

[16] The text is edited by P.E. Easterling & E.J. Kenney, *Ovidiana graeca* (Cambridge
1965); see also Kenney in *Hermes* 91 (1963) 213-27.

[17] On the MSS of Plutarch in question see M. Pohlenz, *NGG* (1913) 388ff, esp. 342 f. One
of the bowdlerising corrections is cited in L.D. Reynolds & N.G. Wilson, *Scribes and
Scholars* (ed. 2. Oxford 1974) 211.

number recovered from elsewhere would not alter the picture seriously) gives the following figures for those authors: Homer 590 (*Iliad* 454, *Odyssey* 136), Euripides 75, Menander 27 and Demosthenes 83.[1] The dominance of Homer is astonishing, and one wonders if many pupils did not proceed further with education than was necessary to acquire the rudiments through the study of this single text. The low figure for Menander needs an explanation; he may have been less popular in some provinces of the empire than others, but at all events it is clear from the frequency with which he is quoted that he must have been read quite often in schools. Other authors were not excluded from the syllabus. The papyri suggest that Hesiod must have been one of them; there are 74 known papyri. Callimachus was also popular, and Plato, Isocrates, Thucydides and Pindar are by no means rare. It is beyond doubt that the other tragedians and Aristophanes also had a place.

Literary education preceded rhetoric and philosophy, but the order in which the books and topics were tackled is not clear, and indeed it is not certain that there was a generally agreed order. We occasionally get a glimpse of school-room practice. In the life of Thucydides by Marcellinus, who has been thought to be as late as the sixth century, it is made clear that the pupils are introduced to this author after they have been initiated into the works of Demosthenes. But on the whole we are ignorant of these matters. The central government, while taking an interest in the literary polish of recruits for its service, made no effort to legislate about details of their studies. On the other hand, since the writings of the authors normally read amounted to an extremely bulky corpus, far greater than could possibly be adopted as a syllabus by the most ambitious school, it was essential to make a selection of texts. At one time it was believed that the selection was made by an enterprising master in the second century A.D., and the popularity of his choice led to general neglect of other texts, so that they ceased to be copied except occasionally by a learned reader, and the occasional copies were not numerous enough to withstand the hazards to which a manuscript tradition is subjected. This account of the process by which Greek literature survived as it did has a good deal to commend it. In Byzantine times the schools used a selection of texts that can be described as a standard syllabus. There is nothing absurd in the idea that the selection is a product of late antiquity. But no plausible suggestion has ever been made about the identity of the master responsible for the choice, and the papyri written later than the second century make it likely that the new syllabus, if it was invented at the date suggested, was not generally adopted at once. A more gradual process, by which a consensus was created among the teachers about the choice of texts best suited for use in the classroom, is an equally possible explanation of the facts.

Adoption of a text was almost a guarantee that it would survive. Among the authors mentioned above there are two who

[1] On the papyri see W.H. Willis, *GRBS* 9 (1968) 205-41; on the standard authors H.-I. Marrou, *Histoire de l'éducation dans l'antiquité* (ed. 6, Paris 1965) 248.

fail to confirm the rule. Menander, although greatly prized for his subtle characterisation and therefore valuable, as was realised by the leading Roman writer on education Quintilian (10.1. 69-71), for the student of the art of public speaking, nevertheless disappeared from the curriculum, and the last trace of his text in circulation is probably to be found in the letters of the historian and rhetorician Theophylactus Simocatta *c.* 600.[2] Aristophanes seems to have gained ground at his expense, if the papyri are a safe guide in this case, in the fourth century and later. The reasons for the change of taste are uncertain; Aristophanes was harder linguistically and required a good deal of historical commentary if he was to be fully understood, and it is difficult to dismiss the suspicion that those were reasons which weighed with teachers anxious to make pupils work hard at their texts. It would require a very optimistic view of the cultural standards of late antiquity to accept instead the explanation offered by Matthew Arnold in his inaugural lecture as professor of poetry at Oxford in 1857: 'The instinct of humanity taught it, that in the one poetry there was the seed of life, in the other poetry the seed of death; and it has rescued Aristophanes, while it has left Menander to his fate.' Callimachus nearly suffered the same fate as Menander; his *Hymns* survived and were perhaps part of the school reading list. His popularity among the papyri, which have almost all been found in Egypt, may be explained by a special factor: he could be thought of as an Egyptian and accorded special favour for that reason, while enjoying a less privileged status elsewhere. The power of the schools to influence the fate of texts is clear: Menander and Callimachus are the two major authors of whom our knowledge has been transformed by the discovery of papyri. Scientific texts had a good chance of being preserved if they were still a source of useful information to specialists. Philosophical texts were required for study in institutions of higher learning. Literature needed the protection of the schoolroom. Exceptions can be found to this rule, but it is fair to say that a work of the classical or Hellenistic period which did not have this protection was very much less likely to be preserved, and the known cases should be thought of as the result of extraordinary chances. The best example is the conservation of ten plays of Euripides known as the alphabetic series because they appear to be part of an ancient collection of his works arranged in that order. Apart from that there are few striking discrepancies between the literary texts read in the ancient schoolroom and what is available for us to read today. The others disappeared gradually; some were perhaps no longer available at the end of antiquity, while others, including a large number of historical writings, could still be read in the ninth century and possibly later.

In the medieval west the curriculum was organised in the system known as the trivium and quadrivium, the first part consisting of grammar, rhetoric and logic, the second of music, geometry, arithmetic

---

[2] J.-M. Jacques, *Bulletin de l'association G. Budé* (1959) 200-15.

and astronomy. The same was true in Byzantium. Ultimately this concept of education goes back to classical Greece, as the seven constituents are named as the interests of the sophist Hippias. When and by whom they were first formally constituted as the proper elements of a liberal education is less clear: the consensus of opinion favours a date *c.* 100 B.C., between the time of the Greek grammarian Dionysius Thrax (*c.* 170 B.C.-*c.* 90 B.C.) and the Roman polymath Varro (116-27 B.C.).[3] It should also be mentioned that the four topics of the quadrivium are discussed as a group in the introduction to mathematics by Nicomachus of Gerasa (between A.D. 50 and 150). In the Greek schools of late antiquity the seven liberal arts were probably recognised as such, but it is hard to find evidence of their arrangement in a systematic programme. The formulation of the trivium and quadrivium in the west goes back to Boethius (*Inst. arithm.* 5.6) and may depend on Roman practice or personal experience of the system in the east. System, however, is not necessarily the correct word to use in referring to a liberal education in either east or west. When the statutes of the university of Paris were drawn up in 1215, the statement of the syllabus indicated a predominance of dialectic over all the other liberal arts.[4]

We should not be surprised to find a similar situation in Byzantium, where there is a reference to the quadrivium (*tetraktus*) as early as the eighth century, in Ignatius' life of patriarch Nicephorus.[5] The biography of St. Cyril who converted the Slavs to Christianity reports that it was necessary for the saint to go to Constantinople in order to obtain higher education, and the subjects he studied are listed in a way which clearly indicates an organisation along the lines of trivium and quadrivium, the only variation in the list being that grammar is represented simply by Homer.[6] There is a treatise written in A.D. 1008, formerly ascribed to Michael Psellos because the date of composition was not correctly understood, which consists of an elementary handbook to five of the seven liberal arts, grammar and rhetoric being left out.[7] The omission is probably to be taken as an indication that those were the first two subjects mastered by the average pupil, and that the author is not concerned with them. The opening words of the text make clear the choice of texts for the study of dialectic: Aristotle's *Categories*, *De Interpretatione* and *Analytica*. That is the order in which they appear in the numerous surviving manuscripts of Aristotle's writings on logic. The other sections of the treatise show dependence on Ptolemy for astronomy, on Euclid for geometry, with a hint that Proclus' commentary was also

---

[3] F. Marx in his edition of Celsus (Leipzig 1915) x.

[4] G. Leff, *Paris and Oxford Universities in the Thirteenth and Fourteenth Centuries* (New York 1968) 119.

[5] *Nicephori archiepiscopi Constantinopolitani opuscula historica*, ed. C. de Boor (Leipzig 1880) 149-50.

[6] F. Dvornik, *Les légendes de Constantin et de Méthode vues de Byzance* (Prague 1933) 25-31.

[7] Ed. J.L. Heiberg (Copenhagen 1929); see also A. Diller, *Isis* 36 (1945-6) 132.

consulted, on Euclid and Nicomachus of Gerasa for arithmetic. The latter was the author of an introduction to the subject that seems to have been widely used; a commentary was written on it in the sixth century by the Alexandrian John Philoponus, but we cannot assume that it had been in use in the schools from a much earlier date, since in that case copies of Nicomachus would have been found among the papyri, whereas not a single one has come to light so far.

In general the existence of commentaries, especially if they are of an elementary character with many explanations of individual words, is a further indication that a text formed part of a school curriculum. The commentaries on Aristotle, particularly the introductory logical treatises, are very numerous. The scholia on Homer are amazingly rich and diverse, and those on Aristophanes of notable proportions. The point is further emphasised by the fact that the plays of Euripides belonging to the school curriculum are accompanied in the manuscripts by commentaries, whereas those of the alphabetic series are not. Both for Aristophanes and the three tragedians it is true to say that the commentaries are much richer for the three plays of each author which by the middle of the Byzantine period had become the normal requirement of a syllabus. We may legitimately infer by the same means that some pagan authors read in the schools had to make way for Christian texts. The Psalms were not merely studied at an advanced level with the aid of learned commentaries, they were subjected to close linguistic analysis of the elementary kind that is used to introduce pupils to the basic concepts of grammar and syntax. These analyses (*epimerismoi*) were drawn up by George Choeroboscus, whose activity can be placed between the approximate limits of 750 and 825, and they are found in several manuscripts.[8] Their frequency is perhaps not such as to prove that they were used in every school, but evidently they were not just the experiment of a teacher that failed to win any approval from his colleagues. It is not possible to be sure whether they were devised because the idea of using the Psalms in the school curriculum was new; it may equally well have been Choeroboscus' intention to replace what seemed to him less satisfactory teaching material. Elementary linguistic notes on the *Iliad* already existed in one collection of material, now known as the D scholia because they were for a long time supposed to be the work of the famous ancient grammarian Didymus. The existence of these ancient notes did not prevent the compilation of analyses similar to Choeroboscus' work on the Psalms; they are thought to have been produced at much the same time. As they are found principally in two manuscripts (Coislin 387 and Oxford, New College 298) they presumably never achieved a wide circulation. No doubt the D scholia continued to be found adequate for the purpose.[9]

[8] Ed. T. Gaisford (Oxford 1842). See W. Bühler and C. Theodoridis, *BZ* 69 (1976) 397-401.

[9] R. Reitzenstein, *Geschichte der griechischen Etymologika* (Leipzig 1897) 208; C. Theodoridis, *BZ* 72 (1979) 1-5.

The other Christian text which won its way into the list of books known to schoolchildren was the selection of sixteen sermons and addresses by St. Gregory of Nazianzus (329-389). Although the date of its adoption is again unknown, the text was closely studied and there is a very substantial corpus of explanatory material, much of it extremely scholarly in nature, but some of it no more than a series of synonyms for difficult words that would scarcely have been necessary for the mature reader. Short vocabulary lists are good evidence for our present purpose. An Oxford manuscript (Barocci 50) contains a glossary of this type. Gregory's poems were also very widely read, and glossaries to them are found (e.g. Oxford, Gr. class. f. 114 and Montecassino 550). All three manuscripts cited here have been thought to be products of the Greek-speaking area of Italy, the first on the strength of inadequate evidence, the other two very plausibly. In the bilingual culture of southern Italy the lists might have been more necessary than in the main part of the Byzantine world, but there is no reason to think that the choice of texts was different in the provinces, and these manuscripts, which represent only a small part of the commentators' work on Gregory, can safely be used as evidence.

Many schools in antiquity and the middle ages seem to have been run by one man. We are fortunate enough to possess an account of one of the few larger schools in session. It is given by Nicholas Mesarites in his description of the church of the Holy Apostles in the capital, composed just before the Fourth Crusade, apparently some time during the years 1198-1203.[10] Most of Mesarites' description is devoted to the series of mosaics in the church but he does not entirely neglect its architecture. The enormous size of the buildings and their surrounding estates, which produced substantial crops of wheat, can be imagined easily by the modern visitor to the Fatih Mehmet Camii on the same site. Outside the church in a colonnade elementary instruction, consisting of grammar, simple arithmetic and singing, was given to the younger pupils of the school. Immediately after the mention of grammar Mesarites refers to the practice of memorising texts, the identity of which he does not reveal, and then to a practice of the more advanced children within this group, the formulation of riddles. That an exercise of this kind should have formed part of education may throw some light on the Byzantine character. Despite, or perhaps because of, the strict discipline imposed the school enjoyed a very good reputation; yet Mesarites, even though writing an encomium, goes so far as to call the masters violent, brutal and ungovernable. The more senior pupils were taught in another part of the buildings. A large crowd, not all of school age, could be seen there, and, if Mesarites is to be trusted, there appears to have been open discussion of rhetoric and dialectic. In one corner was a group studying medicine. Others engaged in arithmetic, geometry and musical theory. It

---

[10] Ed. G. Downey, *Transactions of the American Philosophical Society,* 47 (1957) 855-924.

is evident that the curriculum in this school corresponded roughly with
the programme of the trivium and quadrivium, but not exactly. Perhaps
it is an accidental omission that no mention is made of astronomy.
Medicine is an addition to the programme. It is natural that there should
be no reference to theology; the study of the seven liberal arts was meant
to be a preparation for it, and theology, at any rate at that stage of
Byzantine history, was studied in a special school under the aegis of the
patriarch.

At this point we can briefly summarise the progress of an average pupil
in a good school reading a full range of Greek literature. His first
acquaintance with grammar and syntax would be through the very short
treatise of Dionysius Thrax entitled 'The art of grammar', on which
many schoolmasters wrote their own explanatory notes. It enjoyed a
remarkably long influence, but as it is rarely found among the papyri one
may wonder if it is one of the texts that came into general use only at the
end of antiquity, at which time it was translated into Syriac and,
perhaps soon after, Armenian. Some modern authorities have suggested
that the Byzantine schoolboy also read the works of Apollonius Dyscolus
as his introduction to syntax,[11] but as there is for most of his work only
one manuscript surviving and little trace of scholia, while the text itself
is couched in technical language of the most abstruse kind, this notion
must be rejected. But other textbooks were used in addition to
Dionysius. The twelfth-century teacher John Tzetzes, in a passing
remark in his commentary on Hesiod's *Works and Days* 285, says that
the study of grammar is undertaken in three stages, the first being
Dionysius, the second the *Canons* of Theodosius (*c.* 400?), in which
grammatical forms were listed and rules about them given, and the third
exercises in parsing.

Passing from grammar to literature the pupil would begin with Homer,
especially the *Iliad*, and probably the Psalms. He would then go through
a number of poets; there were selections from tragedy and Aristophanes,
and it is clear that many also read Hesiod, Pindar and Theocritus' *Idylls*.
A verse text whose popularity is unexpected is the hexameter poem of
Dionysius Periegetes (*c.* 130) on the geography of the world. This was
often copied and commented on. It would seem that the Byzantines
retained the ancient taste for didactic poetry and used this text as an
elementary handbook of geography. Among the prose writers Plato,
Thucydides and Demosthenes would be the most important, the last
being used as a model of rhetoric. If we are to accept the evidence of
Marcellinus' *Life of Thucydides* mentioned above, the study of literature
continued after that of rhetoric had begun.

As far as the Attic orators were concerned, Demosthenes was referred
to in the scholia as 'the orator' par excellence, just as Homer was 'the poet'
and Aristophanes 'the comic writer', and there is much less sign of the
others being read. The minor Attic orators were perhaps not included in

---

[11] R.J.H. Jenkins, *DOP* 17 (1963) 43; C. Mango, op. cit. at (ii) n. 5 above, 9.

the syllabus, as the two main manuscripts are both to be dated *c*. 1300 and it is not clear that they were closely studied earlier. Lysias too, despite his simple style suitable for beginners, may not have been read very often. Isocrates was valued for his essays rather than his oratory. There were also handbooks of oratory that every schoolmaster used in conjunction with the original masterpieces. The art of public speaking was a practical accomplishment which could be brought into play in many situations in the Roman empire, even if there was no opportunity for what would nowadays be called party politics. The number of social and official functions at which an address was called for may have declined as Rome was succeeded by Byzantium. One might exemplify the point by observing that representatives of cities did not often meet provincial governors. But oratory lived on in the sermon, and the textbooks remained the same. The two which held the field in Byzantium were by Hermogenes (second century) and Aphthonius (fourth century), on which many commentaries were written. The two treatises commonly known as the work of Menander the Rhetor were also fairly popular, but they did not stimulate any commentators to discuss them. The third element of the trivium, dialectic, was studied, as we have already seen, by means of the first three books of Aristotle's *Organon* together with the commentaries written on them by Porphyry (232/3-*c*. 305) and others.

For the quadrivium, which perhaps fewer pupils were able to study in detail, we can reconstruct the basic list of books. Music, as we saw in the description of the school at the church of the Holy Apostles, might be treated initially as a practical accomplishment. If a pupil passed on to the theory, he might study Ptolemy's *Harmonics* or Cleomedes or Aristoxenus. Arithmetic would be studied through Nicomachus, but the book is more theoretical than practical and would not have been any use for teaching simple everyday calculations. Euclid provided the basis for geometry, and we find Arethas in the year 888, when he was still a young deacon – he later became archbishop of Caesarea in Cappadocia – ordering a copy and writing marginalia in his own hand (Oxford, D'Orville 301). Astronomy at an advanced level would certainly be based on Ptolemy, but as a first step it seems that the schoolboy read the poem of Aratus (*c*. 315-*c*. 240 B.C.) called *Phaenomena*, which appears to have been immensely popular in antiquity and the middle ages. Its continuing utility is demonstrated by the decision of Maximus Planudes (*c*. 1300) to delete some lines that were now known to be factually incorrect and substitute verses of his own composition.

A certain number of other prose authors continued to be read, including some who had no obvious practical value or were not regularly incorporated into a school reading list. Among them were the Atticists of the Roman empire, regarded as the equals of the Attic masters whom they attempted to mimic. For this reason Lucian and Aristides were popular and received the honour of being commented on, especially the latter. Other writers of late antiquity such as Philostratus managed to

survive for the same reason. Although his biography of Apollonius of
Tyana was understandably described by Aldus Manutius as the worst
book he had ever read and Lucian's comments on the Christians were not
appreciated, these writers could all be treated as models of good prose
style, their texts a quarry of elegant expressions and phrases that would
decorate the prose of a consciously literate administrator or man of
culture. Probably the historians were regarded in much the same way as
useful reading matter for anyone with an interest in style. They also
provided a wealth of material for the teacher of rhetoric who wished to
test his pupils by asking them to compose a speech that might have been
made by a famous person on a given occasion. Rather more unexpected is
the survival of the Greek novels. Some in fact depend on such a slender
manuscript tradition that one is probably justified in speaking of a lucky
accident, but Achilles Tatius and Heliodorus enjoyed wider circulation,
as is made clear both by the manuscripts and by the evidence of interest
on the part of Byzantine intellectuals. They were discussed by Photius
and made the subject of a short essay comparing their qualities by no less
a figure than Michael Psellos. Although their stylistic qualities as
Atticists may have helped to give them value in the eyes of Byzantine
readers, it is to be noted that Heliodorus' position may have been
strengthened by the story, usually thought to be no more than a pious
fiction, that he was a Christian and a bishop. But as a whole Greek
authors do not owe their preservation or popularity to mistaken
assumptions about their religious beliefs in the same way as Vergil,
Seneca and Statius did in western Europe during the middle ages.

Christian writers, with the already mentioned exception of Gregory of
Nazianzus, do not seem to have established themselves as literary
models on a par with the pagans. In so far as many of them aimed at the
same Atticist quality of style they could in principle have won as much
approval from the discerning reader. Yet although many of the writings
of such fathers as St. John Chrysostom were very often copied, it is
difficult to be sure that they found the bulk of their readers outside the
monasteries. The absence of commentaries or notes on them is suggestive
rather than conclusive; the simpler style of Chrysostom may have been
more readily understood by the average reader.

The products of Byzantine education show a remarkable fusion of
ancient and Christian culture. A few instances will make this clear. The
envoy Leo Choerosphactes, whom we have previously met on his mission
to Bulgaria, later found himself writing letters from exile begging the
emperor to let him return. They are a mixture of pleas and erudition.
Though he makes a slip in citing a rare poetic word describing mountain
scenery as if it were found in Euripides, whereas it occurs only in
Aeschylus' *Prometheus*, in other respects he succeeds in his object of
displaying a wide knowledge of ancient literature. Letter 21, in which
classical learning is particularly lavishly flaunted, is followed by another
in which Leo begins by saying that his Attic language has had no effect
and so he will show instead his acquaintance with the songs of David and

Christian precepts to see if they have any greater power to move the emperor. A series of eight quotations from the Psalms and eleven allusions to the New Testament follows. They did not have the desired result. For our purposes what is important is that Leo should have regarded the display of either type of culture as equally appropriate in a plea to the head of a Christian state. Sometimes the blend of pagan and Christian is encapsulated within the limits of a single sentence. The patriarch Methodius (d. 847), writing a life of Theophanes the Confessor, records an episode in which Theophanes was able to silence the loud croaking of frogs. The hero of the story speaks of the frogs as 'marsh-loving monsters', using an adjective of exceptional rarity which can only be regarded as an adaptation of the name given to a frog, Limnocharis, in the pseudo-Homeric *Batrachomyomachia*. Hagiography is scarcely the place to look for erudite classical allusions. Equally striking, but perhaps not surprising in an ecclesiastical writer who was also the leading classical scholar of the day, is a passage in the account of the capture of Thessalonica by the Normans in 1185 written by Eustathius, who was at the time the archbishop of the city. He writes of the captured city: 'A deep cloud enveloped it, like a dust-cloud raised by a storm or the feet of innumerable animals, so that one might say that the sun hesitated to shine on those whose brilliant armour outshone his light, and one might paraphrase the ancient Muse "for eighteen days the ship of the city ran its course and on the nineteenth appeared the shadowy mountains" by which the sun of our life was fenced off and darkened the shadow that covered us, in the words of the Psalm.' The quotations are from Homer's *Odyssey* 7.267-8 and Psalm 43:20, and the next sentence continues with a reference to Psalm 88:16.

2

The Schools of Late Antiquity

(i) Antioch

In the most flourishing period of the Roman empire the leading schools in the Greek provinces were at Athens, Ephesus and Smyrna. There were others, a good deal less important, at Pergamon and Byzantium.[1] By the fifth century the situation had changed. Athens was still one of the leading centres, but Ephesus, Pergamon and Smyrna were of no significance. Antioch, Alexandria and Gaza had become prominent, while there was a law school at Beirut. To speak of schools is not always precise: there were professors of rhetoric or philosophy, sometimes employed by the civil authorities, who taught as individuals and attracted pupils by their personal reputation. As the empire gradually declined the schools began to disappear for a variety of reasons, until the position was reached that higher education could not be obtained anywhere except in the capital. The law school at Beirut seems not to have recovered after the earthquake that devastated the town in 551. Antioch suffered earthquakes in 526 and 528, and was captured and sacked by the Persians in 540. It is not known what became of the school at Gaza. In Athens the teaching of philosophy continued well into the sixth century; but although the notorious edict issued by Justinian in 529 may have had less effect than is generally supposed, there is no sign of higher education continuing there much after the middle of the century. In Alexandria traditions lasted longer than elsewhere and there are signs of activity almost up to the time of the Arab conquest in 641.

What is known of the advanced study of Greek texts in the schools? In Antioch Libanius, the most famous rhetorician of his day, some of whose writings remained popular throughout the Byzantine period, taught in the conventional way. He may have read less widely than he would like us to believe, but there is no doubt that he went through the standard authors with his pupils, not neglecting the more recent writers such as Aristides. He is the author of synopses of the speeches of Demosthenes, for him perhaps the most important of all the classics. It has already been mentioned that his fame as a teacher of rhetoric led to his being consulted by Christians anxious to achieve pagan standards of literacy. We may reasonably assume that in matters of scholarship, even if he

[1] G.W. Bowersock, *Greek Sophists in the Roman Empire* (Oxford 1969) 17-22.

made no contribution of any note himself, he introduced pupils to the principles of interpretation and textual criticism developed by the scholars of Hellenistic Alexandria. One of his Christian pupils applied these principles of interpretation to the Bible. Theodore, bishop of Mopsuestia from 390 to 428, is the most important representative of the so-called Antiochene school of exegesis. As far as can be seen he was doing no more than insist on the use of the same methods for the explanation of the scriptures as had been generally accepted for centuries by pagans and had been expounded to him by his teacher.[2] Long after his death, at a church council held in 553, he was condemned as a heretic, and his works, with one exception, have to be reconstructed from fragments that were incorporated, despite his condemnation, into later biblical commentaries. To say that he applied pagan textual criticism to the Bible is true but needs to be qualified in order to avoid the misleading implication that there was a simple opposition between two methods, each identified with one cultural tradition. His opponents, known as the Alexandrian school, favoured extensive use of allegory as a means of interpretation, and allegorical exegesis had been used by some of the ancients, in particular the Stoics. Nevertheless it is fair to think of Theodore as a scholar who used the generally accepted methods of the Hellenistic scholars, originally devised in order to establish accurate texts of classical authors and explain their meaning. How much Theodore learnt from his master and how much he improved on his teaching it is impossible to say. He was in any case not the earliest of the Antiochene interpreters. It is interesting to observe him at work. He and his colleagues appear to have written monographs about problems in the text of the Old Testament in the same style as the pagans used for the discussion of difficulties in their own literature. The Psalms were thought of as originally separate compositions that were not united into a corpus until a man of literary taste and intelligence put them in order. This hypothesis is most naturally explained as an adaptation of the theory advanced to explain how the Homeric poems reached their final form: many originally independent short poems had been put together in an organised form in Athens during the sixth century B.C. under the auspices of Peisistratus. The Antiochenes found themselves in some difficulty when they tried to apply their literal and historical approach to a text such as the Psalms, which the church treated as a book of prophecies. Theodore extricated himself by the suggestion that the Psalms are to be thought of as spoken by people who participated in or were affected by the events foretold by King David; in other words the prophet put himself in the position of men whose experiences he predicted. The speech of an imaginary character was well tried as a weapon in the armoury of classical literary critics (they used the phrase

[2] His studies under Libanius are attested by Socrates, *Hist. eccl.* 6.3. L. Petit, *Les étudiants de Libanius* (Paris 1957) 40-2, is uncertain whether to accept this evidence, but Schäublin (see next note) does so.

ἐκ προσώπου , and it was also a regular feature of instruction in rhetoric). There are many surviving fair-copy pieces (ἠθοποιίαι) composed by rhetoricians to illustrate the proper way of tackling an exercise such as 'write the speech made by Andromache over Hector's corpse'. In the more linguistic part of his work Theodore operates with sound principles. His interpretation of II Corinthians 3:17 'The Lord is the Spirit' depends on the formulation of a rule well known to modern students of Greek but apparently not formulated by classical grammarians of an earlier date, that in a sentence of the type just quoted the predicate does not normally take the definite article. The rule is stated by Ammonius, a commentator on Aristotle of the following century, and both he and Theodore may be indebted to an unknown philosophical commentator for the idea. A point in which Theodore and his colleague Diodorus were evidently not dependent on pagan predecessors concerns the difficulties of translating Hebrew accurately into Greek. They realised that a word in one language has a semantic field such that it cannot be reproduced by a single word in another. This insight probably goes back to Origen's work on the Septuagint.[3] Finally one may note an invention due to the last important member of the Antiochene school, Theodoret, bishop of Cyrrhus in Syria (d.c. 466). He announces in the preface to his dialogue *Eranistes* that he has made it his practice, wherever there is a change of speaker, to name him explicitly. Hitherto it had been customary to indicate changes of speaker merely by a double point like a modern English colon, and the practice is still observable in manuscripts of the Platonic dialogues, which means that Theodoret's excellent idea was not generally adopted for a very long time.[4]

(ii)   Gaza

The Antiochene approach to the Bible did not find favour. It is not necessary to assume that indebtedness to the methods of classical scholarship was in itself enough to invite condemnation of Theodore and his colleagues. But the rationalist basis of their thinking led to the suspicion that they had prepared the ground for the heretic Nestorius, who held that the divine and human elements in the nature of Jesus were strictly separate. A less troubled relationship between Christian and pagan culture is to be found in the school that flourished at Gaza in the late fifth and early sixth centuries. Its main figure is Procopius, and there were several lesser members of the circle. There is no reason to doubt that they were all members of the church and they certainly knew a wide range of pagan authors. Two of them wrote philosophical dialogues modelled on Plato to such an extent that some pages seem almost a cento of Platonic phraseology; the *Theophrastus* of Aeneas deals with the

---

[3] On Theodore see C. Schäublin, *Untersuchungen zu Methode und Herkunft der antiochenischen Exegese (Theophaneia* 21) (Bonn 1974), and his paper in *Würzburger Jahrbücher für die Altertumswissenschaft* 4 (1978) 69-74.

[4] *PG* 83.29B; cf. N.G. Wilson, *CQ* 20 (1970) 305.

immortality of the soul, the *Ammonius* of Zacharias with the creation of the world. It is possible that the existing commentaries on Demosthenes were improved by a minor member of the group, Zosimus, who wrote a brief notice of the orator's life. Another minor member, Timotheus, apart from compiling miscellaneous zoological information in an unscientific spirit, was responsible for a short and trivial set of notes dealing with questions of grammar and orthography, including the correct method of dividing syllables.[1] But it is far from clear that he belongs to the group, as he is stated to have been a pupil of Horapollon, who taught in Egypt and later in Constantinople. More important is Choricius, whose substantial writings allow us to trace the extent of his classical reading. There are few surprises, but it is worth noting that he gives the impression of having read at least one of the mimes of the early Sicilian writer Sophron, and he tells the story that Plato greatly admired them as scenes of ordinary life and conversation (*Apologia mimorum* 14-17). Choricius' knowledge of Menander is also interesting. He refers to leading characters in some of the plays that are now at least in part available to us through the discoveries of papyri, the *Epitrepontes*, *Samia*, *Dyscolus* and *Aspis* (*Apologia mimorum* 73). But his reading list does not tell us anything about his qualities as a scholar.

The chief member of the Gaza school is Procopius, tutor of Choricius and his predecessor as its head. His works do not survive complete and those that have come down to us may owe their preservation to a chance discovery made by a twelfth-century rhetorician, Nicephorus Basilaces, with whose writings they commonly go hand in hand in the manuscript tradition. Procopius has sometimes attracted the attention of historians of science by his description of a remarkable clock in Gaza which struck the hours and had elaborate automata. At each hour a figure of Heracles emerged from one of a series of twelve doors, carrying an object representing one of his twelve labours, and an eagle placed above him bent down to place a victor's garland over his head, to signify the successful completion of the labour in question. After that the figure of Heracles retreated again behind the panel from which it had appeared. It is symptomatic of the mentality of antiquity that Procopius expends most of his descriptive talents on the external appearance of the clock and does not explain the mechanism or write a eulogy of its inventor.

In the ninth century Photius was able to read with approval a much less interesting work that is now lost apart from tiny fragments, a set of paraphrases of the *Iliad*. These belong to a class of literature that reflects classroom activity; pupils' comprehension was tested by a requirement to paraphrase in various ways. The fragments that have come to light concern a famous passage in the *Iliad* (12.322ff), in which Sarpedon urges Glaucus to join him in attacking the Greek camp. 'My friend, if we were destined to avoid this war and live for ever, immortal and unaging, I

---

[1] J.A. Cramer, *Anecdota graeca Parisiensia* IV (Oxford 1841) 239-44; Reitzenstein, op. cit., 296.

would not fight among the leaders myself or send you into battle that
brings glory to men. But as innumerable fates of death certainly loom
over us, which a mortal cannot escape or avoid, let us go, and bring
success to ourselves or to another.' Procopius turns this into cold
rhetoric. 'Through the hope of victory I shall be able to bear even defeat.
I know nature, I am fully aware of the devices of the Fates. Therefore it is
better to fight. I advance in order to perform great deeds, before seeing
old age come upon me and learning all too well that it is not only battle
which can bring death.' Another version follows. 'I wish to kill an enemy
or fall in the assault, I swear by Fate, by whom I shall certainly be caught
even if I attempt to flee. Let us admit that one does not necessarily win
glory by fighting: will old age not be a trial to one who disobeyed orders? I
do not know of any coward who won immortality.'[2] Although the practice
of paraphrase may seem an arid classroom exercise, Procopius can at
least be given credit for directing his pupils' attention to one of the
greatest writers. A comparison with other ancient paraphrases reinforces
this judgment. Hellenistic and later didactic poems, some of which were
read in school, were treated in this way, and we still possess the
paraphrase by an otherwise unknown Eutecnius of the two poems on
snakes and antidotes by Nicander, together with an anonymous
paraphrase of Oppian on species of fish. There can be few who regret the
loss of Marianus' literary productions (*c.* 500) (*Suda* s.v.). He is reported
to have paraphrased Theocritus, Apollonius Rhodius, most of
Callimachus, Aratus and Nicander's *Theriaca*, converting them all into
iambic verse. Although we can be reasonably sure that Procopius used
the paraphrase as a classroom exercise, it is likely that the other
examples of it are more in the nature of tours de force than practical aids
to teaching, and it has been suggested that they represent an attempt to
retrieve the falling popularity of authors who had written in hexameters
by turning them into the iambic trimeter form which remained
acceptable.[3]

   Procopius' paraphrase represents one side of his work. The other is an
achievement of some note, if it is rightly ascribed to him. He is generally
held to be the inventor of the form of literature known as the catena, a
commentary on a book of the Bible which consists of a compilation of
excerpts from various previous commentaries, each excerpt as a rule
prefaced with the name of its author, and the compiler himself
contributing little or nothing. The catenae attributed to Procopius are
not universally accepted as genuine. At his first mention of this author
Photius (*Bibliotheca* 160) does not mention them specifically but cites
the paraphrases of Homer as his outstanding work; for all his interest in
literary studies one might expect him to rate catenae higher. But later
(*Bibliotheca* 206-7) he includes them, without any suggestion that he
doubts their authenticity. In favour of the usual attribution it may be

   [2] Published from Vaticanus gr. 2228 by H. Rabe, *RhMus* 63 (1908) 515 n. 2; see also A.
Brinkmann, ibid. 618-23.
   [3] A.D.E. Cameron, *Historia* 14 (1965) 482.

observed that Procopius was not an eminent figure in other respects, on whom lesser writers or forgers would be likely to wish to father their own productions. Whether the catena is his invention or not, it marks a significant stage in the history of biblical scholarship, and its importance for classical scholarship is that in some degree it resembles the commentaries on Greek literature. These, like the commentaries on books of the Bible, were originally separate books. At some date, probably in late antiquity, it became the custom to make a compilation of them. Since the number of commentaries on some texts was very large and no doubt a good deal of duplication occurred, the new compilation if skilfully undertaken could give the reader the benefit of a convenient synopsis of what the best scholars had thought of the text and its problems. The history of catenae and commentaries is still extremely obscure, but the possibility must at least be considered that Procopius was responsible for the new type of commentary and that he may have been inspired to invent it by what was already being done for classical literature. The priority cannot be established with anything like certainty. It may be remarked that catenae as a rule cite the names of the original authors, whereas the scholia on classical authors only rarely give the names of the authorities being quoted, and almost never do so at the beginning of an excerpt, which is customary in a catena. It is a reasonable but hypothetical inference that Procopius lit upon the idea of regularly citing names as an improvement on the practice followed in commentaries on pagan authors. On the other hand it has to be said that this practice is not found in all the compilations that pass under his name, and until more reliable editions are available the matter must remain undecided.

(iii) Scholia

Because the Gaza school is associated with the invention of the catena, and there is a resemblance between it and the commentaries on classical texts, this is the appropriate point to discuss the formation of the latter.[1] As scholars had been concerned with the exegesis of the classical texts for nearly a millennium, the quantity of accumulated material was huge, and the task of making a satisfactory compilation of what seemed important correspondingly daunting. The names of the men who carried out the task are not known, and it has to be said that they did not always perform it well. Nor is the date of their activity easily established. Modern authorities have mostly supposed that it is to be placed some time in late antiquity, and the usual view is that it was inspired or at least assisted by the important change in ancient book production, the adoption of the modern form, the codex, instead of the roll, which made it much easier to write a large amount of explanatory material in one or

---

[1] For more detailed discussions see N.G. Wilson, *CQ* 17 (1967) 244-56; *GRBS* 12 (1971) 557-8; *CR* 27 (1977) 271.

more of the margins round the text. It can be stated as a general rule that in antiquity commentaries consisting of anything more than brief notes were transcribed as independent texts on a separate roll, whereas in the middle ages they were copied in the margins.[2] The new type of book was introduced gradually and became standard for all kinds of texts by the end of the fourth century. It is an easy inference that the commentaries were rationalised and transferred to the margins of a codex as soon as that type of book came into general use. But the objection has been raised that the scripts in general use in late antiquity were too large to allow any bulky commentary to be included in the margins of a book, and consequently the credit for compiling the extant corpora of scholia should be given to the scholars of the first Byzantine renaissance, as it is sometimes called, when the new minuscule script seen in the manuscripts of the ninth century could be exploited to fit a much greater quantity of text on to a page of given size. The circle of Photius is a milieu in which this kind of scholarly activity can easily be imagined, and although there does not appear to be an explicit mention of it by Photius or his contemporaries, it is plausible to suppose that some work of this kind was still being done in the ninth century or later. In fact one might cite as an example of the process the addition of excerpts from pseudo-Heraclitus' essay on allegorical interpretation of Homer to the corpus of scholia on the *Iliad* found in a Venice manuscript (Marc. gr. 453); the hand which entered these additions is not earlier than the eleventh century.

There are, however, several reasons for thinking that the old view which attributed the compilation of scholia to late antiquity was correct, and although none of them is decisive, collectively they make a strong case. The first, as has been indicated already, is the invention of the catena. The second is that the word used in Greek scholia very frequently to mark the transition from one original source to another is adopted by Latin scholiasts who worked in late antiquity (they used *aliter* in the same way as ἄλλως), and it is difficult to suppose that they did not borrow a convenient formula already available. Thirdly, there are manuscripts and papyri which, while not exhibiting scholia in their fully developed medieval form, are highly suggestive. A leaf survives from a copy of Callimachus transcribed probably in the sixth century (P. Oxy. 2258). It has a large amount of commentary, written in all four margins, and though it may not be an amalgam of commentaries in the way that scholia normally are, it shows what could be done by using a big format and one of the normal types of script. What might be termed scholia in an embryonic form can be found in a more famous manuscript, the wonderfully illuminated Dioscorides herbal that can be dated *c.* 500

---

[2] The Lille papyrus of Callimachus is a recently discovered exception to this rule. It may turn out to reflect a short-lived experiment, but in the meantime it must serve as a warning that a single find can easily upset received opinions. Attention has been drawn to other exceptions by A. Carlini, *Maia* 32 (1980) 235-6. See further my forthcoming paper in the *Atti* of the conference held in Urbino in September 1982 on the theme 'Il libro e il testo'.

(Vienna, med. gr. 1). On a number of folios the scribe copied in the margin extracts from the works of Galen and Crateuas dealing with the same plants, giving the author's name in each case. On four pages he had occasion to add such an excerpt from both the authorities he was consulting, and so produced the effect of scholia or, since the names are included, a primitive catena. It might be argued that scribal practices in the preparation of scientific texts were not necessarily the same as for more literary authors, and that the herbal of Dioscorides, being a practical book essential to doctors and evidently frequently copied, should not be equated with texts of poets. But there is no evidence of such a distinction being drawn between scientific and literary texts, and the medical profession was in any case largely composed of cultivated men and recognised as such; one has only to cite the famous remark of St. Jerome (letter 119) that Luke was the best stylist of the four evangelists partly because he was a doctor. Finally there are grounds for thinking that the palaeographical argument brought against the traditional view has been given too much weight. It is to some extent weakened by the papyrus of Callimachus already mentioned, but a more powerful refutation comes from the existence of uncial script of extremely small size which may have been specifically developed in order to permit the inclusion of lengthy commentaries in the margins of a codex. An early example of it is found on a scrap of parchment containing a Latin legal text with a few notes (P.S.I.1182) and dated tentatively by Latin palaeographers to *c*. 500. There are Greek notes in the margin in a minute hand. A similar minute hand dating from a later period is well known to palaeographers: the so-called half-uncial script of Arethas could be used to transcribe an extensive marginal commentary, the best example being his copy of Aristotle's *Organon* (Urb. gr. 35), in which the opening folios are tightly packed with notes. We do not need to assume that Arethas invented this script; he is far more likely to have learned it from examples like that found in the fragmentary legal text. At some point between 500 and 900, probably later rather than earlier, we find another Greek hand of the same kind. A palimpsest fragment in Leipzig (Tischendorf 2) has an Arabic script, datable to 885/6 covering an earlier Greek script. The Greek marginalia are the work of the grammarian Herodian. Originally it was a book in large format, with scholia in a very tiny hand. A still more minute uncial hand, used for a text rather than marginal notes, has come to light in recent years. The codex containing the biography of Mani, the founder of Manichaeism, has leaves measuring only 45 x 35 mm., with a written surface of 35 x 25 mm., into which the scribe has managed as a rule to cram twenty-three lines (P. Colon. inv. 4780). This appears to be the smallest book surviving from antiquity, and it was probably written in the fifth century.[3]

[3] The Leipzig palimpsest is discussed by R. Reitzenstein, op.cit.299ff; for the date of the Arabic script I rely on I. Kračkovskij, *Viz Vrem* 14 (1907) 246-75. On the Mani codex see A. Henrichs & L. Koenen, *ZPE* 5 (1970) 97 ff, especially 100-3.

When all the facts are taken into account, the balance of evidence entitles us to revert to the view that scholia began to be amalgamated from the earlier monographs and to take on their medieval shape during the late Roman empire. It is possible that the process had started by the end of the fifth century and that Procopius was taking note of it when he invented the catena.

(iv) Athens

If we now turn our attention to Athens we find another flourishing centre of higher education in which pagan traditions were vigorously maintained in the fourth century and, perhaps rather surprisingly, continued despite official discouragement until some time during the sixth. To speak of Athens as a university is misleading if it is taken to imply a degree of central organisation. But in the fourth century it is clear that there were many independent teachers attracting students from all over the empire, and if numbers of students and the establishment of teaching posts funded by the town council are criteria by which to judge, it was a university town. Competition between the professors was intense. They sent their pupils down to the harbour to waylay newly arrived students. Libanius records in his *Autobiography* (16) how he came with the intention of studying under a fellow countryman but was press-ganged into joining another school. As has been mentioned already, pagans and Christians existed together on easy terms. Among the Christian students in the middle of the fourth century were St. Basil and St. Gregory of Nazianzus. It is natural to think of Athens as a centre of philosophical studies, but at this time probably the most celebrated professor was the rhetorician Himerius (c. 310-c.390), who shows no sign of any concern with philosophy. He is fond of showing his knowledge of the Greek lyric poets such as Sappho, Alcaeus and Anacreon, and is in fact the sole source for a few fragments of their poems; this is incidentally further evidence against the view that texts falling outside the basic list of a curriculum ceased to be read after the second century. But Himerius tells us little about education and scholarship. We infer from his own rhetorical productions the example and aim that he set before his pupils; considerations of rhetoric are more important than the contents. It is sometimes alleged that his speech in honour of the proconsul Hermogenes (*Oration* 48) gives a picture of the education to be had in Athens at the time. But although the speech is an encomium, a type of writing that does not easily lend itself to precise interpretation, it is made clear that the proconsul himself, who is praised for his attainments in philosophy, rhetoric, geography and astronomy, came to these studies at a later age than was normal and should not be regarded as an average product of an Athenian education.[1]

Athens was probably at its peak in the fourth century. Its only claim to fame after that date derives from the reestablished Academy of the

[1] I differ slightly from H.D. Saffrey & L.G. Westerink, *Proclus: Théologie platonicienne* I (Paris 1968) xl, on the view to be taken of Himerius 48.20-5.

Neoplatonists. But Academy, if not a misnomer, is misleading. There was a group of Neoplatonists active for several generations, but we are not entitled to suppose that they occupied the original premises of Plato's school or that they inherited property from it. All that we can be sure of is that the group behaved like a small private club or school. The distinction of some of its members and their avowedly anti-Christian stance ensured that it remained well known. Colleagues of a similar outlook in Alexandria appear to have come to some kind of agreement with the local ecclesiastical authorities, which enabled them to continue teaching, presumably on the understanding that they did not state their views too bluntly in lectures. A fragment of Damascius' *Life of Isidore* (316) suggests that the latter disapproved of the Alexandrian Ammonius for having taken this course of action. The most interesting, but not necessarily the most widely publicised, indication of pagan sentiment is found in Marinus' *Life of Proclus* (36), where the death of the master (A.D. 485) is stated to have occurred in the one hundred and twenty-fourth year of Julian, as if the accession of the apostate were regarded as the start of a new era. One of Proclus' lost books was entitled 'Eighteen arguments against the Christians'.

The group possessed an endowment, as a result of which they were able to teach without charging fees. By the sixth century they may have been the only source of higher education in Athens. It is often thought that they were abolished in 529 by Justinian's edict which forbad pagans or heretics to teach and ordered that public funds should not be used for their support.[2] According to a generally unreliable authority, the chronicle of John Malalas (451), the emperor issued a special edict against the Athenian Neoplatonists. A private club could otherwise have continued in existence, if fees were not essential for its maintenance. Either because of the edict or for some other reason seven members decided to leave and seek their fortune in Persia, thinking that they had at last found the incarnation of the Platonic ideal of the philosopher king. The idyll did not last long, and they returned, but not all to Athens. It may be that the club managed to prolong its existence by being very discreet, and there is something to be said for the view that Simplicius, deprived of the opportunity to teach, had time to write his lengthy philosophical commentaries; he filled 1300 pages on Aristotle's *Physics*. But the effectiveness in the provinces of prohibitions issued by the central government is problematical. Perhaps Simplicius could still teach. About 560 the Alexandrian professor Olympiodorus, who seems to have maintained a discreet paganism without having to resign his office, speaks of the Athenians as if he thought they were still active. One cannot be quite sure that he was accurately informed, but the balance of evidence suggests that the edict of 529 was not quite the end of philosophy in Athens. It is difficult to believe, however, that much

[2] On the Academy see A.D.E. Cameron, *PCPS* 195 (1965) 7-29; J. Glucker, *Antiochus and the Late Academy* (Göttingen 1978) 322-9; H.J. Blumenthal, *Byzantion* 48 (1978) 369-85.

cultural life continued in Athens for more than about a generation afterwards. In 579/80 the city was sacked by the Slavs. A Latin source suggests that at the end of the following century Theodore of Tarsus, sent to convert England to Christianity, had studied in Athens. Some modern authorities believe the report,[3] but the Latin author may well be guilty of misunderstanding a Greek source which spoke of his Attic attainments. In the language of educated Byzantines that would mean no more than that he had studied the classical authors with success.

The Neoplatonists dominated Athens. We hear little of other teachers. The Egyptian poet and schoolmaster Pamprepius settled in Athens and taught for a while until a quarrel forced him to move to the capital. He made no secret of his paganism, which at this date was potentially dangerous, although it had not prevented his appointment at Athens. It also ensured him the friendship of Proclus. One of our sources records that he taught grammar and poetry as a propaedeutic to philosophy. But though he is interesting as one of a recognisable category of Egyptian poets who made their living abroad by their literary talents, his place in the history of scholarship is of no importance whatever. He serves only to show that literary education was still available in Athens in the middle of the fifth century.

The philosophers, while concentrating their attention on the exposition of Plato, did not limit their interests as severely as the name applied to the group might suggest. Syrianus, who succeeded Plutarch as the head in 431/2, is the author of commentaries on Aristotle's *Metaphysics* and Hermogenes' rhetorical handbook. Proclus, whose education had begun in Lycia and Alexandria, met Syrianus but was not interested in his lectures on rhetoric. He was attracted instead to Plutarch's classes on Aristotle's *De anima* and Plato's *Phaedo*; the common theme of these two books is significant, for it was the Platonic doctrine of the soul that Christianity found most unacceptable. In the course of two years they read the whole of Aristotle and went on to Plato, taking his dialogues in what seems to have been an order approved by the school (Marinus, *Vita Procli* 11-13). Proclus also had some scientific interests; he wrote an introduction to astronomy. The last important member of the group, Simplicius, wrote four commentaries on Aristotle and one on Epictetus' *Enchiridion*. In the latter hints are dropped (153, 331) that the topic was chosen because Simplicius felt that he was suffering the same fate of oppression under a tyrant as Epictetus, who had been sent into exile by Domitian.

Although the main concern of the group was philosophical, literary interests are quite prominent in the work of others besides Syrianus. Marinus wrote an encomiastic life of his master Proclus, and Damascius one of Isidore, which though known to us only in fragments is full of fascinating detail. The Suda entry for Proclus assures us that he wrote much on literature as well as philosophy, and lists a commentary on the

[3] A. Frantz, *DOP* 19 (1965) 199 n. 78.

whole of Homer, another on Hesiod's *Works and Days*, a study of the gods in Homer and a Chrestomathy or handbook of literary studies. One other work that goes under the name of Proclus in the manuscript tradition but is not listed in the Suda is a set of formulae for letters of various types. Absence from the Suda's list is not a decisive ground for rejection of authenticity, but the lack of any obvious connection between the subject-matter of the treatise on letter writing and Proclus' other interests together with the hints that the author was a Christian invite us to suppose that in this case the Proclus in question is another person of the same name.[4]

The surviving scholia on Hesiod's *Works and Days* include a set ascribed to Proclus, and examination of them suggests that the attribution must be right. It is not simply that he cites Plato quite frequently, which is not customary in other scholia. The language sometimes hints at Neoplatonic authorship, and in one passage we find that Proclus' comment coincides with what he has to say in one of the Platonic commentaries. Hesiod speaks of the men of the golden race who lived in the age of Cronus (*Works and Days* 111). Proclus' comment is: 'Note that the men of the golden age lived a life pure, immaterial and without suffering; and that is what gold signifies, as Plato also (*Cratylus* 398) clearly explained. For gold is not subject to rust or mould and is therefore the symbol of impassibility.' Commenting on Plato's *Republic* (vol. 2 p. 75 Kroll) Proclus refers to the Hesiod passage and says 'Now the race of gold means for him too a certain intellective, immaterial and pure life, of which gold is a symbol because it is not subject to rust or mould.' The identical wording here is sufficient proof. The note also gives some idea of the character of the commentary, which is however not entirely philosophical and contains a good many quotations from a lost work by Plutarch on the same text.[5]

The case of the *Chrestomathy* is not so simple. It is preserved in outline by Photius, who says that it was divided into four books, whereas the figure in the Suda is three, and gives a summary of the first two only (*Bibliotheca* 239). To judge from what Photius says it was chiefly a discussion of the classification of types of poetry, and it looks more like the work of a teacher of literature than a philosopher. There are also some remarks which one would not expect to find coming from the pen of a fifth-century writer. For instance the paean is said to be a form of song now addressed to all the gods (320a21), and the song known as a *nomos* is stated to have received its present form from Timotheus (320b11). In each case the present tense is odd, if Proclus is the author, since even a diehard adherent of pagan traditions might have recognised that such forms of literature were a thing of the past. Similarly the statement that the poems of the Epic Cycle, which when added to Homer gave the Trojan saga in full, are preserved and widely appreciated (319a30), is

[4] H. Rabe, *RhMus* 64 (1909) 294-5.

[5] The commentary on the *Works and Days* has been studied by C. Faraggiana di Sarzana, *Aevum* 52 (1978) 17-40.

very implausible at such a late date. Doubts must also be expressed about the life of Homer and the brief résumés of the poems of the Epic Cycle which are found in a few manuscripts. Nevertheless, if the attribution of the *Chrestomathy* to Proclus now seems unlikely to be correct, it remains true to say that his vast literary output was not exclusively philosophical.

Proclus' main work consists of commentaries on Plato's *Republic*, *Parmenides*, *Timaeus* and *Alcibiades I*. There were also commentaries on the *Cratylus*, which no longer survives complete, and on the *Phaedo*, *Gorgias*, *Phaedrus*, *Theaetetus* and *Philebus*, which are all lost. Apparently they are all the products of a strenuous programme of lecturing. The inclusion of the *Alcibiades* may be surprising to a modern student of Plato, especially as many prominent authorities have declared it to be spurious. It is, however, quite beyond doubt that for the Neoplatonists the *Alcibiades* was important, and may well have been used as an introduction to Plato's thought, for which it was quite suitable as it contains a good example of Socrates' ability to deflate unjustified confidence and refers to his belief that he received instructions from a divinity. Students read as a first series ten dialogues, followed by the *Timaeus* and *Parmenides* to complete the initiation into the works of the master.[6] Proclus' commentaries are devoted largely to the twelve chosen dialogues. They are not regarded as possessing much originality, but rather as the systematisation of Neoplatonic thought. In a history of scholarship, if the definition of the term is strictly interpreted, they do not have a large place. But recent work on his fifth and sixth essays on the *Republic* has thrown fresh light on his thought. These essays are concerned with poetry, and in particular with Homer. Apart from revering Plato, Proclus worked within the tradition that saw in Homer the source of all knowledge, and as Plato had attacked poetry, some ingenious interpretation had to be found in order to preserve the credit of both. The fifth essay is a commentary on problems raised by Plato's discussion in *Republic II*; it tries to find a consistent view both in that book and in other statements by Plato. The sixth is an attempt to reconcile Homer and Plato. As Proclus frequently refers to his teacher Syrianus there is a question about the extent of his originality. Close analysis suggests that Proclus is not doing much more than develop lines of thought already indicated by his master, and in his turn Syrianus was actually following earlier traditions of interpretation. Proclus elaborated Syrianus' distinction between inspired and uninspired poetry, which was based on Plato's *Phaedrus* (245), into a threefold division: inspired, didactic and mimetic. Plato and Homer have to be taken equally seriously and they are made to agree by a process of Neoplatonist metaphysical interpretation. Interest in the texts as literature, though not entirely absent, is subordinated to philosophical exegesis. It may be worth noting

[6] L.G. Westerink, *Anonymous Prolegomena to Platonic Philosophy* (Amsterdam 1962) xxxvii-xxxviii, deals with the Neoplatonic canon.

in passing that Proclus follows Plato in attaching no value to dramatic literature.[7]

Despite official disapproval a large proportion of Proclus' output survived, and some of it was unexpectedly influential. It was not long before an unknown writer attempted the seemingly daunting task of reconciling Platonic metaphysics as expounded by him with the doctrines of Christianity. The author of this synthesis had the daring idea of passing it off as the work of Dionysius the Areopagite, the convert of St. Paul. This deliberate fraud will be mentioned again below.

Of the other Athenians Simplicius is the most interesting. He studied in Alexandria and then came to Athens, and there are a number of other known cases of movement between these two centres of learning in this period.[8] Simplicius is an opponent of Christianity in the same way as the other members of the group. His works were mostly, perhaps entirely, produced after his return from Persia. They are pedestrian and long-winded, and he confesses with agreeable frankness on one occasion that he is following Iamblichus to a large extent, frequently verbatim (*In Categorias* 3.2). He is better known to modern scholars than some of his colleagues because he was able to read certain texts by pre-Socratic philosophers, which he cites verbatim quite often. These texts must have been great rarities by the sixth century, and he is one of our most important sources for the thought of Parmenides and Empedocles, because he took the trouble to transcribe long sections of their poems. In the case of Parmenides Simplicius states explicitly that he is dealing with a rare text (*In Physica* 144.28), and he was doubtless intelligent enough to realise that the same was true of others. The question where he could lay hands on such bibliographical rarities is intriguing but impossible to answer. The only likely places are Athens, Alexandria and the capital.

But it is not only the student of early Greek philosophy who has cause to be grateful to Simplicius. For the historian of science he has the merit of preserving facts of importance. He cites the Hellenistic physicist Strato for a view about the acceleration of falling bodies (*In Physica* 916.10ff). He knows important details of Eudoxus' idea, destined to remain generally accepted until the time of Kepler, that the movements of the heavenly bodies can all be explained as the revolutions of concentric spheres (*In De caelo* 493-506). Once we even find him repeating an experiment designed to show whether air has weight, spurred into action because his authorities, Aristotle and Ptolemy, contradict each other. Simplicius states that the weight of a skin inflated with air is no different from its weight uninflated (*In De caelo* 710.14ff).

Perhaps his quotations have given him greater prominence than he deserved. But such are the accidents of manuscript tradition that he

---

[7] A.D.R. Sheppard, *Studies on the 5th and 6th essays of Proclus' Commentary on the Republic* (Göttingen 1980).

[8] H.-I. Marrou in A. Momigliano (ed.), *The Conflict between Paganism and Christianity in the Fourth Century* (Oxford 1963) 150.

might easily have become important in yet another context. If one copy of Epictetus had not been rescued, probably by the bibliophile Arethas *c.* 900, the text would almost certainly have been lost and Simplicius' commentary on it would have turned out to be valuable, bringing him once again to the attention of scholars.

(v) Alexandria

Alexandria had had a long tradition of scholarship both pagan and Christian. In the first centuries of our era the Christian school was more prominent than the pagan, and the famous library of the Museum, if it still existed, did not stimulate scholarship of the level that had been possible under the enlightened patronage of the Ptolemies. The library, if it did not disappear in the notorious fire caused by Caesar's military operations in 48-7 B.C., may have survived until the late fourth century. From about this time Alexandria gives the impression of becoming once again a centre of scholarship. If we are to trust the Suda (s.v. Theon) the Museum had not disappeared; but it does not follow that it was an institution organised on the same lines as before. A picture of a city with an active student population emerges from the Syriac *Life of Severus*, which we have had occasion to cite already in connection with Zacharias Scholasticus' decision to postpone the beginning of his literary education.

Of all the books produced in Alexandria at this time the one which perhaps proved most useful to successive generations of Byzantines was the commentary by Theon (*fl. c.* 360-380) on the Handy Tables appended by Ptolemy to his *Almagest*. The purpose of the Tables was to permit elementary astronomical calculations, such as the time difference between various towns. Theon wrote two books with the same purpose: one, addressed to competent astronomers, survives only in a few manuscripts; the other, explicitly designed for those who were incapable of understanding the reasoning and mathematical procedures lying behind the calculations, was frequently copied. It is boringly pedagogical in manner, as are many other books by the Alexandrians of this period.[1] Theon's other work includes an edition of the *Elements* and other writings by Euclid, which found favour to such a degree that it nearly ousted the original recension from circulation. He also wrote a commentary on the *Almagest*, which survives. Whatever his merits Theon is probably less famous than his daughter Hypatia, who is alleged to have written a commentary on the mathematician Diophantus, an exceptionally difficult author of algebraic problems, and was torn to pieces by an ignorant mob of Christians.

A less important but more widely used product of the Alexandrian schools was the *Canons* of Theodosius the grammarian. His date is uncertain: a man of that name and profession is mentioned in a letter

---

[1] A. Tihon, *Le Petit Commentaire de Théon d'Alexandrie aux Tables Faciles de Ptolémée* (*Studi e Testi* 282) (Vatican City 1978) offers text, translation and full account of the manuscript tradition of this much read work.

(no. 4) of Synesius (*c*. 370-413) and the identification is usually accepted. His work was often transcribed and even thought worthy of a commentary by George Choeroboscus. This fact, in combination with the statement of John Tzetzes already cited, indicates that it was in regular use in Byzantium. It is a list of the grammatical forms of Greek nouns and verbs with innumerable rules for the pupil to master. The conservatism of educational practice can be amusingly illustrated from one feature of it. The verb used as the standard example, conjugated through all its forms, is τύπτω, and this verb retained its pride of place in grammars until well after the Renaissance, despite the fact that classical Attic authors, who provide the canon of good usage that Theodosius and his colleagues all accepted without hesitation, used this verb only in a few tenses. Improved linguistic knowledge removed it from grammar books of the nineteenth century, but in a new grammar commissioned from a group of experts and published in 1978 one of the phantom forms recorded in Theodosius makes an unwelcome reappearance.

The chance survival of a single manuscript has given perhaps undue significance to a large lexicon compiled by a colleague of Theodosius called Hesychius. His date too is uncertain; the fifth century may be correct. The book is a compilation of previous works, as the author himself says in a dedicatory letter. He claims, however, to have added a substantial amount of material derived from his own reading. To the modern scholar it is of value because it explains some very rare words in classical texts and occasionally gives the correct reading when the direct tradition is at fault. Hesychius' purpose was to provide for the educated reader a dictionary which would help him not only with Attic literature but with dialect texts as well. For reasons which are not clear it seems not to have become popular, and its preservation in a single copy made in the early fifteenth century (Marc. gr. 622) is hard to explain. One would like to know more about the origin of the copy, since the scribe has been identified as responsible for another manuscript of considerable importance, containing the recension of eight plays of Aristophanes made by Demetrius Triclinius *c*. 1300 in Thessalonica (Holkham gr. 88);[2] evidently he had access to a good library and could appreciate the value of its contents. It would be rash to conjecture purely on the strength of this association that Hesychius was unearthed and used by Triclinius, especially as other evidence points in a different direction.

This lexicon was overshadowed in the middle ages by another which may in origin go back to much the same period. It is attributed to Cyril of Alexandria (d. 444), notorious as the instigator of the monks who murdered Hypatia, and though its present form is impossible to reconcile with his authorship it may be that he had a part in an earlier recension. The attribution to a Christian bishop will certainly have assisted its circulation.

[2] O.L. Smith, *Maia* 27 (1975) 205. K. Latte, *Hesychii Alexandrini lexicon* I (Copenhagen 1955) xxiv-xxv, argued that the book was written in Italy; but the script lends no support to that view.

Two other figures of the fifth century whose work is no longer extant in its original form may receive brief mention at this point. Orion, a member of one of the priestly families of Egypt, set up a school in Alexandria, where one of his pupils was none other than Proclus, who had begun his education in Lycia. Later he went to the capital. Some of his lexicographical work is preserved in the medieval lexica. The same is true on a much smaller scale of Horapollon, who compiled a list of the names describing shrines of the numerous pagan deities. Like Orion he moved to the capital. At some stage of his career he taught Timotheus of Gaza, mentioned earlier in this chapter. The Suda credits him with commentaries on Homer, Sophocles and Alcaeus. The last of these, even if it had no original feature whatever, is a further proof of the wide reading of the professional teachers of his time.[3]

An important figure whose activities extend into several fields is John Philoponus. Biographical information about him is scanty and we can only say that he was active in the first half of the sixth century. The name Philoponus appears to be a title indicating a lay person who is very active in the life of the church. His membership of the church is also indicated by his book on the eternity of the universe, arguing against Proclus and his Platonic position, and published in or shortly after 529. It is thought that this may have been intended as a demonstration to the authorities that their measures against the Neoplatonists of Athens did not need to be extended to Alexandria. In fact some of the Alexandrian philosophers were of Neoplatonic leanings but somehow managed to reach an agreement with the church which allowed them to continue to teach. Several theological treatises have been attributed to Philoponus, but the evidence of his authorship does not seem to amount to proof, although some involvement in theological controversy is established if we accept as accurate the notice of him in the Suda which states that he was declared by the doctors of the church to have fallen into the heresy of tritheism. Philoponus is regularly described as a grammarian, which is usually taken to imply that he never succeeded in obtaining the chair of philosophy. His activity as a teacher of literature is shown by some of his writings. The everyday problems of the classroom are revealed by his list of words with identical spelling but different accentuation. Treatises on accentuation and dialects are also ascribed to him. Probably none of these works has come down to us in its original form; their utility invited alterations and abridgments by other teachers.

Other works by Philoponus are more substantial. One of them gives the oldest extant account in Greek of the plane astrolabe. Another is a commentary on the first book of Nicomachus' *Introduction to Arithmetic*, which was a text used in the quadrivium. Some manuscripts attribute to him writings on medicine. That is a mistake, but an influential one, for it seems to have earned him a great reputation as a doctor among Arabic writers.[4] One might consider attributing them to

---

[3] Reitzenstein, op. cit. 312, 348, gives the essential facts about Orion and Horapollon.

[4] M. Meyerhof, *Mitteilungen des Deutschen Instituts für Aegyptische Altertumskunde in Kairo* 2 (1932) 1-21, especially the information from O. Temkin on p. 21.

his namesake who will be mentioned briefly below. But his main work was a series of commentaries on Aristotle's *Organon, De anima, Physics, De generatione et corruptione*, and *Meteorologica*. They are to a large extent his improved version of notes taken at the lectures of his teacher, Ammonius, a fact which is made clear by some of the titles in the manuscripts. Some modern authorities have maintained that the criticisms he makes of Aristotle's physics are of great importance as a landmark in the history of science; others dispute the claim, and it may well be that he appears to be of greater originality than he really was because of a failure to name his sources as regularly as his enemy Simplicius did.[5]

Eutocius of Ascalon, a person of whom we would gladly know more, was probably an older contemporary of Philoponus. He wrote commentaries on Archimedes, Apollonius of Perga's *On Conic Sections*, and Ptolemy's *Almagest*. The last of these three works is lost. One of his books is dedicated to Ammonius, who may be the head of the school in Alexandria. It has been suggested that he succeeded Ammonius, and the idea is attractive, since he would fill a gap between the tenures of Ammonius and Olympiodorus. Eutocius also lectured on philosophy, as is proved by some incomplete lectures of the rather later scholar Elias, on Aristotle's *Prior Analytics*, which open with a sentence mentioning Eutocius along with Alexander (of Aphrodisias) and Themistius as having considered the question whether logic is to be thought of as a part of philosophy or as merely its instrument.[6] Elias' reference by itself does not prove that Eutocius taught in Alexandria, and all that we can say with certainty is that he was there in the year 498, as is shown by a short astrological text.[7]

Eutocius's commentaries on the mathematicians may have turned out to be more important than he expected when he set to work on them. His commentary on Apollonius deals with the first four books; presumably he could not find the remaining four, but a copy survived somewhere in the eastern provinces of the empire and served as the exemplar of the Arabic translation. The existence of Eutocius' commentary may well have helped to guarantee the survival of the first four books in the original language. He dedicated his work to Anthemius of Tralles, the distinguished architect responsible in conjunction with Isidore of Miletus for the construction of Hagia Sophia. By a lucky chance colophons added by a later scribe are preserved and we learn that two of the commentaries on Archimedes, one on the *De sphaera et cylindro*, originally dedicated to Ammonius, the other on the *De dimensione circuli*, came into the hands of Isidore (pp. 48, 224, 260). He used them in classes with pupils. Since Archimedes' works would not have been suitable for use in an ordinary school, Isidore was obviously using them to give his own pupils specialised professional training. Another hint of Eutocius' importance is

[5] On Philoponus see H.D. Saffrey, *REG* 67 (1954) 396-410.

[6] L.G. Westerink, *Mnemosyne* 14 (1961) 126-39, especially 129.

[7] Printed in A. Olivieri, *Catalogus codicum astrologorum graecorum* I (Brussels 1898) 170.

found in a second addition to the original text of his commentary (p. 84). A parabola is under discussion, and the note remarks that Isidore was able to draw it with a compass that he invented, and that he used the parabola in his monograph on a lost book by the ancient engineer Heron on the construction of vaults. For architects concerned with Hagia Sophia, the dome of which collapsed in 558 as a result of an earthquake, the significance of such books is evident.

Some more light is thrown on Eutocius' work by his report of finding in an old book a fragment of Archimedes which he took to be the text making good Archimedes' promise to provide a particular proof. Eutocius says that he made his find after a long search. The fragment was very obscure owing to errors in the text and the diagrams. But it preserved to some extent the Doric dialect in which Archimedes had written and it used old-fashioned technical terms for parabola and hyperbola, 'section of right-angled cone', 'section of obtuse-angled cone' (p. 132). The point about the dialect is of some importance. Part of Archimedes' work has come down to us in Doric, which is what he would naturally write as an inhabitant of Syracuse, but some of it has been converted into a standard Greek more or less corresponding to Attic. One would like to know why the text was tampered with, since on the whole the dialects of Greek literature, although not always understood by the scribes, were reasonably well preserved in the process of transmission, and short guides to the essential features of the dialects used in literature were written for the benefit of schoolchildren.

Although Eutocius perhaps failed to find a complete copy of Apollonius, it is clear from his discovery of the fragment just mentioned and from the number of other writers that he is able to quote that he was at least an industrious researcher and had access to good libraries. Experts in the history of mathematics allow him credit for making explicit the stages of argument in the proofs that he was elucidating. The preservation of his work enables us to see how mathematicians worked together and combined theoretical and practical studies.

Of the other philosophical commentators of the Alexandrian school not much needs to be said. The tradition can be traced from the end of the fifth century until the late sixth or early seventh. The main product of the school consisted of introductory lectures on Aristotle's *Organon*, which follow a fairly regular pattern. The texts which survive are often lecture notes taken down by pupils and revised rather than the words of the master. This is true of all the Alexandrian introductions to the *Categories*. From a philosophical point of view they offer nothing of interest to the modern expert. It is perhaps worth emphasising that Olympiodorus (*c.* 500-*c.* 560) maintains a Neoplatonist position and finds sophistical ways of making it acceptable to his audience, which was presumably entirely Christian.[8] The fact is extremely surprising at such a late date and in a city where religious fervour could assume such ferocious forms as the murder of Hypatia. The last member of the school

[8] L.G. Westerink, *Anonymous prolegomena*, xv-xvii.

is a very shadowy figure called Stephen, who is thought to have been summoned to teach in Constantinople in the reign of Heraclius (610-641). He appears to be the author of commentaries on Aristotle, *De anima III* and *De interpretatione*, and on Ptolemy's *Handy Tables*, the last of which evidently did not replace Theon's similar handbook. His position in the capital is inferred partly from various titles given to him in the manuscripts, which are far from being unambiguous, partly from his use of an era based on the reign of the emperor Constantine, whereas in Alexandria he might have used Diocletian's accession as his starting point.[9] But almost every statement that has been made about him is open to doubt. The fact is that the last days of the school are shrouded in obscurity.

One final point should however be made in order to counter the generally mediocre impression that we are bound to form of the Alexandrian philosophy lecturers. In an otherwise undistinguished preface to his course on Aristotle's *Categories* Elias, who is probably to be dated in the second half of the sixth century, gives an admirable view of the qualities that are desirable in the ideal commentator. The paragraph is worth quoting in full.[10]

The commentator should be both commentator and scholar at the same time. It is the task of the commentator to unravel obscurities in the text; it is the task of the scholar to judge what is true and what is false, or what is sterile and what is productive. He must not assimilate himself to the authors he expounds, like actors on the stage who put on different masks because they are imitating different characters. When expounding Aristotle he must not become an Aristotelian and say that there has never been so great a philosopher, when expounding Plato he must not become a Platonist and say that there has never been a philosopher to match Plato. He must not force the text at all costs and say that the ancient author whom he is expounding is correct in every respect; instead he must repeat to himself at all times 'the author is a dear friend, but so also is truth, and when both stand before me truth is the better friend'. He must not sympathise with a philosophical school, as happened to Iamblichus, who out of sympathy for Plato is condescending in his attitude to Aristotle and will not contradict Plato in regard to the theory of ideas. He must not be hostile to a philosophical school like Alexander (of Aphrodisias). The latter, being hostile to the immortality of the intellectual part of the soul, attempts to twist in every way the remarks of Aristotle in his third book on the immortality of the soul which prove that it is immortal. The commentator must know the whole of Aristotle in order that, having first proved that Aristotle is consistent with himself, he may expound Aristotle's works by means of Aristotle's works. He must know the whole of Plato, in order to prove that Plato is consistent with himself and make the works of Aristotle an introduction to those of Plato.

[9] On Stephen see H. Usener, *Kleine Schriften* III (Graz 1965) 247-322; Westerink, op. cit. xxiv; R. Browning, *CR* 15 (1965) 262-3.

[10] Ed. A. Busse, *CAG* 18.1 (Berlin 1900) 122-3.

Since Elias' lectures do not appear to have enjoyed a wide circulation among later Byzantine students and were not printed until the turn of the last century, he was for long deprived of the opportunity to exercise a beneficial influence on all who expound literary texts. The heterogeneous character of his course prompts the reflection that it may have been a compilation from various sources, so that the present passage is not necessarily the product of his own good sense. The last sentence in fact, assuming that the Greek text is correctly transmitted, indicates a preference for Plato over Aristotle in a way that may be thought somewhat surprising at so late a date. And the preceding sentence is a reference to the well known principle of exegesis, developed in all probability in the Hellenistic period by Aristarchus in his work on Homer, that each author is the best source for illuminating his own writings. Nevertheless Elias' statement of the ideal to be looked for in a commentator merits a prominent place in any history of scholarly method.

One other field of intellectual activity in Alexandria should be mentioned. The city was known as a flourishing centre of medicine. According to the historian Ammianus Marcellinus (22.16.18) it was enough for a doctor to say that he had studied there if he wished to be accepted as a serious practitioner. The comment was made at the end of the fourth century, and there is no reason to doubt its accuracy, both at that date and later. We know that Julian's doctor Oreibasius studied in Alexandria, and later we can trace the writers Aetius and Paul of Aegina practising or studying there. In the sixth and perhaps even the early seventh century the lecturers on philosophy Elias and David when discussing Aristotle sometimes speak as if they also lectured on Galen, combining the professions of philosopher and physician.[11] The same combination of interests is suggested by a papyrus (P. Berol. 11739) which preserves for us the opening paragraph of an almost unbelievably pedestrian commentary on Galen's *De sectis*, written from a Neoplatonist point of view and sharing many features of the better known Alexandrian commentaries.[12] Very little can be said of any positive achievement of Alexandrian medicine. Paul admits openly in his introduction that he contributes practically no original material of his own and depends for the most part on Oreibasius, whose encyclopaedic treatment was too bulky to be convenient for ordinary use. Paul's book had a wide circulation, and its account of ancient surgery is more complete than others. Some of the other texts produced by the Alexandrians survived by the slenderest thread of transmission, which is surprising when the practical utility of medical works is borne in mind. One writer whose works almost disappeared is Palladius; we still have his lectures on Galen's *De sectis*, an account for beginners of various schools of medical thought, and a commentary on the sixth book of Hippocrates'

[11] L.G. Westerink, *Janus* 51 (1964) 172-4.
[12] E. Nachmanson, *Göteborgs Högskolas Årsskrift* 31 part 2 (1925) 201-17. Owing to damage in the papyrus the author's name cannot be restored with certainty.

Epidemics. Another is John of Alexandria, whose commentary on Hippocrates' book about the foetus is preserved only in one Greek manuscript (Laur. 59.14) and a Latin version made at the request of king Manfred of Sicily (1258-66). An almost identical fate overtook his commentary on the sixth book of Hippocrates' *Epidemics*, now found in an anonymous Latin translation. But fragments of the Greek original still exist, entered in the margins of an Arabic medical text translated into Greek. The manuscript in question (Vat. gr. 300) appears to have been written in Palermo in the middle of the twelfth century. As will become clear later, Sicily was sometimes an important staging-post in the journey of books heading for survival.

The Alexandrians of late antiquity have no achievement that can compare with the invention in Hellenistic times of literary scholarship as we know it. But in their modest way they helped to ensure the continuance of certain worthwhile traditions, and several textbooks received the seal of approval by being used long after Egypt had ceased to be a province of the empire. Even if the commentators on the philosophical classics do not have the merit of originality, they were at least concerned to interpret their chosen authorities according to the principles of common sense, which is more than can be claimed for the Athenian Neoplatonists' treatment of their master. In scientific matters their services were, at the most pessimistic estimate, similar to those of Simplicius at Athens; they preserved ideas of importance that had been put forward by their more distinguished predecessors. And the influence of the Alexandrians was felt elsewhere. Some of them went to Athens and the capital, and it is possible that their medical school was sufficiently long-lived to be of interest to the Arabs. In a westerly direction their influence may not have been negligible, for it has been argued that Boethius studied with them; although there is no explicit testimony, the comparison of his thought with that of the Alexandrians suggests very strongly that he had learned from them. But the argument depends in part on a corrupt text where more than one emendation is possible.[13]

(vi) Constantinople

It was not until the south-eastern provinces of the empire had fallen into the hands of the Arabs that Constantinople held an undisputed position as the centre of learning and culture. Its status as the capital, and the foundation of what is sometimes called a university by Theodosius II in 425, had not been enough to set it above its rivals. Once again the use of the term university can scarcely be justified. The emperor's edict gives the impression of being anxious to protect the imperial establishment from private competitors, who are forbidden in future to advertise for custom, whereas a university would not have found itself endangered by

---

[13] P. Courcelle, *Les lettres grecques en Occident de Macrobe à Cassiodore* (Paris 1943) 259-300, was answered by J. Shiel, *Medieval and Renaissance Studies* 4 (1958) 217-44, and *Vivarium* 12 (1974) 14-17.

private institutions. It is safer to assume that there was one privileged secondary school, in which intelligent masters and pupils would sometimes engage in advanced study.[1]

The first person of any consequence is Themistius (c. 317-c. 388), the author of paraphrases of several Aristotelian works and a number of panegyrical addresses to successive emperors. His rhetorical style makes him uncongenial to modern taste, and his position in a history of scholarship is incidental, since he is the source of an interesting report about an imperial initiative that may have turned out to be very influential. In an address to the emperor Constantius on the first of January 357 (*Oration* 4, pp. 59-61) he describes a plan to guarantee the survival of ancient literature. A scriptorium for the production of new copies of the classics, whose survival is alleged to be threatened by neglect, will ensure that the new capital becomes a centre of literary culture. One point of considerable interest which is clear on a careful reading of the text is that the leading authors – Plato, Aristotle, Demosthenes, Isocrates and Thucydides are named – are of such standing that they do not require official support in order to guarantee their position. In other words Themistius is saying what we are in any case entitled to infer, that the major school authors did not need any protection beyond their place in the school syllabus, which ensured that they would continue to be copied. But, continues Themistius, the successors of Homer and Hesiod, and philosophers such as Chrysippus, Zeno and Cleanthes, together with a whole range of other authors, are not in common circulation, and their texts will now be saved from oblivion. The suggestion that the poets apart from Homer and Hesiod are in danger is an exaggeration, one of many that a panegyrist can permit himself; he can scarcely have thought or wished to suggest that the schools of the capital did not read tragedy or comedy. But the general point he is trying to make is clear; none but the central authors will be read in future unless something is done to increase the number of copies available, and the emperor is now taking the necessary steps. To a more impartial observer the threat may not have seemed to be so pressing, but it was convenient for the panegyrist to overlook the existence of other centres of education where there were good supplies of books. One city could probably still boast of a library much larger than was needed merely to supply the needs of the average teacher, but that library, which was in the Serapeum at Alexandria, seems to have been destroyed by fire c. 390, an accident which lends an importance to the measures of Constantius that could not have been predicted with confidence at the time they were announced.

Themistius' report taken by itself is lacking in clarity and could be taken to show that the emperor intended to found either a library or an unusually well equipped school or a bookshop. The suggestion that from

---

[1] P. Speck, *BZ* 67 (1974) 385-93, reviewing P. Lemerle, *Le premier humanisme byzantin* (Paris 1971).

now onwards Constantinople will export Greek culture raises a question: does it mean that books will be copied to order and sent off, or more simply that a student attracted by the new supply of books will come to the capital and take away with him a mind improved by his experience? On either view the accessibility of the scriptorium and the books to the public seems to be presupposed. To that extent the new foundation, even if not producing copies for customers, might come near to serving as a bookshop by allowing them to transcribe their personal copies. The proof that a new library was the emperor's plan comes from an order issued in 372 to the city prefect Clearchus to appoint four scribes skilled in Greek and three in Latin to undertake the transcription and repair of books (*Theodosian Code* 14.9.2). One wonders what had been going on during the fifteen years intervening. It is customary to speak in glowing terms of Constantius' initiative, but the words of a panegyrist need to be treated with reserve. Perhaps the emperor did conceive a grand scheme, and the execution of it turned out to be slower than anticipated. Or perhaps we may suppose that the order of 372 marks an alteration in the staffing of a flourishing institution. Was it intended to be the library of a special school, a kind of university? That is possible, but the other information that we possess about such institutions is so fragmentary that the idea must remain hypothetical; there is no unequivocal sign of such a school at the time.

If one attempts to draw up a list of the works or activities of scholars resident in Constantinople from the time of its designation as the capital in 330 until the accession of Justinian in 527, the result is meagre. Probably the only figure of any great importance is the grammarian Priscian, excluded from the present survey because his work is entirely in Latin. A complication arises from the careers of one or two known scholars who, having established their reputations elsewhere, finished their working lives in the capital; this is true of Horapollon, who had made his name in Alexandria, and Pamprepius, who had been employed by the city of Athens. In such cases it is difficult to feel sure that their best work had not already been done before they moved. Of those who appear to have spent their whole career in Constantinople there is nothing exceptional about men like Orus (*c.* 450) and Eugenius (*c.* 500), two of the rather small number who are anything more than names to us. The former wrote a long book on orthography, a topic which became an increasingly tiresome necessity to the Byzantines as the gradual changes in the pronunciation of Greek made spelling harder. A small section of it has come down to us (Messina gr. 118); it lists words written with the iota which the modern learner is invited to call subscript, but which in fact was often not written at all by ancient scribes, as is proved by the papyri, or if written was always given a normal position in the line alongside the preceding vowel, not below it. Orus' work was therefore a product of the grammarian's problems in teaching children to write accurately. It happens that he is valuable to us because he justifies his rules by quotations from a wide range of authors, some of whom are now lost. He did not necessarily know them at first hand. A long list is preserved of his other writings (Suda s.v.). They include some on orthography, one on enclitic words, one on vowels that may be scanned either long or short, and one on propositions in the grammar of Herodian, whose work, although it has not come down to us, was certainly the standard reference book and no doubt stimulated a large proportion of the minor grammatical literature of late antiquity. There are two other works by Orus of which we can gain some idea from their fragmentary remains. One was a list of words which have more than one meaning; excerpts of it exist, and suggest a careless compilation of elementary nature, full of inaccurate information. The other was a list of geographical names, and is quoted by more than one later authority. The scraps that remain make it clear that Orus was interested in the etymology of place names and the myths that were connected with them. The etymologies are sometimes given as alternatives; he is prepared to consider for instance that the Adriatic derives its name either from a town Adria founded by the Sicilian tyrant Dionysius or that the town and the sea both received their name from a Messapian called Adrius (*Et. gen.*, s.v. Adria). A great variety of sources are cited, including commentaries on Euripides' *Hecuba* and the poet Lycophron. It is impossible to say whether his show of learning is the result of first-hand reading, which might have been possible in the libraries of the capital at the time, or the product of compilation from the writings of a few genuinely learned predecessors of an earlier age. But we can say with certainty that etymology and mythology were topics dear to the heart of the average ancient teacher, and all Oros' work gives the impression of being produced to meet the requirements of the classroom. Recent research has thrown a great deal of light on one of Oros' main works, a lexicon of Attic diction designed to controvert the doctrine available in Phrynichus' work on the same subject. Oros exploits a wider range of authors, including Menander, Lysias and Xenophon, while he seems to neglect Aeschylus, Sophocles and the writers of the Second Sophistic as potential source material. In both these respects he shows good sense. It is also interesting to note that in the long-standing controversy between proponents of analogy and anomaly as the key to solutions of grammatical questions he stood on the side of the anomalists.[2]

The same educational concerns characterise the work of Eugenius (Suda s.v.). He is stated to have become famous at an advanced age in the reign of Anastasius (491-518). Stephanus of Byzantium (s.v. Anaktorion) refers to him in such a way as to imply that they may both have held the same official position. Some of his work was provoked by problems of orthography, and he compiled a lexicon. There are also signs of an interest in metre, in particular a study of the choral lyrics in Greek tragedy, taken from fifteen plays. It is tempting to see in the number

---

[2] On Orus see Reitzenstein, op. cit. 316-48; K. Alpers, *Das attizistische Lexikon des Oros* (Berlin 1981), especially 87-101.

fifteen a selection of nine from Euripides and three each from Aeschylus and Sophocles, which might have been the prescribed reading list in a school.

The age of Justinian (527-565) is a brilliant epoch in many respects. The reconquest of many of the territories that had belonged to the Roman empire, the architecture of Hagia Sophia and the codification of Roman Law were extraordinary achievements. It can hardly be said that literary scholarship reached the level attained in other fields of activity. What is perhaps most interesting is that we can see the principles of scholarship being put to use in debate by theologians. The ancients had been much concerned with the detection of forgery, probably stimulated in the first instance by a number of forgeries offered to the librarians of Hellenistic Alexandria when they attempted to form a complete collection of Greek literature for the library in the Museum. According to one possible interpretation, which was certainly known to the Byzantines, Dionysius Thrax in his little treatise on grammar had defined the ability to distinguish the genuine from the false as the highest aim of the grammarian. Questions of authenticity took on a more serious aspect when theological doctrines were at stake. Theologians had not disdained philological methods in the past. Dionysius, bishop of Alexandria and a former pupil of Origen (d. *c.* 264), had argued from the language and style of the Apocalypse that it could not be by the same author as St. John's Gospel; while not wishing to accept the verdict of critics who removed it from the biblical canon because of the obscurity of its contents, he found the character of the Apocalypse quite different and its style full of unacceptable expressions (Eusebius, *Hist. eccl.* 7.25). But now the emperor himself took an active interest in such questions, and we find him considering problems of authenticity in a letter sent to the monks of Alexandria in which he tries to refute the Monophysite heresy.[3] The Monophysite position had been defended by the citing of propositions favourable to it from writings by Pope Julius of Rome and Athanasius. Justinian argues that they are forgeries because their doctrine coincides with that of Apollinaris, which was generally agreed to be heretical. As far as the alleged papal letter is concerned, he argues first that the popes have never lapsed from orthodoxy, secondly that the form of address in the heading of the letter uses an incorrect style, and finally that he had written to Rome to ask if the letter could be found in the archives there, and the reply was negative. As to the letter of Athanasius addressed to the emperor Jovian, for Justinian it is betrayed as a forgery by not being cast in the style appropriate to a letter and not adopting the tone that would be proper in addressing the emperor; and furthermore the question of the incarnation was not a cause of controversy at the time. Justinian's scholarship does him credit. One might ask whether research in the archives of the capital would have been possible in order to show that no such letter had been received by

---

[3] Ed. E. Schwartz, *Abh. München* 18 (1939) 18-21, sections 70-86.

Jovian, but perhaps the records were not complete. It could also be suggested that, if critics were capable of detecting features of style suitable for a letter and obtaining the agreement of other qualified judges, a sceptic might reply that a letter on so important and delicate a topic would be almost certain to adopt the tone of a formal treatise. Nevertheless the discovery of comparable texts, the insistence on verification of sources and the investigation of historical facts are proof of high quality scholarship.

The emperor's standards of scholarship contrast favourably with those of one of his best known civil servants, John the Lydian (b. 490). This man tells us (*De magistratibus* 3.29) that he left his home town Philadelphia and moved to the capital in his twenty-first year. He spent a short time studying philosophy, which amounted to an introduction to Aristotle and Plato. Shortly he was able to enter the bureaucracy, in which he served forty years. During that time his literary tastes became known to the emperor, and he was allowed to hold in plurality an official teaching position. Unfortunately, despite his discursive manner, he does not give us any details of the terms on which he held the post or of the instruction he offered. Three antiquarian books survive from his pen: *On the magistracies*, *On the months*, *On omens*. He was particularly interested in the Roman origin of Byzantine institutions and clearly had read widely in both Greek and Latin in order to collect his information. But his scholarship, especially in Latin, is not of a high order, and he has too great a taste for astrology to please modern rationalist attitudes, not to mention those of Christians. Photius (*Bibliotheca* 180), who rightly thought that a lot of his material was pure nonsense, questioned whether he was genuinely a Christian. As is shown by his willingness to write on a topic such as omens, he was of anything but a sceptical turn of mind. In literary matters his credulity is demonstrated by his willingness to accept as genuine the collection of hexameter verse known as the' Sibylline oracles, which included prophecies of the birth of Christ. He does, however, make up for his credulity to some extent by his comments on the poor versification of the oracles. Being unwilling to accept that such faults could be due to the Sibyl herself he suggests that they are to be attributed to the shorthand writers who failed to keep up with her as she gave her prophecies. When the prophetess came out of her trance she was unable to remember the correct wording and they were incapable of reconstructing the verses (*De mensibus* 4.47). John's misplaced ingenuity could have served him well in dealing with difficulties in some texts: there were in circulation sermons by leading church fathers whose texts depended ultimately on transcripts made by shorthand writers.

Another episode from Justinian's reign deserves mention. In 532 a convocation was held before the patriarch to deal with the doctrines of the heretic Severus. The authenticity of several documents brought forward as evidence was challenged. Hypatius, bishop of Ephesus, argued that Dionysius the Areopagite should not be cited, as the works

attributed to him were not genuine.[4] Although the forgery was produced
c. 500 and had not had much time in which to acquire the status of a
classic, this scepticism is extremely remarkable. There is practically no
other trace of such an attitude until the Italian Renaissance, and the
forger, who adapted Neoplatonic metaphysics to Christian needs, must
be one of the most successful members of his profession ever to have
existed. He ranks with the author of the Donation of Constantine.
Hypatius asked a simple question: if the works are genuine, how is it that
they are not exploited by Cyril and Athanasius? Although the objection
does not constitute a proof, it is a notable instance of justified scepticism
based on a properly scholarly approach. The report of the debate is
perhaps incomplete, because the objection mentioned is the first of four
which an otherwise unknown Theodore tried to refute in a pamphlet on
the genuineness of Dionysius' work. This is known to us from the résumé
of Photius (*Bibliotheca* 1), which states the four objections that
Theodore attempted to answer. Apart from the one already mentioned
they were: (2) why does Eusebius make no reference to it in his review of
books by the fathers? (3) how does it come about that Dionysius, a
contemporary of the apostles, describes in some detail traditions that
grew up gradually in the church? (4) why should Dionysius quote
Ignatius, who lived in the reign of Trajan? Photius tells us nothing of the
means by which Theodore tried to weaken the force of the objections and
leaves the impression that, while not wishing to commit himself openly,
he found them convincing. Presumably the defence would have had to
make much play with the concept of interpolations in an otherwise
genuine text. It is difficult to think that the case can have seemed very
plausible, but Theodore's importance is that he unwittingly
demonstrates the sound scholarship of an opponent, who was in all
probability Hypatius.

While the emperor and theologians argued in support of what they
believed to be the truth and the architects of Hagia Sophia studied
higher mathematics, the more ordinary literary studies of the period
bring us back to traditional and less exalted pursuits. One substantial
monument remains from the scholarship of the Justinianic age, the
geographical lexicon of Stephanus Byzantinus. In its original form it
must have been enormous; entries beginning with the letter omicron
were in book 36, which, even allowing for the modest proportions of what
the ancients called a book, indicates great length. As so often length
militated against survival, and what remains is an epitome, not quite
complete, but large enough to fill several hundred pages of a modern
printed edition. The epitomator is presumably the Hermolaus recorded
in the Suda lexicon (s.v.) as having performed this feat and dedicated
the result to Justinian. Within a generation Stephanus' work had been
found too cumbersome and suffered the usual fate. Its objective can be

---

[4] Ed. E. Schwartz, *ACO* tom. 4 vol. 2 (Strasburg 1914) 173.

simply described. It was to provide a geographical gazetteer, with a note of the correct spellings for the names of places and the adjectives by which their inhabitants should be described. The emphasis is throughout linguistic, and its interest to the modern reader is, as so often with ancient lexica, that it quotes from a wider range of literature than is now available to us. It was intended to serve as a reference book, more useful to the teacher than to officials of the foreign office or provincial administrators. But in view of the education and attitudes of Byzantine civil servants it would not be surprising if they in fact consulted it. Though its bulk may have ensured the merit of being a more or less complete guide to the inhabited world, Stephanus' industry was perhaps less meritorious than it seems. It is known that some of his predecessors had taken an interest in geographical names. In the entry for Anaktorion he records a disagreement with Eugenius, suggesting that the latter had accepted a faulty spelling from an uncorrected manuscript. A more important predecessor was Orus, whom he quotes three times. The exact relation between the two is masked by the fragmentary nature of what has come down to us, but it is clear that a great deal of Stephanus may derive from Orus. Stephanus is more concerned with the linguistic and lexicographical aspect of the material.[5] It is hard to avoid the suspicion that he is a compiler with little to add of his own.

An important writer whose career falls partly in the reign of Justinian deserves brief mention here. Agathias (*c.* 531/2-*c.* 580), although inferior as an historian to his predecessor Procopius of Caesarea, is not only a source of some information about other scholars but had literary pretensions of his own. A lawyer by profession, he complains that he had to spend the day from morning till sunset poring over legal texts, whereas he would rather have read the classics in order to improve his own prose (*History* 3.1). The modern reader may well feel that the deliberate imitation has produced a turgid result, but the book is not without interest. He is our sole source for the story of the seven Athenian philosophers seeking asylum in Persia, and he tells an amusing if obscure story about the architect Anthemius managing to take revenge on a troublesome neighbour in the apartment above his own by means of steam channelled through pipes leading from containers of boiling water. Agathias also wrote epigrams in elegiac verse in the fashion that had been traditional for centuries, and his interest in this form of literature led him to make his own collection of recently composed epigrams that were not easy to obtain. This operation marks a stage in the history of the collection known as the *Greek Anthology*. Agathias' *Cycle*, as he called it, seems to have been published a year or two after Justinian's death.[6] It was divided according to subject matter into seven sections: dedications to the old gods of paganism, descriptions of statues or other works of art, epitaphs, episodes of daily life, satire, love, wine and dinner parties. In

[5] Reitzenstein, op. cit. 316-332.
[6] Averil Cameron, *Agathias* (Oxford 1970) 12 ff.

order to collect poems for an anthology of this kind Agathias might be thought to have gained access to the best libraries of the capital. Very little is known, however, about public libraries at this date, and even assuming that he could have used his position to obtain entry to the imperial library or a collection in the imperial high school, the privilege might have been useless. The epigrams that he sought to put together in a single corpus were probably difficult for a reader to find because there was no organised publishing trade at the time and that kind of literature did not necessarily reach the libraries. It is more likely that Agathias gathered a few texts from the monuments on which they were inscribed, others by personal contact with the authors or members of their families who would probably retain a master copy.[7]

Brief mention should be made here of another Hesychius, a historian born in Miletus who wrote a chronicle of world history up to the death of Anastasius (518), followed by a supplement on Justin and part of Justinian's reign. A few pages on the history of the capital have come down to us, but the reason for including him in the present account is that he was also the author of a biographical dictionary of pagan writers and scholars. In its original form this is no longer preserved, but an abridgment of it served as one of the sources of the Suda lexicon in the tenth century, and it gives a large amount of valuable information. Hesychius probably did not collect all the information himself but his sources have not been identified with certainty. Once again we are apparently dealing with a revised and improved version of an existing reference book.

Since we have referred to medical studies as part of the achievement of Alexandria in late antiquity, it is necessary to add a brief note about the doctors whose career was passed in the capital. Their work seems to have been, like so much else produced at the time, almost entirely in the nature of compilation, and as such of interest to the modern scholar only in so far as it preserves earlier work that would otherwise have been lost. The first writer of any note is Oreibasius, already mentioned as Julian's physician who had studied in Alexandria. His work was an encyclopaedia of medicine in seventy books, of which rather less than half has come down to us; very large books, unless they proved to be exceptionally useful, were exposed to the dangers of abridgment or neglect. His main source was Galen. Late in his career he put together a shorter synopsis of medical practice and a still shorter book aimed at the layman, telling him of certain basic remedies he could employ when he was travelling or found himself for any other reason unable to obtain a doctor's services. Oreibasius's shorter books were translated into Latin, and so like John of Alexandria he had some influence in the medieval west, which as a rule was unable to use Greek texts in the original language.

Oreibasius served as one of the main sources for Aetius of Amida,

---

[7] See further N.G. Wilson, 'Books and readers in Byzantium', in *Byzantine Books and Bookmen, a Dumbarton Oaks colloquium* (Washington 1975) 1-15.

whose compilation in sixteen books is thought to date from the reign of Justinian. Photius (*Bibliotheca* 221) preferred his work to Oreibasius' short guides on grounds of clarity and a wider selection of material, but admitted that Aetius did not stand up to comparison with Oreibasius' major work. Nevertheless he recommended Aetius to the medical profession of his own day as a good practical guide, despite its weakness on the theoretical aspects of the subject. A modern judge would be bound to take the opposite view, because it is in Aetius that the scientific attitude of previous Greek doctors begins to yield to some extent to magic and superstition. His work enjoyed quite wide circulation in Byzantium, either because it was thought more up to date than Oreibasius or because its character appealed more. The lapse into superstition is a sign of the times, and is found also in the work of Alexander of Tralles (*c.* 525-*c.* 605), one of the brothers of the architect Anthemius, whose collection of twelve books entitled *Therapeutica* had a certain popularity and was also translated into both Latin and oriental languages. In the case of Alexander the recommendation of magical practices appears to be due to a mistaken belief (II 475 ed. Puschmann) that they had been accepted as efficacious by no less an authority than Galen, who had discussed them in a treatise on medical practice as described in Homer. A sentence is quoted by Alexander in which the putative Galen says that his initial scepticism was overcome by long experience. The treatise in question is not extant, and the mere fact of its willingness to concede the utility of magic is enough to prove that it cannot have been genuine. Galen himself had been much exercised by the incorrect attribution to him of books that were either not his or had not reached a stage of completion that justified publication, and the librarians of the Alexandrian Museum had had to develop criteria for the identification of forgeries. In the present case we see how the inability to maintain an accurate canon of the genuine writings of a leading author was a significant factor in permitting the resurgence of superstition.

As the sixth century draws to a close there is less and less sign of literary life. One symptom of decline is the disappearance of knowledge of Latin. At the beginning of the century the capital at least had been, if not a bilingual city, one in which both languages were well understood. The great grammarian Priscian wrote in Latin. It is certain that it was Justinian's first language. The codification of the law, one of the greatest achievements of the reign, required a professional knowledge of it. But by the middle of the century the law students seem to have needed a crib of Justinian's *Code*, the so-called κατὰ πόδας. John the Lydian laments that the use of Latin was abolished in the bureau for European affairs by order of John the Cappadocian, Justinian's minister (*De magistratibus* 3.68). One does not know exactly what inference to draw from the work of Corippus, formerly a schoolmaster in Carthage, who in 566-7 wrote a Latin poem in praise of the emperor Justin's accession and early acts in office. Could he have been sure of being understood even by all members of the court? Whereas the historian Procopius had been a versatile linguist, there is much less sign that Agathias, who must have known of Corippus' composition, had similar talents. The loss of linguistic competence may have happened quite suddenly at the end of the century. The most striking proof of it is the story of Pope Gregory the Great who, in a letter dated 597, says that in Constantinople it is not possible to obtain a satisfactory translation (*Epistles* 7.27).

There is some reason to think that book production may have begun to decline in quantity during the reign of Justinian. A survey of papyri and manuscripts that can be attributed to the period from the end of the fifth century to the end of the sixth has led one recent writer to the conclusion that already under Justinian fewer books were being copied.[8] This conclusion depends on an ability to date scripts accurately to within half a century or less, which in the case of uncials is not generally agreed to be possible. But although there is inevitably a subjective element in the palaeographical judgments which are the basis of judgments about the level of culture, the conclusion in this case deserves serious consideration.

The darkness is not much illuminated by the figure of Theophylactus Simocatta, a historian whose family had come from Egypt. He wrote an account of the wars against the Persians in the reign of Maurice (582-602), which is useful as a historical source but chiefly noteworthy for the rhetorical bombast of the style. Curiously enough, in view of what has just been said of the decline of linguistic knowledge in Byzantium, he reports some correspondence between the Persian king and his rebellious general Baram in such a way as to suggest direct translation from the Persian (4.7-8). But rather than attribute a knowledge of the language to Theophylact we may find it easier to believe that he had availed himself of the skill of some professional interpreter or a friend at court in the diplomatic service. He is a man of some learning, anxious to display it by quoting Callimachus (fr. 620 in the prologue § 2). He tantalises us with the bald statement that Maurice promoted learning and literature (8.13), and there are some annoyingly allusive indications that steps were taken to restore education and culture after the overthrow of the usurper Phocas. A curious dialogue between the personified abstractions philosophy and history which prefaces his book tells us that the study of philosophy and of Atticism had now become possible again. It is also said that the patriarch had given new life to history. A reference is made to the story of Alcestis, which may be meant as a sign that Theophylact was proud of knowing a play of Euripides that remained outside the list read in the schools. But the wording of a sentence about the patriarch suggests that he had created a teaching post, perhaps for the historian himself. Although it is not now fashionable to believe in the existence of a theological seminary under the aegis of the patriarch at this date, it would be perverse to deny that such a seminary may be what

[8] G. Cavallo, 'La circolazione libraria nell' età di Giustiniano', in G.G. Archi (ed.), *L'imperatore Giustiniano, storia e mito* (Milan 1978) 213-15.

Theophylact in his contorted way is referring to. If his testimony is taken in isolation it is equally possible to suppose that the patriarch's patronage was a more limited act, setting up the historian perhaps as the head of a school. But we also know from an epigram by George of Pisidia that the same patriarch created a theological library and it is tempting to see a link between that and the help given to Theophylact.[9]

[9] No. 46, ed. L. Sternbach, *Wiener Studien* 14 (1892) 55. In Theophylact's preface the words βῆμα εὐμενῶς ἱδρυμένον suggest to me a teaching post; Lemerle, op. cit. 79, is more sceptical.

3

Dark Ages and Iconoclasm

(i) Interlude

In the opinion of some historians the reign of Heraclius (610-641) marks the end of the ancient world; it was in his reign that Islam made its great initial conquests which, by closing much of the Mediterranean to international trade, put an end to the economic basis of the Roman empire. We have mentioned the slight indications of literary and scholarly activity in Constantinople during the early years of the seventh century. One literary figure whose career extends a little further into the century is George of Pisidia. His verses are partly theological in theme and partly a celebration of the campaigns of Heraclius against the Persians. George shows some indebtedness to the classical tradition in that he is apparently the last Byzantine capable of writing iambic lines that preserve the rules of classical prosody intact. He had admirers, and as will be explained in more detail in a later chapter he inspired someone in the eleventh century to ask whether his verse was superior to that written by Euripides, a question which was considered in a short essay by the leading intellectual of the time, Michael Psellos. But from the end of the reign of Heraclius, which coincides with the loss of Egypt and other provinces to the Arabs, until the early years of the ninth century there is a period traditionally known as a dark age. Whether the iconoclastic controversy, which broke out half way through this period, is responsible for a decline in culture is a question that has been variously answered. What seems to be clear, to judge from the biographies of numerous saints who flourished in the late seventh and eighth centuries, is that the basic structure of the educational system remained unaltered.[1] When intellectual life begins to blossom again after the final defeat of the iconoclasts all the indications are that the schools were still using almost all the same books for the same purposes as they had in the reign of Justinian. In the meantime there had been little time or energy to spare for the higher concerns of scholarship. We will mention briefly the few incidents that appear to constitute exceptions to the general rule.

The first is the story of a certain Tychicus, who was a native of Trebizond, born probably c. 560. Greek sources do not refer to him, but in the Armenian autobiography of Ananias of Shirak it is stated that he

---

[1] Lemerle, op. cit. 97-104.

studied in various cities and, despite the invitation of the patriarch
Sergius to remain in Constantinople, decided to return to Trebizond.
Some years later he declined another invitation from the emperor
Heraclius. As a result students seem to have been willing to make the
voyage from the capital in order to be able to sit at his feet. The story
may be true. It is not incredible that he should have studied at
Alexandria or been to Rome for a year. Nor is it out of the question that
in the capital he should have been able to hear the lectures of a teacher
from Athens, if some activity had continued there after 529; but of the
two versions of the autobiography that have so far been made known the
longer and more complete omits this detail. The fact arouses suspicion,
and one may wonder whether the rest of the picture has been exaggerated
by the loyalty of a pupil towards his teacher.[2] Even if it is not
exaggerated the text gives no informative details about Tychicus'
accomplishments and teaching.

In periods when men have had little time for literature and the arts the
requirements of theological debate have usually ensured that certain
basic techniques of scholarly procedure are preserved. The skills shown
by Justinian and others during his reign in dealing with forged texts were
not entirely lost. At the church council held in 680 these skills were
brought into play more than once, and one modern authority has called it
the council of the antiquarians and palaeographers. A communication
from patriarch Menas of Constantinople to Pope Vigilius was challenged
by the Roman delegates on the ground that Menas had died several years
before the council at which the text had allegedly been approved. On
inspection the volume in question proved to contain extraneous matter
in the form of three quires written in different script, and the serial
numbers of the quires did not form part of the series found in the rest of
the book. Another volume produced at the same council proved to
contain a quire added at some later date and full of suspicious material.[3]
About a century later elementary but necessary techniques were used to
expose crude forgeries which the iconoclasts had been able to exploit at
the council of Constantinople in 754. At Nicaea in 787 these were shown
to be false. Some texts had had whole passages cut out.[4]

Forgery and its detection is the theme of a story told by a little-known
writer of the late seventh century, Anastasius of Sinai. In his book called
Hodegos ('The Guide') he refers to a governor of Alexandria about a
hundred years before his own time who had maintained a staff of
fourteen professional scribes. The task of this scriptorium was to falsify
the texts of the church fathers, especially St. Cyril. Anastasius cites some
instances of the alterations made by this group. With regard to one of
them he tells us that he was unable to find any exemplar of the genuine

---

[2] Lemerle, ibid. 81-4, deals with the text in some detail.

[3] G.D. Mansi, *Sacrorum conciliorum nova et amplissima collectio* (Florence-Venice 1759-
98) 11.225 and 591; W. Speyer, *Die literarische Fälschung im heidnischen und christlichen
Altertum* (Munich 1971) 199.

[4] Mansi 13.36 and 184-92; Speyer, op. cit. 277.

text in Alexandria until the patriarch's librarian showed him one.[5] This suggests considerable success for the forgers in achieving their aim. A scriptorium of fourteen is uncommonly large; for though we have no descriptions of these organisations it is possible to make a reasonable inference from the fact that manuscripts written by more than half a dozen scribes are rarities, and some of them may be the product not of a scriptorium but of a school where the master divided a task of transcription between his pupils. While the number fourteen is specific and not a round number or one of the other types that are most open to suspicion,[6] a sceptic may reasonably offer the alternative explanation that the scribes in question were simply the clerks of the governor's office, diverted from their normal administrative duties.

(ii) Two changes in production: paper and a new script

The dark ages were not uneventful for the history of the book. Two changes took place, both of extreme importance. They occurred at the end of the period. It is impossible to say which came first, and in any case no long interval separated them. The one which in the short term was less influential was the arrival from the orient of a new writing material. Paper became an alternative to papyrus about the end of the eighth century, since the Arabs are believed to have learned the technique of manufacture from some Chinese prisoners of war taken after a battle at Samarkand. The latest papyri from Egypt are found to contain some scraps of the new material, but it is difficult to give an account of the stages of its adoption for use in Greek texts. The oldest Greek book written on paper that is now extant is a famous codex in the Vatican Library (Vat. gr. 2200), usually dated *c*. 800. It is famous because of its eccentric script, which we shall have occasion to refer to again. At one time it was thought to have been written in Damascus, but this view was based on the identification of the hand with that found in a single leaf of another manuscript and the erroneous supposition that a certain Thomas of Damascus mentioned in some verses on that leaf could be regarded as the scribe.[1] We must be content with a less definite location in one of the eastern provinces of the Byzantine world. There is no way of dating the script precisely, and a margin of at least a quarter of a century in either direction should be allowed. A single leaf survives from another literary text copied on paper at about the same time; it contained the hymns of Andreas of Crete (P. Vindob. G. 31956).

It is a hypothesis rather than a legitimate inference to suggest that the use of paper rapidly became normal in the main part of the Byzantine empire. It will certainly have needed a little while to spread from the original centres of production to other Mediterranean countries. The length of time required for the general acceptance of the new material

---

[5] *PG* 89.184-5.

[6] D. Fehling, *Die Quellenangaben bei Herodot* (Berlin 1971) 155-67.

[1] E. Follieri, *Codices graeci Bibliothecae Vaticanae selecti* (Rome 1969) 21-3.

will have depended partly on its quality and partly on the supply of the material that it displaced, papyrus. There are two grounds for thinking that the process may have been rapid. It is possible that the Byzantines had been short of supplies after the fall of Egypt, which had always been for practical purposes the only source. But we do not know whether the Arabs raised the price or discouraged exports. Although one embargo was imposed in the seventh century, it seems to have been a purely temporary measure. Another reason for supposing that the Byzantines may have welcomed paper quickly is the possibility that the papyrus plantations had been overworked and no longer produced as much good quality material as they had done in the past. Some Byzantine papyri are very coarse, but they do not provide conclusive evidence in favour of this view.[2] Papyrus was still being used later in the middle ages, even in the eleventh century in western Europe, but references to it and surviving examples are by no means a proof that it was still a common or easily available commodity after c. 800.[3]

As paper is less durable than parchment, extant manuscripts do not give an accurate statistical reflection of its use in the early Byzantine period. The next tangible signs of the use of paper do not occur until the eleventh century, by which time it is found in a few manuscripts (e.g. Athos, Iviron 258 and Lavra Θ 70) and in documents from the imperial chancery (the oldest dating from 1052: Athos, Lavra no. 31).[4] We may consider it likely that paper was available in the tenth century, perhaps even in the ninth, rivalling papyrus as an acceptable and cheap alternative to parchment. But there is no certainty, and the only statement by a writer of that period which is relevant may well be thought to justify a different conclusion. Among the minor works of Arethas, archbishop of Caesarea in Cappadocia, there are letters exchanged between him and Stephen, head of the imperial chancery, which concern some writing material that Stephen had evidently promised to obtain from Egypt.[5] Arethas complained of the delay in its arrival. There is no doubt that it is on order from Egypt, and the usual interpretation of his words is that he had in mind a consignment of papyrus, since the word used is *biblos*. This may be the correct view, but as Byzantine writers are incorrigibly archaic in their language it would not be out of the question for him to refer to the new writing material in this way, if only because there was no obvious and acceptably Atticist word available to describe the new invention. Arethas qualifies the noun with an adjective meaning 'from the Nile', but even so a doubt remains, because he may have known or believed that paper was manufactured near the Nile. It is therefore difficult to use Arethas' letters as evidence

[2] N. Lewis, *Papyrus in Classical Antiquity* (Oxford 1974) 58.

[3] *Pace* the implications in Lewis, op. cit. 93.

[4] J. Irigoin, 'Les conditions matérielles de la production du livre à Byzance de 1071 à 1261', *XV Congrès international d'études byzantines, rapports et co-rapports* (Athens 1976).

[5] Opuscula 38-40, ed. L.G. Westerink (Leipzig 1968).

for the present purpose. All they prove is that *c*. 900 it was possible for a man of letters to await anxiously the arrival of the next cargo of imported writing material. Since the chancery has been mentioned in this context, we should note that *c*. 840 it issued a document on papyrus, a letter from the emperor to the king of the Franks (Paris, Archives nationales, Musée K7 n. 17). But this single example gives us no basis for inferring what the general practice was.

It seems that the Byzantines imported from the Arabs instead of making their own paper. No doubt the method of production was kept secret as long as possible. By the thirteenth century the Italians also had a flourishing paper industry, and their product gradually replaced the oriental paper. After the middle of the fourteenth century oriental paper was rarely used in Greek books, and probably only in the lands of the eastern Mediterranean. The suggestion that in the tenth century there were papermakers at Corinth depends on a dubious interpretation of a text that refers almost certainly to parchment manufacturers.[6]

At about the same time as shortages of writing material were alleviated by the prospect of the new invention coming into general use another helpful step was taken to reduce consumption. Traditionally the script used in books had been fairly large, of the type usually called uncial, although that term was originally applied to Latin script and has no particular merit as a description of Greek. For practical purposes it can be regarded simply as capital letters, and though such a script can be written in minute letters the extant examples show that most scribes did not attempt to do so. Such a script is not conducive to economical book production, especially when parchment, the most durable writing surface, can only be produced by the slaughter of animals. For trade, official business and other everyday concerns more practical scripts were in use, saving both space and time. These cursive hands are seen in the papyri from Egypt; the latest examples come from the early years of the eighth century, showing Greek still in use after more than half a century of Arab rule. Experiments were made with these cursive hands, using them for literary texts. One such experiment has been found in the cache of manuscripts uncovered behind a partition wall in St. Catherine's monastery at Sinai in 1975. Another is seen in the manuscript already alluded to, which was thought until recently to come from Damascus (Vat. gr. 2200). In this case the hand is adapted from the script employed in documents and the result is exceedingly difficult to read. Practically no other examples are known, and it rightly failed to find favour. How many other experiments were made, and whether they were directly due to economic pressures, we do not know. A few notes in scripts of this general category are found in margins or flyleaves of manuscripts (e.g. Laud gr. 35, Helmstadt 75a), and there are some manuscripts and fragments that may also be regarded as belonging to the experimental stage of the new hand (e.g. Laur. 28.18 and the fragments in Paris Coislin

---

[6] Lewis, op. cit. 92 n. 9, has a confused and unhelpful note about this.

8, 120, 123 and supp. gr. 1156). The important fact is that one form of the new script, which has not so far been found in any documentary text, was almost universally adopted as a book hand by the end of the ninth century. The first precisely dated example is the famous Gospel book named after the archimandrite Porphyrij Uspenskij, who acquired it on one of his visits to monasteries in the Levant (Leningrad gr. 219). It belongs to the year 835, and as the handwriting does not look in any way primitive or experimental, the origin of this new hand, which is regularly termed minuscule, may need to be placed as much as half a century earlier. Another example of minuscule which is perhaps earlier than the Uspenskij Gospels but is not datable with the same degree of precision, is a collection of astronomical texts in Leiden (B.P.G. 78). A few leaves of this book are written in minuscule, and it has been assigned to the years 813-820, the reign of the emperor Leo V, on the strength of a list of emperors that was subsequently amended by a later owner of the volume. Once again the script is not primitive and it is difficult to decide on palaeographical grounds whether a date in the second decade of the ninth century is acceptable.

Not only is the date at which the new script was invented uncertain; its place of origin is unknown. One hypothesis which held the field for a long time is that the Stoudios monastery in the capital deserves the credit for the invention. The idea is based on circumstantial evidence. A leaf at the end of the Uspenskij Gospels records the obits of certain members of the community, and some of them are known to have been expert calligraphers. The monastery itself had a flourishing scriptorium, regulated by elaborate rules in the revised version of the statutes governing the house. A number of fine manuscripts, some of them dating from the early part of the tenth century, can be attributed to it. But the number of such manuscripts has been exaggerated, owing to the false belief that they can be identified by the habit of certain scribes who marked the top margin of the first page of each new quire with the sign of the cross, usually written two or three times. This pious trait is not in fact a peculiarity of the monks of Stoudios. It also has to be recognised that during the period at which the new script came into use the monastery suffered from Iconoclast persecution and some of its members were exiled. The possibility must be left open that the oldest dated specimens of the script may be the product of another place.[7]

The consequences of adopting the minuscule hand as the regular means of producing books were of enormous importance, and as with the introduction of paper the new invention took some time to achieve its full effect. From *c*. 850 onwards, whenever a fresh copy of a text was required, the chances were that the scribe would use the new script; after *c*. 950 it

[7] On the Stoudios monastery as the source of minuscule see T.W. Allen, *JHS* 40 (1920) 1-12, supported by C. Giannelli, *StudBizNeoell* 10 (1963) 225. On the false inferences made from the sign of the cross, N.G. Wilson, *Medieval Greek Bookhands* (Cambridge, Mass. 1972-3) 18 and plate 26.

was almost inconceivable that he would do otherwise. Few books in capitals are now extant. Copying from them into the new script is often stated to have been a difficult process that scribes would not have wished to undertake on more than one occasion, and it has been suggested that as a rule only one manuscript served as the basis from which all subsequent minuscule copies were made. In fact, however, copying was only likely to become difficult when the new script was so well established as a standard that the average reader began to find the old capital letters less easy. But until that point was reached one capital letter script was much the same as another, and indeed initially it will have been easier to work with the traditional script than the new one. It often happens that all extant copies of a text seem to derive from a single archetype, and the fact may be due not so much to the unwillingness of scribes to use different capital letter exemplars as to the survival of only one such exemplar in a conveniently accessible library, whether private or institutional. Such a situation is of course not commonly found in the textual transmission of works that formed part of the school curriculum. For the textual critic the real importance of the new script is that whereas in capital letter script certain confusions of letters had been particularly easy to make if the exemplar was damaged or the scribe careless, now with the minuscule hand a different set of errors arose from the same causes. For the preservation of literature as a whole the new invention was of great significance, as it allowed a much larger number of words to be fitted on to a page, even without the use of abbreviations, which at first were used sparingly by the majority of scribes. So the cost of the material needed for each volume was substantially reduced. There was also some gain in the time required to copy a text, because minuscule included several combinations of letters by ligature and did not demand laborious tracing of each one individually.

There are certain other features of books written in minuscule which must rank as important improvements in the standard of book production. They are sometimes associated with the new hand in such a way as to suggest that they were an immediate consequence of its adoption, but early minuscule manuscripts datable to the ninth century demonstrate that the changes did not come about at once. One of them was the regular use of accents and breathings. Although the papyri show that these aids to the reader were occasionally employed, it is impossible to see any system in their application, and the same applies to their use in uncial manuscripts. Probably the best view of the question is to suppose that they were not normally used unless the text was difficult and was expected to fall into the hands of an inexperienced reader.[8] In other words copies of some of the harder texts read in schools might be written with accents and breathings, and one famous example from

[8] H.-I. Marrou, *Histoire de l'éducation dans l'antiquité* (ed. 6, Paris 1965) 602 n. 30; an up-to-date report on the history of accentuation is given by C.M. Mazzucchi, *Aegyptus* 59 (1979) 145-67.

antiquity supports this view: a papyrus of Pindar's *Paeans* (P. Oxy. 841) shows not only these diacritical signs, but also the signs indicating long and short syllables, a refinement which the Byzantines did not normally avail themselves of. Most ancient and early medieval books gave little help to the reader except rudimentary punctuation. Greek texts from late antiquity onwards exhibit a diaeresis over iota and upsilon, which is not much help, and occasionally an apostrophe is added after a consonant if that consonant is in final position but does not often occur in it. In general, however, it may be said that reading was a skill acquired with some difficulty, and aids to the reader were of real value as long as the script continued to be written without divisions between the words. In practice the scribes began to mark word division at the end of the ninth century at much the same time as they made it their regular practice to add accents and breathings. But since the division was never rigidly enforced as a rule of good penmanship as would now be thought appropriate their policy was less contradictory than it seems at first sight. Because minuscule was essentially a cursive hand it was by nature less easy to master than its predecessor, and the price that had to be paid for its economy and speed was reduced by offering some guidance to the reader. Guidance in the form of accents and punctuation was made a regular part of book production at the Stoudios monastery; the rules laid down by St. Theodore for the conduct of his house prescribe penalties for copyists who fail to be accurate in these details.[9]

(iii)   Fresh signs of activity
The violent struggles arising out of the Iconoclast movement did much to destroy the conditions in which literary and scientific study might flourish. Scholarship retained its utility chiefly as a means of unmasking forgeries advanced in defence of theological propositions. But the effect of the controversy is perhaps overestimated, since we do not have to wait until the end of the dispute in 843 in order to find evidence of scholarly activity once again. As has been noted already, from the ninth century onwards Byzantine schools continued to use as the basis of education essentially the same selection of ancient texts which had been in use in the time of Justinian, and what little we know of teaching in the dark ages suggests a continuity of practice. There are teachers of grammar of uncertain date who have left some tangible proof of their activity. The first to deserve mention is John Charax, whose date cannot be given more precisely than by saying that he is later than the Alexandrian John Philoponus and earlier than George Choeroboscus, who will be dealt with in the next paragraph. Charax has been placed in the sixth century by some modern scholars, but the mere fact of his possessing a surname should make us hesitate to accept such a dating. Three of his writings have come down to us, and there is evidence that he wrote more. All three show clearly the same concerns of the school classroom that we

---

[9] *PG* 99. 1740 (section 54).

have seen in the work of the grammarians of late antiquity. The first is a short essay on enclitics and is considered to be no more than a compilation from material contained in a chapter of one of Herodian's major works. The same derivative character is seen in another short piece on orthography, Herodian's treatise again being the main source. A few other works, probably no more than brief pamphlets, are lost: we hear for instance of one on infinitives. A somewhat longer text suffered the fate of abridgment: he gave lectures on Theodosius' *Canons*, and the course survives in a shortened form prepared by Sophronius, patriarch of Alexandria in the years 848-60. It may seem surprising that this task should have been undertaken in a part of the Byzantine world that was no longer under the control of the emperor, but in fact the leading centres of Greek monasticism continued to exist in the Arab territories after the conquest. What is perhaps more remarkable is that the abridgment was made by Sophronius when he was a monk, at the request of John bishop of Damietta. This fact is made clear by the title and dedicatory letter, which explicitly refers to the bishop's concern that beginners should have a satisfactory guide to the *Canons*. It is sometimes stated that Byzantine monasteries did not maintain schools. A bishop's employment of a monk to revise a textbook could be taken as a hint of an exception to such a general rule, and the circumstances in Egypt could have led to a change of policy. But there is reason to think that monasteries might have a school, subject no doubt to the proviso that it should provide for boys destined to follow a monastic career and not be open to the general public. No less a figure than St. Basil had laid it down that monasteries could accept children, providing that they did not at once become full members of the community.[1] And in the rules of the Stoudios monastery drafted by St. Theodore the list of punishments for misbehaviour includes a section on the teacher of the children, which indicates his duty to ensure their spiritual and material well-being, without giving any hint of the nature of the instruction provided.[2] Alternatively it is possible that the bishop of Damietta had in mind the needs of a school attached to a church; we have already referred to the school that flourished in the twelfth century at the church of the Holy Apostles.[3]

Charax is not a man of much importance; he serves as an example of the way that the Byzantines continued to draw on what were to them the standard authorities and give their pupils the traditional instruction in Greek grammar. His works are not found in many manuscripts. Rather more significant is George Choeroboscus, whose date has recently been established within somewhat closer limits than had been possible before. At one time he oscillated between the sixth and tenth centuries, and the early date was upheld by an appeal to an apparent citation of him in

---

[1] *Regulae brevius tractatae*, PG 31.952.

[2] PG 99.1745 (section 96). See also A. Moffatt in A. Bryer & J. Herrin (edd.), *Iconoclasm* (Birmingham 1977) 88.

[3] On Charax see L. Cohn s.v. in *RE* III 2123-4, A. Hilgard, *Grammatici graeci* IV.2 (Leipzig 1894) cxxiii-vii.

Stephanus Byzantinus. But his surname aroused suspicion and the single quotation now has to be regarded as an interpolation, outweighed by several quotations in Choeroboscus that have been identified as coming from hymns by St. John Damascene, who died in 754, and consequently his career should be placed between the middle of the eighth century and the beginning of the ninth. The lower terminus is guaranteed to be approximately correct by the fact that Choeroboscus is quoted in the dictionary known as the *Etymologicum Genuinum*.[4]

Choeroboscus is described in the titles of his works as a deacon and ecumenical teacher. The meaning of the latter term is uncertain. It has frequently been interpreted to mean that he taught in a patriarchal seminary in the capital. The title would then derive from the nomenclature of the patriarch himself. But it could also be given to teachers who had no connection with the church, such as the professors of law at Beirut, and so Choeroboscus may be a teacher in a purely secular institution. At an earlier date Stephanus of Alexandria perhaps belonged to the same category; and at much the same time as Choeroboscus there is an obscure figure called Ignatius of whom the same is true.[5] There is, however, one more fact to be taken into account. One copy of his lectures on Theodosius' *Canons* (Marc. gr. 489) describes him in the title as holding the post of chartophylax, which, given that he was in any case a deacon, should probably be interpreted as meaning that he was librarian and archivist in the patriarchate. If that is correct it tilts the balance of evidence in favour of the view that his teaching activities were conducted under the aegis of the church. But though the manuscript in question offers a text of good quality, one cannot be sure that the information in its heading is not based on some error made at an earlier stage of the tradition. The point needs to be considered in detail because of its implications. The interpretation of the evidence makes a significant difference to our view of the organisation of education, and we have an example of the way in which our understanding of important facts about Byzantine cultural history depends on slender and ambiguous primary sources.[6]

Choeroboscus' surviving works suggest a preoccupation with the textbooks used in the early years of schooling. A very long commentary on Theodosius' *Canons* has come down to us. The title invites us to believe that the text consists of notes taken at his lectures or classes. If so – and there is a formulaic expression used at irregular intervals which seems to be a prayer offered at the end of a lecture – the extremely detailed nature of the rules expounded suggests that he must have followed the practice, not unknown even in the university of Oxford a generation ago, of dictating all the essential facts to the class. Whereas

---

[4] W. Bühler & Chr. Theodoridis, *BZ* 69 (1976) 397-401.

[5] Lemerle, op. cit. 88.

[6] J. Darrouzès, *Recherches sur les Offikia de l'église byzantine* (Paris 1970) 22-3, 68 n. 1, remains sceptical, perhaps unduly so.

Theodosius had listed the forms of Greek nouns and verbs with a limited number of explanatory notes, the whole of his text occupying ninety-nine pages in a modern printed edition, Choeroboscus' self-indulgence is such that his explanations amount to 685 pages. It is difficult to believe that young children, even in an age untouched by the modern prejudice that nothing should be done to tax their minds, were exposed to such an exhaustive treatment of the subject, and one must wonder whether Choeroboscus had some occasion for instructing a more advanced class. The general impression created by his work is one of tedious mediocrity. The obvious is usually stated at considerable length. Some of the doctrine offered is inaccurate. There is for instance a distinction drawn between the perfect and pluperfect tenses, according to which the perfect regularly refers to an act that has recently taken place (IV.2 p. 12. 19ff, repeated at 13.7ff). It scarcely needs to be said that in his discussion of the tenses he shows no sign of appreciating the distinctions that are now referred to by the technical term aspect. He is also guilty of a misconception that is widespread and which he may have found asserted in what seemed good authorities, namely that Homer writes an early form of the Attic dialect. This leads him to criticise Aristarchus (ibid. 86.7-24) for failing to understand the difference between early and late Attic, as a result of which he left uncorrected in the text of Homer a form found only later. Needless to say, the criticism is quite misplaced. An interesting point arises from his notes on accentuation. He explains that unaccented syllables are barytone, that is to say they can be marked with a grave accent, but he advises against marking each one, and at the same time says that signs for long and short vowels should not be used except in the ambiguous cases of alpha, iota and upsilon (IV.1 p. 117-18). The use of accents and the diacritical signs is clearly presupposed by his discussion, and yet their use in books earlier than *c.* 900 is sporadic. This apparent contradiction is further evidence in favour of the view that copies of texts used by schoolchildren were different in these respects from copies prepared for the average adult reader.

Choeroboscus refers to other books that he had written or hoped to write. He mentions Apollonius Dyscolus as one of his sources (8.19) and states an intention to comment on his doctrine about verbs and pronouns (11.21, 13.7). Similarly he says that he plans to deal with Herodian's treatment of the Greek noun (3.19), and he cites it when giving a list of rare monosyllabic nouns that Theodosius, perhaps out of a desire not to confuse beginners with a large number of rare and special cases, had left out of his account (IV.1, p. 116.12). There are in fact numerous references to both these leading ancient authorities on grammar. Dionysius Thrax is also mentioned, and among the great mass of scholia on that small treatise there are a few that can be identified as due to Choeroboscus. It has been held that one set of such scholia, which now passes under the name of an otherwise unknown Heliodorus, is a compilation drawn from Choeroboscus' notes. That is at best an inference from some inconclusive evidence, which consists chiefly of the similarity between what

Heliodorus says and what Choeroboscus might be expected to say. But it must be remarked against this view that the name Heliodorus is not likely to have occurred in Byzantium as late as the eighth or ninth century. In addition Choeroboscus appears to quote from Heliodorus in his notes on Hephaestion's handbook of metre.[7]

In any case we must admit that we do not know much about Choeroboscus' notes on Dionysius Thrax with the exception of a short note occupying about four printed pages (*Grammatici graeci* III 124-7) on elementary principles of accentuation and prosody. It is unremarkable except in so far as it deals briefly with three diacritical signs not regularly found in manuscripts, apostrophe, hyphen in the sense of a mark beneath a compound word linking the two component parts, and hypodiastole in the sense of a sign like a comma separating two words that could equally well be taken together as one in a text without spacing between the words. Once again it appears likely that special conventions applicable more often to school texts than other books are being discussed. An identical list of diacritical marks, consisting of the accents, macron and short sign, breathings, apostrophe, hyphen and hypodiastole, occurs at the beginning of the treatise on weights and measures by Epiphanius, bishop of Salamis in Cyprus. This work, no longer fully extant in Greek, dates from the year 392. Epiphanius begins by saying 'some have put punctuation marks in the text of scripture' (one would like to know who he is referring to), lists the diacritical marks and goes on to a discussion of the other critical signs used in the margin of the Septuagint. Either Choeroboscus is copying Epiphanius or they are both dependent on a common source; in either case one is left with an uncomfortable feeling that Choeroboscus may be referring to conventions no longer in regular use.[8]

His work on the Psalms is no more than a series of parsing exercises and it does not appear to contain interesting quotations from the sources that he used. But the commentary on the metrical treatise by Hephaestion, which had been composed in the second century and had already been commented on in late antiquity, deserves more attention. Choeroboscus begins with some remarks largely based on a similar introduction by the third-century sophist Longinus. It may be noted that these included two examples of sentences in Demosthenes which happen to be capable of scansion as lines of Greek verse, a hexameter from the *De corona* (143) and an ionic verse from the third Olynthiac oration(4). Choeroboscus adds to these an iambic trimeter from the first Olynthiac (5). He then makes two revealing remarks. The first is an admission that Hephaestion's handbook is not valuable to everyone, but only to those

---

[7] A. Hilgard, *Grammatici graeci* III (Leipzig 1901) xv; Hephaestion, ed. M. Consbruch (Leipzig 1906) 204.21.

[8] For the Greek text of Epiphanius see P. de Lagarde, *Symmicta* II (Göttingen 1880) 149-83, especially 153. A translation of the (complete) Syriac version was edited by J.E. Dean (Chicago 1935); his plate on p. 87 shows the signs and their Greek names written alongside the Syriac in British Library MS. Add. 17148, dated between 648 and 659.

who are going to write verse. He does not suggest that metrical knowledge might be of service to a reader of ancient poetry. A modern reader is bound to ask what types of verse were still being written in eighth-century Byzantium. The answer is that many litterati tried their hand at iambics, while a few attempted hexameters, elegiacs and even anacreontics. Another indication of such instruction being given in schools comes from a contemporary source: Ignatius the deacon, writing the life of his master the patriarch Tarasius (d. 806) says that he was initiated by him into trimeters, tetrameters, trochees, anapaests and the metre of epic.[9] After the tenth century, however, these forms of literary virtuosity died out almost completely. Hephaestion's handbook did not disappear without trace; it was one of the basic sources of Isaac Tzetzes' essay on Pindaric metres written early in the twelfth century (he died in 1138), and was brought to light once again *c.* 1300 by Demetrius Triclinius. Choeroboscus' second revealing remark throws light on him not as a medieval schoolmaster but as a critic in the classical tradition: he assures us that the handbook is a genuine work of Hephaestion because of the unambiguous testimony of the commentators on it and because of Hephaestion's references to it in another shorter work. The concern with authenticity, of no direct consequence for Byzantine schoolboys, is a result of the tradition established by Dionysius Thrax, for according to one interpretation he had defined the grammarian's highest task as the proof that a poem is genuine.

The rest of Choeroboscus' introduction is a medley of mainly derivative observations that need not concern us, except to note his rejection (p. 182) of the idea that the metrical handbook ought to be studied before pupils reach the stage of dealing with any verse text and the *Iliad*. The comments on individual chapters of Hephaestion are sketchy and not free from error; although he deals with most of the book, there is no treatment of the last two chapters on asynarteta and polyschematist metres. He is much concerned to explain apparent oddities of scansion in Homer. He appears to make bad mistakes in speaking of the choliambic line (p. 193.12-14) and in the treatment of synizesis (p. 210.13). The only other points of note are his claim to knowledge of Hephaestion's longer books, which do not survive now (p. 229.17 and 246.16), and the occurrence in one of the manuscripts of indications that the text is really a set of lectures (MS. U has the word πρᾶξις meaning 'lecture' at p. 198.13 and elsewhere).

All Choeroboscus' other work shows the same pedagogic objectives that have been clear throughout our discussion of him. There is an abridgment of what may have been a very substantial guide to orthography, a subject that presented increasing problems to the Byzantines as more and more vowels came to be sounded identically.[10] Apart from the signs of an interest in the rules for accentuation which

---

[9] Ed. I.A. Heikel, *Acta Societatis Scientiarum Fennicae* 17 (1891) 391-439; see p. 432.
[10] Edited from MS. Barocci 50 by J.A. Cramer, *Anecdota graeca* II (Oxford 1835) 167-281.

have been mentioned already, there is a treatise on this topic which claims to derive from Choeroboscus, Aetherius and Philoponus.[11] The work which earned him most fame, if its survival in the mansucripts may be accepted as a rough guide, is a list of twenty-seven poetical figures of speech. The first in the list is allegory, and among the others occur such well known devices as syllepsis, synecdoche, catachresis and metonymy. They are briefly defined, and examples are given of some. One gets an idea of the spirit in which the classical texts were read at school: pupils had to be able to say what figure a poet was employing when his language departed from the norms of prose. Choeroboscus' guide received the honour of being translated into Slavonic by c. 900, which is a fairly sure sign that it had established itself as a useful tool for the teaching profession. Not that Choeroboscus was original: collections of figures had been made in the ancient world; one passes under the name of Tryphon and lists fourteen tropes, while another by the totally obscure Cocondrius makes up a list of thirty. Choeroboscus seems to have been found more acceptable by his colleagues and successors.[12]

We have dealt with Choeroboscus at rather more length than he might be thought to deserve. One reason for this is simply the value of taking a mediocre but possibly typical figure and indicating clearly the limitations of his objectives and achievements. On the whole our aim should be to reserve detailed discussion for outstanding scholars, which brings with it the risk of creating the impression that their appreciation and use of classical Greek literature was not unusual. Another reason for giving Choeroboscus some prominence is that he is one of the first men active again after the dark age of iconoclasm and civil war. One might suspect him of being the first to raise standards of secondary education, but there is another claimant for that honour, Ignatius the deacon, whom we have already met as the biographer of the patriarchs Nicephorus and Tarasius. His date of birth has been calculated as falling about 770-80, and it is customary to assign to him an epigram in the *Greek Anthology* (15.39), in which he claims to be learned in the wisdom of poetry and to have rescued from a sea of oblivion the art of grammar, bringing it to light once more. The relative dates of Ignatius and Choeroboscus are not known, and there has been a good deal of argument as to how works assigned to Ignatius in manuscripts should be apportioned between several holders of the name. A case in point is the set of quatrains paraphrasing the fables of Babrius. But leaving aside these difficulties it may be noted that Ignatius' estimate of his own importance will not automatically have been shared by his colleagues. There is one respect, however, in which the biographer of the patriarchs merits mention at this point. He is, as far as we can judge, the author of a dramatic dialogue on a biblical subject, written in iambic trimeters which suggest an acquaintance with Greek tragedy. The linguistic parallels, one might

[11] Ed. W.J.W. Koster, *Mnemosyne* 59 (1932) 132-64.
[12] W.G. Rutherford, *A Chapter in the History of Annotation* (London 1905) 200 ff.

almost say borrowings, can reasonably be taken as an indication that texts of tragedy were not lying totally unused and collecting dust in Byzantine libraries. Probably Ignatius had acquired his knowledge of them at school. But the inference is not quite certain. While the failure to understand certain rules of the iambic trimeter is no evidence against direct acquaintance with the classical originals, it has to be borne in mind that there was a skilful and apparently popular Byzantine writer in this metre, George of Pisidia, and imitation of him rather than Euripides may be enough to account for the existence of Ignatius' curious production.[13]

But there is another side to Ignatius. His letters provide a fine demonstration of the degree of classical learning that might be acquired by a member of the generation before Photius. Whether or not Ignatius seemed unusual to his contemporaries, he proves more effectively than Choeroboscus that Photius did not grow up in a society utterly devoid of culture. Ignatius' correspondence is full of allusions to Homer and classical proverbs, and there are several letters which exploit a more recherché knowledge of pagan literature. Two of these deal with questions of metre, one referring to the correction of iambic trimeters, while the other mentions, with what must be almost certainly an empty show of pretension, the *ionic a maiore* (nos. 32 and 60). There is what looks like an extensive quotation from Herodian's doctrine on the accentuation of monosyllabic adverbs (no. 36). Ignatius surprises us with a quotation of Euripides' *Orestes* 140; since this play was scarcely read in Byzantium, one must wonder if he knew the line only as a quotation, which it undoubtedly was (no. 59). Some comments on literary style include mention of the inevitable Aristides and Hermogenes (no. 64). Most curious of all is a letter of consolation. Here Ignatius quotes from Ctesias' *Persica* an episode in which a messenger gradually breaks the news of Cyrus II's death to his mother Parysatis. Ctesias' book still existed and was read by Photius, but the passage we are dealing with happens to be known, in a version with substantial differences of wording, from Demetrius *On Style* 216. One is bound to ask whether the differences arise because the quotation has been made from memory and whether Ignatius drew on Demetrius or the full original text.[14]

Nor is Ignatius the only other teacher whose name at least is known to us. A man who must have been approximately his contemporary in due course became the last iconoclast patriarch, occupying the throne for an uncertain number of years until he was deposed in 843. He is regularly known as John the grammarian. Unfortunately nothing whatever is known of his education or his activity as a teacher. His theological

[13] Various problems about Ignatius are discussed by W. Wolska-Conus, *Travaux et mémoires* 4 (1970) 329-60; see 335-9 for Babrius. On the dramatic dialogue see R. Browning, *REG* 81 (1968) 405-7.

[14] On the letters see C. Mango in F. Paschke (ed.) *Überlieferungsgeschichtliche Untersuchungen* (Berlin 1981) 403-10. He has also very kindly shown me his forthcoming text.

opponents represent him as a magician, which may be an indication that he was interested in natural science and read some of the classical authors who were still the best authorities. The suggestion gains some support from the existence of several manuscripts of scientific texts that may belong to the first half of the ninth century and also from the assertion, in a hymn composed to celebrate the restoration of icon worship, that John 'showed himself indistinguishable from the pagans, priding himself on his knowledge of their writings, which the voices of the just have rightly crushed'. One episode from his career has occasionally, but quite unjustifiably, been taken to have some significance for the history of literature. For about a year before the Iconoclast Council held at Santa Sophia in 815 John was responsible for conducting a search for old books in a large number of libraries. It is perfectly clear that the motive for the search was to find texts that would serve the purpose of the iconoclasts, and the most that can be inferred about other texts is that they may have come to light in the course of the search and been recognised as of some value by the person who happened to unearth them. That there was any attempt to salvage classical literature or even to find lost masterpieces of patristic thought is not a legitimate inference.[15]

Two other members of this generation are a little better known. Theognostus compiled a book on orthography, which he dedicated to the emperor Leo V (813-820). He also wrote a history, which is now lost, and he is perhaps to be identified with an officer of the court who was sent on a diplomatic mission to Charlemagne at Aachen in 812. His surviving work is a cross between a guide to spelling and a list of difficult words. In the letter of dedication he says that no other such work exists; so much for Choeroboscus. He claims to have drawn his material from Herodian, which is not out of the question, and there appears to be a lacuna in the text in which he mentioned his other sources; it would seem that one of them was the lexicon ascribed to Cyril of Alexandria. Although he seems to have been a source of material for one of the later Byzantine lexicographers, Theognostus did not succeed in writing a popular book. The tradition rests mainly on two early copies (Barocci 50 of the tenth century and Patmos 109A, *olim* 737, of the tenth or early eleventh) and one of the fourteenth century (Laur. 56.37). The Patmos manuscript, which was not studied until quite recently, turns out to contain a reference to the obscure grammarian Aetherius, who was one of the sources for Choeroboscus and is now proved to have been available to Theognostus as well.[16]

Vastly more popular, and designed as a textbook rather than a work of reference, was the guide to syntax by Michael Syncellus. It is known to

[15] On John see Lemerle 135-46; on the search for MSS 139-40; on that see also N.G. Wilson, *CQ* 54 (1960) 204, arguing on the same lines.

[16] For Theognostus see K. Alpers, *Theognostos Peri orthographias Überlieferung, Quellen und Text der Kanones 1-84* (Hamburg 1964); W. Bühler, *BZ* 58 (1965) 369-70 and *JOB* 22 (1973) 49-91.

exist in about a hundred manuscripts, and the text varies a good deal, suggesting that it was found useful enough to be thought worthy of revision. The first printed editions ascribed it to the much later writer George Lecapenus, but this must be regarded as a mistake, apparently due to a misapprehension on the part of the editor of the first printed edition. Some manuscripts tell us in the title that it was written in Edessa, and there is reason to think that the composition should be placed in the years 810-13. It is a fairly short and routine production, designed to give schoolchildren help with some of the usual problems of grammar and syntax. The preface refers to Apollonius Dyscolus, Herodian, Apollonius the younger (it is not clear who this is; can it be Apollonius the son of Archebius, the author of the Homeric dictionary preserved in Coislin 345?), the Atticists, and Arcadius of Byzantium, and it may be that Michael was able to use all these authors as his sources. A good deal is known of his later career: he was sent to Rome to hold discussions on the Filioque question, but on the way Leo V had him arrested and imprisoned; he was freed in 820 on the death of the emperor but found himself in prison again in the years 834-42. Then he became syncellus or private secretary to the patriarch Methodius and was appointed abbot of the Chora monastery. He is also known to have been a friend of Theodore, the famous abbot of the Stoudios monastery. But the remarkable thing about him is that he should have composed his book in a town in Mesopotamia which was no longer in the Byzantine empire. If we are to trust the manuscripts which say that he wrote it in Edessa – and it is difficult to see why this statement should be an invention – we receive an unexpected proof of the vigour of Greek culture and the availability of texts in the most far-flung areas of the Byzantine world. A small piece of confirmatory evidence can be seen in the report that in Edessa there was a teacher called Sophronius who held a public appointment, probably in the early years of the ninth century.[17] One might also cite as a parallel the other Sophronius mentioned earlier in this chapter, who was patriarch of Alexandria later in the century and made an abridgment of the textbook by John Charax.[18]

Two more episodes from the career of Michael Syncellus should be mentioned; the first gives some impression of his own education, and both add to our picture of cultural activity in the eastern part of the Byzantine world. His biographer says that when he received the tonsure the patriarch of Jerusalem, which was his birth-place, invited him to pursue his studies in grammar, rhetoric and philosophy. We are told that he mastered the best poetry and astronomy. It rather looks as if Michael familiarised himself with the subjects of the trivium and quadrivium, imperfectly understood by his biographer. This reference to poetry does

---

[17] Cited by Moffatt (supra n. 2) 89 n. 32 from section 6 of the life of St. Theodore of Edessa, ed. I.V. Pomialovskij (St. Petersburg 1892).

[18] A survey of the tradition of Michael's treatise is given by D. Donnet, in the ·duction to his new edition, *Le traité de la construction de la phrase de Michel le Syncelle de Jérusalem* (Brussels-Rome 1982).

not stand alone. While living near Jerusalem under the auspices of the monastery of St. Saba he taught two brothers, Theodore and Theophanes Graptos, and apart from grammar and philosophy we find mentioned 'a large number of questions relating to poetry'. Again it looks as if the writer does not fully understand what happened, but it is not unduly rash to infer that Michael was giving lessons on part of the standard literary education.[19] In this context it may be worth mentioning a fragment of Aristotle's *De interpretatione* written in ninth-century minuscule script, formerly belonging to the Umayyad mosque in Damascus, even though there is no certainty that it was written in that region.[20]

The discovery of a large number of manuscripts, many of them very early, in a disused cell in the monastery of St. Catherine on Sinai, made in 1975 and concealed from the public as long as possible, has not yet added significantly to our knowledge of cultural life in this area of the Byzantine empire. But even the first report given to the learned world,[21] although prepared under the most adverse conditions, shows that an important find has been made, perhaps more important for the types of script, especially early minuscule and a curious mixture of uncial and minuscule not previously known, than for the texts themselves. The identification of the texts is not easy, as the manuscripts are mostly incomplete, in many cases no more than tiny fragments; but at present it looks as if only one is relevant to our present purpose. It consists of four leaves, with a text of the *Iliad* in which each line is followed by a prose paraphrase. Doubtless it comes from a schoolbook of a type once common; but despite its palaeographical interest it does not modify the picture outlined above.

[19] The biography is edited by Th. Schmitt, *Izvestija russkago arkheologičeskago Instituta v Konstantinopolje* 11 (1906) 227-59; the passages important for the present purpose are on pp. 228, 230-1, 242 and 265.

[20] P. Moraux et al., *Aristoteles graecus* I (Berlin 1976) 121.

[21] L. Politis, *Scriptorium* 34 (1980) 5-17.

4

A New Start

(i) Leo the Philosopher

The first figure of real importance in the middle Byzantine period is a man whose career begins under the iconoclasts and ends at a time when the controversy was dead and buried. Leo, generally known as 'the philosopher', was probably born *c.* 790 and lived at least until 869. He was a cousin of the iconoclast patriarch John, and may be supposed to owe to this connection his preferment to the archbishopric of Thessalonica, which he held from 840 until 843. The virulent hatred of the orthodox for the iconoclasts, often expressed in terms which make it look as if they were regarded as worse enemies than pagans or Muslims, would lead one to expect that Leo's career could have had no future after the restoration of orthodoxy and his enforced resignation from his see. But Leo did not suffer much if at all from the vindictiveness of the iconodules, and after what may have been an interval of as much as twelve years or even longer we find him put in charge of a newly established school enjoying imperial patronage and with premises in the Magnaura palace. This promotion must indicate not only that he had been extremely lukewarm in his feelings on the issue of the icons, despite being appointed by iconoclasts to his previous position, but also that he was regarded as a person of exceptional attainments entitling him to exemption from the treatment handed out to others.

A few words must be said about the first part of his career. His elementary education was acquired in the capital. According to our best source he used to recall that after his studies of grammar and poetry he went on to tackle rhetoric, philosophy and mathematics on the island of Andros, where he found a man able to teach him the elements of these subjects but no more, or at least not enough to satisfy him. So he crossed over to the mainland and searched for books in the monasteries, studying by himself in a mountain retreat. It is very odd that anyone should have had to leave the capital in the early years of the ninth century in search of secondary education, and one can reasonably infer that the story as it has come down to us is incomplete. It is odder still that Leo should have made his way to Andros, not noted as a cultural centre at any time. On crossing to the mainland he will have found himself in Attica, another intellectual desert for most of the middle ages. After a certain time, having acquired as much learning as he wanted or could master in such unpromising conditions, Leo made his way back to the capital and taught privately in humble circumstances. He had had a number of pupils for several years when his name was suddenly and unexpectedly brought to the notice of high authority. One of his pupils was appointed secretary to an officer serving in the campaign against the Arabs on the eastern frontier. The secretary fell into the hands of the enemy, and while a prisoner was allowed to be present at a discussion between the caliph and his advisers on some questions of geometry. He was able to show that he understood the principles underlying Euclidean propositions better than the Arabs, who asked him how he came to know so much. The caliph made an attempt to secure Leo's services, sending an invitation back with his pupil. Leo, afraid of being caught in possession of an incriminating document from a foreign power, took it to a government minister who passed it to the emperor. Recognition of his talents followed, and he was given an official position with a salary and a room for teaching at the church of the Forty Saints (more usually known as the Forty Martyrs). The caliph made further vain efforts to tempt Leo away. The story is attractive and may be true. It must be admitted that the notion of a Greek giving lessons to an Arab on a mathematical topic does not accord with generally received ideas about the history of science in the middle ages, but it seems that the episode occurred shortly before the Arabs obtained their excellent knowledge of Greek mathematics through the translations of Hunain ibn Ishaq, and the story therefore becomes much more plausible. It has to be placed in the years 829-33, as the emperor and caliph are named as Theophilus and Mamun and their reigns overlap in those years only. But the story continues by relating that in order to be sure of retaining Leo the emperor asked the patriarch to find him ecclesiastical preferment, which resulted in Leo being made archbishop of Thessalonica for three years, and it is known from other sources that he held the see from 840 until 843. An alternative account of the episode concerning Leo's pupil places it *c.* 838/9, which makes the sequence of events more logical in one sense, avoiding the long interval before the caliph's attempts to entice Leo away, but introduces the difficulty that there is now scarcely time for Leo to take up his new teaching post.

After the restoration of orthodoxy in the matter of icons Leo's position is obscure. He eventually became head of a new school established in the Magnaura palace under the patronage of the assistant emperor Bardas. As the latter was in power from 855 to 866 the foundation of the school is usually placed in these years, which has the result of leaving Leo unemployed for at least twelve years, possibly much longer. Although he perhaps took some time to live down the disgrace of having held a see under the auspices of the iconoclasts, the interval appears too long. Perhaps the foundation of the new school should be placed earlier, on the assumption that Bardas was already very influential. The date of Leo's death is not known; it is certain that he was still alive in 869, when he was one of the survivors of a severe earthquake.

The part of his career that is of least concern to us is his tenure of the archbishopric. One product of it may be a homily on the Annunciation usually ascribed to Leo. But the reasons for attributing this mediocre performance to him rather than to a later namesake are anything but convincing.[1] The only other notable report about this period of his life is that he used his astrological knowledge to forecast that if the local population, which had been suffering severely from a series of droughts, sowed a fresh crop at a certain time, there would be a fine harvest, which turned out to be the case. Astrology was normally disapproved of by the church, but there is no doubt of Leo's interest in it, since we know that he owned a copy of the introductory treatise by Paul of Alexandria, on which he wrote a brief epigram (*Anth. Pal.* 9.201).

It would be interesting to know how he would have defended himself if challenged to justify his enthusiasm for a pseudo-science. He would probably have pointed to his empirical success, and with the benefit of hindsight we may be tempted to suppose that he would have emphasised the uncertainty of the dividing line between astrology and astronomy, as a result of which a treatise like that of Paul contained a modest amount of scientific information.

Leo's most famous exploitation of scientific knowledge was his invention of a system of beacon lights designed to carry messages from a point near Tarsus to the capital within a short space of time. A fire lighted at any given hour (it is not certain that the system could be operated during the day as well as at night) was relayed over a number of stages and indicated a different message according to the time, so that a fire lit at one o'clock signified an Arab raid, at two o'clock a declaration of war, and so on. Details such as the problem of visibility and the time required to light a beacon remain unclear. But two identical clocks were the basis of the system. Leo would have been able to make the necessary calculations about the difference of time between the eastern front and the capital and the varying length of the hour in each month by means of the procedures explained in Theon's commentary on Ptolemy's Handy Tables. This is perhaps a better hypothesis than the alternative, which is to assume that the clocks were synchronised and divided the day into twenty-four equal hours.

Another display of technical skill from the early years of the ninth century is less certainly associated with Leo's name. During the reign of Theophilus (829-42) some automata were made for the reception room in the royal palace. The next emperor, Michael III, is said to have had them melted down, but if the story is true it is clear that a fresh set was made. They are best described in the words of a western envoy received by Constantine Porphyrogenitus in 949. Liutprand of Cremona writes:

A tree made of bronze but covered with gold leaf stood in front of the

[1] *Pace* V. Laurent, in *Mélanges Eugène Tisserant* II (*Studi e Testi* 232) (Vatican City 1964) 282-3.

emperor's throne. Its branches were filled with similar golden birds of various types, which emitted various notes according to their species. The emperor's throne was cleverly constructed so that at one moment it was on the floor level, at the next it seemed raised to a great height. It was guarded by lions of enormous size, which may have been made of bronze or wood but were gilded. They swept the floor with their tails, opened their mouths, moved their tongues and emitted a roar. I was taken into the emperor's presence, carried on the shoulders of two eunuchs. During my entry the lions roared and the birds sang appropriately, but I had no feelings of terror or surprise, as I had carefully questioned everyone who knew about these things.[2]

Other envoys, less well informed in advance, will no doubt have been suitably impressed by the display of mechanical objects. The Byzantine writers who refer to them add that besides the lions there was a pair of griffins, and two organs are mentioned. Only one chronicler, probably the least reliable of our sources, says that these toys were constructed by Leo, while two others suggest that Theophilus ordered them from his chief jeweller. This would not exclude the possibility that Leo had produced the designs, which the emperor simply passed on to the craftsman. But it is a trifle odd that Leo should be denied the credit if he deserved it. Whatever the truth it should be noted that automata of this kind could be made by following the designs in the ancient manuals by Philo and Hero of Alexandria, which had perhaps survived by accident and were now exploited. It is not certain whether the gadgets had ever been made in antiquity, and in some cases it has been doubted whether ancient technology would have allowed Hero and his colleagues to make a prototype. It is worth offering the hypothesis, which at present can be no more than speculative, that Leo or one of his contemporaries first put into practice some of Hero's inventions.

The final stage of Leo's career, in which he presided over a school which had three other teachers, is presumably the most important, as it will have given a renewed impetus to the study of the ancient authors. But it has to be admitted that we know next to nothing of the school and its activities. We cannot even say how long it continued in being. The names of the three other members of the staff are known, but that is almost all. Theodore and Theodegios, who taught geometry and astronomy respectively, are mere names, which is not surprising; they were bound to be overshadowed by Leo, who was probably better qualified in both subjects. Grammar was assigned to Cometas. His epigrams, preserved in the *Greek Anthology* (*Anth. Pal.* 15.36-8), prove that he was interested in Homer, as any teacher of his subject must have been. Two of the epigrams could be taken to mean that he had arranged for copies of the text to be made in the still fairly novel minuscule script, but the interpretation is not certain. A third epigram was composed for a copy that he may have transcribed himself; alternatively it was an old

[2] Liutprand, *Antapodosis* 6.5, ed. J. Becker (Hannover-Leipzig 1915) 154-5.

copy in which the ink had faded in many places and Cometas had retraced the letters. Whichever view is correct, he certainly claims to have introduced punctuation into the text. As we have noted earlier, the first minuscule manuscripts were not fully punctuated, and it may be one of them rather than an old uncial copy that Cometas refurbished.

Leo must have had a good private library, and it is possible to infer some of the titles that it contained. Once again the epigrams of the *Greek Anthology* come to our aid. Leo seems to have composed verses to put on the flyleaf or the last page of his copy. So we know that he owned Apollonius of Perga *On Conic Sections* and some lost treatises on mechanics by the unknown authors Marcellus and Quirinus (*Anth. Pal.* 9.578 and 200). Another volume seems to have contained a geometrical treatise by Proclus and a work by the astronomer Theon (*Anth. Pal.* 9.202); we have already seen how some of Theon's works could have been useful to Leo. More precise identification of the two texts is impossible owing to the obscurity of the verses. The reference to Alexandria is unintelligible as it stands, and what Leo says of the common theme of the texts would be easier to understand if he were speaking of Theon of Smyrna, author of a guide to mathematics for students of Plato. Still in the scientific field one may note a text of Archimedes. This manuscript may have survived until the Renaissance, for it is likely to be the very old codex which caused difficulty to the copyists of that period because of its archaic script and numerous abbreviations. It had a note in which a reader or pupil expressed his best wishes to Leo.[3] There can be little doubt that Leo also possessed his own copy of Ptolemy's *Almagest*. It used to be identified as a famous and highly calligraphic manuscript now in the Vatican collection (Vat. gr. 1594), but the supposed ex-libris is written in a hand of much later date and can only be a pen-trial.[4] His reading of Euclid is attested by a note in the Bodleian copy added as a comment on *Elements* 6.5, which is the proposition that two triangles with sides that are in the same proportion will be equiangular. Leo's note discusses proportions, and it has been claimed that since he uses the Greek letters as algebraic symbols rather than as numbers he should be credited with an important step towards the development of algebra.[5] This may be true, but the truth is more complex than the account given by recent authorities. In the first place we may note that the text of Leo's observations is by the scribe of the manuscript himself, not by its first owner Arethas, and it forms part of a series of supplements to book VI of the *Elements*. Secondly, although Leo states elementary rules about proportions in general terms, it is not true that the scribe uses letters without the accent or stroke written above which normally indicates numerical value. However, it does seem that his intention was to give the rules in what we should call an algebraic notation, and he follows his

---

[3] Archimedes, ed. J.L. Heiberg, III (Leipzig 1915) x-xv.

[4] N.G. Wilson, *GRBS* 14 (1973) 223.

[5] K. Vogel, *Akten des XI internationalen Byzantinisten-Kongresses München 1958* (Munich 1960) 660-2.

rules with specific examples. To what extent he has made a step forward is uncertain. There is a sense in which Diophantus can be regarded as an exponent of algebra, and Leo might have been able to read more of him than we can today. There are also passages in Theon of Smyrna that could have set Leo thinking along these lines and it will be recalled that some of Leo's verses about his library would be easier to understand if he could be assumed to have confused the two Theons.

Turning to other types of literature we find that Leo knew Porphyry, probably the introduction of Aristotle (*Anth. Pal.* 9.214), and perhaps the novel by Achilles Tatius (*Anth. Pal.* 203), not a rare possession in Byzantium, as will become clear later. Literary rather than scientific motives led him also to Plato. All we know of Leo's dealings with this author is that he went through the *Laws* correcting the text up to a point in book V (743b). A note to this effect is found in no less than three manuscripts (Vat. gr. 1, Paris gr. 1807, Vat. gr. 1031). It is a pity that we do not know how much his activity of correction amounted to and why he gave up when he was less than half way through his task.

Less creditable to our way of thinking is his ownership of Paul's *Introduction to Astrology*, already mentioned above. His liking for this subject led him to write on it; if the titles in the manuscripts are to be trusted, which is not by any means guaranteed, he may be the author of various short works, including one showing how to use the Gospels and Psalter for the purpose of prediction. Whether shocked by this deviation from orthodoxy or because of general prejudice against pagan learning, a pupil of Leo called Constantine published two short attacks on him.[6] The pupil, although evidently hostile to classical culture, wrote in classicising verse, using first elegiac couplets and then iambics. As if this concession to the pagans were not enough he incorporated in the second poem unmistakeable allusions to Herodotus (6.127-9, the story of Hippocleides) and Orestes.

No discussion of Leo's place in Byzantine culture is complete without a mention of the tradition that Constantine-Cyril, the apostle of the Slavs, studied under him and Photius. Its source is the Slavonic life of the apostle, and though it seems explicit enough there must be doubt as to its accuracy. While there is nothing implausible in the idea that Constantine, having failed to find teaching in Thessalonica, came to the capital and studied grammar, Homer, geometry and philosophy, there is no proof that Photius ever held a teaching post in an institution. Although he uses the words teacher and pupil to describe his relations with correspondents, close informal contacts, such as regular meetings of a reading club in his house, would be enough to justify them. This argument, if valid, casts doubt in turn on the assertion that Constantine studied with Leo. It is easier to assume that he had informal contacts with both men.[7]

---

[6] *PG* 107. LXI-LXIV and 661-4.

[7] My account of Leo owes a good deal to Lemerle, op. cit. 148-76. See also I. Ševčenko, *American Historical Review* 79 (1974) 1533-4, for the point discussed in the last paragraph.

(ii) The evidence of manuscripts from c. 800-c. 875

The picture of cultural life that can be inferred from what we know of Leo must be complemented by two other sets of evidence. The first, to be dealt with here, is provided by manuscripts; the other comes from Photius, and will be the subject of the next chapter. Although many manuscripts have survived through lucky accidents, it cannot be entirely coincidence that has led to the preservation of a number of copies of ancient authors transcribed in the ninth century. The criteria for dating uncial and early minuscule hands admittedly do not allow much precision. But is is a fair presumption that Leo's lifetime saw the production of the texts in the list that follows, and it is quite possible that all were written in the first half of the century.

In view of what we know about Leo it is not surprising that literature is less prominent than science. There is an uncial copy of Homer with the mainly short and elementary notes that were useful in the schoolroom (Madrid 4626 & Rome, Bibl. Naz. gr. 6). There are also some palimpsest leaves from an uncial copy of Herodian (Leipzig, Tischendorf 2) and a set of lexica in minuscule (Coislin 347). In addition there is one tiny fragment which should probably be assigned to this period and which adds a vital element to our overall picture. It is a scrap of parchment with a few lines from book III of the *Argonautica* of Apollonius Rhodius (P. Strasburg 173), a text which did not normally form part of the school curriculum. The discovery of a few more scraps of this kind would force us to revise drastically our reconstruction of the intellectual world of the ninth century, but from the evidence available at present it seems that pride of place was given to scientific writers.

If we are tempted, however, to pass an enthusiastic verdict on the intellectual atmosphere of the period, a reservation must be expressed. The scribe who penned the magnificent copy of Ptolemy's *Almagest* (Vat. gr. 1594) turns out to have written another much less edifying volume (Laur. 28.27). It contains two poems on astrology by Manetho and Maximus. Despite condemnation and elaborate refutation by the church this pseudo-science continued to claim adherents. Few astronomers had the strength of mind to disregard it entirely; and if challenged to justify themselves they had an easy reply, since one of Ptolemy's other works, the *Tetrabiblos*, was much used as a manual of astrology. It is only to be expected that medical books should enjoy a wide circulation. Dioscorides' manual of herbal remedies, which has the distinction of being preserved in two copies earlier than the period that we are now concerned with, the Vienna codex of *c.* 512 and the Naples copy generally placed in the seventh century (Naples, supp. gr. 28), not to mention two other copies now reduced to tiny fragments (one in Erevan (Matenadaran 141) the other in some palimpsest leaves in Naples lat. 2), exists in yet another uncial copy that may reasonably be assigned to the ninth century (Paris gr. 2179). Another text of value to the practitioner was Paul of Aegina. It is found in some stray leaves that

survive from a very early minuscule copy (Paris Coislin 8 and 123, supp.
gr. 1156), and has been identified in the uncial text of a palimpsest
recently acquired by the Belgian Royal Library (Brussels IV. 459).

Other sciences are well represented, with Ptolemy's *Almagest* to the
fore. An uncial and a minuscule copy of the full text (Paris gr. 2389 and
Vat. gr. 1594) are accompanied by two uncial copies of the tables that
went with it (Vat. gr. 1291 and Leiden B.P.G. 78). The second of these
may belong to the years 813-20, and contains the commentary by Theon.
A second, more academic, commentary from his pen is extant (Laur.
28.18); in the same manuscript a similar work by Pappus, another
mathematician of late antiquity, is preserved. Euclid's *Elements* exist in
an early undated copy (Vat. gr. 190, containing also a fragment of
Theon's longer commentary on Ptolemy), as well as the copy dated 888
written for Arethas, which will be discussed later. The interest of the
Vatican copy is that it appears to be the only one which preserves the
original text of Euclid; all others exhibit alterations due to Theon.
Another book which can be assigned fairly confidently to the ninth
century brings together a large collection of mathematical and
astronomical treatises (Vat. gr. 204). It includes such advanced works as
Eutocius on Apollonius' *Conic Sections*, some writings by Euclid, and
Aristarchus' essay on the sizes and distances of the sun and moon. The
other authors in this codex are Theodosius (*Sphaerica*, *De
habitationibus*), Autolycus (*De sphaera*, *De ortibus et occasionibus*),
Hypsicles (*Anaphoricus*), and Marinus (commentary on Euclid's *Data*).

Interest in Aristotle at this time seems to have been as much scientific
as philosophical. While there are fragments of an uncial copy of the
Sophistici elenchi (Paris supp. gr. 1362) and fine early copies of the
Nicomachean Ethics, *Magna moralia* (Laur. 81.11) and the *Organon*
(Ambr. L 93 sup.), there are also three early manuscripts which offer
selections from his scientific work, and only one of them has in addition
items of philosophical content. There is a fragment in Paris of the
Historia animalium (supp. gr. 1156), an Oxford codex of several of the
biological writings which for a long time was believed to be of the twelfth
century (Corpus Christi College 108), and a very famous Vienna codex,
which besides the *De generatione et corruptione* offers the *De caelo*,
Physics, *Meteorologica* and *Metaphysics*, along with Theophrastus'
short essay on the same subject (phil. gr. 100).

The greatest palaeographical contribution to the reconstruction of the
intellectual milieu of ninth-century Byzantium was made by T.W.
Allen.[1] He identified a large and important group of manuscripts on the
basis of the idiosyncratic hand of the main scribe and the use of a rare
abbreviation. For convenience we may refer to these books as the
products of 'Allen's scriptorium'. Their date is not certain, but some time
in the middle of the century seems likely. It is difficult to conceive of
them being produced anywhere except in the capital. One of them

---

[1] *Journal of Philology* 21 (1893) 48-55.

contains a tiny treatise on the nature of time by Zacharias of Chalcedon, friend and pupil of Photius. The person responsible for their production must have been an uncommonly expert student of philosophy, if indeed it is legitimate to suppose that all the books were written to order for the same person. From what we can infer about the practices of Byzantine calligraphers and scriptoria the possibility of two or more patrons should not be excluded, but it is not unduly adventurous to imagine the philosophical texts produced as a set, and in any case it is the production of the scriptorium as a whole that gives us evidence for the activity of intellectuals at the time. The surviving volumes can be divided into various categories, of which the largest is devoted to Plato and consists of (i) Plato's *Republic, Timaeus, Critias* and *Laws*, together with various minor, mainly spurious, items from the Platonic corpus (Paris gr. 1807); (ii) Proclus' commentary on the *Timaeus* (Paris supp. gr. 921);[2] (iii) his commentary on the *Republic* (Laur. 80.9 and Vat. gr. 2197, which originally formed a single volume); (iv) Damascius' commentary on the *Parmenides* and his short essay on the first principles of philosophy (Marc. gr. 246); (v) Olympiodorus' commentaries on the *Gorgias, Alcibiades I, Phaedo* and *Philebus* (Marc. gr. 196); (vi) Albinus and Maximus of Tyre (Paris gr. 1962). Considering the dangers occasionally attendant on the close study of Plato from a philosophical as opposed to a strictly linguistic and literary point of view, this group of texts is a remarkable phenomenon. Most of the other books from Allen's scriptorium are less notable. Simplicius on the Aristotelian *Physics* (Marc. gr. 226) could not tempt a reader away from orthodoxy. Probably the same may be said for treatises on physics and the nature of the soul by Alexander of Aphrodisias (Marc. gr. 258, a volume not in the same script as the rest of the group but containing marginal notes by the characteristic hand).[3] There is also nothing unconventional in pseudo-Dionysius the Areopagite or Theodoret's attack on pagan culture (Vat. gr. 2249). But the last member of the group has some surprises for us (Heidelberg, Pal. gr. 398). It is the unique witness for some of the texts it offers and the selection is to say the least unusual. It begins with several minor works, mainly of a geographical nature, including the so-called *Periplus of the Red Sea*, a valuable document for the history of ancient trade with the Orient, and an abridgment of Strabo's *Geography*, which perhaps not surprisingly was found inconveniently long by the average reader. The second main section of the volume contains mostly the writers known as the paradoxographers, who collected a mass of curious and almost entirely fictitious lore. One of the items is Antoninus Liberalis' collection of stories from mythology involving a

---

[2] Identified by A. Jacob, *Revue des bibliothèques* 9 (1899) 376-7; cf. also D. Serruys, *Revue de philologie* 38 (1914) 290 f.

[3] The script of Marc. gr. 258 is probably identical with that in the copy of the *Almagest* already mentioned in connection with Leo, Vat. gr. 1594. – I leave out of account Marc. gr. 236, Philoponus' *Reply to Proclus* on the eternity of the universe, as it seems to me that Allen was right to exclude it, although his view has not always been accepted.

metamorphosis, and another is the abridgment of a similar collection by Phlegon of Tralles. A third, probably the most famous, is the little book by Parthenius, the Greek man of letters who is believed to have helped Vergil in his reading of Greek literature. The book consists of a series of short mythological tales, all involving an unusual and frequently perverted love interest, which Parthenius dedicated to the poet Gallus, saying in a covering letter that he hoped these tales would be useful material when Gallus was looking for themes to write on. The third main section of this rich miscellany of texts contains four collections of ancient letters, attributed to Hippocrates, Themistocles, Diogenes the Cynic and Brutus. Such collections of letters, many of them spurious, were popular in Byzantium, as the letter was a literary form which the Byzantines cultivated with great care, and so this third part of the Heidelberg codex is not remarkable in the same way as the others.

In seeking the origin of these manuscripts one has to be content to be guided by extremely slender hints. Just as the interest in Plato might be thought to point to Leo and his acquaintances, so the works of paradoxography suggest a connection with Photius, who in his *Bibliotheca* devotes more space to this kind of literature than might be thought appropriate. Although there is no precise correspondence between any section of the Heidelberg manuscript and the contents of the *Bibliotheca*, an argument has been put forward in favour of assuming Photian influence in this context. The abridgment of Strabo has a number of details added from other authors, including Ptolemy, Arrian and Diodorus. The last two are prominent in Photius. It is also apparent that the style of the abridgment is very much the same as that found in Photius.[4] Another palaeographical observation has added a tantalising piece of knowledge. The main hand in Allen's scriptorium has been found in some marginal notes in the Vienna Aristotle. One gains a hazy impression of contacts between intellectual readers; more pieces are required before the jigsaw puzzle becomes intelligible.[5]

---

[4] A. Diller, *The Textual Tradition of Strabo's Geography* (Amsterdam 1975) 38-40.
[5] J. Irigoin, *JOBG* 6 (1957) 5-10.

5

Photius

(i) Introduction

We now come to the man who must probably be reckoned the most important figure in the history of classical studies in Byzantium. Although some later scholars may have been his equals or even superiors in various branches of scholarship, Photius must be considered more important, not merely because of the influence he exercised over his contemporaries, which was strong enough to restore a lasting tradition of scholarship, but because he must be presumed to have read more ancient literature than anyone has been able to since his day.

His biography is obscure at the points where we should most like to have information. The best view seems to be that he was born *c*. 810 and lived until *c*. 893. He had a distinguished career as a civil servant and was chosen to serve on an embassy to the Arabs, which is perhaps to be placed in 855. In 858, while still a layman, he was elected patriarch, according to his own account against his will, and held the throne until 867. After being deposed and sent into exile he was restored to favour and became patriarch again for the years 878-86, but was then deposed once more. To church historians he is famous as the man who widened the gulf between the Greek and Roman churches, the enduring consequences of which are enough to make him one of the leading figures in European history. His importance in the history of scholarship is of the same order.

We know nothing of his education. As he came from a family of some standing – the patriarch Tarasius was his uncle – there is a presumption that he will have enjoyed the best education available in the capital in the first quarter of the ninth century. There is a temptation to suppose that such a remarkable figure needs to be explained as the product of contact with a notable teacher, and the only person generally accepted as corresponding to that description is Leo. As there is very little sign of contact between the two of them the idea must be treated with reserve. It is odd that neither Photius nor the historians who had cause to mention him should say anything about his education, especially when he was recognised as a person of prodigious learning. One hostile source describes him in terms reminiscent of the Faust story, saying that his erudition was the result of a pact with a Jewish magician, who invited him to give up his faith in return for knowledge and worldly success.[1]

[1] Pseudo-Symeon, *PG* 109. 732BC.

This picturesque fiction is perhaps a good reason for thinking that Photius owed little to any teacher. It is not likely that he conceals the name of his master because the man was an iconoclast and an avowal of indebtedness to such a tainted source would have been dangerous. There is positive evidence in one of his own letters that Photius and his father and uncle were condemned by the iconoclasts, presumably at their last synod in 837.[2]

(ii)   The Lexicon

We will deal first with the *Lexicon*, particularly as there is reason to think that it is an early work. In his later *Amphilochia* Photius refers to a dictionary which he had compiled when still a young man, and a careful interpretation of his words allows us to identify it with the surviving work. The dedicatory letter, addressed to an otherwise unknown pupil Thomas, protospatharios and governor of Lykotomion, evidently a man of some standing, is not a decisive objection to this view.[1] Although at first sight a lapse of some years would be required to allow for Thomas' rise to a position of importance, there are two considerations which weaken the force of the argument. One is the possibility that the *Lexicon* was compiled some time before Photius saw fit to let it circulate; the other, which has more weight, is that at the time of dedication Thomas had not yet acquired his titles, which have been added by a later copyist in the light of his subsequent career. The letter itself gives us some valuable indications of Photius' aim. After a title which may be translated 'Alphabetical list of words which lend particular elegance to the compositions of orators and prose-writers' he begins by saying that most poetical vocabulary has been usefully collected for those interested by Diogenianos. The statement is notable for two reasons, first that it presupposes the possibility that someone might wish to read the classical poets or imitate their metres, and secondly that Photius knew a lexicon now lost and not included in the substantial list reviewed in his later *Bibliotheca*. He must have had access to a copy, as he continues by saying that as faɪ as he knows no other comparable work of reference is superior, and there are two passing references to it in the *Bibliotheca*. He then turns to his own concern, the vocabulary of orators and Atticist prose-writers, in fact any writer avoiding the constraints of verse, together with the vocabulary of Christian writers in so far as it needs explanation. Admitting that a complete dictionary requires more time than he can spare (was he already occupied as an administrator?) and that a promise to make one would be pretentious, he offers his own compilation to his friend with the remark that he has not entirely omitted poetic usage, just as the authors of lexica to the poets have not excluded prose words. Here the argument seems to miss the point;

---

[2] Letter 2,64, *PG* 102. 877BC; V. Grumel, op. cit. above at Ch. 1 (iv) n. 8, no. 413.
[1] *Pace* I. Ševčenko, *American Historical Review* 79 (1974) 1534.

Photius should either say that he is trying to help readers of verse or that prose sometimes contains words that are more characteristic of poetry. In fact his *Lexicon* is notable for including much vocabulary from Old Comedy, which in its iambic verse seems to have used essentially the words current in ordinary prose. After another remark which breaks the train of thought, in which he offers his book as a token of past and present friendship, he reverts to the poetic words he has included. He asks that they should not be taken as evidence of a desire to appear learned or as conflicting with his main purpose; when a standard word is not available, a poetic one may have to be used instead, even if it is a great rarity. It is better to use words than deny oneself power of expression; writers of elevated style are accustomed to make poetic vocabulary serve their purposes. If asked to prove this statement by an example he could have cited the elaborate style of the myths in Plato's dialogues. He is evidently thinking here of the utility of his lexicon for the writer of formal archaising prose rather than for the reader of the classics. The point of the title is now made explicit, and his intention is confirmed by the remark that he has been at pains to cite authorities, especially for the words of whose meaning there is no doubt, while for obscure expressions, which by their nature are not useful to the writer, he has tried to unravel the obscurity. In other words he is not recommending to his pupil the use of such vocabulary but wishes to help him in his encounters with it in the classics. In conclusion he invites his friend to consult the lexicon carefully to see whether it comes up to expectations. The last sentence, though difficult to interpret, appears to express the hope that his friend's studies will lead him to achieve better results as a writer.

The sources of the lexicon are numerous, and a precise identification of them would lead to a more complex discussion than can be attempted here.[2] The ultimate source appears to be the glossary attributed to Cyril, and various additions have been made to it. One of these derives from a lost dictionary known as 'the enlarged *synagoge*', of which reflections are seen in two Paris manuscripts (Coislin 345 and 347). The earlier of the two is written in a hand of archaic appearance that might be regarded as contemporary with Photius himself. By using these sources he was in practice drawing on various Atticist lexica; apart from Diogenianos, mentioned by him in the dedicatory letter, he was using at second hand material from Aelius Dionysius, Pausanias, and Phrynichus. It can be seen how Photius took short series of entries first from one source, then from another, without blending them so as to respect alphabetical order precisely. Phrynichus in particular seems to have contained a rich store of quotations from Old Comedy, and one of the many reasons for awaiting impatiently the publication of the full text of Photius is the expectation that it will provide a substantial number of additional

[2] On these questions see K. Alpers, *Das attizistische Lexikon des Oros* (Berlin 1981) 69-79.

fragments from Aristophanes and his rivals.[3]

A later reference to his youthful production throws some further light on his aims and methods. In *Amphilochia* 21 he notes that a very long book would result if someone were to make a list of common words with more than one meaning – to make a complete list would be difficult if not impossible; then he adds the phrase 'the sort of list I made myself, as you know, when I was little more than a youth'. Since the extant *Lexicon* is not designed purely as a list of words with more than one meaning it might seem that it should not be identified with his early work. But some of the words cited in *Amphilochia* 21 recur in the lexicon, and Photius' phrasing need not imply that his scope was limited to words of variable meaning. The identification is probably correct.[4]

Despite Photius' importance both as a scholar and a churchman his lexicon does not seem to have been widely used. The number of surviving manuscripts is small, and the lexicon generally known as Cyril's together with the later compilation wrongly ascribed to John Zonaras are much commoner. In fact no complete copy of Photius was known until the discovery of one in a large collection of manuscripts unearthed in a deserted monastery at Zavorda in Macedonia in 1959. This turns out to be a copy of the celebrated Cambridge codex (Trinity College O.3.9), from which many pages are now missing. The copy was fortunately made while it was still complete.

At one time it was believed that Photius' lexicographical activities were more extensive. He was thought to have had a hand in or to have been primarily responsible for the production of two other dictionaries (known as the *Etymologicum Genuinum* and the *Etymologicum Gudianum*). The evidence cited in support of this belief consisted of what appeared to be Photius' name written in the form of a monogram in the margin alongside a large number of entries. Other monograms found in these lexica were interpreted as meaning George Choeroboscus and Nicetas, presumably to be identified with a bishop of Heraclea of rather later date. The application of more expert knowledge of Byzantine culture led to an amusing refutation: the monograms are all found adjacent to texts occurring in the liturgy, and they indicate not the names of scholars but of the feasts at which the liturgical texts in question were sung or recited, Epiphany, Christmas and Pentecost.[5]

What is clear, however, is that later in his career, when he was patriarch, Photius made a number of additions to the *Etymologicum Genuinum*. At the end of the entries for most of the individual letters there is a small supplement of other words. Some of these clearly indicate Photian authorship; in one case it is stated 'this is by me, Photius the

[3] R. Reitzenstein, *Der Anfang des Lexikon des Photios* (Leipzig-Berlin 1907) xxxix, and note also his description of the lexicon as a 'Hilfsmittel für den Schreibenden oder Redenden'. The first volume of the long awaited new edition has now appeared: C. Theodoridis, *Photii patriarchae lexicon* I (Berlin 1982).

[4] K. Alpers, *BZ* 64 (1971) 71-84, esp. 79-80.

[5] E.L. De Stefani, *BZ* 16 (1907) 52-68, L. Cohn, ibid. 20 (1911) 215-16.

patriarch'.[6] We shall find other signs that Photius did not lose his linguistic interests when he ceased to be a layman.

(iii) The Bibliotheca

Photius' literary fame depends on the *Bibliotheca* or *Muriobiblos* (neither title has any authority in the manuscript tradition, but they are convenient and well established terms). The work consists of 280 chapters, each normally referred to as a codex, as if corresponding to a volume on the shelf in Photius' personal library. They vary in length from two lines to seventy pages, and are a record of his reading over a number of years. The whole amounts to some 1600 printed pages in the only modern edition. The presentation of the chapters is not uniform, but the usual pattern is a résumé of a text accompanied by a few biographical details about the author or a criticism of him from the stylistic point of view. Photius is in effect the inventor of the book-review.

The *Bibliotheca* is perhaps the most important work in the whole of Byzantine literature. It deals with a wide range of classical, late antique and early Byzantine writers. Theology is slightly better represented than secular literature. The number of lost books reviewed is substantial; for these Photius is often the best or the only source. Many questions about the *Bibliotheca* are still not satisfactorily answered. Fortunately it is not necessary for the present purpose to find an answer to them all. The account that follows gives an outline of them and then passes on to deal with Photius' scholarship.[1]

According to the dedicatory letter and the concluding paragraph Photius compiled the work for his brother Tarasius before setting out on an embassy to the Arabs. The date of this embassy has not been firmly established. It has usually been assumed that it must have taken place before 858, the year in which Photius was elevated to the patriarchal throne. The earliest possible date appears to be 838, when the author may have been in his late twenties.[2] This hypothesis raises the question whether he could possibly have read so much while still so young, and is prima facie in conflict with the remark in codex 189 (Nicolaus of Damascus) that he is dealing with a book read 'long ago'. Other hints of composition at a much later stage of his career have been detected. He refers to a life of Pope Gregory the Great which is believed to have been adapted from a Latin version composed as late as 875 (codex 252).[3] He recalls his personal experience in dealing with Messalianist heretics, an experience not easily located in his career as a layman (codex 52).[4] These

---

[6] R. Reitzenstein, *Geschichte der griechischen Etymologika* (Leipzig 1897) 53-60.

[1] The best treatment is by K. Ziegler in *RE*, s.v. Photios.

[2] So Lemerle, op. cit. 179-80, following a suggestion by Mme. H. Ahrweiler.

[3] F. Halkin, *AnalBoll* 81 (1963) 414 ff, anticipated by E. Dekkers, *Sacris Erudiri* 5 (1953) 215.

[4] C. Mango in *Byzantine Books and Bookmen, a Dumbarton Oaks colloquium* (Washington 1975) 40-1.

are not the only instances of material more likely to appeal to the patriarch than the layman, but none of the others provides such a strong argument.

Our inability to date the embassy in question is perhaps not very surprising, since the sources for the history of Byzantium in the ninth century, though less sparse than for some periods, leave something to be desired. But two observations may be offered. First, it does not follow from what Photius says that the embassy actually took place; it may have been called off at the last moment. Secondly, we might consider the possibility that Photius was asked to serve during one of the two periods when he was no longer patriarch; the mission was potentially dangerous, just the kind of task that might be assigned to someone not fully in favour with the government.

An attempt has been made to reconcile the conflicting indications by supposing that the text which we now have is a revised version, enlarged by Photius after a considerable lapse of time. But this seems most unlikely; in such a revised version it would be very strange if Photius allowed the many duplicated entries to stand (there are more than a dozen works dealt with on two separate occasions). One of the duplications is exceptionally hard to credit: codex 185 and codex 211 consist mainly of lists of chapter titles in a medical book by Dionysius of Aegae, with brief comments that vary slightly between the two versions. It is impossible to believe that a repetition of this nature would have escaped the attention of an author preparing a new edition of his book.[5] And to anticipate a point that will arise in due course, some of the lacunae in the text appear to be inconsistent with the view that the *Bibliotheca* has undergone revision.

It therefore has to be admitted that the date of composition remains uncertain. The next question concerns Photius' sources: where did he find all the texts, a high proportion of which have since been lost? Once again a satisfactory answer is impossible. Although Photius remarks from time to time that the copy he read was old (codex 77), that he has seen more than one copy (codices 77, 88, 111, 199, 200), or that he has not so far found a complete copy (codices 35 and 224; cf. also 40, 41, 42), he gives no further information. It is sometimes assumed or asserted that he must have found all the texts he read in the capital.[6] While that is no doubt true of most, and especially for heretical texts which probably could not be found outside the library of the patriarchate, it is by no means clear that it has to be true of all. The chronicle of Theophanes, a compilation from a number of sources, was written in the early ninth century by a resident of the Megas Agros monastery on the southern shore of the sea of Marmara.[7] It may have been worth Photius' while to look outside the capital; one should not forget that historical texts are

[5] *Pace* Mango, op. cit. 42-3.
[6] Lemerle, op. cit. 190.
[7] C. Mango and I. Ševčenko, *DOP* 27 (1973) 265.

very prominent in the *Bibliotheca*. Other possibilities of finding books in provincial collections may be inferred from the search ordered by the iconoclast emperor Leo for texts to support his heretical views and by the activity of such writers as Michael Syncellus.

The *Bibliotheca* is a record of Photius' reading of Greek literature over a period of many years. He says in the dedicatory letter that it covers the books read when his brother was not present. In the postscript there is a remark which probably indicates that he read the books when alone. Certain consequences follow. We can now see why many of the texts normally read at school, especially the poets, are notable by their absence from the *Bibliotheca*. Perhaps the only central school text to be included is Demosthenes (codex 265). But the exception is more apparent than real, because what Photius does in this codex and the others about the Attic orators is to give an account of the author's life and work rather than an ordinary review of the speeches themselves. Probably we should infer that he also omitted all the texts discussed at the informal club which met in his house; but the identification of them is uncertain, and we may simply note in passing that Plato and Aristotle, who do not figure in the *Bibliotheca*, are found in the *Amphilochia*. In one codex (268, the orator Lycurgus) Photius admits that he has not yet had time to read the author he is commenting on. This confession is followed immediately by the remark 'but we have learned by inquiry that fifteen speeches exist'. In view of his success in locating copies of obscure books we may plausibly infer that he later read at least the one speech which still survives. But his candour, although reassuring in other respects, creates a difficulty. Both here and at the end of the preceding codex, where he sums up his remarks on the other nine orators, he fails to make clear the difference between the complete works of an author as reported by the ancient critics and the number of speeches he had read himself. That may be pardonable in a book composed hastily. But real doubt must attach to his claim to have read Hyperides, despite the alleged survival of a copy of that author as late as the Renaissance.[8] In general, however, it should be accepted that the *Bibliotheca* is an accurate and truthful account of private reading. A possible exception is codex 165 (Himerius), where Photius appears to say that he has read the declamations in the company of his brother. But the wording of the Greek text here is difficult and the two main witnesses diverge (108 b 28-30), so that it would be rash to base an argument on this passage.

The method of composition has been a subject of controversy. Photius is usually imagined reading texts pen in hand, making notes as he went along. The *Bibliotheca* is taken to be a revised version of the notes. But what he says is that he wrote from memory. Modern scholars, who are almost unanimous in their refusal to believe that he is telling the truth, have failed to notice that the word used in the dedicatory letter and in codex 267 could in principle be translated as 'memorandum, written

---

[8] N.G. Wilson, *GRBS* 16 (1975) 98-101.

record' rather than 'memory'. There are other signs of composition in normal fashion. In codex 234 there are questions at the end of two paragraphs which look like verbatim transcripts of notes made by a reader (293 a 40-1, 293 b 21). In codex 186, at the end of the third mythological story from Conon's handbook, Photius asks, 'But why should I practically copy them out, when they ought to be dealt with in a much more summary fashion?' If he means 'copy out' literally, then he has a text in front of him; but if he were working from memory, he might in fact still use the same term. Perhaps a better argument can be derived from codex 167, where Photius lists about 450 authors from whom Stobaeus compiled his anthology. It may be doubted whether even a photographic memory would imply such a power of recall; but those who are not endowed with such powers should be cautious in passing judgment until they meet someone who is. Similarly codex 185, strangely repeated in almost identical terms as codex 211, is little more than a list of chapters. But this case of repetition is even harder to account for on the assumption of composition based solely on extensive notes. One would be forced to believe that Photius had read the book twice, listing each time but in slightly different wording the contents of the chapters. Better pointers to the use of the original texts or extensive notes have been found by a detailed examination of codex 241.[9] The second part of it contains a fair number of examples of choice phraseology from Philostratus' *Life of Apollonius of Tyana*; they are distributed approximately evenly throughout the length of the text, which is somewhat unexpected if they were recalled by memory. There is also the fact that an error of the inferior class of manuscripts, which Photius evidently depended on, is reproduced literally, although it creates a serious breach of syntax. Though it is odd that Photius did not correct this, it would probably be odder still if it had survived as such in his memory.

The grounds for believing that Photius may be telling the truth can now be explored. The first is simply an argument from analogy; other men of exceptional powers of memory are known, the best recorded case being perhaps Lord Macaulay, of whom his biographer states that 'During the first part of his life he remembered whatever caught his fancy without going through the process of consciously getting it by heart ... At one period of his life he was known to say that, if by some miracle of

---

[9] T. Hägg, *GRBS* 14 (1973) 213-22. Hägg thinks that when an author refers to his own memory, he may be doing no more that exploit a standard *topos*, as was argued by Immisch in *RhMus* 78 (1929) 113-23. But Immisch's argument is flimsy. It consists essentially in a denial that certain statements by the Elder Seneca can be taken literally, together with an argument derived from Cicero's *Topica*, the preface of which is prima facie in conflict with what Cicero himself says in *Ad Fam*. 7.19 (now no. 334 in Shackleton Bailey). Immisch makes a crass blunder in citing Cicero's letter, quoting the words *eum librum tibi misi Regio scriptum* as if *scriptum* were to be taken with *Regio* and meant 'at Reggio', for which the Latin is *Regii*; *scriptum* governs words that follow. One might add the a priori argument that authors' prefaces tend to advertise the quality of modesty; boasting about powers of memory is rare.

vandalism all copies of *Paradise Lost* and *The Pilgrim's Progress* were destroyed off the face of the earth, he would undertake to reproduce them both from his recollection whenever a revival of learning came ... Macaulay thought it probable that he could rewrite *Sir Charles Grandison* from memory.'[10] It is important to note the unspoken implication that his ability was not fully maintained in later life. If the analogy is valid, the same may be assumed to be true of Photius, and there certainly are mistakes in the *Bibliotheca*.

Another argument can be derived from the errors and oddities of presentation. Appian's *Roman History* (codex 57) receives a muddled treatment. An incomplete summary of book I is followed by a brief account of the whole work, then some notes on the civil wars, after which come notes on Rome's origins as a Trojan settlement. This does not look like the work of a man using systematic notes made during his original reading; it may also militate against the idea of a man with a photographic memory. There are also mistakes of detail, many of which can no doubt be put down to scribes rather than the author. But some are difficult to account for. Codex 195 deals with a dialogue by Maximus the Confessor on the two wills and energies in the person of Christ. Photius says that the dialogue is set in Rome after the self-imposed exile of Maximus. In fact Maximus was sent into exile in 641 and the dialogue is set in north Africa. The first mistake does not necessarily depend on the text itself, but the second is very peculiar if we are meant to imagine that the *Bibliotheca* depends on notes made during reading. In fact the work ends with a statement that one of the characters made good a promise in Rome, travelling there with Maximus.[11] Two other such errors may be cited. In codex 240 Photius says that Philoponus dedicated his work to Sergius, patriarch of Constantinople. In fact he was patriarch of Antioch. Perhaps even this error is scribal; if Antioch was given its alternative name of Theoupolis and this was abbreviated, confusion might have arisen. Nevertheless the error looks more like one of memory. Another case occurs in codex 37, a dialogue on political theory. The names of the speakers are reported as Menas and Thomas; as far as we know they should be Menodorus and Thomasius.[12] There are also very strange

---

[10] N.G. Wilson, *GRBS* 9 (1968) 454-5, cf. also 12 (1971) 559-60.

[11] *PG* 91.353.

[12] The argument is valid if we are right to identify the fragments found in Vat. gr. 1298 as coming from the dialogue; cf. H. Hunger, *Die hochsprachliche profane Literatur der Byzantiner* I (Munich 1978) 301 n. 72. (His reference to Vat. gr. 73 appears to be an oversight.) The identity is virtually certain if we accept that Thomasius is an Atticist equivalent of Thomas, while Menas is an example of a common type of abbreviated nickname ending in -as; the pair Menas/Menodorus is given by Michael Syncellus, *Syntax* 33, and A.N. Jannaris, *An Historical Greek Grammar* (London 1897) 110. It might be possible to argue that rather than making an error Photius deliberately adopted the colloquial form of the names. – The text is now to be read in the edition of C.M. Mazzucchi, *Menae patricii cum Thoma referendario De scientia politica dialogus* (Milan 1982). Its author's provisions for education, medical, general and elementary, of which a public library is a necessary adjunct (V 83), are not indicated in detail and probably do not reflect contemporary reality.

errors in the résumé of Heliodorus' novel (codex 73), in which Athens is wrongly mentioned instead of other parts of Greece. Photius in addition fails to point out how superior Heliodorus' novel is in comparison with other Greek novels in the construction of its plot.

A further argument is palaeographical. In the text as we have it there are a number of lacunae, where the manuscripts leave blank spaces. These would normally be taken to indicate a damaged archetype, nothing unusual in the history of texts. The present case is different. Some of the lacunae are not mechanical. In codices 11, 12, 19, 20, 21 and 68 spaces are left blank for the insertion of numerals. As the text is otherwise sound at these points, the absence of the numerals cannot be due to coincidence. Photius had evidently failed to record them and could no longer remember them accurately enough to satisfy himself. As he failed to insert them it is scarcely possible to believe that the present text is the product of two stages of work; such gaps, like the repetitions, could not be tolerated in any work which the author claimed to be issuing in revised form. One must in strict logic go further and say that they could not be tolerated in any book intended for normal publication. The *Bibliotheca* can only have been published in the sense that the author's master copy or the presentation copy to Tarasius, if there was one, was somehow made available to friends who thought that its value far outweighed the drawback of its being incomplete. The absence of a few numerals is a minor blemish. One has to bear in mind, however, that other lacunae in the text, which could in principle be due to mechanical damage, may instead be further proof of the incomplete state of the author's autograph. The balance of probability inclines strongly in favour of this alternative explanation. As the lacunae occur almost without exception at the ends of the codices – the small gaps in codices 124 and 137 can be due to other causes – the explanation of them as due to mechanical damage implies a coincidental series of accidents in the archetype as implausible as such a coincidence would have been in the case of the missing numerals. About twenty codices are incomplete in this way. The gaps vary in length from a line or two to more than a page; as is only natural, the two manuscripts differ slightly, but there can be no doubt of their derivation from a single source.

Let us try to imagine our author at work. At certain points he stops and leaves a blank space. Various explanations can be considered. They are not all mutually exclusive. Perhaps he had lost or mislaid the rest of his notes, and did not trust his memory to make good the loss. Perhaps he had failed to make notes on the whole of the text in question and was not confident of making an adequate summary without referring back to it. Perhaps he had not read all the texts right to the end. A cynical observer might suspect that he anticipates a bad habit of modern reviewers. Finally we may suppose that he was working from memory and his memory failed him.

However that may be, the blank spaces are strange, indeed they are nothing short of bizarre in a work designed specifically for presentation to the author's brother. Eleven of them are long enough to be regarded as more than trivial blemishes that could easily be put right later. Why were they left? Presumably Photius hoped to fill them, if necessary reading what he had not yet read. It was in a way reasonable to leave room at the end of codex 63 to allow for comment on the six books of Procopius that he had not dealt with, and the same applies to codex 239, where only the first two of the four books of Proclus' *Chrestomathy* are outlined. But a man with a deadline to meet does not leave many gaps that can only be filled by reading texts through as opposed to checking details in them. The embassy's departure could not be delayed; perhaps it even had to be brought forward. Photius was unable to put the finishing touches to his work, and gave it to his brother as it was. Another possibility is that the embassy was cancelled at the last minute. The urgency to complete the text then disappeared. In either case Photius might well have been distracted by other cares and so prevented from completing a task which no longer claimed first priority.

The usual view is that Photius cannot have worked from memory because he leaves mistakes that he found in his text uncorrected. It may seem special pleading to infer that he had a special kind of photographic or eidetic memory which would have preserved mistakes in this way. But I find the more normal view equally open to objection. It assumes that Photius read his faulty text, did not see any need to correct it, and made excerpts incorporating erroneous readings. Many years later, writing the *Bibliotheca*, he went back to his notes and took from them the passages in question, once again leaving the errors as they stood. In other words he failed twice to make the necessary correction. That is not a simpler hypothesis. A third possibility is that he marked passages when reading them and later gave instructions to an amanuensis to copy them out. Errors that had eluded his attention in the first place might equally well escape the notice of the scribe. But in practice Byzantine readers did not normally mark their books in a way that could have been used later by a scribe to make a compilation; the signs σημείωσαι and ὡραῖον are not accompanied by marks to show exactly where each passage begins and ends. And one cannot believe that Photius from a youthful age read with the intention of writing the *Bibliotheca*.[13]

It is now time to consider what the *Bibliotheca* tells us of Photius as a reader and scholar. As a reader he dealt with slightly more theology than secular literature, and the long and complex accounts of some theological works such as Job on the incarnation (codex 222) or Ephraim on questions arising out of the teaching of St. Cyril of Alexandria (codex 229) show a grasp of the subject that may have been not quite as impressive to the Byzantines as it is to us. He was much interested in heresy, and if the *Bibliotheca* is a product of his early middle age it

---

[13] On the composition of the *Bibliotheca* one can now consult W.T. Treadgold, *The Nature of the Bibliotheca of Photius* (Washington 1980), reviewed by N.G. Wilson, *Speculum* 57 (1982) .

suggests that he was given the run of the patriarch's library and acquired such an extensive knowledge of the subject that he was an obvious candidate for the patriarchal throne when a vacancy was created. The fact most frequently emphasised in accounts of the *Bibliotheca* is the absence of poetry, from which it has usually been inferred that the poets were not being read in Byzantium at that time. It would be more accurate to infer that Photius did not read them for pleasure. Even that is not quite correct: the *Bibliotheca* refers to two verse paraphrases of the Old Testament (codices 183-4) and the end of codex 279 shows acquaintance with some verse texts by obscure grammarians of late antiquity. But Photius had read some classical poetry, as will become clear when we deal with his letters. Despite the loss of ninth-century manuscripts of poets other than Homer it seems clear that the curriculum still included such texts. Photius did not need to describe them to his brother or to any other educated man.

Another obvious and frequently stated fact about the *Bibliotheca* is the prominence given to historians. Although Thucydides is missing and Herodotus treated only briefly, there are valuable résumés of many less eminent authors. This does not mean, however, that Photius was a student of history in the ordinary sense of the term. Admittedly he was prepared to take the trouble to acquire a large amount of chronological knowledge by reading the lists of dates compiled by Phlegon of Tralles (codex 97), and we cannot criticise him when he confesses that having worked through five books of such dry information covering the period from the first Olympic games in 776 B.C. to the year 68 B.C. he could not bring himself to read any further. Although he regards Herodotus as a contemporary of the events he narrates, Photius will certainly have been much better protected against anachronistic misunderstandings of the ancient world than most Byzantines. But his motives for reading historians were mixed. He was clearly conscious of their stylistic qualities: his judgment on Arrian, for instance, is one of his longest and most interesting criticisms of style. This consideration was one of the most important for him in reading any text, as is proved by the frequency of such criticisms. There are signs that his interest in the contents was, if not limited, at least one-sided. Several reviews of historians (codices 63-5 and 72) show an overriding concern with the affairs of the orient. A striking case is the account of Procopius' history of Justinian's wars. Photius deals with only the first two books, which have as their subject the campaign on the eastern front against the Persians. And there are other signs of the fascination that the orient held for him. The summary of Philostratus' *Life of Apollonius of Tyana* (codex 241) concentrates on curious facts about the east and Africa. He devotes a good deal of space to an extraordinary novel, the *Babyloniaca* of Iamblichus (codex 94). Part of the attraction was the strangeness of the information, which explains the inclusion of several other texts. Although he expresses little liking for a silly tale involving metamorphoses by Lucius of Patras (codex 129), he was fascinated by such diverse books as the collection of paradoxical information by Damascius (codex 130) and Conon's handbook of fifty unusual stories from classical mythology (codex 186). It is difficult to see why these fantastic tales should have induced Photius to write one of his longer summaries; the brief appraisal of the author's style does not suggest that that was the reason. In the same volume Photius found and read the much more elementary handbook of mythology by Apollodorus; he commented that it was a valuable guide for anyone wishing to know about the subject. But he could scarcely have felt the same about Conon. More collections of bizarre pseudo-information are recorded in codices 188 and 189. To Photius' credit it must be said that he found some of these texts less plausible than others. He concludes his survey of the novel by Antonius Diogenes (codex 166) by saying that it was better than many in this respect (109 a 10-12), and he reveals more of his outlook by the remark that the author has the merit of portraying the unjust paying the penalty in the end after seeming to escape scotfree, while the just are saved after a series of dangers. A further indication of his views occurs in codex 190, an extraordinary collection of bizarre and probably for the most part false information put together by Ptolemy Chennos. Despite having justifiable reservations about much of it, Photius unexpectedly commends this book on the ground that it is a compendium of information which would otherwise require a lifetime to collect. We ought to view charitably a thirst for knowledge tempered by at least a grain of scepticism, a quality difficult to exercise in the limiting circumstances of the early middle ages.

Since the Byzantines regarded their state as the continuation of the Roman empire it is only natural that an educated man should wish to read histories of Rome. The choice of many texts in the *Bibliotheca* can be explained in this way. When Photius confines his résumé of Appian's *Roman History* mainly to the mythical period of early Rome, he shows no more than a proper concern with the ultimate origin of his own society. Yet not all his historical reading is easily explained. To devote fifty pages to Memnon's history of the city of Heraclea Pontica (codex 224) argues a different motive; there was not enough Roman history in it to make it an obvious choice. Nor can it have appealed to him specially on stylistic grounds or as a source of information about the geography of the Levant. This text more than most others proves that Photius was an omnivorous reader.

In philosophy Photius had read more widely than the *Bibliotheca* shows. Despite a passing reference to Plato in codex 212, which could imply a familiarity with his writings, and a mention of the Aristotelian commentator Ammonius son of Hermias in codex 187, Plato and Aristotle are neglected. So are the Epicureans and Stoics. Most of Photius' concern is with the philosophical issue of greatest interest to theologians, free will. So we find him giving two accounts (codices 214 and 251) of Hierocles, a Neoplatonist of the early fifth century who wrote on predestination, trying to reconcile the opinions of Plato and Aristotle on this subject and on the immortality of the soul. Photius also devoted forty pages to the treatise of Diodorus of Tarsus against predestination, which contained an extensive critique of astrology (codex 223). While being perfectly well aware that Diodorus was a heretic, Photius notes that this book was free from all traces of Nestorian doctrine.

It is less easy to understand why he should have given an account of the book by Aenesidemus on arguments in favour of philosophical scepticism (codex 212). Photius remarks that Plato and other philosophers have shown that its contentions are without foundation. But he concludes by saying that it could be of some use to students of dialectic provided their judgment is steady and not affected by specious arguments. He also deals with a treatise of Nicomachus of Gerasa on number symbolism (codex 187). To judge from his résumé this was barely intelligible and he honestly confesses how difficult he found it to understand. One might wonder how he could bear to read such nonsense. It may be that Nicomachus' authorship of an introduction to arithmetic which seems to have been used in schools led Photius to attempt this much more abstruse text.

One does not expect natural science to figure largely in Photius' reading, particularly in view of his penchant for tales of the miraculous. There are reviews of a few medical texts. The herbal of Dioscorides (codex 178) is praised as the best source of information on the appearance, nature, and origin of plants. He is compared with Paul of Aegina, Aetius, Oreibasius and Galen. The final words of the review suggest that Photius had conversed with medical men about the relative merits of the various available handbooks. It is worth recalling that Dioscorides was, to judge by the surviving manuscripts, much used by doctors. Of the two most famous ancient writers Hippocrates is absent, while Galen is represented only by the *De sectis* (codex 164), but Photius makes it clear that he had read more. The writers of late antiquity are more fully treated, and they give additional evidence of Photius' contacts with members of the profession. In codex 217 he recommends the huge compilation by Oreibasius in seventy books for its clarity and comprehensive coverage, urging practitioners to use it. When he comes to deal with a shorter book by the same author in the next codex he says that he would have recommended it as being of some use but for the fact that he had seen the results of its incautious use by inexperienced and hasty practitioners (174 a 38-175 b 4). Another voluminous compiler of late antiquity was Aetius (codex 221). Although he does not deal with anatomy or offer a summary of Galen's opinions, he may be superior in other respects, says Photius, and he adds the surprising remark 'in view of the laziness of the present generation, who are more interested in other things than curing the sick, this handbook ought to be studied in preference to others'.

Two other facts should be mentioned in this context. Codex 163 is devoted to a book on agriculture by Vindanius Anatolius. Photius says that this has been proved by experience to be the best book on the

subject. He uses the word 'we have seen', which is rather hard to take
literally; he is not usually thought of as an active member of the land-
owning class. Less unexpected is a statement quoted from Diodorus of
Tarsus (217 b 25-7), which though written at the end of the fourth
century may be thought to typify the attitude of the Byzantines towards
science: 'Men used to invent new arts, but now they are content with
those that exist and do not have any idea of proceeding further.'

Much of Photius' reading of literature seems to have been done with
the intention of maintaining and improving his command of prose style.
Other considerations appear from time to time. We have already seen
evidence of his desire to accumulate information. He also shows himself
aware of another use to which literature could be put. Commenting on a
miscellany which exploited Plutarch's biographies and essays (Sopater,
codex 161) he noted their tendency to encourage high ideals and moral
behaviour. Some texts struck him as having undesirable effects. He
complains of the indecency of Achilles Tatius' novel *Clitophon and
Leucippe* (codex 87) and yet surprisingly concedes that the author's style
deserves high praise. Moral considerations might have been expected to
colour his view of an author such as Lucian (codex 128), who had made
uncomplimentary references to the Christians and did in fact rouse a
reader of the next generation, Arethas, to heap abusive epithets on him.
But Photius overlooks Lucian's anti-Christian sentiments and values
him highly. This is partly due to his admirable style, partly to his skill in
mocking the follies of pagan religion and culture. Paganism as such did
not make an author objectionable to Photius; he seems to have objected
more to heretics. But it should be noted that he did find unattractive the
blend of pagan and Christian elements in the work of Choricius, the
sophist of the Gaza school (codex 160). It may be significant that he
approves in principle of the attempt of an anonymous author (codex 170)
to show that non-Christian cultures contain some elements consistent
with Christianity.

Photius' overriding concern with style is shown in three ways. First is
the comment on the usefulness to writers of lexica such as that of
Helladius (codex 145). Secondly there are two codices (241-2) in which
having given his normal review he appends a list of phrases and
sentences chosen, as a fresh heading makes clear, for their stylistic
quality. In the first case, Philostratus' *Life of Apollonius of Tyana*, these
stylistic pearls fill ten pages, whereas his account of this long text had
occupied only twenty-one. In the second, Damascius' *Life of Isidore*, they
again fill ten pages, but the text itself had been summarised at greater
length, in almost forty pages. Photius is here listing for his own benefit
and that of his brother features of Attic or Atticist style which can be
exploited in order to give the correct archaising veneer to their
compositions. That the choice should fall on two Atticists rather than
ancient writers is not surprising; in the *Bibliotheca* the highest praise
seems to be reserved for Atticists. Photius' enthusiasm, however, is not
unlimited, and he is prepared to admit that imitation can go too far and

degenerate into hyperatticism. In a favourable judgment on Diodorus
Siculus' universal history (codex 70) he says that it is clear,
unpretentious and very appropriately written for a history, adding that
'it neither seeks what one might call hyperattic or archaic syntax nor
leans too far towards the spoken language'. Curiously this last comment,
however apt in its application to Diodorus, mentions as faults qualities
that Byzantines in practice regarded as essential merits. Similarly the
historian Herodian (codex 99) is said to avoid 'hyperatticism and
violence to the natural grace of ordinary language'. Commenting on
Heraclianus, author of a denunciation of the Manichaeans (codex 85),
Photius says 'his diction is concise, sober and elevated, and he does not
sink into obscurity; clarity is blended with grandeur in that he mixes the
spoken language with atticism and is a guide to children engaged in a
competition of what might be called hyperatticism'. One is surprised to
see here the suggestion that an author whose style is worthy of praise
can include features of the spoken language; it is now clearly a desirable
quality. As to excessive imitation, if the translation offered above of an
obscure sentence in the Greek is correct, we are given a glimpse of
conditions in the Byzantine school classroom where pupils competed
with each other to produce the best imitation of Attic Greek. It is a pity
that Photius does not attach the label hyperatticist to a surviving author
so that we can try to see what he meant by it.

His literary judgments have been discussed often, particularly with a
view to discovering the sources of his critical terms and the extent of his
originality. In a case of this kind it is easy to fall into the trap of assuming
that there must be sources and that once they are identified Photius loses
all claim to being an independent thinker. As far as the judgments
themselves are concerned, Photius is usually dealing with authors who
had not been subjected to this kind of inquiry by the well-known critics
of antiquity, and there is no sign that there had been any critical
literature in the early Byzantine period from which he might have
derived his opinions. Were there for instance critics who had commented
on such late authors as St. Basil and Eunomius, on each of whom
Photius passes judgment in detail? Although one modern authority has
given it as his opinion that there very probably were,[14] it seems to me
doubtful in the extreme. When it comes to the choice of critical terms,
Photius clearly owes a great deal to his predecessors, and it would be
extraordinary if it were not so. His debts are chiefly to Demetrius,
Dionysius of Halicarnassus and Hermogenes.[15] Hermogenes in particular
is a powerful influence, as is only to be expected, since he was the author
of a standard textbook of rhetoric used in the schools.[16] Photius has been
criticised on the ground that he offers 'most often a mechanical
attribution of literary categories derived from Hermogenes'.[17] There is

[14] Ziegler, op. cit. col. 723.

[15] G. Hartmann, *Photios' Literarästhetik*, Diss. Rostock 1928 (Leipzig 1929) 6-10.

[16] G.L. Kustas, *Hellenika* 17 (1962) 136-7. But his views on the Christian element in
Photius are too vague to be useful.

[17] R.J.H. Jenkins, *DOP* 17 (1963) 48.

some justification for taking that view of a number of his shorter criticisms, which prove nothing more than a sensitivity to style normal in a well read man.

The willingness of critics to recommend to others something that they do not regularly practise themselves is seen in Photius' praise for writers who use short sentences, such as Basil of Seleuceia (codex 168), and the correspondingly adverse comment on the opposite feature in Galen (codex 164) and Theodore of Mopsuestia (codex 177). He has a weakness for aspects of Byzantine style that are almost unbearable for the modern reader. His comment on Theophylact Simocatta (codex 65), though not concealing disapproval, is still too lenient for one of the most affected and stilted of all Byzantine writers. 'His diction has some grace, except that the excessive use of metaphorical language and allegory leads to a certain frigidity and juvenile lack of taste. In addition the inappropriate insertion of moralising reflections is a sign of officious and excessive self-confidence. Otherwise there is nothing to criticise.' But we should not fail to recognise that he sometimes hits the mark. Here is his criticism of Isocrates (codex 159).

> He has a special gift, as the reader notices at once, for limpidity and purity. He displays great care in the preparation of his speeches, to the extent that his careful arrangement even becomes excessive. The exaggerated workmanship throws into relief not so much his fluency of argumentation as a lack of taste. Character, truth and vigour are entirely lacking. Grandeur, in so far as it suits political oratory, is well blended in equal proportions with clarity; but the style lacks the necessary power. The boring regularity of his evenly balanced clauses lays him specially open to a charge of hair-splitting. But we make these comments on his literary merit, drawing attention to the shortcomings and unevenness in his works, because even his failings might count as merits when he is compared with some people who have the presumption to become authors.

Since there is no detailed comment on any other surviving author of the classical period, it is worth giving his judgment on two important writers of the early Roman empire. In codex 209 he has this to say of Dio Chrysostom, the fluent philosopher who gives us in his seventy-eight extant essays a lively picture of politics and culture at the turn of the first and second centuries.

> He is sharp in his argumentation, maintaining a compact manner in accordance with his style of writing, rich in vigour, and fertile. He is excellent in his illustrative examples, fluent with them on all occasions, selecting them from every sphere and adapting them well to a context. He particularly enjoys interlacing his exhortations with mythological stories, and so gives the impression of aiming at simplicity. One will not often find him imitating Plato, as he does in his Borystheniticus, and using extensively myths that impart elevation and grandeur to his style. For the most part he is simple, as I said, in his ideas; his vocabulary is from the spoken language and obvious; his syntax makes no innovations designed to add depth or to entertain. In the choice and arrangement of words one

would hope for a writer to aim at clarity; but because the exposition of his thought proceeds at length and the exposition is very greatly complicated by (?) the approaches to the subject, he is far removed from such a style. These features mark a change of literary form and a special quality of style, but are perhaps not evidence of a fault. Yet the very great length of his introductions, or what amount to introductions, cannot leave him free of the charge that he changes unobtrusively from a style suitable to oratory or formal prose to a conversational manner, and that he makes the head of his essay too large for the body that accompanies it.

In this criticism Photius once again surprises us by his approval of ordinary language. The truth is that although Dio writes in a straightforward style, he resembles all authors of formal prose in his day. He expresses his admiration for the great past of classical Greece by attempting to write in the language of its authors. Everyday language was rather different, as can be seen from the Gospels and the letters preserved among the papyri. He is therefore an archaist, and his success is due to his deliberate simplicity. Photius is wrong to say that his language is ordinary; but given that archaism was prescribed by fashion, which Photius no doubt takes for granted, Dio has the merit of not being pretentious and elaborate. He has in addition the advantage of being an honest man with something to say on the main political problems of his day; but that consideration has more weight with a modern student of the Roman empire than it did with Photius. Subject to these reservations the criticism can be regarded as competent.

In codices 91-3 Photius deals with works by the second century writer Arrian: his account of Alexander's campaigns, the history of events after Alexander's death, and a history of Bithynia. On the second of these Photius offers one of his most detailed and flattering judgments.[18]

This author is not inferior to any of the best historians. He is excellent in concise narrative and never spoils the continuity of his account with ill-timed digressions or insertions. He innovates more in the arrangement of the words than the choice of vocabulary, and does so in such a way that the account could not be more clear and vivid by any other means. Using to the full limpid, euphonious and well-rounded diction he achieves a blend of smoothness and grandeur. Novelty in the use of words is not taken too far; it is very close to normal usage and most expressive, resulting in figurative usage rather than the replacement of ordinary words. So he also achieves clarity, not by this means alone but by the order, arrangement and especially the presentation of the narrative. That is the skill needed for clarity. For the straightforward use of periods is a feature often found even in dilettante writers and reduces their work to an unduly humble and modest level because it is entirely without variation – a fault which this author, despite his reputation for clarity, has not committed. Of figures he

[18] Accurate translation is not easy; I have derived some benefit from the version by Larue van Hook in *CP* 4 (1909) 181, but in both this and the preceding passage there is room for doubt about the meaning of several terms.

uses the ellipse, not of periods but of words, in such a way that the ellipse is not even noticed. If one tried to add what is missing, it would seem to verge on pleonasm rather than supply what is lacking. His abundance of figures is excellent, not abruptly changing from natural unaffected usage, but woven in gently from the beginning, so that they do not annoy by their excess or cause difficulty by their sudden appearance. And in a word, if one were to approach history through his works, one would see that many of even the ancient writers stand on a lower level than he does.

The enthusiasm of our critic is not shared by modern readers, however much they may value the account of the most spectacular military operation in history. But it has to be pointed out that Photius' remarks refer to the lost work about the years following Alexander's death, which may well have differed from the extant narrative of Alexander's expedition. It was a convention of ancient literature that style should vary according to the model that an author selected to guide him in the composition of a particular work. Arrian's *Anabasis* takes Xenophon's *Anabasis* as a model, as Photius himself noted in passing in codex 58, but its sequel, *Indica*, being as much concerned with ethnography as military history, is cast in Ionic dialect intended as an acknowledgment of Herodotus' standing in this field. There is no reason why the lost history should not have been written in a third style, and the scanty fragments that remain hint at imitation of Thucydides.[19] Yet Photius seems curiously unaware of the connection between dialect and subject matter. He does not mention the Ionic of the *Indica*, just as he fails to add comment or explanation when recording the use of the same dialect by other writers of the Roman imperial period (codices 62 and 68). He also fails to make clear what Arrian's stylistic model in the *Anabasis* was. Apart from that it is difficult to tell how accurate his comments are.

Because of his undeserved popularity throughout the Byzantine period, which makes it necessary to refer to him frequently in the course of this account, the impression made on Photius by the second-century sophist Aristides should be recorded here. To the average medieval reader he seems to have been a figure of the stature of Demosthenes, with whom in fact he is explicitly compared, not entirely to his disadvantage, by the Palaeologan scholar Theodore Metochites. It is worth seeing whether Photius by his comments reveals the same exaggerated regard for an author whose productions are, with a few important exceptions, thoroughly mediocre. His codices 246-8 consist of lengthy excerpts from some of these mediocre works. There is no critical comment except that the passages have been chosen on account of their stylistic merit. But in commenting on Demosthenes in codex 265 he gives one hint of a better appreciation of the relative merits of the two authors. Some critics had expressed reservations about the invectives in Demosthenes' speeches against Meidias and Aeschines, on the ground that frequent repetition of the same ideas made it look as if the author was competing against

---

[19] A.G. Roos, *Studia Arrianea* (Leipzig 1912) 66-9.

himself in a rhetorical contest, not a real lawsuit. Photius' reply is 'What would critics of these speeches say of Aristides, who obviously employed this method to the point of satiety, going beyond moderation in his treatment and continuing at undue length beyond what was reasonable?' (491 a 40-b 11).

Another extant author about whom Photius has given us his opinion is Himerius, the fourth-century Athenian professor of rhetoric. The text is as follows.

> Throughout he preserves his type of diction and the same style, employing amplification and figures; the clever application and aptness of these figures does not create satiety. To the best of my knowledge no one has exploited figures so well and succeeded so agreeably. His works are full of examples from history and all kinds of myth, given as proofs or parallels or to add pleasure and elegance to what he says. With these he guides and decorates his exposition. His proems and conclusions, sometimes even what one might call his argumentation, are manufactured from these elements. He is fond of giving a preliminary outline. But while possessing these literary qualities he is clearly pagan in his religion and imitates the hounds who secretly bark at us.

To the modern reader Himerius has the saving grace of preserving a few fragments of Greek lyric poetry. Otherwise he is a man with little to say whose allusions to classical culture come from a standard repertoire. His style is very mannered and Photius' admiration for it can be understood if not shared. Admiration is all the more remarkable as Photius took exception to his religious stance. It is to be noted that he does not allude to the rhythmical clausulae; but one can hardly believe that he failed to notice this feature, given its importance for all Byzantine writers.

Prejudice against pagans influences Photius less than might have been expected. But although there is nothing specifically Christian in his literary outlook, it does not come as a surprise that his highest praise is reserved for a Christian writer. Two codices (141 and 191) describe St. Basil's stylistic merits. The first deals with his commentary on the *Hexaemeron*.

> Basil the Great is excellent in all his works. More than anyone else he is able to use diction that is pure, limpid, exact, altogether worthy of oratory and public speaking. In the arrangement and purity of his ideas he is seen to be the first, inferior to no one. He is a lover of persuasion, sweetness and brilliance. He is fluent and the stream of his oratory seems to flow spontaneously. His persuasive power is so great that if one were to take his discourses as a model for public speaking, studying them closely and gaining experience of the rules that contribute to success in this genre, I think there would be no need of any other model, neither Plato nor Demosthenes, whom the ancients encourage us to study at length, in order to become an orator in political life or on other public occasions.

There is no sign of any attempt to bring about the change in the school curriculum implicitly recommended in the last sentence. The rest of the judgment is little more than an expression of enthusiasm. More detail is given when Photius deals with the ascetic treatises.

> In his work the customary impression of the author's character and the purity of his style stand out. But in the treatment of certain problems an emphasis is sometimes scattered over his text, not by juvenile innovations in vocabulary, not by obscuring the composition through amplification, nor yet by any elaboration and forcefulness that is foreign to or departs from his personal manner or oratorical style. Indeed, maintaining these last qualities in his usual way, he as it were tosses in emphasis, not creating any impression that this is his regular habit but bringing it into prominence briefly(?). Since he aims at a summary exposition he does not often descend to precise details (?), not having an occasion for it. His solutions of problems are often sharp and persuasive, always salutary and edifying. Clarity, however, is damaged not only by his brevity, but equally because arguments leading to a solution are not expressed in syllogistic form; propositions are carelessly presented, proofs are disjointed and uncoordinated, the direction of the argument uncertain.

The reservations expressed here are unexpectedly strong, but are perhaps intended to apply only to this one work by St. Basil. As with other criticisms of this type it is a pity that examples are not quoted to illustrate each point being made. Photius missed the chance to combine criticism with a selection of passages that had struck him as admirable or faulty. Had he revised the *Bibliotheca* it might have occurred to him to relate the criticism of Damascius' *Life of Isidore* given in codex 181 to the list of fine expressions collected from it in codex 242, and although we no longer have more than excerpts from the text the result might have been illuminating.

Of adverse comments perhaps the most instructive is that applied to Eunomius (codex 138), against whom he was probably prejudiced by doctrinal considerations.

> Eunomius has no idea of charm and grace in style, but is anxious to produce pompous bombast and ugly sound with a succession of consonants and words difficult to pronounce, full of consonants, which belong to the poetic style, or more accurately to the dithyrambic manner. His sentences are put together in a way that is forced, compressed and jerky, so that the reader must beat the air with his lips if he is to enunciate clearly Eunomius' rough, condensed, tortured, jumbled, and mutilated product.

That is a fine indication of the Byzantine sensibility to the sound of words and suggests that reading aloud was still normal practice in Byzantium as it had been in the ancient world.

Finally it is time to deal with the evidence that the *Bibliotheca* provides of its author's scholarship. A number of passages allow us to infer something about his competence in dealing with problems of authenticity, textual criticism and interpretation.

Photius is naturally aware of the problem of forgery. Already in antiquity this had created serious difficulties for scholars, so much so that many of them interpreted the 'criticism of poetry' declared by Dionysius Thrax to be the grammarian's highest task as the ability to judge whether a work was genuine or not. It is also obvious that no one with a knowledge of the history of the Christian church could fail to be aware of such problems. Photius deals with them several times. The most important example is in codex 1, where he reproduces the arguments against the authenticity of the work of Dionysius the Areopagite. Here he adds nothing of his own.[20] But elsewhere he expresses his own views. In codex 201 he reports finding something not to his liking in Diadochus of Photice and says that he hopes it is not a genuine part of the text. He allows for the possibility of deliberate forgery or accidental inclusion (163 b 25-9). In codex 230 he reports that Severus falsified a text (271 b 13, 23). He rejects the attribution of a sermon to St. John Chrysostom because the style of argument and the author's familiarity with scripture are not good enough (codex 274, 510 b 9). It may be said that these grounds are subjective, and Photius does not enlarge on them, but they are not necessarily invalid because of being subjective. He has the sense to realise that a stylistic test is not infallible: dealing with Demosthenes' speech *On the Halonnesus* (no. 7) he admits (codex 265, 491 a 10ff) 'some assign this speech to Hegesippus, but I know that different authors have similar styles, while individuals can vary their own style, and so I cannot confidently declare whether this speech is by Demosthenes or Hegesippus'.

Problems of authenticity lead to an interest in the history of texts. The identification of a text or an author was sometimes hard. In codex 88 Photius discusses three authors called Gelasius, all bishops of Caesarea in Palestine, and tries to decide which of them wrote the text in question. In this codex he uses the incipit to help, and he does the same in codices 89 and 111. He was aware that some books existed in more than one edition. A good case is codex 77, Eunapius' *History*. He read both editions, noting in each case that the manuscript was old, but unfortunately not giving his reasons for the assertion.

Mistakes by scribes occasionally concerned him. One possible example has been already mentioned. More important is a discussion in the review of Helladius (codex 279), where the question at issue is the correct spelling of a word in *Iliad* 4.412. Some scholars had thought that a faulty variant reading arose from a confusion of letter forms. They claimed that a lambda was misread because the shorter stroke looked like the upright of a tau, and the longer one like the crossbar. At first sight one might think that this palaeographical argument is an addition by Photius, since the form of the letter being discussed is clearly not the uncial one

[20] Except perhaps a hint of personal scepticism; see J. Stiglmayr, *Historisches Jahrbuch* 19 (1898) 91-4 and I. Hausherr, *OrChrPer* 2 (1936) 484-90.

that is associated with antiquity. But the reference books show that in antiquity the form of lambda was quite often similar to the one in use in modern versions of Greek script, composed of two unequal strokes. As a result we should probably infer that Photius is here reproducing ancient scholarship; it may well be the earliest such discussion on record, and it is very much to his credit that he takes note of it.[21]

Larger issues of interpretation arise from time to time in the *Bibliotheca*. One of great importance in the history of the church is the allegorical treatment of scripture. Photius notes that this appears to derive from the influence of Philo (codex 105), and he goes so far as to say that Philo forces such interpretations on the texts – the word used implies violence. Another principle of general application is the requirement that texts should be interpreted within a context. It is cited from various ecclesiastical authorities in codex 225. Among others St. Basil is quoted as saying that ambiguous or obscure passages of scripture are explained by others that are of undisputed interpretation. A very similar point occurs in codex 229, where Ephraim quotes Athanasius, Cyril and Chrysostom in support of the principle that one must not examine words only and with malicious intention, but also consider the pious intention of the author. Unfortunately this presupposes that one already knows whether an author is orthodox or not. A better statement is found in the adaptation of a famous principle of pagan scholarship: 'Who could be more eloquent or more reliable to interpret Cyril than Cyril himself?' This is stated twice in codex 230. Here we see the Christian version of the rule attributed to the Hellenistic critic Aristarchus, that Homer should be interpreted by means of Homer.[22] Just as Photius had shown his reservations about the allegorical approach to scripture in the course of his remarks on Philo, hinting thereby at a certain sympathy for the Antiochene school of exegesis, so here he employs a principle of classical criticism that will have been accepted in the same school. In assessing the leading member of it, Theodore of Mopsuestia, Photius notes that he avoids allegory as far as possible (codex 38) and gives him credit for close study of the Bible, even though he frequently strays from the truth (codex 177). Despite the heretical element in their doctrine Photius was not blind to their scholarly merits.

(iv) The letters

Photius' knowledge of and interest in classical literature is usually inferred from the *Lexicon* and *Bibliotheca*. But the other works can yield valuable information. His letters, some of which were subsequently

[21] One of the publisher's (anonymous) readers kindly points out that there is an earlier discussion of this type in Galen 14.31-2K, where the question at issue is the confusion of letters representing numerals. Galen was very much aware of bibliographical and textual problems and it would not be surprising if other examples were found in the vast corpus of his writings.

[22] N.G. Wilson, *CR* 21 (1971) 172 and *PCPS* 202 (1976) 123.

incorporated verbatim as chapters of the *Amphilochia*, enable us to add to the picture provided by the two works best known to classical scholars and correct it in one respect. To all intents and purposes Photius disregards poetry in his book reviews. But in his letters he does sometimes refer to the classical poets. There are allusions to the Prometheus story and the *Plutus* of Aristophanes (196 and 127 in Valettas, 82 and 150 in Montacutius). These letters are addressed to a tax collector and an admiral. The *Prometheus vinctus* of Aeschylus and the *Plutus* of Aristophanes were the first plays of their respective authors to be read by schoolchildren in Byzantium, and it is not surprising that Photius should allude to them and expect to be understood. But it may well be that he, like his pupils and correspondents, had no more positive interest in the texts that they had been obliged to study at school, and it is perhaps significant that another letter (134 V., 55 M.) begins with a mention of the idea that poets are the authors of falsehood. On the other hand it is striking that he calls the abbot Theodore an admirer of Homer (100 V., 142 M.) and conveys his message by an allusion to the effectiveness of Odysseus and Palamedes as ambassadors, citing the story of Odysseus going unsuccessfully to ask Anios for provisions, whereas Palamedes later succeeded. Photius writes as if he expected Theodore to know his Homer well, but curiously the episode from the story of the Trojan war is not known in this form from Homer or any other source.

Other classical topics occur in the letters. There is a mention of Oedipus and the sphinx (Papadopoulos-Kerameus 21), which may imply knowledge of Sophocles' *Oedipus tyrannus*. A letter (129 V., 209 M.) which became chapter 107 of the *Amphilochia* acquired the misleading title 'Why do poets represent both Hermes and Hercules as possessing the horn of Amaltheia, the symbol of plenty?' The letter is not in fact about poetic symbolism; it is nothing more than an encouragement to his correspondent to realise that not only the active life but sound learning can bring happiness. Photius specifies what kind of learning he has in mind by inviting the addressee to 'study our Muses, which are as much superior to the Greek ones as freedom is to slavery or truth to flattery'. There is no exaggerated enthusiasm for pagan antiquity here.

Another letter (64 V., 151 M.), which later became a chapter of the *Amphilochia* (83), deals with the passage in Acts 16.16 that describes the girl possessed by a spirit of divination. Photius unexpectedly cites a fragment of Sophocles and a passage of Plato (*Sophist* 252c) in his explanation of the scriptural text. The classical authors had been concerned with ventriloquism, which had been dishonestly exploited with the pretence that the practitioner possessed a familiar spirit with powers of prophecy.

Photius offers stylistic comments on the writings of his friends (244 and 114 V., 204 and 242 M.), correcting their Attic usage and idiom, and in response to an inquiry from Amphilochius, who wished to know whether the letters of Plato were a suitable stylistic model, he expressed the view (233 V., 207 M.) that whereas Plato's other works are models of civilised[1] style, with only the reservation that the use of the vocabulary is sometimes slovenly, the letters are inferior both as letters and stylistically. Aristotle's letters are written in better style than the rest of his works, but fall short of Plato's. Demosthenes' letters are no better than Plato's. Instead Photius recommends, as a selection from a wide range, the letters ascribed to Phalaris (can he have had an inkling that they were not genuine?), and those of Brutus and Libanius. He concludes his advice by noting that if one wishes to read texts that are beneficial from the point of view of their contents, then Basil, Gregory (of Nazianzus) and Isidore (of Pelusium) are to be recommended.

One letter raises the question whether Photius had access to more classical poetry than now survives (227 V., 156 M., chapter 86 of the *Amphilochia*). He is writing to George, metropolitan of Nicomedia, and reproves him for not knowing that a rare word found in I Peter 5:5, (ἐγκομβώσασθαι , meaning 'wear') is good Greek. The opening words are 'I am very surprised that you, a teacher of grammar conversant with the study of the poets, should think that this word is part of a foreign language and not a Greek word'. The remark incidentally proves that a fair range of poets was being read in the schools, even if it deliberately exaggerates the learning to be expected from an average teacher. Photius then remarks that the word is to be found in Apollodorus of Carystus and Epicharmus. This information coincides with an entry in two Byzantine lexica (*Etymologicum Magnum* and *Genuinum*). But Photius adds that in Epicharmus the word is used in many different parts of its conjugation. One might be tempted to think that he had read one or more of the plays of Epicharmus, but the notion is so implausible that one must prefer the alternative explanation, which is that he is drawing on a more informative lexicon entry than any now surviving.

There is also a difficult question about Photius' knowledge of a lost prose text. He ascribes (Papadopoulos-Kerameus 16) to Aesop a fable about Dionysus, according to which the god provides three cups of wine for the sensible man – the first for health, the second for love and pleasure, the third for sleep. The surviving collections of Aesopic fables do not include this story and it has been inferred that Photius must have read it in the collection made by Demetrius of Phalerum.[2] Although he does not mention Demetrius, there is perhaps a reference to him in a letter of Arethas, which will be discussed in the next chapter. The two points are closely linked, and here I shall anticipate my conclusion about Arethas, which is that he did not have access to Demetrius' collection. That increases the probability that Photius did not either. Can the appearance of the story in his letter be explained in any other way? The Photian version may conceivably be a deliberate remoulding of an idea

---

[1] πολιτικός is difficult to translate; in some contexts 'oratorical' is correct, but it seems less suitable here.

[2] B.E. Perry, *BZ* 46 (1953) 308-13; cf. also *TAPA* 93 (1962) 287-346. Lemerle, op. cit. 222, was sceptical.

known in various sources, the earliest of which, Panyasis and Eubulus, both of the classical period, are found together in a passage of Athenaeus (36 B-D). But Photius' attribution to Aesop is explicit and not hedged about with any reservation or irony.

The last letter to concern us is addressed to Leo the philosopher (77 V., 208 M., *Amphilochia* 106). It is the only obvious sign of contact between the two men and its tone suggests either that Photius had never been his pupil or that relations between them had become cool. The purpose of the letter is to reply to the suggestion that pleonastic use of εἰμί 'I am' in the scriptures is a stylistic solecism. Photius says that the idiom is common, but the only example that can be easily located is II Kings 11:5 (ἐγώ εἰμι, ἐν γαστρὶ ἔχω). His defence is to say that other pleonastic expressions are not held to be blemishes in pagan authors. Photius speaks of them as 'your sophists', i.e. 'the men you admire', making it quite clear that his addressee is known to have a liking for classical culture, and this may be taken as confirmation, if any is thought to be needed, that Leo the philosopher is indeed the addressee of the letter, as the best manuscript (Barocci 217) indicates both in its title and the index of contents. The examples given by Photius are ἔνιοί τινες, σφᾶς αὐτούς and various expressions with ἔχων. This last category is exemplified by verbs such as ἀπῆλθες, βαδίζεις, σπεύδεις in conjunction with ἔχων, and it demonstrates an interesting and significant failure on Photius' part to appreciate the nuances of Attic idiom. In the case of the first verb ἀπῆλθες it is impossible to see what he had in mind, and with the others he fails to see that the participle has the effect of implying continuous action. But then he finds a better example to support his case, the Attic idiom ἑκὼν εἶναι, in which the infinitive of the verb 'to be' adds nothing to the meaning. Few Atticists fail to use this expression as an ornament of their style. Leo himself has done so, and so he should not comment adversely on the style of the scriptures on account of a similar idiom. Photius concludes: 'But knowing your impartial character I have hopes that in future you will not behave like this and will deter others from such ignorant criticisms. Ignorance, the mother of temerity, has inspired and spurred them on.' One might infer that Leo had a number of pupils who seemed to Photius to be exposed to undesirable intellectual influence. It should be noted in passing that the last sentence begins with a phrase reminiscent of Thucydides 2.40.3.

(v) The Amphilochia

The *Amphilochia* is a collection of over 300 chapters, most of them very short, on a variety of topics. The great majority deal with theological matters. The collection derives its name from Amphilochius, metropolitan of Cyzicus, and can be dated to the period of Photius' first exile.

Despite its predominantly theological content the collection can tell us a good deal about the author's interest in classical antiquity and his qualities as a scholar. It supplements for instance our picture of his reading of classical philosophy, which had a relatively minor place in the *Bibliotheca*: chapters 137-147 are a commentary on Aristotle's *Categories*, and there are clear signs of an acquaintance with Plato in chapter 101. This deals with the biblical precept to sell one's belongings and give the money to the poor. The emperor Julian had pointed out the practical difficulties of universal adherence to this principle. Photius tells us that he had written on this topic before (*PG* 101. 617A) and will now repeat what he can remember of his previous essay. Part of his polemic with Julian consists of an accusation that he unduly admires Plato's Utopias (625a). 'And yet ought not a writer who almost worships Plato's ideal states, filled though they are with innumerable forms of immorality and innumerable contradictions, utterly opposed to every constitution known to man, unrealised and non-existent throughout the course of history – if a writer calls these to mind and takes pride in doing so, ought he not to be ashamed of letting the very word "constitution" pass his lips?' Whereas Plato had usually been suspect to Christians because of his views on life after death, here religious fervour is directed against the bizarre provisions of the *Republic* and *Laws*. For our purpose it is enough to note that the combined weight of these objections was still not sufficient to remove Plato from the reading list of educated Byzantines.

A few chapters are scientific or antiquarian. No. 131 deals with magnets. The statements correspond with an entry in the *Etymologicum Genuinum*, and there is a reference also in the *Bibliotheca* (codex 279). It is no surprise that the treatment is anything but scientific; Photius tries to draw a moral from the power of attracting iron, and invites us to admire the skill of the divine creator. One chapter deals with medical matters (113 in the Athens edition), and such authors are not neglected in the *Bibliotheca*. Four deal with miscellaneous antiquarian topics: 242 is a brief and inaccurate explanation of the Roman calendrical terms Kalends, Ides and Nones; 134 discusses the various dates for the beginning of the year, January, March and September; 150 enumerates the Sibylline prophetesses, and includes an allusion to Euripides' lost play *Lamia*; another (114 in the Athens edition) deals with points of Roman antiquities. One or more of these chapters may derive from the sixth-century writer Johannes Lydus.

There is very little here to show us the scholar at work. The allusion to Euripides is simply the reproduction of facts given in Photius' source, and a virtually identical statement is preserved in the anonymous prolegomena to the extant collection of Sibylline oracles.[1] We get a little closer to the scholar in Photius when we find him listing the editions of the scriptures, in this case the Old Testament. A list of seven Greek versions fills chapter 154, and it corresponds closely to the text printed in

---

[1] *Oracula Sibyllina*, ed. A. Rzach (Vienna 1891) 3-7; B. Baldwin, *ByzModGrStud* 4 (1978) 9-14, is slightly misleading.

the works of Athanasius (*PG* 28.433-6) and Theodoret (*PG* 84. 28-32).
This is of interest only in that it clearly refers to copies of the Greek Old
Testament found as geniza deposits in Jericho and at Nicopolis near
Actium. But Photius does no more than reproduce his source, and that
statement is valid for a large number of chapters; even when we cannot
trace the source we may suspect that he is not being entirely original.

No. 151 deals with quotations from pagan authors in the New
Testament. The passages mentioned are (i) Acts 17:28, with its reference
to Aratus, *Phaenomena* 5, (ii) I Corinthians 15:33, the line from
Menander made famous in the translation 'evil communications corrupt
good manners', (iii) Titus 1:12, the alleged oracle of Epimenides stating
that the Cretans are 'always liars, evil brutes, idle bellies'. Photius or his
source notes that the line is referred to by Callimachus (*Hymn* 1.8). An
oddity in this chapter is the suggestion that in I Corinthians 15:32 the
words 'Let us eat and drink, for tomorrow we die' are a Spartan proverb.
Photius corrects himself by noting that they are also a quotation from
Isaiah 22:13.

Several chapters show linguistic interests. 21 deals with words that
have more than one meaning. A list of about twenty-five examples from
pagan texts is given, the first of them drawn from Plato's usage
(*Theaetetus* 149b), and Photius then goes on to consider similar
phenomena in biblical texts. Three chapters deal with more specific
questions. In 133 the meaning of rare words in Matthew 26:27
(ἐκολάφισαν) and I Corinthians 4:13 (περίψημα) is considered, while in
227 Photius deals with a delicate point of trinitarian theology, whether
the Son should be said to have been born or to have come into existence
(γεννώμενος, γενόμενος). Despite the authority of Gregory of
Nazianzus Photius advises against the first formulation, which is
distinguished by having double instead of single nu in both its spoken
and written form (the difference between omicron and omega had ceased
to be noted in speech).

We have not so far been able to detect Photius practising the art of
textual criticism. Yet as an intelligent reader, with what must
admittedly be thought a somewhat one-sided interest in many of the
authors he read, he can hardly have been unaware of the problems that
inevitably arise in the transmission of texts, and there is a fascinating
but tantalisingly brief discussion in the first chapter of the *Amphilochia*
(*PG* 101. 84ff.) Photius is considering difficulties in three passages of
scripture. He writes:

> Not only does a single word, and a short one at that, applicable to many
> subjects but wrongly interpreted, obscure or destroy the meaning of correct
> statements; but the change of a letter, or its addition or subtraction, even if
> not difficult to correct, nevertheless frequently gives rise to an absurdity.
> Leaving aside other instances, the word ἔκτησεν with a long vowel, if
> one were to write it or understand it as having a short vowel in the verse
> 'The Lord possessed me in the beginning of his way, before his works of old'

(Proverbs 8:22), and if one also inclined towards the views of Arius, one would be sharpening one's tongue against the divinity of the Son. To beat down and refute the blasphemy of this view is quite easy, but none the less it is also the case that the person who demonstrates that ἔκτησεν is pronounced not with an iota but with an eta will drive the insolent loquacity of heretical arrogance into shamed silence.

The verse is not chosen at random; it had been the cause of christological debate since the time of the early Christian apologists Justin and Athenagoras, and Arius' great opponent Athanasius had dealt with it at length.[2] After some further discussion Photius comes to the conclusion that 'many other examples, both in pagan literature and in scripture and the prophecies of Christianity, could be detected and subjected to the same kind of inquiry'. This is remarkable enough in itself, but Photius goes a stage further by saying:

> It is not only the addition or subtraction of a single letter that creates wholesale confusion and misrepresentation, but the inexact use of an accent can turn one word into another although the spelling is identical, and can alter the sense to an utterly inappropriate meaning or produce an impious notion or laughable nonsense. Why speak of letters? After all, even the smallest of signs, the mark of punctuation, wrongly used or overlooked or misplaced, creates great heresy of every kind.

He then deals with the awkward question raised by the interpretation of II Corinthians 4:4 'The unbelievers whose minds the god of this world has blinded, to stop them seeing the light shed by the Good News of the glory of Christ, who is the image of God'. This text, as he goes on to explain, had been seized on by heretics anxious to see in Paul's words evidence of Manichaean dualism. Photius thinks that, although the heretics can be refuted on their own ground, the problem would not have arisen if punctuation had been correctly inserted in the text. His attitude is unexpected for two reasons. First of all, manuscripts of late antiquity and the early Byzantine period have only rudimentary punctuation, and it is difficult to imagine that Photius expected to find copies superior in this respect, or that if he did, he could have given any reason for believing them to be trustworthy. Secondly, the punctuation required by Photius consists of the insertion of a point, indicating a very slight pause, in a highly implausible position, between the words 'God' and 'of this world', with the result that the words can be taken to refer to God blinding the minds of the unbelievers of this world. This view is not contrary to the rules of Greek syntax but requires the assumption of a totally unnatural word order. As an interpretation of the Greek it had been recommended by previous writers, but whereas they had concentrated on the word order Photius argues that the sense should be guaranteed by the punctuation.

[2] P. Walters, *The Text of the Septuagint* (Cambridge 1973) 223; R.P.C. Hanson in *The Cambridge History of the Bible* (Cambridge 1970) 416, 441-3, 445-6.

Once again we have to ask whether Photius deserves credit for an original observation. Hergenröther[3] included the first chapter of the *Amphilochia* in the list which he considered to be original, and he may have been right with regard to most of it. But this section of the chapter has a certain resemblance to chapter 152 entitled 'The reasons why the scriptures are obscure', and Hergenröther himself[4] acutely noted that this is essentially a transcript, with some slight amendments, of a text by Polychronius, bishop of Apamea (d. before 431) and brother of the well known Antiochene biblical commentator Theodore of Mopsuestia. All authorities are agreed that Polychronius followed the same principles of historical and rationalist exegesis as his brother, and the text in question supports that view of his work. In his enumeration of the factors that have created problems in the text of the Bible the fourth concerns difficulties created by punctuation and the fifth those resulting from accentuation. His text as we have it is probably abbreviated, and it gives no example of the two factors in question except a case of difficult punctuation in Proverbs 2:21, which is not intelligible as it stands. There can be no doubt that this is the basis of Photius' ideas and that he developed it into the fuller formulation that we find in the first chapter.

Let us now examine in more detail the background and implications of his statement of principle. First of all the traditional punctuation of Greek texts can be inferred partly from papyri and early manuscripts, partly from explicit statements of authors. Dionysius Thrax (section 4, 630.14 Bekker) laid it down that there were three punctuation signs, *teleia, mese, hupostigme*, in descending order of magnitude. But in most papyri the scribes seem to content themselves with two stops rather than three, and it may be that the text of Dionysius has been interpolated.[5] For most texts this will have been the standard practice; for Homer, but only for him as far as we know, a sophisticated system was invented by Nicanor, recorded in the A-scholia to the *Iliad*. That being so it was scarcely likely that Photius and his contemporaries could find copies of scripture more accurately punctuated, unless one believes that the Antiochene interpreters won general acceptance for their views on the subject, which seems most implausible. There are however occasional signs of concern for punctuation and accents. In the seventh century Anastasius of Sinai, writing the preface to his *Hodegos* (*PG* 89.36B), asks the reader to excuse the fact that he had written directly on the pages of a quire without the preliminary stage of a rough draft, and then invites readers to mark their texts in various ways. He mentions *tonoi, stigmai, hupostigmai*, and complains that ignorant copyists have caused confusion in one of his statements on a theological topic. In the biography of Theophanes the Confessor by Methodius we read that he

---

[3] *Photius Patriarch von Konstantinopel* (Regensburg 1867-9) III 48.
[4] ibid. 58.
[5] E.G. Turner, *Greek Manuscripts of the Ancient World* (Oxford 1971) 11.

was an expert scribe who made no mistakes in accentuation.[6] That is evidence for the latter part of the eighth century; shortly afterwards the Studite rule laid an obligation on scribes in that monastery to be accurate in writing accents and punctuation. This instruction may well have been known to Photius.

What of the manuscripts of the Pauline Epistles? Examination shows that most are punctuated in the way that we should expect, but after inspecting a number of copies I have been able to find three that follow Photius' recommendation. Two are tenth-century copies in Paris (gr. 216 and Coislin 224), the third is an illuminated copy probably of the twelfth century in Cambridge (University Library, Add. 6678). The Cambridge copy has no marginal commentary that might throw light on the text, and in the two Paris copies the catena, which discusses the correct interpretation of the sentence, considers the various possibilities without mentioning the punctuation.[7] It is unfortunately impossible to say whether these three books reflect the influence of Photius or are evidence of an older tradition.

The fact remains that we cannot absolve Photius from two serious errors in his treatment of II Corinthians 4:4. There is no reason at present to believe that he could obtain biblical manuscripts with a reliable tradition of punctuation. There is also no reason that can possibly justify the hyperbaton which he accepted as the price of making St. Paul's statement theologically sound. Yet despite these faults we must admire the statement of a principle that is correct. It has a famous analogy. In 1519 Erasmus added an Apologia to the reprint of his edition of the Greek New Testament, towards the end of which we read (p. 67): 'Quid minutius hypostigma? at tantula res haereticum gignit sensum'. He cites as his authority Augustine, *De doctrina Christiana*, book III. Presumably he did not know Photius or Polychronius; neither text was printed until long after his death. We may conclude that great minds think alike.

[6] Ed. B. Latyshev, p. 16 (*Zapiski of the Russian Academy* 13 (1916) no. 4).
[7] No further light is cast on this matter by K. Staab, *Pauluskommentare aus der griechischen Kirche* (Münster 1933) 287-8.

6

Arethas

(i) The extant manuscripts

In the generation following Photius scholarship is best represented by a man who may have been his pupil. Arethas, born probably *c*. 850, could have come under Photius' influence, but most recent authorities deny that there was any link between them.[1] The only sign of a possible connection is that Arethas addressed some verses to Photius. They are listed in the contents of MS. Barb. gr. 310, and owing to damage to the manuscript the leaves in question are now lost. It has to be admitted that Arethas might have written verses, perhaps an epitaph, about an eminent man with whom he had no personal link. Arethas too had a distinguished career in the church, becoming archbishop of Caesarea in Cappadocia. Once again we have an example of the rule that churchmen of the highest standing were liberal and tolerant in their attitude towards the literature of the pagan past. As will be seen later, there is one reservation in the case of Arethas. His prominent place in the history of scholarship may be due to a lucky accident, the survival of several volumes from his personal library, whereas it has never been possible to identify any book that belonged to Photius. It is also possible, thanks to Arethas' habit of adding notes in the margins of his books, to identify transcripts of several other volumes which he possessed but have subsequently been lost. His private library may have been much smaller than Photius', but it has the advantage that we can see a collector at work and assess the value of his books for the preservation of classical authors. His writings give further evidence of his classical learning.[2]

Eight volumes survive from his library. They are all fine examples of calligraphy on high quality parchment, and the prices he paid for some of them prove, when related to the annual salaries of civil servants, that book collecting was not a hobby for men of modest income.[3] The earliest of the eight appears to be the Euclid (D'Orville 301), written in 888 by the scribe Stephanos, perhaps the most accomplished of all Byzantine

---

[1] Lemerle, op. cit. 209, is very firm in his denial. H.G. Beck, *Kirche und theologische Literatur im byzantinischen Reich* (Munich 1959) 614, words his judgment more prudently.
   [2] With the exception of his scholia and the commentary on the Apocalypse they are to be consulted in the edition by L.G. Westerink, two volumes, Leipzig 1968, 1972.
   [3] N.G. Wilson, in *Byzantine Books and Bookmen, a Dumbarton Oaks Symposium* (Washington 1975) 3.

calligraphers. The cost was fourteen gold pieces. The text is not the original version but the revision made in the fourth century by Theon, which enjoyed a much wider circulation, and so Arethas' manuscript is not of great importance as a witness to the text of Euclid. But it is the only copy to preserve the note referred to earlier which records Leo's use of Greek letters as algebraic symbols. Arethas' interest in Euclid presumably derives from a wish to study geometry as one of the subjects of the quadrivium. Among the marginal scholia in this manuscript about fifty notes written by Arethas do not occur in any other copy and may therefore be his own additions. They are mostly short and straightforward, and modern authorities do not suggest that they are of any significance.[4]

In 895 Arethas, who had now become a deacon, commissioned from the calligrapher John a copy of Plato (E.D. Clarke 39) containing twenty-four of the dialogues, in fact all the important works except *Republic*, *Laws* and *Timaeus*. It cost him twenty-one gold pieces; the higher price makes sense in view of the greater length and larger format. This volume is one of the three or four most important witnesses to the text. Only a small proportion of the extant scholia[5] have been copied into the margins by Arethas. The reason for this is not clear. Perhaps he did not have all the scholia at his disposal; but as Plato was not an uncommon text that seems unlikely. It may be that he was less interested in Plato than some other authors. What he wrote in the margins of the Clarkianus was for the most part not of his own composition, even if in some cases it cannot now be found in any other manuscript. His notes are mainly devoted to the *Theaetetus* and *Gorgias*. Nearly all the comments on the *Theaetetus* correspond to notes found in other manuscripts (T and W, Venice, app. class. 4.1 and Vienna, supp. gr. 7). Those on the *Gorgias* are not found elsewhere, but it has reasonably been conjectured that they derive from a lost commentary by Proclus.[6] The derivation of several other notes is clear. Pollux' *Lexicon* allows him to give an appearance of learning, which he does not acknowledge, on the subject of the Athenian archon basileus (on *Euthyphro* 2a) and the board of eleven prison commissioners at Athens (on *Phaedo* 59e). Similarly unacknowledged are even more learned notes on ball games (on *Theaetetus* 146a) and knuckle-bones (on *Lysis* 206e). These both come from an ancient monograph by the Roman historian Suetonius, written in Greek and transmitted by three manuscripts.[7] The ocurrence of the geographical name Elea in *Sophist* 216a leads him to observe that this is probably the place in Italy, not Ionia, if one is to accept the authority of Strabo (6.252). Here his information coincides partly with a note in Eustathius and may derive

[4] J.L. Heiberg, *Om Scholierne til Euklids Elementer* (*Mémoires, Académie Royale de Copenhague*), 6th series 2 (1888) 36 and 75; T.L. Heath, *The Thirteen Books of Euclid's Elements* (Cambridge 1925) I 72.

[5] Edited by G.C. Greene, *Scholia Platonica* (Haverford, Pa. 1938).

[6] E.R. Dodds, *Plato: Gorgias* (Oxford 1959) 60-1.

[7] Edited by J. Taillardat (Paris 1967).

from the atticist lexicon of Aelius Dionysius. Another lexicon, which he cites by name, was that of Diogenian; it gave him some information about Hermes (on *Lysis* 206d). A note on the tragic poet Agathon (on *Symposium* 172a), now partly illegible in the Clarkianus, seems to coincide in all essentials with one of the scholia on Lucian (*Rhetorum praeceptor* 11, Rabe p. 178). If its original home was in the Lucian commentary, which Arethas perhaps did not acquire until later in his career, we might have evidence of him returning to Plato after an interval of years and adding notes during his fresh reading. But the note does not occur in any Lucian manuscript that is certainly independent of Arethas, and so the process of transfer from one corpus of scholia to the other may have run in the opposite direction.

This is perhaps the best moment to deal with another argument which has been brought forward in support of the idea that Arethas returned to Plato long after first acquiring his copy. A passage of the *Phaedo* (96, on folio 46 verso), which occurs also in Eusebius, a text he obtained in 914, has several corrections that coincide with the secondary tradition as given by Eusebius.[8] But unfortunately the argument is not cogent: the corrections could have been obtained from almost any other source, since they restore the normal text, and there are corrections elsewhere in the Clarkianus that must have come from other sources.[9] What has not previously been remarked, to the best of my knowledge, is that of the corrections in question at least three are not in the handwriting of Arethas, as has been claimed. They are corrections by the scribe John, part of the routine of the calligrapher before handing over his product to his patron.

Four learned notes on the *Apology* preserve a wealth of information derived from Old Comedy about the prosecutors of Socrates, Anytus and Meletus, his pupil Chaerephon, and the poet Aristophanes. The source is not known; Arethas must have compiled the material from one or more ancient reference books. The information about Aristophanes (on 19c) is particularly valuable; it includes a comment by the poet himself, and another by his rival Cratinus, in which his intellectual affinity to Euripides is identified. We must be grateful to Arethas for being the only source of facts that are crucial to the understanding of Aristophanes.

Arethas' own additions to the corpus of scholia are few and far between. From time to time he makes a remark about some feature of syntax. A note adducing Callimachus, *Hymn* 6.3, as a parallel to *Symposium* 218b may be due to him. But there are four notes of more importance. First, in the *Apology* Socrates, defending himself against the charge of atheism, says (27d): 'If the demigods (*daimones*) are illegitimate children of the gods, either the result of unions with nymphs or others, as indeed they are said to be, could any man believe that offspring of the gods exist but that the gods themselves do not? It would

---

[8] E.H. Gifford, *CR* 16 (1902) 16 and 391.
[9] J. Burnet, ibid. 276.

be just as ridiculous as if someone were to believe that the offspring of horses and asses, I mean mules, exist, but that horses and asses do not.' This prompted Arethas to say, 'You are quite right, Socrates, to compare the gods of the Athenians to horses and asses.' Of course Socrates is doing nothing of the kind; the remark serves only to warn us not to expect from Arethas the intellectual distinction of a philosopher.

In the *Charmides* (155d) Socrates is made to confess that he was put into a state of excitement by catching sight of Charmides' body as his cloak opened. The admission of a homosexual feeling provoked our Christian reader to say 'A curse upon you, Plato, for so cunningly leading astray simple souls', by which he presumably means the commendation of such feelings implicit in their attribution to Socrates. Later in the same dialogue Arethas complains, and here we can have sympathy with him (159c): 'Socrates, you are cheating in argument, confusing the noble Charmides by sophistry. For even if he did not give an adequate account of temperance (*sophrosunē*), still it was not absolutely at variance with the truth. It is at least a part of temperance to act in quiet and orderly manner; I mean quiet in the sense of not violent; but you take it as the equivalent of lazy and are obviously playing tricks with the reasoning.'

Finally in the *Theaetetus*, where the digression begins about the difference between the unworldly student of philosophy and the man who devotes his energies to speaking in the law courts (172c), Arethas notes: 'From here for the next fourteen columns one ought to learn the text by heart.' If the word 'columns' has already undergone the semantic shift to mean pages as in the modern language, fourteen pages of the Clarkianus take us up to Stephanus' page 189, well beyond the end of the digression. Perhaps Arethas meant to write four instead of fourteen, but one must also wonder whether this note is derived from an earlier stage of the tradition, when the text was laid out in a papyrus book in relatively short columns. The passage is memorable not so much for the anecdote about Thales, who was so engrossed in thought that he fell into a well, as for the intervention by Theodorus, who says to Socrates 'If you could persuade everyone, Socrates, of what you are saying as you persuade me, there would be more peace and less evil among men', to which Socrates replies 'It is impossible that evil should disappear, Theodorus, for there must always be something opposed to good, nor can evil establish itself among the gods, but it circulates of necessity among mortal natures in this world. Hence one must try to escape as quickly as possible from here to that other place. Escape is by likening oneself as far as possible to god; and to become like him is to become holy and just and wise.' Let us hope that we are right to believe Arethas moved by this passage to express his unqualified approval. It may suggest that his reason for reading Plato was not simply a desire to study him from the stylistic point of view, as must have been the case with so many authors.

His next purchase was Aristotle's *Organon* (Urb. gr. 35), commissioned while he was still a deacon, from Gregory, who was himself a sub-deacon. The date cannot be established more precisely. The book is further proof of Arethas' study of the subjects that formed the quadrivium. He wrote an extremely large quantity of notes on folios 2-29, covering Porphyry's *Eisagoge* and part of Aristotle's *Categories*. Whether he gave up at that point out of boredom or for some other reason is not known. The cost of the parchment for this volume was six gold pieces, and the figure for the transcription is lost owing to damage of the folio giving the colophon.[10] This book is the oldest copy of the texts it contains and is also one of the best. The scholia appear to be a mixture compiled from various sources; it is not certain how much if anything Arethas himself contributed to them.[11]

The library contained two Atticist writers. Lucian (Harley 5694) was written for him by the scribe Baanes. The date is not known. One of the notes mentions the death of Leo VI, which occurred in 912, but the text of Lucian could have been transcribed some years earlier. Once again we are dealing with the oldest surviving manuscript of an author, and as a source for the scholia it is obviously important, but not the only important witness.[12] As will be seen later, Arethas was provoked by Lucian into writing outspoken replies to some of his propositions, and these are also transmitted separately in the corpus of his own writings.

His Aristides (Paris gr. 2951 and Laur. 60.3) was produced for him by the same John who had written the Plato.[13] Once again the date is uncertain. A note by Arethas refers to the disastrous leadership of the Byzantine army that led to its defeat by Symeon of Bulgaria. There is no general agreement that the defeat is to be placed in the year 917,[14] and in any case the text may have been copied long before. It is the oldest manuscript, but not of outstanding importance for the constitution of the text. One might expect some relation between its readings and those attested by Photius in his résumés of four of the orations, but investigation proves that they are not close; so one more potential proof of a link between the two men is denied to us.[15] As to the scholia, it seems that Arethas for the most part took over the commentary which goes under the name of Sopater, making some additions and adjustments to it. Pending the appearance of a new edition of the scholia it is difficult to say how much he altered. One intervention is known: when Aristides refers to an ivory statue of Athena, Arethas says he thinks it is the one standing in Constantinople in the Forum Constantini at the entrance to the senate, opposite which there is one of Thetis with crabs decorating her hair, as a result of which the ignorant imagine that the two represent

---

[10] E. Follieri, *Archaeologia classica* 25-6 (1973-4) (actually 1975) 262-79.

[11] See A. Busse's editions of Porphyry and Ammonius on the *Categories* (*CAG* IV i and iv) (Berlin 1887 and 1895) vi, x, xl, xli and x respectively.

[12] H. Rabe, *NGG* 1902, 735.

[13] Aristides, ed. B. Keil II (Berlin 1898) vii-viii; ed. F.W. Lenz & C.A. Behr I i (Leiden 1976) xxvi-xxvii.

[14] Lemerle, op. cit. 220 n. 52.

[15] F.W. Lenz, *Aristeidesstudien* (Berlin 1964) 167-97; cf. Lenz-Behr, op. cit. lxxviii with n. 9.

the earth and the sea.[16]

Finally there are three volumes of Christian literature. First comes a copy of writings by early apologists for the church (Paris gr. 451). This was written by Baanes in 914 and cost twenty-six gold pieces. The authors are Justin, Athenagoras, Clement of Alexandria and Eusebius. For most of the texts it contains the Parisinus is either the unique source or one of the most important. Several quires have been lost, but from the surviving copies it can be inferred that when it was complete the book also contained the *Apology* by Tatian. There are a number of scholia added by Baanes and Arethas. Apart from quite detailed comments of a theological character on Athenagoras the notes are scanty on all the texts except the *Protrepticus* and *Paedagogus* of Clement of Alexandria. Most of these notes are in the hand of Baanes, and it has been suggested that they were composed as far back as the fifth century.[17] Arethas made a small number of additions. A few of these are prefixed by his name; one or two others which are not have a personal character which makes it at least likely that they are due to Arethas. The great majority of the notes in this manuscript relate to Clement of Alexandria. Two of those on his *Protrepticus* show Arethas copying out a passage of Photius' *Bibliotheca*. One of these, from codex 239, Proclus' *Chrestomathy*, proves that Arethas was using a manuscript related to Marc. gr. 451 (M), which is generally inferior to the other witness. So although we may admire Arethas for his own and others' calligraphy, we must note that he did not always obtain the best text. Once again the notion of a close link between the two men receives no support; in such a case his text of the *Bibliotheca* might have been expected to be closer to the original. The notes on Clement include information about the ancient theatrical device known as the eccyclema, which is borrowed from Pollux 4.128. There are also quotations from tragedy, Herodotus, Thucydides, Euphorion and Callimachus.

Arethas' own additions to the notes are not all scholarly. When Clement recommends a simple diet including bulbs, Arethas, quoting Homer (*Iliad* 4.350), exclaims 'Father, what a word has escaped the barrier of your teeth. What more difficult and indigestible food can there be?' The suggestion that a limited amount of food is good for growing children is met by the comment that this is advice suitable for dwarves, who could hope by following it to achieve normal stature. Clement's rule that hair should not be cut or removed is rebutted by a quotation from St. Paul.[18]

The next book that we can trace from Arethas' library is a collection of texts dealing with ecclesiastical law (Vallicellianus gr. F. 10). It is not

---

[16] Aristides, ed. W. Dindorf II (Leipzig 1829) 710.

[17] O. Stählin, *Untersuchungen über die Scholien zu Clemens Alexandrinus* (Diss. Nürnberg 1897) 45-8.

[18] Scholia on Clement, pp. 164.23, 166.19, 248.1, ed. O. Stählin, *Clemens Alexandrinus* I (Berlin 1972, 3rd ed.) 293-340.

dated and the scribe is unidentified. Arethas' marginal notes, which are fairly numerous, have not yet been fully edited.[19]

Lastly comes a volume written in 932 by the deacon Stylianos (Moscow, Hist. Mus. 231). It is a collection of theological treatises in which the writings of Theodore Abucara are prominent, but it also contains the pseudo-Aristotelian *On virtues and vices*. There are marginal notes, some of them marked by Arethas with his own name, but they contain nothing of real interest for our present purpose.[20]

(ii) Other texts

In this section we will deal first with a group of texts that evidently formed part of his library, the proof being provided by notes in extant copies.

First we may mention Dio Chrysostom. A tenth-century manuscript (Urb. gr. 124) has among its notes some attributed to Arethas. They include a preface about the author.[1] Most of it is concerned with Dio's orations on kingship. As Arethas had the delicate task of expressing opinions on a matter of state, namely whether remarriage is permissible, to a man who still used the title of Roman emperor, Dio's vicissitudes in his relations with Domitian and his successors had an obvious interest. Arethas comments on Dio's technique of assembling unimpeachable authorities in favour of his propositions. He adds of his own accord an apposite quotation from Hesiod, *Works and Days* 295. At the end of his last paragraph, an imperfect account of Dio's career with an anecdote explaining the origin of his nickname Chrysostomos, Arethas adds a few words on his style. He regards it as a mixture of the styles of Plato and Lysias, in which the distinctive features of each are retained. It will be noticed that neither this judgment nor the preceding matter coincide with what Photius had said about Dio, but some of the brief statements in the scholia about the theme of an oration do coincide. A high proportion of the short, unattributed notes deal with points of grammar and syntax; a few remark on the simplicity and clarity of Dio's Greek. There are two references to Marcus Aurelius, one to Aristophanes' *Clouds* and one to Apollonius Rhodius. An oddity is the suggestion that Lycurgus first brought Homer's poetry to Greece from Crete. Assuming that all the notes are due to Arethas, which is not certain, since we cannot know whether all were written in the margins of his copy and whether he drafted them all himself, our picture of him as a reader is not much affected.[2]

One note among the very few scholia on Pausanias' guide to ancient Greece reveals that Arethas had read this book. His comment is simply

---

[19] A. Meschini, *Il codice Vallicelliano di Areta* (Padua 1972).

[20] Edited by L.G. Westerink, *Byzantion* 42 (1972) 196-244.

[1] Printed in von Arnim's edition, ii 325-8.

[2] The notes were printed by A. Sonny, *Ad Dionem Chrysostomum analecta* (Kiev 1896) 83-130; he also argued for Arethas' authorship.

that Patras is his birth-place. It is worth observing that this is a text of which there does not seem to be any sign in Photius, but perhaps the argument from silence should not be pressed. Among the other notes there is one in which the writer gives the text of an inscription that he had seen among some ruins in Patras. One might be tempted to see in this a proof that Arethas occasionally occupied himself with epigraphy. Although there is in a sense a parallel to such activity recorded in the notes to the Palatine manuscript of the *Greek Anthology*,[3] the inference must remain uncertain. So too must the inference commonly made from another of the notes on Pausanias, that Arethas was acquainted with Philostratus' essay on gymnastics. Although the note quite clearly refers to Philostratus, it occurs in only one manuscript (Paris gr. 1399), written and signed by Peter Hypsilas of Aegina in Milan in 1497, and this late scribe is just as likely to be the author of the note as Arethas.[4]

Another work which may not have been known to Photius is Epictetus. The notes in the archetype (Oxford, Auct. T. 4.13) appear to go back to Arethas. The chief argument is a quotation from Marcus Aurelius in exactly the same form as occurs in the notes to Dio Chrysostom. There are also a number of remarks that seem characteristic of Arethas. Some of them are directed against monks; when Epictetus says 'I want to see a Stoic', Arethas adds 'And I want to see a monk' (2.19). On 3.24 he makes the unlikely suggestion 'I think he has read the Gospels'. Perhaps the most interesting note is one containing a hexameter line which used to be attributed to Heraclitus but can now be seen to belong to the so-called Chaldean Oracles.[5]

Among more specialised texts one may note Pollux's *Lexicon*. It looks as if Arethas copied out parts of this when compiling his notes on Plato and Clement of Alexandria; if this is really the case, and he did not find these excerpts already made by some previous scholar in one of the copies that he consulted, we may infer with a fairly high degree of probability that Arethas owned the archetype of Pollux.[6] The usefulness of this compilation to a student of Attic literature does not need to be emphasised.

It is convenient to deal at this point with the suggestion that Arethas, although he is not the scribe, was responsible for the production of a large collection of lexica (Coislin 345). This hypothesis has received some support from the belief, which in my view is mistaken, that one marginal note in this book addressing a certain Tarasius is a greeting to Photius' brother, the addressee of the *Bibliotheca*, and is written in Arethas' own hand. I would deny the attribution to Arethas because the general appearance of the script is not the same, since it contains some

---

[3] See the next chapter.

[4] See F. Spiro's edition (Leipzig 1903) i 16, iii 218-22, and A. Diller, *TAPA* 87 (1956) 84-97.

[5] H. Schenkl's edition (Leipzig 1916) lxxix f. deals with the scholia; for the line of 'Heraclitus' see M.L. West, *CR* 18 (1968) 257-8.

[6] E. Bethe, *NGG* (1895) 336-8.

minuscule letters, and because it differs in one of the features which I believe to be characteristic of Arethas, the shape of the compendium for the word καί. The other argument for suspecting Arethas' involvement is that the contents of the manuscript imply the use of the *Etymologicum Genuinum* and Hesychius. The only person active at this date who is thought to have had access to both these sources is Arethas, if we may accept his authorship of notes on Pausanias 1.1.3 and 1.1.5. Since we cannot claim to be fully informed about literary and intellectual life at the time it is rash to believe that Arethas was certainly the moving spirit behind the compilation of the lexica. But it is at least possible that he should be given the credit for it, and that in turn carries with it the implication that we owe to him the abbreviation of some of the most important contents, such as Phrynichus and Apollonius Sophistes.[7]

A good case has been made for attributing to Arethas the short and mainly uninformative notes found sporadically in copies of Plutarch's *Lives* (I say mainly because the note on *Solon* 9.14 makes suggestions about the ἄξονες and κύρβεις, on which Solon's laws were inscribed, that at least have to be discussed by ancient historians). The language and general tone certainly conform to the style known from his notes on other authors. There are also suitable chronological indications, pointing to a date between 917 and 922. One can strengthen the argument in favour of attribution by exploiting a hint given by the note on *Solon* 1.6. Plutarch there deals with Solon's leanings towards homosexuality, and the scholiast urges the reader not to take offence at Plutarch for mentioning such unpleasant topics, because even Plato for all his greatness says things far worse in the *Charmides*. Since we have already noted how Arethas was roused by Socrates' confession in that dialogue, it is difficult to avoid the conclusion that the note is the work of Arethas.[8]

We come now to a category of texts where the evidence of Arethas' ownership is less easy to evaluate. A good example of the difficulty is provided by a small collection of philosophical writings, transcribed by John the grammarian in 925 (Vienna, phil. gr. 314). It consists of three introductions to Plato, the first being by Albinus, and the so-called *Golden Verses* attributed to Pythagoras with the commentary by Hierocles. There are marginalia which, though not in Arethas' own hand, may well have been copied from his autograph. Some of the notes are uncannily similar in wording to other notes by him, and the tone of the writer, who alternately abuses and patronises, is not unlike Arethas. The last two texts in the volume were in any case known to him. But his name is not prefixed to any of the notes.[9]

---

[7] On all this see K. Alpers, *BZ* 64 (1971) 83-4; K. Latte's edition of Hesychius I (Copenhagen 1955) xviii.

[8] M. Manfredini, *Siculorum gymnasium* 28 (1975) 337-50 (taking up a statement made without supporting evidence by A. Sonny, *Ad Dionem Chrysostomum analecta* (Kiev 1896) 93 n. 2).

[9] L.G. Westerink & B. Laourdas, *Hellenika* 17 (1962) 105-131; Lemerle, op. cit. 216, is perhaps too sceptical.

Another copy of Plato which has given rise to a good deal of discussion is an early manuscript of the *Laws* (Vat. gr. 1). The text itself was not written by John the calligrapher or Baanes, as has been variously assumed, but can be identified in a Demosthenes of the tenth century (Paris gr. 2935).[10] Once it is clear that the text is not written by a scribe known to have worked for Arethas, it becomes easier to reach the conclusion that the marginalia are not in his hand. But it has to be admitted that they are very similar. However, if Arethas did not read the *Laws* in this copy, we can easily admit that he may have read it in another.[11]

The unique manuscript of Athenaeus was written by John the calligrapher.[12] One is tempted to look for evidence that he undertook this commission for his only known patron. But there are no marginalia or other signs of Arethas' ownership. It can be observed that he cites (Westerink 41) a tiny fragment of Greek lyric verse that he could have derived from this source (5.217C, Page *PMG* 1020), but it was a tag which he could equally well have found in Lucian, where it occurs twice, not to mention another occurrence in Dionysius of Halicarnassus.

Various other manuscripts have been attributed from time to time to Arethas, but there are no other cases that seem to me worthy of serious discussion.[13] One should simply note the possibility that he wrote some notes on the *Letters* and *Amphilochia* of Photius. The manuscript which was once thought to be his copy of the commentary on the Apocalypse by his predecessor at Caesarea Andreas (Barocci 3) does not contain his autograph, but is not much later.

An attempt has been made to add to the archbishop's library a copy of the mathematical compilation of Pappus, a fourth-century writer whose account of his most important predecessors is valuable to historians (Vat. gr. 218). The reasons adduced in support of the attribution are the minuscule script, which is supposed to hint at origin in Constantinople, and the subject matter, which has been thought to coincide with one of Arethas' interests.[14] The flimsiness of this hypothesis is such that it would scarcely need to be discussed had it not been quoted with tentative approval.[15] A moment's reflection must convince us that, although most scientific activity took place in the capital, it is at once unduly optimistic and pessimistic to assign the volume in question to Arethas' collection. We must not imagine Arethas as being rich enough to commission or acquire all the important or calligraphic manuscripts produced in his lifetime, nor should we think so ill of the culture of the

---

[10] N.G. Wilson, *CQ* 54 (1960) 200-202.

[11] But Lemerle, op. cit. 215, is wrong to bring Paris gr. 1807 into the discussion.

[12] N.G. Wilson, *JHS* 82 (1962) 147-8.

[13] They are dealt with very satisfactorily by Lemerle.

[14] A.P. Treweek, *Scriptorium* 11 (1957) 206 f.

[15] M. Sicherl, *JOB* 15 (1966) 201-29, an article published in revised form in D. Harlfinger (ed.), *Griechische Kodikologie und Textüberlieferung* (Darmstadt 1980) 535-76; see n. 8, pp. 560-1.

capital as to suppose him the only man of his generation willing to explore abstruse areas of mathematics.

(iii)   Arethas as a reader

Photius' wide reading and the existence of a group of friends meeting in his house for discussion[1] will have ensured in all probability the survival of some texts that might otherwise have been consigned to oblivion. Can any similar claim be made for Arethas? It is usually held that he is responsible for preserving the *Meditations* of Marcus Aurelius, having found a damaged copy and ordered a transcript. There is a letter (Westerink 44), written before he became a bishop, in which he offers the transcript to a certain Demetrius, metropolitan of Heraclea. There is nothing in it to suggest that he thought of the text as a great rarity or had brought it to light himself. But as he is sending a present to a senior colleague he may have thought it tactful not to boast of a discovery. He reveals only that he had possessed the text for some time, that the condition of his copy made it difficult to consult, and that he has now been able to make a fresh copy to pass on to posterity (the wording does not rule out the idea that he had made the transcript himself). We should notice with approval how he regards himself as a kind of trustee with the responsibility to transmit literary treasures to future generations. On another occasion, in a letter to the emperor on the question of his remarriage (Westerink 71), Arethas quotes from 'the wise Marcus' two recommendations: 'to read accurately' and 'not to give assent lightly to fluent talkers'.

Apart from Marcus Aurelius it does not appear that Arethas can be credited with the preservation of any classical author. Nor does he show signs of reading many who have since been lost. It is uncertain whether his brief tirade against Julian (Westerink 24) implies a reading of a complete work by the apostate that is now lost. There is one piece of evidence to suggest that he may have read the Greek version of the account of the Trojan War by Dictys of Crete.[2] A more difficult case is the collection of fables from Aesop made by Demetrius of Phalerum. The evidence is a single reference in a letter addressed to Arethas by Stephen, Keeper of the Inkstand, from whom he had asked for a supply of writing material (Westerink 39). Stephen says: 'Have you put out of your mind the saying that dogs in a hurry give birth to blind puppies? Have you left out of account the man of Phalerum who said that judgments also give birth to similar results?' One modern authority took this to refer to a fable about a sow and a bitch which has the moral 'things are not judged by the speed with which they are accomplished but by their perfection'.[3] In that case the reference to Demetrius of Phalerum points to the existence of his collection of fables. But the

[1] *PG* 102. 597 AD.
[2] A. Sonny, *BZ* 1 (1892) 590.
[3] B.E. Perry, *BZ* 46 (1953) 308-13.

inference is extremely doubtful. The combination of a curious piece of folk-lore and the maxim about hasty judgments is ascribed to Demetrius elsewhere in a collection of pithy sayings attributed to philosophers (Gnomologium Vaticanum 253), and acquaintance with that collection is probably sufficient explanation for Stephen's allusion.

Is there any other indication of a knowledge of lost classical texts in Arethas' writings? Occasionally he seems to quote from poetry that we can no longer read. Four allusions to the miniature epic poem *Hekale* by Callimachus are taken to imply that Arethas had read it. The allusions occur in scholia that Arethas entered in the margins of his copies of Eusebius (Paris gr. 451) and Pausanias. But scepticism is in order; there is nothing to prove that these references are due to Arethas himself, and unless better evidence is forthcoming one should assume that he did no more than copy an existing note on each of the four passages. There may in fact be better evidence, but it depends on conjecture. One of his polemical pamphlets, a tirade against Leo Choerosphactes, contains an extremely obscure passage in which Hecuba is mentioned just after Icarius. Since Icarius was famous for having given hospitality to the god Dionysus, perhaps the train of thought should be continued by reading 'Hekale' for 'Hecuba', a change of a single letter, since Hekale gave hospitality to the hero Theseus. But this suggestion must remain tentative, and even if it is right the question would still arise whether Arethas knew the story from Callimachus' poem or some other source.[4]

The extent of his reading was none the less considerable, even if we are sceptical enough to exclude a number of possible allusions on the ground that they could derive indirectly from an ancient author, having become standard or semi-proverbial expressions recommended by handbooks or lexica. Although we do not have his copies of the ancient poets we know that he read some, partly because he composed three short epigrams, two in elegiac couplets and one in iambics (*Anth. Pal.* 15.32-4, Westerink 79-81), partly because he quotes them or makes unmistakable allusions. His quotations include *Anthologia Palatina* 10.30, pseudo-Pythagoras, *Carmen aureum* 7, and Aristophanes, *Peace* 525-6, the last being from a play that was not one of the most popular in Byzantium. He is willing to mention Hesiod and Pindar in an after-dinner speech delivered before the emperor Leo VI on July 20 902 (Westerink 61). It is a panegyric of the emperor's military successes, and the exploitation of classical literature is not confined to mention of poets. Plato and Aristotle are also cited, the former for his belief (*Republic* 5. 473) that humanity will only be happy when philosophers become kings or kings take up philosophy, the latter for a remark about external factors that contribute to happiness (*EN* 1099a 31-b7). There is also a comparison of the emperor with Alexander the Great.

Plato, Aristotle and Homer are the three authors Arethas most often alludes to. Homer he is prepared to quote from even on occasions that do

---

[4] N.G. Wilson, op. cit. above at (i) n. 3, 14-15.

not seem appropriate for the display of classical culture. In a letter to a synod which he was unable to attend personally he applies the famous lines of *Iliad* 3. 156-7 'it is no disgrace that Trojans and well-greaved Achaeans should endure sufferings for such a woman' to a trivial dispute, and shortly afterwards he adds another Homeric phrase. Some authors could provoke him to an outburst. Twice he added a short essay of his own to the existing commentaries on Lucian (Westerink 54-5). Both these essays are couched in intemperate language. Lucian had made one speaker in a dialogue suggest that the universe is not like a ship under the command of an intelligent captain, while another claimed that the orderly system alleged by the Stoics to exist in the world is proof that everything is determined by preordained necessity. These propositions were anathema to a pious Christian.

The attack on Julian in another short essay (Westerink 24) is no surprise; in view of the long tradition of hostility to the apostate what is remarkable is that a large proportion of his literary output survived. Julian had complained that the advent of Christianity had not brought any reduction of the amount of evil in the world. Arethas replies that this is because free will has been given to mankind by his creator. He concludes: 'If the autonomy of the logical soul were destroyed how would man differ from an ass? It would have been far better for you to be an ass than to belch forth such arguments.' Whether this essay results from a reading of a complete work by Julian or is designed merely to be an answer to a quotation already made by some previous church father remains uncertain. But it may be worth mentioning that there are some hostile notes of a type that would be consistent with Arethas' authorship found in the manuscripts of Julian, as if he had once possessed a copy.[5]

The same kind of abusive language, coupled with an outburst against Julian, is found in the tirade aimed at Leo Choerosphactes (Westerink 21), the ambassador whose ingenious and pedantic negotiations with Bulgaria have been noticed earlier. Choerosphactes fell from favour after a diplomatic mission to the Arabs, and from Arethas' text it is possible to gather that he had had the temerity to enter a church and make public his views on theological questions. Exactly what he said and how he found a suitable occasion cannot be inferred from Arethas' intemperate ranting. But after much abuse, including the suggestion that his powers of oratory are to be compared with those of Demades and Hyperbolus, and that he is an Epicurean, the parting shot is: 'Go your own way to destruction with the old man from Tyre, with the impious Julian, whose works you admire and copy. You are already counted as their partner. Go to the Acherusian lake, to Cocytus, to Tartarus, to Acheron and Pyriphlegethon, where your Plato consigned your companions. This is said seriously, not in jest; why should one jest when the unholy hatred of God shown by these intrigues has led the champions of piety to justified abhorrence?' The reference to Demades and Hyperbolus implies an

⁵ J. Bidez, *Byzantion* 9 (1934) 391-408, especially 399-404.

audience or readership well versed in classical culture, capable of recognising these two Athenian politicians as notorious demagogues. Similar demands are made by speaking elliptically of Porphyry, the third-century philosopher whose most offensive work, an attack on Christianity in fifteen books, probably did not exist even in Arethas' day. Plato receives an epithet intended to mark the gap separating him from Christian attitudes, a gap which nevertheless did not prevent Arethas from reading him attentively.

There is not a great deal more to be said about his classical reading. Standard authors are referred to from time to time in a way that does not arouse suspicions of fraudulent claims to learning. Among them are Herodotus and Thucydides. There is also a mention of Antiphon's *Tetralogies*, not a prominent text in Byzantium. He may also have known Strabo; the scanty scholia include references to Patras, his home town, which might be his additions. He seems to have been acquainted with Lesbonax' short treatise on rhetorical figures. Various other claims made on his behalf cannot be substantiated at present.[6]

Although Arethas does not regularly pass judgment on the style of classical authors as Photius had done, stylistic questions were of some importance to him. He criticises (Westerink 32) a panegyric of St. Gregory of Nazianzus by Nicetas Paphlagon, saying that it is like a pile of precious stones in total disorder, as if the quantity of material rather than its arrangement guaranteed a distinguished product. This is to disregard the precept of the handbooks, to use not every topic that we can find but everything that we judge suitable. The comment turns out to be a quotation from Hermogenes. Arethas also criticises the text for its obscurity, its unduly close imitation of mannerisms found in St. Gregory, and excessive use of comparisons between him and biblical figures.[7] Here Arethas cited Hermogenes again, this time explicitly, saying that certain principles are clear even if one has only dipped into his handbook. Once again the pagan textbook is accepted without question as the proper authority.

The comment on his friend's inability to write clearly is a good case of the pot calling the kettle black. Arethas is certainly open to the same charge and was in fact criticised by some contemporaries. A six-page essay gives his reply (Westerink 17). A friend had called on him the evening before, bringing back one of his essays, and reported that some people criticised him for obscurity. Arethas says that perhaps they do not know when obscurity is in order and for what audience. If the criticism comes from experts in ancient literature and rhetorical style, he will make alterations without any feeling of shame; but if the critics are unqualified, he remains unmoved. To the point that the fathers of the church write simply he replies that this may be true when they are giving moral exhortation, but it is not always the case, as is shown by St.

---

[6] They are sensibly discussed by Lemerle.

[7] See the edition by J.J. Rizzo (Brussels 1976), especially 8-10.

Gregory's 44th Oration, *On Encaenia*. Yet Gregory is not the less appreciated for that; he presents a challenge to the cultivated reader. Arethas notes that Gregory himself had expressed the wish that he might possess the training and the linguistic skill of Thucydides and Herodotus in order to expose to posterity the wickedness of Julian. Arethas then defends his own style in terms which owe something to Hermogenes. He assures his friend of his peaceable intentions in this controversy, emphasising the point by a quotation from Aristophanes' *Peace*. Most of the remainder of the essay amounts to an assertion of the merits of his own writings, which is not argued or demonstrated by examples. He quotes an anecdote which he presumably found in Aelian's *Varia historia* 2.2,[8] comparing his critics to the Persian Megabyzus, who visited the studio of the painter Zeuxis and admired the paintings in bright colours but showed little appreciation of the darker works painted with greater skill and laughed contemptuously at the slaves who were grinding pigments to make the colours. But for all his display of learning Arethas cannot persuade a modern reader that he has any defence against his critics. He fails to exploit the possibility of appealing to the ancient critic Demetrius, *On Style* 254, where it is stated 'obscurity often produces forcefulness'.

Arethas' procedures as a reader have been illuminated by an attentive study of a number of his books. When he read the early apologist Athenagoras he did his best to remedy faults in a number of places, and it is clear that his alterations do not coincide with those recommended by modern scholars.[9] Similarly the manuscript now in Moscow reveals that at least in his old age he read rather carelessly and made notes based on misundings.[10]

One should perhaps conclude this dicussion by taking note of two remarks in his commentary on the Apocalypse. This was a reworking of a commentary by Andreas, one of his predecessors in the archbishopric of Caesarea, and comparison of the two texts allows us to infer that the remarks are his additions. Commenting on Apocalypse 2:24-9 he says 'if the syntax is un-Greek (indicatives are never combined with subjunctives) this will not worry people who obtain salvation through the mind alone and not by the precision of words'. And on 3:22 he notes 'it has already been said that Greek culture treats such syntax and word order as solecisms, about which the church is less concerned'.[11] The different emphasis here suggests that he so to speak wore a different hat when reading scripture, which is not surprising.

There is no sign that Arethas deserves consideration as a literary or textual critic. His tone is often irritable and unedifying. He read widely

---

[8] It looks as if the reading *Μηλιάδα* implies dependence on the V-family of Aelian manuscripts (cf. Dilts' edition).

[9] See E. Schwartz's edition in *Texte und Untersuchungen* IV part 2 (Leipzig 1891) iv-vii.

[10] L.G. Westerink, *Byzantion* 42 (1972) 199-200.

[11] Ed. J.A. Cramer, *Catenae graecorum patrum in Novum Testamentum* VIII (Oxford 1844) 218, 236. The edition of Andreas is by J. Schmid (Munich 1955-6).

in ancient literature, but if he assumed that the result of this process would be an ability to express himself clearly in the language of great writers of the past he was seriously mistaken. There is no evidence that he had pupils with scholarly interests. His collection of books, however important it seems to us through the accident of its partial preservation, may not have been remarkable in its own day, except in so far as any private collection not consisting of copies made by the owner himself argues a degree of wealth. Almost all extant manuscripts transcribed at that period are inevitably among the most important for the texts they transmit; the Bodleian Euclid is a rare and striking exception. What Arethas himself added to the scholia on various authors is not on the whole of great importance. In short Arethas enjoys a more flattering reputation than he deserves.

7

From Arethas' Contemporaries to the End of the Tenth Century

(i) The activity of copyists

Arethas was not the only scholarly reader of his generation. In the last chapter we had occasion to mention various books which have been attributed to his library for no good reason or indeed no reason at all. There are a few others which deserve to be recorded here. First we may mention the oldest surviving copy of Isocrates (Urb. gr. 111). It has many distinctive readings and is generally regarded as the most reliable witness to the text of this influential author who, it may be noted in passing, is not frequently cited or alluded to by Arethas. The script of the Isocrates suggests a date near the turn of the century. A slightly more archaic impression is created by the angular and idiosyncratic script of four other books, one of which is even more important for the classical scholar: the oldest surviving copy of Demosthenes (Paris gr. 2934), again a book which presents many distinctive readings and is accepted by almost all editors as being by far the most important manuscript. One would like to know where it was produced, but there is no clue, and certainly no inference should be made from the fact that several centuries later it belonged to a monastery which can be located in Asia Minor. Very similar and presumably deriving from the same copyist or scriptorium are copies of the two ninth-century chronicles of George Syncellus and Theophanes (Vat. gr. 155 and Christ Church, Oxford, Wake 5)[1] and Stephanus' commentary on Hippocrates' *Aphorismoi* (Escorial C-II-10).

The practical side of medicine is brought to our attention by another book which can be dated to the end of the ninth century or the early years of the tenth. It is a collection of ancient writings on the treatment of broken bones and dislocations, which is well known to art historians on account of its illustrations of patients in bandages or strapped down on various ancient equivalents of the operating table (Laur. 74.7). The standard of the illustrations is high enough to point to origin in Constantinople itself, and a later note of possession, which admittedly needs to be supplemented by conjecture, says that it belonged to the hospital attached to the church of the Forty Martyrs, which is known to have been installed in a converted imperial palace at the end of the

---

[1] N.G. Wilson, *DOP* 26 (1972) 357-60.

twelfth century.[2] How often the Byzantines, or indeed the ancients, practised the techniques outlined in the treatises is uncertain. One would like to know who the original owner of the volume was, all the more so because the main manuscript of Theophrastus' botanical writings (Urb. gr. 61), which are of more theoretical than practical significance, is written in a script so similar that both volumes must have been produced, if not by the same copyist, certainly in the same scriptorium. Both questions receive at least a partial answer from three sets of verses added to the Laurentian manuscript by contemporary hands. The verses include an invitation to practitioners to follow the advice given. All three poems praise a doctor called Nicetas for having rediscovered, put together, and transcribed in his own hand, this collection of neglected texts. But most of the texts do not appear to have been copied again during the Byzantine period, and it may well be that the rate of success obtained by using the treatments recommended was low enough to discourage their general application. Nicetas can, however, take the credit for preserving these treatises, and he probably deserves the thanks of all students of the history of botany for having copied the manuscript which is the archetype of one if not both Theophrastus' chief works.[3]

After the death of Arethas, no scholar of outstanding ability can be identified for some time. The middle of the century was nevertheless a period of considerable activity, the significance of which has tended to be underestimated owing to the unduly low datings which were at one time given to some of the manuscripts that serve as the main evidence.[4] It is possible to identify a number of scribes, but we cannot say whether they were working for themselves or undertaking commissions for wealthy book collectors.

From the second quarter of the century onwards we find texts of classical poets: the earliest copies of Theognis (Paris supp. gr. 388) and Musaeus (Barocci 50, a miscellany containing a wide range of texts) may be as early as *c.* 925. To the middle of the century one can assign the celebrated codex now in the Medicean Library in Florence which alone of the medieval manuscripts contains all seven plays of Aeschylus and is of fundamental importance also for Sophocles and Apollonius Rhodius (Laur. 32.9). The only copy of Aristophanes to transmit all eleven plays (Ravenna 429) belongs to this time. It has been suggested that the scribe can be identified with the man who wrote the Sophocles text in the Medicean manuscript, but this is not quite certain.[5] Both these manuscripts have marginal scholia; those in the Aristophanes turn out to be much inferior to the scholia found in later copies, and from this point of view the book is disappointing. On the other hand there is a

[2] R. Janin, *Géographie ecclésiastique de l'empire byzantin* I tome iii (ed. 2, Paris 1969) 564.

[3] B. Einarson & G.K.K. Link, *Theophrastus De causis plantarum* I (London-Cambridge, Mass. 1976) lix.

[4] A. Diller in *Serta Turyniana* (Urbana-Chicago-London 1974) 514-24.

[5] Ibid. 523; I am not quite convinced.

particularly rich collection of scholia in the margins of the copy of the *Iliad* written about this time (Marc. gr. 454). They constitute a unique source of information about ancient scholarship which, when published in 1788, led to a better understanding of the genesis of the Homeric poems. Much less important, but of the same date, is a copy of the *Odyssey* (Laur. 32.24). The last important verse text copied at this time, probably *c.* 930-950, is the *Greek Anthology*, usually known as the *Palatine Anthology* because of the library where most of it is preserved (Heidelberg gr. 23; a small section has been detached and is now Paris supp. gr. 384). This collection of Hellenistic and later poems, almost all elegiac, is a great treasury of Greek epigrams. The circumstances of its compilation are difficult to work out in detail,[6] but one fact should be emphasised. The epigrams include some inscriptions from Byzantine churches. It looks as if these were collected by a certain Gregorios Magistros of Campsa in Macedonia; the fact is revealed by captions to some of the epigrams. They have been taken to imply visits to Thessalonica (*Anth. Pal.* 7.340), Larissa (7.327f), Megara (7.337), Corinth (7.347), Magnesia (7.338), Cyzicus (7.334f) and Phrygia (7.330-3). The suggestion has been made that extensive journeys were undertaken at the request of the compiler of the *Anthology*, Constantine Cephalas, of whom nothing is known except that he appears to be the person with the rank of palace chaplain mentioned in the account of the year 917 by Theophanes Continuatus 6.10 (p. 388.23). It is certain that Gregory transcribed one epigram direct from the monument (7.327), and of two others it is said that they were found in Cyzicus (7.334) and Thessalonica (7.340). But one may doubt whether the journey was undertaken specifically for this purpose. It is more likely, but still noteworthy as an example of a scholarly pursuit, that a man who had to travel made it his hobby to collect epigrams.

The appearance of several poetic texts should not lead to the belief that prose literature suddenly went out of fashion. The tenth century produced manuscripts of equal importance for these authors as well. The best known may be recorded here. There are five copies of Demosthenes: Paris gr. 2935, Laur. 59.9, Marc. gr. 416 and 418, and Munich gr. 485. The first of these was written by the same scribe as Vat. gr. 1 of Plato's *Laws*,[7] the second is probably in the same hand as the Ravenna Aristophanes.[8] The most active scribe of this period, who also achieves a very high standard of calligraphy, is the monk Ephraem. His products include: (i) the main witness to the text of Polybius (Vat. gr. 124), probably written in 947; (ii) an important copy of Aristotle's *Organon* (Marc. gr. 201), dated 954; (iii) the Acts and Epistles (Athos, Lavra B 64), a most remarkable manuscript because one of its ancestors may have been in Eusebius' library in Caesarea and because it gives valuable

---

[6] See the forthcoming study by Alan Cameron.

[7] N.G. Wilson, *CQ* 54 (1960) 200-2.

[8] But this is denied by Diller, op. cit. 523.

indications about the work of Origen on these texts;[9] (iv) the Gospels (Athos, Vatopedi 747), dated 948; (v) one of the leading witnesses for the text of Plato (Venice, app. class. 4,1).[10]

Other authors represented in codices of this date are Strabo (Paris gr. 1397 and Dio Cassius (Laur. 70.8), written by the same scribe;[11] Thucydides (Laur. 69.2 and Heidelberg, Pal. gr. 252);[12] Herodotus (Laur. 70.3); Lucian (Vat. gr. 90); Plutarch's *Lives* (Laur. Conv. Sopp. 206); and Aristotle (Paris gr. 1853, a substantial collection of his writings,[13] Barb. gr. 87, the *Organon*, and Paris gr. 1741, the main manuscript of the *Poetics* and *Rhetoric*, also containing a large number of other texts on rhetoric, notably Dionysius of Halicarnassus and Menander Rhetor).[14] Among texts written at this time or a little later one may also note a second copy of Dio Cassius (Marc. gr. 395), Xenophon's *Cyropaedia* (Erlangen gr. 1 and Escorial T-III-14), his minor works (Vat. gr. 1335), Plato (Pal. gr. 173) and Hippocrates (Marc. gr. 269). In addition one should mention here Paris gr. 2036, the main witness for the pseudo-Aristotelian *Problemata*, which curiously enough is also the principal source for the most famous ancient essay of literary criticism, pseudo-Longinus '*On the Sublime*'.

This list is not complete; it is meant simply to give an idea of the intense activity in the middle years of the century. While the texts mentioned are, with only one exception, literary, it is clear that scientific studies were not entirely neglected. The same scribe was probably responsible for a copy of the late mathematicians Anthemius of Tralles and Pappus (Vat. gr. 218)[15] and a book, now a palimpsest in rather poor condition, from which previously unknown works of Archimedes were published by the Danish scholar J.L. Heiberg early this century (formerly Istanbul, Metochion of the Holy Sepulchre 355, but now in a private collection; one leaf has strayed to Cambridge, University Library, Add. 1879.23).[16] But for this manuscript we should only be able to read a medieval Latin version of the essay *On Floating Bodies*, in which the science of hydrostatics is invented, and we should have no knowledge of the essay entitled *Method of Mechanical Theorems*, in which he developed a procedure very similar to the integral calculus. The progress of both subjects would no doubt have been quicker if the two

[9] H. Chadwick, *JTS* 11 (1959) 11-12.

[10] Usually dated to the twelfth century, but cf. B.L. Fonkič, *Thesaurismata* 16 (1979) 158. Two other books have recently been attributed to Ephraem: Urb. gr. 97 (Plutarch) and Urb. gr. 130 (rhetorical handbooks). For a detailed study, concluding that Urb. gr. 130 comes from Ephraem's pen and rejecting the other attribution, see L. Perria, *StudBizNeoell* 14-16 (1977-9) 33-112.

[11] A. Diller, *TAPA* 78 (1947) 184-5.

[12] Pal. gr. 252 may well be as early as *c.* 900; so Diller, *Serta Turyniana*, 523.

[13] Described by P. Moraux, *Scriptorium* 21 (1967) 17-41.

[14] Described by D. Harlfinger & D. Reinsch, *Philologus* 114 (1970) 28-50.

[15] Illustrated by R. Browning, *Justinian and Theodora* (London 1971) 85.

[16] J.L. Heiberg, *Hermes* 42 (1907) 235 ff; the identification of the Cambridge leaf is my own.

texts had been known in the original in the Renaissance.

Modern research has revealed one other interesting palimpsest in which the original script is of the tenth century (Vienna, hist. gr. 10). It contains the great grammarian Herodian's *Katholike prosodia*, books 5-7, in a slightly abbreviated version. His other works, with one exception, were gradually lost or replaced.[17]

In the second half of the tenth century a wide range of literary interests continues to be attested. Without making any attempt to give a complete survey it is worth noting a few significant manuscripts which appear to have been produced at this time. One is the oldest extant copy of Hesiod's *Works and Days*; it also contains the didactic poem on geography by Dionysius Periegetes; both texts have copious marginal scholia (Paris gr. 2771). One can probably assign to this period the oldest and best copy of Nicander's poems on snakes, which has a large number of illustrations (Paris supp. gr. 247). There is also an important copy of John Stobaeus' *Anthology* of verse and prose literature (Vienna, phil. gr. 67). A copy of Aristides deserves notice (Vat. gr. 1298), not because the text was in any way unusual but for two other reasons. In the first place some of the folios are palimpsest and the original texts have been identified as Aristotle's *Politics* and the anonymous Byzantine dialogue on political theory which was edited by Cardinal Angelo Mai and is probably the book mentioned by Photius in codex 37 of his *Bibliotheca*. It is something of a surprise to find that the handwriting of these original texts is not of great antiquity, as might be expected in a palimpsest, but reminiscent of the codex Urbinas of Theophrastus' botanical writings, which should probably be dated *c*. 900. The second reason why the Aristides volume is noteworthy is that one of the scribes can be identified elsewhere, in a collection of prose texts (Coislin 249) which includes a speech by Lysias, two by Aeschines, Gorgias' *Encomium of Helen*, six essays by Synesius and, most notably, Marinus' *Life of Proclus*. For all these writings it is the earliest witness. One cannot see any particular reason for the choice of texts; it is best to imagine the scribe or owner of the book as a collector who took every opportunity to enlarge his library. Yet one would like to know more about a man who wished to read the biography of a Neoplatonist of openly pagan views.

(ii)   Education and patronage

Book production was stimulated by the existence of schools and the benevolent interest of the emperor Constantine Porphyrogenitus (912-959). The surviving correspondence of a schoolmaster whose career falls in the first half of the century gives a tantalising glimpse of the educational world.[1] It reveals a state of uneasy rivalry between the writer and his professional colleagues. His methods of instruction do not appear

[17] H. Hunger, *JOBG* 16 (1967) 1-33.

[1] R. Browning, *Byzantion* 24 (1954) 397-452; further bibliography and discussion in Lemerle, op. cit. 246-8.

to have been unusual. Pupils were expected to learn by heart rules of grammar. His own reading extended to the letters of Synesius, which he asks a friend to lend him for a week. Although the master charged fees, he seems to have been in receipt of a subsidy from the church authorities. The intervention of higher authority in the affairs of schools is seen once again in the biography of St. Athanasius, the founder of the Great Lavra on Mount Athos.[2] As a young man, when his name was Abraamios, he had come from Trebizond to study in the capital with a master called Athanasius, who in the biography is given the unique and mysterious title of 'president of the schools'. A sceptic might say that the expression means no more than 'a leading schoolmaster' and is only given in this form because of the writer's difficulty in handling a formal archaising style. But if he means precisely what he says the title must be the result of an initiative by the emperor, either Romanus Lecapenus or Constantine Porphyrogenitus; there is no suggestion that the schoolmasters of the capital formed an association and elected a president. The future saint made such rapid progress that he was unanimously chosen by his fellow pupils to be assistant master in the school and subsequently, by a fresh vote of the school and with the good will of the emperor, promoted to the rank of full teacher, which meant that he left the school. His new establishment was so popular that relations with his former school became difficult, and it is said that the emperor had to intervene. It is hard to see exactly what Constantine could do in the circumstances. But his concern for education is beyond doubt. He appointed four professors, one in each of the subjects that had been studied in the school set up by Bardas in the preceding century.[3] The fortunes of the school in the intervening years are obscure, and it may be that Constantine was reviving an institution that had ceased to exist. His nominees were Constantine protospatharios in philosophy, Nicephorus patrikios in geometry, Gregory asecretis in astronomy, while the chair of rhetoric was given to Alexander the metropolitan of Nicaea. This man is the only one of the four of whom any trace remains. He owned and corrected a manuscript of Lucian (Vat. gr. 90), marking the book in eight places and stating on each occasion the name of the person with whom he had made the corrections, as if to suggest that the process involved a reading of the text by one of the pair while the other checked the text in a second copy.[4] One fact from his correspondence may be worth brief mention. A letter from Nicetas Magistros says that the writer has derived great benefit from Zosimus' notes on Demosthenes' *Philippics* and *Olynthiacs*, but that he always has difficulty in understanding the two famous orations against Aeschines (*On the Crown* and *On the False*

---

[2] Discussed by Lemerle, ibid. 257-60.

[3] Theophanes Continuatus 6.14, p. 445-6.

[4] The passages may be found through the index in H. Rabe, *Scholia in Lucianum* (Leipzig 1906) 287. Other information about Alexander is collected by P. Maas, *BngrJ* 3 (1922) 333-6 (= *Kleine Schriften* (Munich 1973) 467-72) and J. Darrouzès, *Epistoliers byzantins du Xe siècle* (Paris 1960) 27-32.

Embassy) and oration 22 (*Against Androtion*) because of the lack of scholia. So he asks Alexander to send him any scholia that he can.[5] But if the four professors did nothing that entitles them to a significant place in the history of scholarship, it has to be recorded that the emperor appears to have been satisfied with the results of his appointments. He arranged for the school's students to have grants and to eat at a common table, and before long he had a supply of suitable candidates for high positions in church and state.

The emperor had literary ambitions. He wrote a good deal himself and commissioned a number of substantial works. Four books by him are well known. Three of them, *De ceremoniis*, *De administrando imperio* and *De thematibus*, constitute an attempt to describe the empire. The fourth is a biography of his grandfather, Basil I (it is now known as book V of Theophanes Continuatus). In the preface Constantine says that he had wanted to write a complete history of the Roman empire of Byzantium, for the benefit of serious readers, but not having the time or a large supply of sources ready to hand he contented himself with the biography of just one emperor, his grandfather, adding that if his poor health improved he hoped to continue the story down to his own day. Various minor texts are attributed to him with differing degrees of certainty.[6] The later historian Zonaras (16.21, iii 482-3) remarks of his letters that though they were not products of the highest rhetorical quality they displayed some skill. Zonaras also tells us that he was capable of verse; there was an elegy on the death of his wife.

As a writer Constantine did not always try to achieve the polished Atticism which was the aim of the average man of letters. He apologises for his style in the first chapter of the *De administrando imperio*, which is addressed to his son, saying that his purpose is to teach rather than give a display of literary skill. It might be added that he was composing a strictly confidential document, which would never be released to the public and therefore never submitted to the critical eye of the litterati. There is, however, some reason to suspect that he may have had reservations about Byzantine literary conventions. One of the authors who wrote at the emperor's request was Theophanes Nonnos. He put together a collection of medical knowledge, to which he added a supplement on diet. The prefaces to the two books of the supplement both dwell on the use of ordinary language, which is justified by the argument that it is essential to make sure of being understood by people who are not fully acquainted with classical literature.[7] The author would probably not have allowed himself this degree of stylistic freedom if he had thought it would be unwelcome to his patron. But imperial patronage for a commonsense view about literary style was not sufficient to alter fashion.

[5] Letter 9, ed. L.G. Westerink (Paris 1973), lines 43 ff; see the note on p. 78.
[6] Lemerle, op. cit. 270-1.
[7] Text printed by L. Cohn, *BZ* 9 (1900) 154-60.

It is the attempt to compile encyclopaedias which makes Constantine most interesting to historians. The survey of medicine mentioned in the preceding paragraph was accompanied by another devoted to veterinary science. The author is unknown. It exists in a manuscript in Berlin famous for its luxurious ornamentation (Phillipps 1538), a luxury which strongly suggests that it is the copy prepared for the imperial library. Folios which could have contained decisive evidence, such as a dedication and a frontispiece of the writer handing his book to the emperor, are now missing. One may note in passing that the handwriting and some features of the ornament are identical in a collection of anacreontic verse by various authors (Barb. gr. 310). The emperor's collection of veterinary treatises might have been expected to oust all others from circulation, but it is not so; there are manuscripts of similar content belonging to a different tradition.[8] Nor does it seem that the encyclopaedia of ordinary medicine, based largely on the famous doctors of late antiquity, Oreibasius, Aetius and Paul of Aegina, enjoyed a wide circulation.

The scientific works recorded so far do not exhaust the list of undertakings promoted by the emperor in this field of knowledge. A collection of material on zoology passing under his name reveals the reality of its authorship by the phrase 'I will dedicate to you'. It admits to being derived from Aristophanes of Byzantium's epitome of Aristotle, Aelian and Timotheus (of Gaza) and others. Two manuscripts survive (Paris supp. gr. 495 and Athos, Dionysiou 180).[9] More substantial is the collection known as the *Geoponica*, an encyclopaedia of agriculture. The exact identification of all the sources is problematic, but it is at least clear that a good deal of the material corresponds to what Photius had listed in codex 163 of his *Bibliotheca*. The difference between the *Geoponica* and the other works commissioned by the emperor is that it appears to have had a wider circulation, if the number of extant manuscripts and the existence of a translation into Syriac may be taken as evidence.

A practical aim of another kind was served by putting together in a single collection some handbooks of military technique, both ancient and medieval. The surviving manuscript of this corpus (Laur. 55.4) looks like a product of the imperial scriptorium. Apart from containing two works by the emperor himself it is the most important witness to the text of a number of treatises, including the oldest of all, by Aeneas.[10] But for the emperor's initiative it is quite possible that this and other handbooks by military commanders of antiquity would not have come down to us.

Paradoxically Constantine's main enterprise has for the most part been lost. Our ignorance of this projected encyclopaedia of human activity in fifty-three sections is such that we do not even know the titles

---

[8] L. Cohn, ibid.
[9] Lemerle, op. cit. 296-7.
[10] See the edition by A. Dain and A.-M. Bon (Paris 1967) xxxi-xxxiii.

of more than twenty-five. One cannot be absolutely certain that the plan was brought to a successful conclusion; the fact of possessing part of the fiftieth section 'On virtue and vice' does not guarantee that all were completed. We also have one complete section, the twenty-seventh, 'On embassies', and substantial amounts of two others, 'On ambushes' and 'On gnomic statements'. Their place in the series is unknown. The surviving portions fill six volumes in a modern edition. Since they can only be a tiny percentage of the whole – exactly how tiny is difficult to say, since the material available for an account of diplomacy might have been much greater than for, say, inventors – the encyclopaedia was conceived on a vast scale. The first section dealt, perhaps not unexpectedly, with the proclamation of kings. Others ranged over such topics as the succession of kings, emperors, military stratagems (one is prompted to ask what relation MS. Laur. 55.4 bears to this), letters, political oratory, hunting and marriage.

Each section consists of verbatim extracts from named sources, which are listed at the beginning. In the sections we possess they number twenty-six, all but one being historians, some of whom no longer survive in the direct tradition. The research needed to collect all the source material may have been considerable, even if in these sections a number of the lost sources had been known to Photius and were perhaps still easy to find. The preface to the excerpts on diplomacy tells us that the emperor decided to collect books from all over the world in order to make his selection.[11] The only detail to throw light on the search is that in the *De ceremoniis* he records how he found a text in a monastery at Sigriane, on the south side of the Sea of Marmara, where a former civil servant had retired. The reason for making the collection is stated. It inspires a feeling of sympathy in the modern reader who feels himself overwhelmed by the mass of printed literature. Constantine evidently felt, even without the aid of printing, that a point had been reached where the bulk of what had been written was too great. The books in themselves were admirable, but the great number of them and the rarity of some encouraged weak-minded people, who stood most in need of the moral examples contained in them, to lose their enthusiasm for reading. In order to remedy this situation he decided to collect texts and choose from them everything that seemed morally beneficial and arrange it under subject headings. To the obvious objection that this method will lead to the loss of historical perspective he makes the unconvincing reply that each event will be recorded in a place appropriate to the moral lesson that it conveys.

The modern reader is grateful to Constantine for preserving most of what is now known of the work of seven historians, ranging from Nicolaus of Damascus (1st century) to John of Antioch (7th century); the others, of early Byzantine date, are Eunapius, Priscus, Malchus, Menander Protector and Peter patrikios. The value of the fragments so preserved is

[11] See the edition by C. de Boor (Berlin 1903) 1-2.

not greatly reduced by the observation that the compilers have occasionally abbreviated known texts in a way that creates misleading impressions.[12] But the medieval reader to whom the emperor claimed to speak seems to have felt no gratitude. The encyclopaedia almost disappeared without trace, and no other fate could have been anticipated unless Constantine had been able to give orders for the production of a number of complete sets. Only imperial patronage, and perhaps not even that, could have organised the necessary resources. One may reasonably wonder whether a plan of this kind, though not indicated in the preface, may have crossed his mind. It would have been consistent with his plan of subsidising students. We must suppose that his relatively early death put an end to the project. As it is, the two early manuscripts both give the impression of being copies prepared for the palace library, where they could probably not have been consulted and copied by members of the public.[13]

(iii) The Suda

Far less ambitious and much more popular than the emperor Constantine's enterprises was another large compilation produced after his death. The date is not certain; two entries which refer to Byzantine emperors without stating the length of their reigns point tentatively to the reign of Basil II (976-1025). A further hint is given by some rude remarks about the patriarch Polyeuctus (956-970). They occur in two places and refer to him as a contemporary. The fact that they seem to be an addition to the original text tends rather to increase their value as evidence; a time would soon arrive when a reader making such a note in the margin of his text would no longer think it appropriate to speak of the misdeeds of Polyeuctus as occurring 'in our own time', and the composition of the *Suda* must be at least slightly earlier than the note. The work is variously known as the *S(o)uda*, which is the title apparently guaranteed by the manuscripts and used by a twelfth-century commentator on Aristotle,[1] or Suidas, which is given as if it were the author's name by other Byzantine writers from Eustathius onwards. The dispute about the name and its etymology is unprofitable, and nothing is known of the work's authorship. A superficial interpretation of the note accompanying the title might suggest that we are dealing with the product of a syndicate. Although that may in fact be the case, it does not follow from the words in question, which accompany a list of learned authors alleged to be responsible for the collection of material. The names prove to be at best those of indirect sources, obviously intended to give a spurious air of authority. This unattractive feature is fortunately of little importance, as the real sources of most articles can be identified.

The most interesting feature of the *Suda* is that, while being based

[12] P.A. Brunt, *CQ* 74 (1980) 483-5.
[13] Tours 980 and Vat. gr. 73; cf. J. Irigoin, *Scriptorium* 13 (1959) 177-81.
[1] Stephanus on the Rhetoric, ed. H. Rabe (*CAG* XXI ii) (Berlin 1896) 285 line 18.

largely on two lexica of conventional type, one the so-called enlarged *synagoge* and the other similar to the *Lexicon Ambrosianum*, it incorporates a mass of articles that are intended to be informative rather than lexicographical, and the result is a cross between a dictionary and an encyclopaedia. It marks a significant stage in the evolution of this type of reference book, since ancient encyclopaedias had not been arranged in this way. There are about 30,000 entries, filling 2,785 pages in the most recent printed edition.[2] They are arranged in a special variant of alphabetical order which takes account of the changes that had occurred in the pronunciation of Greek. This massive quantity of material proved so useful to Byzantine readers that it was transcribed fairly frequently, despite the great effort and amount of writing material required, which would otherwise have acted as a serious deterrent. The compiler or compilers of the *Suda* demonstrate by their choice of material that they had unusual tastes in literature or access to a library with a strange stock of books. The modern reader cannot fail to be struck by the predominance of quotations from the text of Aristophanes and the scholia on his plays. For the editor of that author they provide some readings of value, as the source was evidently akin to the famous Ravenna manuscript, the oldest and in some ways the best witness. For the present purpose, however, it is to be noted that of 30,000 entries over 5,000 derive from the Aristophanic text and scholia, a proportion which can scarcely be justified even by an enthusiastic assessment of the undoubted value of Aristophanes as a source of Attic diction of the classical period. That there should also be a very large number of entries drawn from the scholia on Homer is no surprise in view of the unchallenged position of the epics, especially the *Iliad*, in the educational system. Much less expected are the quotations from Greek historians, which turn out to be derived from the excerpts made for Constantine Porphyrogenitus. Their presence proves either that the excerpts were in circulation for a time or that a compiler somehow had access to them, perhaps through having collaborated personally in the enterprise rather than being allowed to consult a copy in the imperial library itself. If that were the case, a relatively early date, say *c.* 975-80, would be indicated for the composition of the *Suda*. A few of the fragments of the historians have been lost in the direct tradition of the excerpts, so that the *Suda* is the only source for them.[3] It is also the source of fragments from a few other lost books, the most notable being perhaps Callimachus' short epic poem *Hekale*. Among texts which had only very restricted circulation in Byzantium the *Suda* cites Babrius' fables, Marcus Aurelius and Athenaeus' *Deipnosophistae*, the last in a better form than is known from the main manuscript (Marc. gr. 447), which is the best part of a century earlier. But the most frequent reason for consulting the *Suda* is that it draws on a dictionary of literary

[2] By A. Adler (Leipzig 1928-38). See also her article in *RE* s.v. Suidas.
[3] Adler, vol. i, p. xx.

biography by Hesychius, which had already been reduced to an epitome. Even so it can be reckoned a valuable source for the literary history of the Roman empire.

Although the *Suda* is not one of the major achievements of Byzantine scholarship it receives one famous mention in English literature:

> For Attic phrase in Plato let them seek,
> I poach in Suidas for unlicens'd Greek.

> (Pope, *Dunciad* 4.227-8)

Pope's attack on pedantry naturally shows no concern with the original purpose of the *Suda*, which was in part to indicate the areas of Greek vocabulary that were licensed for imitation.

8

The Eleventh Century

(i) Introduction: the schools

The intellectual history of the eleventh century is dominated by Michael Psellos and his friends and pupils. Psellos was born in 1018, towards the end of the long reign of Basil II (976-1025). In his *Chronographia* (1.29) he remarks that despite the lack of encouragement from the emperor this period was a good one for literary studies, and that there were a number of 'philosophers and orators'. Who these literary men were remains a mystery. It is not even possible to identify with certainty many manuscripts of classical authors written during Basil's reign. One may point to a copy of fourteen of Plutarch's *Lives* dated to the year 997 (Laur. 69.6). The same scribe probably wrote a copy of the so-called Scholia minora on the *Odyssey*, a series of short explanations of the vocabulary of Homer corresponding to the D-scholia on the *Iliad* (Oxford, Auct. V.1.51).[1] Without doubt there are a number of other books which cannot be precisely dated but belong to this period. One which, despite the difficulty of dating, appears to fall into this category should perhaps be mentioned here in view of its connection with topics that occur later in this chapter. It is Laur. 59.15, which apart from some lesser productions of the Second Sophistic age contains various writings by the critic Dionysius of Halicarnassus. It is important for the text and is the only copy to preserve his essay on Deinarchus. Dionysius was one of the authors exploited by Psellos in his short essays on rhetoric, and there is reason to think that he had access not to the Laurentian manuscript itself but to one of its ancestors.[2] Other valuable manuscripts which are likely to be products of Basil's reign contain Lucian (Vienna, phil. gr. 123), Hippocrates (Vienna, med. gr. 4), and a richly illuminated text of Oppian's didactic poem on hunting (Marc. gr. 479). Much more tentatively one may add a copy of Plato of rather uncertain date (Vienna, supp. gr. 7).

Yet the explanation of Psellos' enthusiasm may not be far to seek. If we are right in thinking that his great friend John Mauropous was born about the turn of the century, he will have completed his education while Basil II was still on the throne. The emergence of such an able and

---

[1] *Greek manuscripts: catalogue of an exhibition held at the Bodleian Library Oxford 1966* (Oxford 1966) 29 (and plate XX).
[2] G. Aujac, *RevHistTextes* 4 (1974) 14.

cultivated man, to whom Psellos felt enormously indebted, goes some way towards explaining his favourable judgment on the period. Not that the schools of the time were distinguished; the masters are not named, and Psellos gives the credit for Mauropous' education not to eminent teachers, but to two uncles, and in similar vein claims that he himself owes everything to Mauropous.[3] Confirmation of this low opinion of schoolmasters is found in the funeral oration for his schoolfriend Nicetas, who later became head of a school called St. Peter's. Psellos makes it plain that when they were at school together they learned very little from their masters, but a great deal through their own initiative. He adds, perhaps prompted by his feelings to some exaggeration, that Nicetas, who was a little older than he was and acted as a kind of second master in the school, helped him with his study of rhetoric.[4] Elsewhere he says that the transition from literature to rhetoric occurred at the age of sixteen.[5] His primary education appears to have been obtained at a school run by a monastery near his home in the capital, and though he later felt a sufficient debt of gratitude to help the monastery he does not say anything which would justify the inference that the teaching it offered was above the average.[6]

It is worth pausing for a moment to give by way of contrast Psellos' view of what a literary education should be like. This can be inferred from his idealised description of his lifelong friend Nicetas, the head of the school called St. Peter's. Holding him up as a model of how to teach Psellos says:[7]

Since he knew that the Greeks hold the key to mysteries and can initiate us into many things, keeping truth hidden under an unattractive exterior, he took off the veil and revealed the ideas concealed beneath it. So with him the golden chain that is let down in Homer (*Iliad* 8.19) seemed to be a halt in the revolution of the universe,[8] Ares bound in chains (*Odyssey* 8.295ff) was recognised as the spirit overcome by the ineffable power of reason, both the didactic type that reaches the soul through the ears and that which springs up from within; the homeland towards which Odysseus and his companions hastened after leaving the witch was understood by him to be the celestial Jerusalem, where this world of suffering received the first created beings (?), the present world where we are converted from a nobler form into beasts if, deceived by the lure of pleasure, we do not hasten towards Jerusalem. Such an expert in Homer was Nicetas, not adhering to the letter as most teachers do, not allowing his ears to be enchanted by the metre nor yielding to appearances, but seeking hidden beauty, by reason and intelligence penetrating the matter and entering inside the shrine. In

[3] The encomium of Mauropous is edited by K.N. Sathas, *Mesaionike Bibliotheke* V (Paris 1876) 142-67; see especially 143, 148.

[4] The encomium of Nicetas is edited ibid. 87-96.

[5] Ibid. 28.

[6] See a letter edited ibid. 378; the monastery was τὰ Ναρσοῦ.

[7] Ibid. 92. A query marks a passage of doubtful meaning, where the text may be in need of correction.

[8] This notion derives from Plato, *Theaetetus* 153d.

the same way he was acquainted with authors like Epicharmus, Archilochus, Nicander and Pindar, and all the other poets who went to work under the inspiration of the Muses.

One can only read such praise with mixed feelings. The insistence on the merits of allegorical interpretation is found in some of Psellos' own work. Although this type of exegesis had a long history and had been provoked by difficulties in the texts, its excessive use does not do credit to Psellos. It contributes to the impression that the Byzantines were never content with a simple explanation where a complex one could be found. The description also makes it clear that Nicetas did everything to ensure that pupils would have no literary enjoyment of Homer. The claim that he read such authors as Epicharmus and Archilochus is hardly to be taken seriously; similar boasts by Psellos will be dealt with in due course.

A curious fact which should be mentioned at this point concerns pseudo-Longinus. As was stated above, the archetype (Paris gr. 2036) was written in the tenth century, and not long after we find the only other trace of its existence in Byzantium, two references by John the Sicilian, an otherwise unimportant schoolmaster, who wrote commentaries on rhetorical textbooks and has been dated in the first half of the eleventh century.[9] In one passage John deals with the exaggerated description of Boreas in a tragedy entitled *Orithyia* in terms which recall 'Longinus' 3.1. He says that there is a detailed discussion in book 21 of Longinus' *Philological Discourses*. At first sight he would seem to support the traditional and barely tenable view that the author of the extant treatise was the third-century rhetorician who makes a brief but glorious appearance in Gibbon. But John's words are not specific enough to prove that he is thinking of the treatise at all, and even if he is he may have made a mistake. The second reference is to 9.9, the famous quotation from Genesis 1:3-9, one of the very few places where a pagan writer takes note of the Bible for purposes that are not polemical. John states that Longinus and Demetrius of Phalerum admired the passage. As Demetrius is not mentioned in the treatise, the natural inference is that John is either inaccurate in his recollection or relying on another source. Research on manuscripts of rhetorical handbooks has brought to light some unexpected nuggets of ancient learning, and probably one should assume that John does no more than exemplify this phenomenon. I see no reason to adopt a cynical alternative hypothesis, that John exploited the extant treatise, knowing that it was an extremely rare text and quoting it with spurious additional details.

---

[9] On John see the evidence cited below, Ch. 10 (i) n. 7, and H. Rabe, *Prolegomenon sylloge* (Leipzig 1931) cxiii. For the Longinus quotations see D.A. Russell's edition (Oxford 1964) xxvi-xxviii. The usual date cannot be quite right, since there are a few marginal notes on Aristides ascribed to John in Paris gr. 2950, and they appear to be of the late tenth century. Such a date is not in fact inconsistent with his autobiographical remark about an oration given in the presence of Basil II.

(ii)   John Mauropous

Although he exercised a great influence on Psellos, Mauropous has no right to anything more than a very modest place in the history of classical studies. He owes his fame chiefly to two facts. One is that in some dodecasyllabic verses he prays to God to be merciful to the souls of Plutarch and Plato, excepting them from the fate that awaits unbelievers because 'both of them in word and character adhere closely to your laws'.[1] In view of the disaster that later overtook Psellos' pupil John Italos because of his admiration for Plato, these verses are highly significant. Intellectual and religious tolerance are fragile, and were temporarily lost towards the end of the century.

Mauropous' admiration for Plutarch makes this the appropriate moment to record the popularity of this author in the middle Byzantine period. Copies of the *Moralia*, many of them containing no more than the first twenty-one of the essays, are numerous. We can list one that is perhaps a little earlier than Mauropous' lifetime (Marc. gr. 250), three that belong with little doubt to the eleventh century, although more precise dating is out of the question (Barb. gr. 182, Paris gr. 1956 and 1957), and no less than five which belong either to the eleventh or to the twelfth century (Paris gr. 1955, Vienna, phil. gr. 129, Laur. 69.13, Marc. gr. 249 and Moscow, Hist. Mus. 501). There is also one that is generally assigned to the twelfth century (Riccardiana gr. 45). The *Lives* were also much studied. After five copies produced in the tenth century (Laur. Conv. Sopp. 206, Laur. 69.6, Urb. gr. 97, Paris gr. 1678 and Coislin 319) there are several more from the following period (Seitenstetten gr. 1, Vat. gr. 138, Heidelberg, Pal. gr. 168-9 and 283, Marc. gr. 386, and Vienna, hist. gr. 60). As with the *Moralia* it has to be borne in mind that these volumes usually contain far less than a complete set of the *Lives*. But it is probably fair to say that no other classical author, apart from those occupying a central place in the school curriculum, was so frequently transcribed.

Mauropous also wrote a series of some 470 dodecasyllabic verses giving etymologies of various Greek words. These prove to derive from an extremely early text, probably dating back to the reign of Augustus (31 B.C.-A.D. 14). Mauropous seems to have done no more than abbreviate it and convert it into verse, without adding any significant contribution of his own.[2] The use of a text now lost is nothing extraordinary.

It has been suggested, on the strength of a remark made by Psellos in an encomium of him, that Mauropous had a knowledge of Latin, which would have been a great distinction. But there is no trace of it in his writings, and it is better to assume that the reference is to Roman law. The same phrase 'Italian wisdom' is used in that sense and without

---

[1] Item 43 in *Iohannis Euchaitorum metropolitae quae in codice Vaticano graeco 676 supersunt*, ed. P. de Lagarde (Göttingen 1882).

[2] The full text was edited from MS. Cairo 296, written *c.* 1600, by R. Reitzenstein, *M. Terentius Varro und Johannes Mauropous von Euchaita* (Leipzig 1901).

ambiguity in Psellos' encomium of his mother.[3] Although he was for a time bishop of Euchaita, a town to the west of Amaseia and not far from his birthplace in Cappadocia, Mauropous was also a trusted adviser to the imperial court, and one item in the collection of his own writings (preserved in Vat. gr. 676) is the draft decree for the appointment of a new professor in a law school set up by Constantine IX Monomachus, perhaps in the year 1047.[4] Civil servants were proud of compositions of this kind; Psellos' collected works include a number of similar state papers or speeches written for emperors.[5]

It is worth quoting in full a letter sent by Mauropous to a schoolboy.[6] The name of the addressee is not known, but we shall not be far wrong if we imagine that this was the kind of encouragement that Mauropous gave Psellos. The pupil is evidently about half way through his school career and the letter casts light on the order in which books and subjects were tackled at least in the eleventh century and probably for much of the period that we are concerned with. Sophocles, Aristophanes and Aratus are apparently read in that order, the last of the three being intended to give a little elementary knowledge of the constellations. The pupil is about to begin geometry, passing from the trivium to the quadrivium. The line of verse is an adaptation of Aeschylus' *Seven against Thebes* 592 and did not need to be identified, as the boy would have read that play recently.

> What sort of grammarian do we now have among us, and of what style? Is he Sophoclean? Or by now Aristophanic? I should be glad to learn that he is Aratean or still further advanced and therefore closer to the end of his general education. So hasten towards this target with all speed. Flitting ably with the sharp wings of your mind over these pure pastures of learning, head towards the perfection of wisdom. Without loss of time devote care to your talents in their most noble enterprise, because life is short and there are many arts (I mean intellectual ones that are for you to learn), and you must go through them all, provided God in his love of humanity consents, if you are to achieve human perfection and to become worthy of your family and the great hopes and prayers you inspire. Do not let your progress be an advance which has length without breadth, as in the definition of slender lines that you will learn in geometry. In that case you would only attend to, let us say, parsing or poetry or some other single branch of education, neglecting the remainder although they are so numerous. Instead you should extend yourself in depth, breath and length in the manner of solid bodies, attending equally to all necessary branches of study and taking up a large area of knowledge, so that you flourish like

[3] The passages in the two encomia are printed by Sathas, op. cit. 148 and 160. Gudeman's idea in *RE* s.v. Ioannes (20) that he knew the Latin saying *incidit in Scyllam qui vult vitare Charybdin* does not survive examination of Leutsch & Schneidewin's notes on Apostolios 16.49.

[4] For the question of the date see J. Lefort, *Travaux et mémoires* 6 (1976) 265-303, especially 285.

[5] Items 28-33 in E. Kurtz & F. Drexl, *Michaelis Pselli scripta minora* I (Milan 1936).

[6] Letter 74, item 173 in de Lagarde.

the fruit-bearing palm-tree and not like a barren reed (cf. Psalm 91:13). This is what I would ask you to do:

> Wish not to seem the best, but best to be,

advancing as deeply as possible in your education, not running superficially over the ground and not simply performing a perfunctory duty towards your studies in the way that most ignorant and ill educated people do. In this way you will not deceive yourself when put to the test or be deceived by others, you will not unwittingly store away a treasure of thin air and gather barrenness with your hands (cf. Proverbs 9:12). May such a fate remain far away from you and yours, may you be thought and at the same time become complete and equipped for all tasks, and when your time comes may you yield abundant fruit like the trees in the Psalm (1:3) which was planted by streams of water.

(iii)　John Italos

From Psellos' chief master I turn to his most important pupil, John Italos, occasionally referred to as Longibardos. He is sometimes declared to be a philosopher worthy of study in his own right, but that aspect of him is outside the scope of the present work. What is important is the episode which has already been mentioned in the first chapter: Italos' enthusiastic study of Plato led to one of the rare occasions when the Byzantine church formally objected to the study of classical authors.

Italos' career can be reconstructed in broad outline.[1] He was, as his name implies, of Italian origin, and though the Italo-Greek communities were in principle bilingual John seems never to have lost the accent and type of speech that marked his provincial origin. When Psellos got into difficulties in 1055 and had to resign his post of professor of philosophy, John appears to have been appointed in his place. This in itself is worthy of note, since it shows that despite being Psellos' pupil he was not regarded as dangerous or unsuitable. It was only much later that his lectures on Plato began to cause offence or were seized upon as an excuse for conducting another attack on Psellos and his circle. There seem to have been two sets of proceedings against John, the first in 1076/7, the second in 1082, as a result of which he was ordered to give up teaching and live in a monastery.[2] After this sentence nothing more is heard of him. It is possible that the adverse outcome of the second trial was due to lack of protection from Psellos, who may have died in the meantime. The ecclesiastical authorities took the opportunity to add formal condemnations of John to the order of service for Orthodoxy Sunday. He is named only in the last of a series of eleven anathemas, but all are aimed at him. Here is a translation of four of them.[3]

---

[1] P. Joannou, *'Christliche Metaphysik' in Byzanz I: Die Illuminationslehre des Michael Psellos und Joannes Italos* (Ettal 1956) 9-30.

[2] J. Gouillard, *Travaux et mémoires* 2 (1967) 188-90.

[3] Edited by T.I. Uspensky, *Zapiski imperatorskago novorossiskago universiteta* 59 (1893) 420-3.

1.   Anathema on those who make any attempt to apply new inquiry or teaching to the mysterious incarnation of our Saviour and God, or to inquire how the Divine Word itself came to be united with a human frame and how it gave divinity to the flesh it had assumed; and on those who attempt to argue dialectically about the nature and status of the innovation, which is beyond nature, concerning the two natures of God and man.

2.   Anathema on those who claim to be pious but shamelessly or rather impiously introduce the ungodly teachings of the Hellenes into the orthodox catholic church concerning human souls and heaven and earth and other created objects.

7.   Anathema on those who go through a course of hellenic studies and are taught not simply for the sake of education but follow these empty notions and believe in them as the truth, upholding them as a firm foundation to such an extent that they lead others to them, sometimes secretly, sometimes openly, and teach them without hesitation.

8.   Anathema on those who of their own accord invent an account of our creation along with other myths, who accept the Platonic forms as true, who say that matter possesses independent substance and is shaped by the forms, who openly question the power of the creator to bring all things from non-existence to existence, and as their creator to impose a beginning and end on all things in the manner of their lord and master.

Although Italos disappears without trace after being anathematised, the result of the trial was not as drastic as it would be in a modern society capable of exercising greater control. Some of his philosophical discussions, a series of nearly a hundred short pieces, survive, and there are fragments of commentaries on Aristotle, which are less likely to have caused offence than his Platonism. One might have expected the church authorities to press for a change in the system of education, but there is no sign that they made any effort to do so, and the wording of the third of the anathemas just cited suggests a resigned acceptance of the status quo.

John's writings show a few signs of philological concerns. He answers in philosophical style a question put to him about the meaning of an obscure sentence in Hermogenes dealing with the elements which go to make up rhetoric.[4] Another question put to him, allegedly by 'Andronikos the emperor', who may be the son of Constantine X, relates to a notorious puzzle in the *Odyssey*. Penelope says (19.562ff): 'There are two gates for insubstantial dreams, one made of horn, the other of ivory. Those which come through the carved ivory deceive and bring messages that are not fulfilled. Those which come through polished horn tell the truth when mortals see them.' This strange passage, which became proverbial and was adapted by Virgil in *Aeneid* 6.893ff, is not easy to explain, and John's attempt consists mainly of implausible irrelevancy. It ends: 'Dreams from ivory are from perception or rather

---

[4] Quaestio 62. The editions are by P. Joannou, *Ioannes Italos: Quaestiones quodlibetales* (Ettal 1956) and N.N. Kechakmadze, *Ioann Ital: Sochinenija* (Tiflis 1966), which adds a few items.

from earth, the mother of dark-winged dreams; those from horn are from the celestial and highest vantage-point. To put it briefly, one category depends on mind and the intellectual state, the other on some phyiscal and irrational forces. Hence the one set are true, coming from places of truth and leading to imagination, the others rise up to it from below, muddying what is genuine and obscuring its purity.'[5]

Of more concern to us is a brief essay addressed to 'the Abasgian grammarian'. It is in part a gentle riposte to an assertion that two verbal expressions which John had used were grammatically incorrect. They are a rare perfect form and a prohibition constructed with an aorist imperative instead of the normal subjunctive. For the second John inappositely cites in his own defence examples of the prohibition with the present rather than the aorist imperative, as if he did not appreciate the difference. This kind of linguistic argument is typical of Byzantine literary life, but John because of his provincial upbringing was probably more exposed than most to such criticism. It is interesting to note, however, that on this occasion he appears to have been corrected by someone from another part of the periphery of the Byzantine world.[6]

Among Psellos' writings is a defence of his pupil. While it contains an assertion that his faith was sound and makes a plea for tolerance of his literary style, it is mainly a justification of John's position in a controversy with an unnamed opponent. There is a remarkable passage in which John is credited with the view that Greece has been deprived of its cultural heritage, which has passed to the east. The text runs as follows:

> Having made it his purpose to praise the wisdom of the Hellenes he regrets, with good reason, that aliens and barbarians have inherited the wealth of this wisdom, which does not belong to them, whereas the legitimate heirs of philosophy should be the successors. Almost all Greece and its colonies in Ionia have been entirely cut out of the family property, the inheritance has passed to the Assyrians, Medes and Egyptians. There has been such a reversal of roles that Hellenes are now barbarians and the barbarians Hellenes. Suppose a Hellene goes to Susa or Ecbatana, the ancient palace of Darius, or talks to the inhabitants of Babylon: he will hear of things which despite his Hellenic culture he had never heard of, he will admire everyone he meets, and he will perhaps then learn for the first time that wisdom has directed their affairs. But if a pretentious barbarian visited us and talked to people in Hellas or any part of our continent, he would treat the majority of men not as asses but as of mulish stupidity. The greater part of the population know nothing of the world of nature or of what lies beyond it, the remainder think that they know everything but do not in fact even know the route towards knowledge. Some claim to be philosophers and a great many more are anxious to learn. But the teachers sit with smug faces and long beards, looking pale and grim, with a frown,

---

[5] Quaestio 43 (J) = 55 (K).

[6] Quaestio 64. The grammarian is identified by Kechakmadze (p. xix) as John Petritsi, on whom see below.

shabbily dressed. They dig up Aristotle from the underworld, from the depths of Hades, and give the impression of passing judgment on everything that he covered in a cloud of obscurity. When they ought to be expounding at length his confusing brevity, they give instead many brief explanations of the broad range of his researches. Our barbarian visitor is convinced that this is a childish game, gloats over our incompetence, and departs, with no addition to his knowledge but reduced to a state worse than ignorance.[7]

As we shall see shortly, Psellos did have pupils from the Islamic world, so that it was possible for an intelligent Byzantine to gain some idea of intellectual life in the near east. One may be permitted to wonder if John made himself unpopular as much by the assertion of the superiority of oriental culture as by his unusual philosophical position.

(iv)   Michael Psellos

Psellos was born in 1018. His baptismal name was Constantine, but he is usually referred to as Michael, the name he took on entering a monastery *c.* 1055, departing from the normal Byzantine practice of choosing a monastic name with the same initial as the baptismal one. Although this episode marked a temporary fall from favour, he seems to have had no difficulty in returning to his previous activities after a short interval. Most of his career was spent in the service of the emperors, and if the account given in his *Chronographia* is to be trusted he was for many years the power behind the throne. His activity and influence were not confined to the imperial palace. As professor of philosophy, holding a post established by the government, he was well known as a lecturer and attracted many students, who treated him as a polymath with a rich store of knowledge about every field of human activity. The view that he was a prodigy who knew Homer by heart is probably mistaken; the passage from the encomium of his mother sometimes quoted to show this does not seem to prove more than a very close acquaintance with the poems.[1] Nevertheless he was without any doubt uncommonly versatile, as is attested by the range of his writings. The most important are: the *Chronographia*, a history beginning in the reign of Basil II, full of gossip and intriguing sketches of important people and events, perhaps better described as memoirs than as a formal history; funeral orations on various friends, relatives and important contemporaries; a large correspondence; the collection known as *De omnifaria doctrina*, a set of brief outlines of various notions in philosophy, science and theology, much of which derives from Plutarch's *De philosophorum placitis*. It is probably fair to say that philosophy was his main concern. His enthusiasm for Plato, which he shared with his pupil Italos, was unusual and in the end led to trouble. The Platonic aspect of his thought may

[7] Kurtz-Drexl, op. cit. I 51.
[1] Sathas 5.14

have been exaggerated, however, and it has recently been maintained that in some important respects his views were firmly Aristotelian.[2] The date of his death is uncertain; 1078 and 1096 are the dates most often advanced.[3]

Psellos' literary output was vast. Some items in it have yet to be printed. Of those that have been printed only a few have received the care required to produce a serviceable edition. Much remains obscure, and the difficulty of giving an account of Psellos' thought on any given issue is increased by his discursive manner, which allows him to digress frequently into unexpected topics. My attempt to describe his reaction to the classical heritage is divided into three parts, the first general, the second and third devoted to his critical essays, since these offer a more substantial body of such writing than can be found in the work of any other Byzantine scholar.

His attitude to the classics and to other non-Christian cultures is difficult to assess. At one moment he seems to say that he is an orthodox Christian who finds answers to all intellectual problems in the teaching of the church. At other times he shows a curiosity about pagan culture and the much more dubious fields of magic and astrology which must have aroused the suspicion of conventionally minded contemporaries. To assume that Psellos wavered in his views is not necessarily the right solution of the puzzle. It is equally likely that he was employing the practice known to theologians as economy, which is exemplified by some fathers of the church. In other words he presented to his immediate audience the opinions or arguments which he thought would be most effective with them. Since the concept of economy is not rare Psellos must have been acquainted with it from his reading of patristic literature; he will not have needed any inducement to take a lead from St. Basil and others. It follows that his enemies will have had little difficulty in interpreting correctly the true meaning of his boasts that he had read the literature of other cultures. Psellos did his best to fend them off with assertions of loyalty to the church. In general he succeeded, and although there was a period of his career when he ran into difficulties he never suffered long eclipse. His talents were too outstanding to be suppressed. The fate of the less able is shown by what happened to Italos.

The doubts entertained by his enemies receive tangible expression in the profession of orthodox faith which he was obliged to make during the reign of Constantine Monomachus.[4] A more spontaneous and balanced statement of principle, which may nevertheless have been affected by the emotional strain of the moment, is to be found in the funeral oration for his mother.[5] Here he asserts that the Christian faith can provide answers to all problems. But having made the assertion at some length

[2] L. Benakis, *BZ* 56 (1963) 213-27, esp. 218, 221.

[3] P. Joannou, *BZ* 44 (1951) 283-90; D.I. Polemis, *BZ* 58 (1963) 73-5; P. Gautier, *REB* 24 (1966) 159-64.

[4] A. Garzya, *EEBS* 35 (1966-7) 41-6.

[5] Sathas 5.58.

he continues: 'Since however the life allotted to me is not meant to be sufficient for itself alone, but is at the service of others, to be drawn on as from an overflowing vessel, for this reason I dabble in pagan culture, not simply its theoretical aspect but also its history and poetry.' One of his notes on the allegorical interpretation of Homer includes the remark: 'The customs of the Mysians and the Phrygians do not differ as much as the false Hellenic doctrine and our true one; and if someone converts their bitter salt water into the sweetness of our faith, he in my opinion is wise, indeed the noblest of the wise.' The object of the essay is explicitly stated to be that of changing a false pagan story into a Christian truth.[6] The metaphor of salt water recurs in the last chapter of the *De omnifaria doctrina*, where Greek culture is again recommended with reservations. Psellos is here speaking to the emperor, and discretion was in order. His concluding words are: 'You should know that the roses of Christian scripture are quite genuine, but others have a poisonous element in the flower.'[7]

In a letter to the future patriarch Xiphilinus Psellos affects a tone of injured innocence when he denies that he is totally under the influence of Plato.[8] But he protests too much to be entirely convincing. In the course of his reply to the charge he says that he is following the example of the great luminaries of the church, St. Basil and St. Gregory of Nazianzus, in accepting certain elements of pagan culture as valuable. The extent of Psellos' acquaintance with pagan literature, especially some unedifying types that had generally and with good reason earned the disapproval of orthodox members of the church, including almost certainly the eminent authorities whom Psellos cites in his own defence, suggests that his assertions should not be taken at their face value.

The conventional contrast between Christian and pagan does not do justice to the complexity of Psellos' intellectual outlook. He tells us that his curiosity extended to five cultures: Chaldean, Egyptian, Greek, Jewish and Christian.[9] The antiquity of Egyptian civilisation had soon been recognised by the Greeks, and from the time of Herodotus onwards never ceased to fascinate them. It was often debated whether Greece was indebted to Egypt. Psellos joins in the discussion. He believes that Pythagoras, apart from being the inventor of musical theory and the first person in Greece to maintain the immortality of the soul, introduced Egyptian culture into Greece.[10] Elsewhere, writing a brief note on Hermes Trismegistos, the putative author of the *Hermetica*, treatises on gnosticism, astrology, magic and alchemy, Psellos claims that Plato was wrong to assert that the Greeks borrowed ideas from foreign nations and improved them. Rather the Greeks were lazy in the pursuit of truth,

---

[6] Sathas, *Annuaire de l'association pour l'encouragement des études grecques dans la France* 9 (1875) 211-15.

[7] L.G. Westerink's edition (Nijmegen 1948), cap. 201, pages 98-9.

[8] Sathas 5.444-51 (more recently edited by U. Criscuolo (Naples 1973)).

[9] Kurtz-Drexl I 441; cf. Sathas 5.152-3.

[10] Kurtz-Drexl I 442.

especially truth about God. Intelligent Greeks realised this, as is shown by Porphyry in his *Letter to Anebo*.[11]

As will be seen shortly, Psellos is always open to the suspicion that he is making a great display of knowledge when his acquaintance with the primary source material is less extensive than he would like his readers to believe. How much he read on the subject of ancient Egypt is uncertain. He claims to have read Chaeremon, an author no longer extant who wrote on the history of Egypt and on hieroglyphics. Whether Psellos knew him at first hand or through quotations cannot now be determined. In another essay he says that he understood the symbolic meaning of hieroglyphs, without giving the name of his source; it may have been Chaeremon or the surviving book by Horapollon, but as John Tzetzes a century later claims to know Chaeremon, who is not cited by Horapollon, one may probably accept what Psellos says at face value.[12]

Alchemy might well have been included in the account of his debt to Egypt, since Zosimos of Panopolis can be regarded as its founder. Psellos certainly knew of Zosimos and refers to another Egyptian author, Theophrastus, but he thinks of it as 'the wisdom of Abdera', owing to the existence of some treatises falsely ascribed to Democritus, the philosopher of that city. His own involvement with the subject went far enough for him to compose a short essay on it, and his long denunciation of the patriarch Cerularius includes a charge of practising it.[13] Psellos gives the impression that he had personally visited practitioners of the art.

The Chaldean legacy consisted of astrology and magic. As far as the former is concerned, Psellos issued a brief denial of its validity on the ground that it conflicts with divine providence and free will.[14] That was the position adopted but not always successfully maintained by the church. With regard to magic, however, Psellos will have found it much harder to reconcile his professions of orthodoxy with an interest in a topic at best nonsensical and at worst sinister. He is evasive on this question. At one point he remarks: 'I will not tell you how to make charms that ward off illness; you might not imitate me correctly.'[15] What Chaldean wisdom meant to him was the collection, complete in his day, but now surviving only in fragments, known as the Chaldean oracles.[16] They are cast in the form of hexameter verses and are attributed to a certain Julian who lived in the Antonine age. If the attribution is correct they are as much a product of the Greco-Roman world as the Orient. They are concerned with theurgy, including prescriptions for a fire and sun cult and for the magical evocation of gods. Psellos wrote several essays about

---

[11] J.F. Boissonade, *Michael Psellus De operatione daemonum* (Nürnberg 1838) 153-4.

[12] Kurtz-Drexl I 444 and 370. Tzetzes' quotations occur in his exegesis of the *Iliad*.

[13] J. Bidez, *CatMssAlchGrecs* VI (Brussels 1928) 26-43 and 71-89 (cf. Kurtz-Drexl I 322).

[14] M.A. Šangin, *CatMssAlchGrecs* XII (Brussels 1936) 167.

[15] Kurtz-Drexl I 447.

[16] See the Budé edition by E. des Places (Paris 1971), esp. 46-52 and 153-6; also E.R. Dodds, *The Greeks and the Irrational* (Berkeley 1956) 283-9.

them. His interest in such matters is strange. It must be explained as a consequence of his Platonism. The Neoplatonists had openly admitted their belief in theurgy, and Proclus had written a commentary on the Chaldean oracles, which Psellos evidently used. He expresses elsewhere great admiration for this author (*Chronographia* 6.38). How he managed to avoid ecclesiastical and indeed general disapproval remains a mystery. It may not be entirely without significance that in his long speech of accusation against the patriarch Cerularios there is a charge of exploiting the techniques of theurgy. It is very doubtful whether one should give any credit to the accusation, but one may speculate that Psellos is replying to criticism of his own interests by suggesting that the church by its methods of dealing with paranormal phenomena lays itself open to unflattering comparisons. Psellos displays far more knowledge of the subject than was discreet, and fabricates a series of insinuations against his enemy, who had investigated, perhaps impartially and with a genuine concern for her well-being, the apparently prophetic utterances of a medium.[17]

Although Platonism as such could lead to a serious conflict with Christian doctrine because of the different view it took of the human soul, it was Neoplatonism which led Psellos into more dangerous areas of thought and seems to have interested him more. Another sign of its influence has been seen in an essay on demons, *De operatione daemonum*. Although there is reference to the Euchite and Manichaean heresies, this short treatise establishes a hierarchy of six categories of demons which derives rather from Pythagorean numerology, a fashion which Iamblichus and his school succeeded in imposing on Platonism. Porphyry is once again a source, and Psellos, if he is in fact the author, thinks of the subject as having its origin in Chaldean thought.[18] But recently his authorship has been denied, and one must hope the sceptical view is correct.

It is time to turn from pseudo-science to the products of a healthier imagination. While Psellos is notable for a curiosity extending to many subjects that scarcely deserved his attention and are not normally reckoned as parts of the classical heritage, he was also fully conversant with more conventional subjects of study. Not that the knowledge he imparted to his pupils was always accurate. For instance, when talking about the involvement of Plato and Aristotle in practical politics, of which his own double career as teacher and civil servant might seem a faint reflection, he makes bizarre statements about each of the ancient philosophers. According to Psellos Plato's stay in Syracuse enabled him to distribute the tyrant's treasures to many Academic and Stoic philosophers. In fact Plato's visits to Syracuse were notorious failures and the reference to Stoic philosophers is an anachronism which must be

---

[17] Kurtz-Drexl I 236 ff.

[18] Boissonade, op. cit. in n. 11 above; see also Bidez, op. cit. in n. 13 above, 97-113, esp. 100. Psellos' authorship is denied by P. Gautier, *REB* 38 (1980) 105-94.

regarded as serious even by the low standards to be expected from the Byzantines. This misconception is at once followed by another. Aristotle is said to have accompanied Alexander on his campaigns and to have been the master mind responsible for his military successes.[19]

The essay that reveals these alarming weaknesses of general knowledge is valuable for the account that Psellos gives of his teaching. He lists a series of topics and authors. It begins with Aristotle and continues with astronomy, geometry and arithmetic. All that is part of the standard programme of secondary education. Next he mentions optics and the study of mirrors. The texts implied are presumably those current under the name of Euclid, and it is quite possible that they were studied in conjunction with geometry. Then Psellos names Hero (of Alexandria) and Archimedes and claims personally to have done various experiments. The first involved siphoning of water, the second two liquids that do not mix. The third and fourth were demonstrations of models, one of an ox that drinks water, the other of a bird that sings and moves its wings. Finally he demonstrated the use of a mirror as a burning glass. Experiments of this kind were certainly unusual, but perhaps not quite as unusual as Psellos might have wished us to believe, and in particular one must doubt whether he can take much credit for the two models, as these mechanical toys are described in Hero's book *Pneumatica* (1.15, 2.32) and existed in the audience room of the imperial palace; Psellos may have done no more than ask the technicians to put on a display for his pupils.[20]

By no means all the instruction that he gave was formal, and he himself tells us of the other demands that were made on him.[21] He was asked to give advice on medical matters, law and geography. 'I never cease to allegorise the Greek myths', he adds. 'But still people tug and pull at me, loving to hear my voice above all others because I know more than everyone else.' Many of his writings are cast in the form of letters, which suggests that his wide circle of friends and admirers treated him as a brains trust.

In the use of allegory as the key to understanding Homer Psellos followed the practice that he admired so much in his friend the schoolmaster Nicetas. Several short pieces survive to demonstrate his ingenuity in this bizarre genre.[22] One deals with the cave of the nymphs at Ithaca, as described in *Odyssey* 13.102, and turns out to be little more than a précis of an essay on the same subject by Porphyry.[23] Another discusses the bow of the archer Pandaros, in terms which make it scarcely intelligible to a modern reader. A third deals with the famous puzzle of the Golden Chain (*Iliad* 8.19-27), which Nicetas had tried to solve. Psellos begins by saying that he has been asked to give an

[19] Kurtz-Drexl I 362.
[20] Ibid. 368.
[21] Sathas 5.60.
[22] Four are edited by Sathas, op. cit. in n. 6 above, 205-22.
[23] Boissonade, op. cit. in n. 11, 52-6.

allegorical interpretation of the passage and to convert a Greek mystery
into Christian terms. He asserts that Homer knew the Orphic mysteries
and 'does not reveal naked truth but wraps it in the dung of myth'.
Psellos names as sources Iamblichus, Proclus, Porphyry and the Julians
who lived in the time of Marcus Aurelius, saying that they were the
Greeks best versed in theology. In the *Iliad* passage Zeus has to be
interpreted as The One, while the golden chain is a symbol of the links
and connections between the other gods. Stranger still is the treatment of
the first four lines of *Iliad* 4, where the gods sit with Zeus, having their
cups filled with nectar by Hebe, toasting each other and looking down on
Troy. Once again Psellos makes it explicit that his purpose is to convert a
false Greek myth into Christian truth. Zeus' name is derived from the
word for life (ζωή). 'Life and the steward of life – who can that be except
the universal God, the God who said in the Gospels "I am the truth and
the life"?' Who are the gods who sit by Zeus? 'Who else but those who
have first and immediate priority of existence, whether one calls them
Cherubim or powers or rulers or authorities or liturgical spirits sent to
serve, for the benefit of those who are to inherit the kingdom, spirits who,
just as they share to the full in all his wonders, so too his name. For God
is not jealous of those who wish to be marked by his greatness ... ' 'Troy is
the state of this world, contemptuous of intellectual beauty, seizing upon
the perceptible and much talked of form of Helen, which is a deception
and a falsehood, and then making war in order to keep it ... ' Hector and
the Trojan horse are explained with the help of pseudo-etymology and a
pun.

There is also a brief note on Circe and her attempt to metamorphose
Odysseus and his companions into pigs (*Odyssey* 10.316ff). Circe, we
are told, is to be interpreted as pleasure. She offers men a draught which
causes them to forget themselves. Their souls drink a potion of sin.
Finally there are two notes on famous figures of Greek mythology, the
Sphinx and Tantalus. Tantalus the son of Zeus is mentioned at the
beginning of Euripides' *Orestes* (5ff), and it is no doubt this passage
which spurred a friend or pupil to ask for an interpretation. Psellos
spends some time on the meaning of Zeus, coming to the same conclusion
as he had in the other essay referred to already, and then he passes to
Tantalus, of whom Euripides says 'fearing the rock that rises above his
head he floats in the air'. Psellos thinks he should be taken to be ethereal
fire. As for the Sphinx, she represents the composition of mankind from
three diverse elements, bestial, human and divine. In this essay one may
note in passing a factual error: Psellos says that the Eleusinian mysteries
occurred only at intervals, not every year, in order that their secrets
should not be divulged to too wide a public.[24]

Since it will be more convenient to consider Psellos' handling of other
literary texts in a separate section, we can now deal with the question

[24] These three pieces are printed as an appendix to Boissonade's edition of Tzetzes'
Allegoriae Iliadis (Paris 1851) 343-65.

whether he was able to read much more classical literature than is available to us today. His remarks have to be interpreted with care. When he quotes from book XVII of Theopompus he would probably like us to infer that his acquaintance with the text was direct. But we can tell that he derived his knowledge from Athenaeus' *Deipnosophistae*. Nevertheless he had access to the fuller version of the first two books of Athenaeus, now missing from the Venice manuscript and known from the epitome generally attributed to Eustathius.[25] A similar explanation will presumably account for his boast of having read the poems of Parmenides and Empedocles.[26] There are substantial fragments of these presocratic philosophers embedded in Simplicius' commentaries on Aristotle, which Psellos might well have been able to lay his hands on. More notorious is his allusion to Menander, Archilochus and Sappho.[27] Here there is no difficulty in defending him from a charge of falsehood. All that he says is that he explains to some of his pupils who various Greek authors were. There is no suggestion that he had the texts in the classroom. It was once believed that he knew a lost work by the physician Galen, but closer examination of his wording proves that the reference is in fact to Aristotle.[28]

Apart from the Chaldean Oracles and some Neoplatonic writings Psellos knew little more of Greek literature than we do. A brief essay on rhetoric cites verbatim fragments from Longinus, the ill-fated prime minister of queen Zenobia of Palmyra, who is best known from the pages of Gibbon's *Decline and Fall*, partly because in the eighteenth century he was still believed to be the author of the essay *On the Sublime*. Psellos evidently knew more of the genuine Longinus than we do.[29] There is also evidence that he knew the obscure chronographer Julius Africanus.[30] But is difficult to acquit him entirely of a desire to suggest that he knew more than he had actually read. Some of his opuscula turn out to be nothing more than a reworking of a classical text: examples are the essay on the cave of the nymphs at Ithaca, various philosophical essays exploiting Neoplatonic literature, a note on electrum, which comes from Ctesias via codex 72 of Photius' *Bibliotheca*, and another on a series of place names in Attica, which derives from Strabo 9.1-2.[31] In these cases he does not acknowledge his sources. It is also a serious weakness that his technique of abridgment has been found hasty and slapdash.[32] The verdict on his reading and his accuracy cannot be as favourable as one would like, given that he has been described as the most interesting and important

---

[25] P. Maas, *Kleine Schriften* (Munich 1973) 475-6.

[26] Sathas 5.57.

[27] Ibid. 59.

[28] P. Maas, *BZ* 34 (1934) 402.

[29] P. Gautier, *Prometheus* 3 (1977) 193-203.

[30] A. Westermann, *Paradoxographi graeci* (Leipzig 1839) 146.12-13.

[31] Boissonade, op. cit. in n. 11; D.J. O'Meara, *AJP* 102 (1981) 26-40, esp. 33; Maas, op. cit. in n. 25.

[32] Gautier and O'Meara, op. cit. in nn. 29 and 31; also G. Aujac, *REB* 33 (1975) 257-75.

personality in the whole of Byzantine history.

Psellos' influence is difficult to estimate accurately. In his own day he must have been something of a magnet. According to one of his letters students came from many foreign countries to listen to him. He mentions Celts, Arabs, Persians, Egyptians and Ethiopians.[33] While modesty and a love of unembroidered truth were not part of his character, this remarkable claim, which no other Byzantine ever made, has some basis. Whereas leading participants in theological controversy with the Roman church could become known in the west, Psellos' reputation as a polymath lecturer made him famous elsewhere. Among his pupils was a Georgian called Petritsi, who translated into his own language Josephus, Proclus' *Elements of Theology* and Nemesius' *De natura hominis*. The choice of a text by Proclus is no surprise considering the nature of Psellos' interests, and the *Elements* is a systematic treatment of the whole Neoplatonist system of metaphysics. The Georgian version is believed to have served in its turn as the basis for one in Armenian.[34]

Whether Psellos can have had any more direct influence in Armenia is uncertain. It has been suggested that he had a part in stimulating the translation of Plato into Armenian by Gregorius Magister (*c.* 990-*c.* 1058).[35] The evidence about Gregory is not sufficiently clear to permit the assertion with any confidence. Although he spent some time in Constantinople during the reign of Constantine Monomachus, the difficulty in believing that he was a pupil of Psellos is that he returned to his family estates in 1048, when Psellos was aged thirty and probably only just beginning to make his mark. One of Gregorius' letters informs us that his translations of Plato included the *Timaeus* and *Phaedo*, and that he had begun work on Euclid. In addition he gives a curious fact which is worth a moment's digression. He claims to have found that Armenian versions already existed of Olympiodorus' philosophical commentaries, Callimachus and Andronicus. From the context one would be inclined to infer that the last of these authors is the Rhodian head of the Peripatos who began the tradition of commentaries on Aristotle *c.* 70 B.C.. But no genuine work by him survives in Greek, and it is not very plausible to imagine that it was translated into Armenian. As to Callimachus, it is difficult to suppose that his poems can have been a suitable choice for anyone wishing to present Greek culture to a foreign audience, and it is not much more likely that the section on philosophy from his bibliographical guide to Greek literature had survived.[36]

It is also possible that we should see Psellos' influence in the report

[33] Sathas 5.508.

[34] E.R. Dodds, *Proclus; the Elements of Theology* (ed. 2, Oxford 1963) xli-xlii, 342-4; M. Tarchnishvili, *Geschichte der kirchlichen georgischen Literatur* (*Studi e Testi* 185) (Rome 1955) 211-25.

[35] R. Klibansky, *The Continuity of the Platonic Tradition* (London 1939, revised reprint Munich 1981) 20.

[36] M. Leroy, *Annuaire de l'Institut de philosophie et d'histoire orientale* 3 (1935) 263-94 (cf. also *BZ* 36 (1936) 189-90).

given by two historians (Attaleiates 110.19 and Scylitzes Continuatus 129.6) that one of the leading figures in Antioch during the reign of Romanus Diogenes (1067-71) was Peter Libellisios (or Libellios),[37] 'a man of Syrian stock who was fully at home in Roman and Saracen culture'. 'Saracen' is the adjective used by Attaleiates, 'Assyrian' is given by the other, slightly later, source. The imprecision implicit in Byzantine classicising language makes it hard to translate the phrase exactly. 'Assyrian' if taken literally would imply Syriac culture, and it is difficult to believe that a leading resident of Antioch did not speak Syriac; but the adjective is used by classical historians, whereas 'Saracen' is not, which tilts the balance in favour of treating the latter as the more accurate description. Psellos himself claims that his audience included Arabs. If Peter was a Christian Arab Psellos was perhaps referring to him. One other curious fact should be mentioned in this context: a Greek gnomology translated into Syriac turns out to contain a quotation from Psellos.[38]

Contact with the East, particularly if promoted by someone with the open mind of John Italos, should have been beneficial to Byzantium in scientific fields. There are slight indications that astronomy did so benefit. A note written originally in 1032 and now found in an important codex of Ptolemy's *Almagest* (Vat. gr. 1594) draws comparisons between the *Almagest* and *Handy Tables* on the one hand and the work of Ibn al-A'lam on the other.[39] That is too early to be the product of Psellos and his circle; it shows that there was already contact between specialists in Byzantium and elsewhere. One cannot tell whether it was the same specialists or Psellos and his circle who were responsible for a treatise composed *c.* 1060-72 (now found in Paris gr. 2425); this draws on Arabic astronomy.[40] There is one clear indication that relations between Byzantine scientists and their eastern colleagues were not of the closest: at this date there is no sign that the Byzantines were using Arabic numerals.

These questions might be nearer to a solution if we knew more of the career of Symeon Seth, a native of Antioch who held an official rank at the court in Constantinople and translated the story of Kalila and Dimna from Arabic into Greek. This work is addressed to Alexius Comnenus. He also wrote on medicine, dedicating a short dictionary of foodstuffs to Michael Ducas, and is presumably the person mentioned by Anna Comnena (*Alexiad* 6.7) as a mathematician and astronomer. Very little else is known about him, except that he made a visit to Egypt *c.* 1058, when he observed an eclipse.[41]

Even if we take an optimistic view of Psellos' influence during his own

[37] The form Libellisios receives some support from the evidence cited by G. Weiss, *Byzantina* 4 (1972) 13 n. 9.

[38] C.E. Sachau, *Syriaca inedita* (Halle 1870) vii.

[39] J. Mogenet, *Osiris* 14 (1962) 198-221.

[40] O. Neugebauer, *Mémoires de l'Académie royale de Belgique* 59 (4) 1969.

[41] L.-O. Sjöberg, *Stephanites und Ichnelates* (Stockholm 1962) 87-99.

lifetime, it did not last. The condemnation of his enthusiastic pupil Italos signified the reassertion of ecclesiastical power and the suspension of freedom of thought. As to Psellos' writings, although they appear to have enjoyed great popularity, the fact is that the majority survive in one or two copies only. This is true even of his masterpiece the *Chronographia*, whereas other history books were recopied frequently. In other words his work suffered the same fate as that of the average Byzantine author. The main exception is that his more conventional and unadventurous lectures on Aristotle seem to have been found useful by successive generations of students; they probably held their own until the end of the thirteenth century, when similar textbooks by Nicephorus Blemmydes replaced them. It is perhaps worth adding that his collection of the Chaldean Oracles was of some importance to the most original and eccentric figure produced by Byzantium in the fifteenth century, George Gemistos Plethon.

By way of appendix, although there is no positive evidence of a link with Psellos, one should mention two manuscripts of some note written while he was at the height of his career. The Towneley Homer (British Library, Burney 86) was for a long time rated more highly than it deserved as a source of the scholia on the *Iliad*. In fact it is only one of several copies of the so-called exegetical scholia which emphasise the ethical content of Homer and do not preserve much valuable ancient learning. The Towneley Homer has a colophon, now damaged, which seems originally to have included the date 1059.[42] From the year 1063 we have a copy of Isocrates (Vat. gr. 65), which in date and importance as a witness to the text is second only to the Urbinas (cf. above, p. 136). Both these books exemplify a new tendency in handwriting, a more cursive style which is often found in copies of pagan texts and suggests that the copyists were scholars writing for their own personal use.[43]

(v)   Some critical essays on Christian authors

If philosophy was the field to which Psellos gave his best energies, he did not lack the ability to read and enjoy literature. We have seen his approach to Homer, which does not inspire confidence in the quality of his response to other texts, and it is legitimate to ask whether he had any liking for texts outside the normal range read either in the schools or by a cultivated adult with a taste for the classics of patristic literature. Seven of his essays help to provide the answer to this question. They consist of one on a Byzantine author, three on fathers of the church, in which there are some comparisons between them and authors of pagan antiquity, and three on pagan authors. Of these last three one includes an autobiographical account of his own formation as a writer, the second

---

[42] *Pace* H. Erbse, *Scholia graeca in Iliadem* I (Berlin 1969) xxvi n. 28, the script is scarcely consistent with the theoretical alternative date of 1014.

[43] N.G. Wilson in *La paléographie grecque et byzantine, Actes du Colloque No. 559* (Paris 1977) 221-40, esp. 223.

compares and contrasts two Greek novels, and the third, which is the only one to deal with poetry, compares Euripides with the early Byzantine author George of Pisidia. It will be best to deal with these texts in the order just given.

The essay devoted to a Byzantine author is an encomium of Symeon Metaphrastes, whose career is probably to be placed in the second half of the tenth century. His great work had been to revise the lives of the saints. Many of these were written in a plain style, sometimes very close to the spoken language, and so were no longer acceptable to the fastidious educated reader. Symeon recast the text in a polished form, which won general admiration. The result was that his recensions were adopted by the church and displaced the previous texts, which almost disappeared from circulation. Psellos makes it clear that Symeon had a staff of shorthand writers, scribes and correctors made available to him by order of the emperor in order to facilitate his enormous task. 'What could one compare with such an enterprise?' asks Psellos, and with typical hyperbole he continues: 'What Greek antiquarian lore or survey of the whole world? The successes of the Persians and before them the Babylonians, after that the noble exploits of Alexander of Macedon? These too are worthy topics, especially for eloquent stylists, but most people read them for the literary skill of their authors. On the other hand all the works of the noble Symeon, describing in appropriate language the martyrs and saints, have two purposes, the imitation of fine style and the formation of character by the best models. I would add a third, no less important than the others but more specific and elevated: for those who support the message of the Gospels the written memorial of the saints is the foundation of other achievements.' Psellos in fact concedes that even Symeon does not satisfy the most demanding critics of style, and he does not think Symeon should be compared with pagan writers in this respect. 'I do not think it right to compare his efforts with those of pagan sages. What if the latter composed Panathenaic orations, or described the war between the Peloponnesians and the Athenians in pompous language? Others wrote pleas for and against the art of rhetoric. In all of them skill is clear and obvious, but the useful element is small and feeble. These are not the authors against whom I would choose to set my hero as a rival. Rather, if the chance were offered, would I put him in the same class as those who have studied the message of the Gospels and interpreted the profundity of the divine word.'[1]

Of the three essays on patristic authors the first is a short defence of St. John Chrysostom against the criticism that his writings display no rhetorical skill. Psellos begins his defence by drawing a distinction between two types of rhetoric, the one exaggerated, the other modest and orderly. Chrysostom is an example of the latter, and he would be the example par excellence had he not been preceded by such models of the

[1] Kurtz-Drexl I 94-107; the key passages are 101.10-23, 105.16-27, 106.7-18.

simple style as Lysias, Isaeus, Plato and Dio. (It is surprising to see Plato in this company, and one of the two manuscripts of this essay in fact omits both his name and that of Dio.) Nevertheless Chrysostom is much superior to his predecessors. Psellos notes that despite having to treat similar topics on many occasions he manages to achieve variety. His proems are exactly right for someone with a didactic purpose and bring him immediately into the best relation with his audience. The narratives are neither too short nor too long, and the digressions are better controlled than in Herodotus. Stylistic success is achieved by the simplest language, and merely gives the impression of unstudied writing. A reference to criticisms levelled at Euripides and Thucydides follows, but Psellos' exact point is unclear and the text is perhaps corrupt. The essay as a whole, though correct in its implicit contrast between Chrysostom and some of the more elaborate patristic writers, suffers from a total absence of citations from or references to specific passages.[2]

Next we may deal with another short piece on the style of John Chrysostom and the three Cappadocian fathers of the fourth century. This turns out to be a reply to the question 'Which Christian writers deserve to be compared for their literary merits to Lysias and Demosthenes?' The answer is that many Christian writers are excellent, but there are four outstanding authors who deserve to be put on a par with the best pagans, whom they surpass in some but not all respects. The qualification in this last phrase is emphasised by the parenthesis 'the truth has to be admitted'. Psellos observes that many people are capable of seeing the merits of the pagans but are unwilling to admit their literary value out of dislike for their beliefs. He goes on to say that the best authors in their respective spheres are Demosthenes and Gregory of Nazianzus, the former especially in deliberative and judicial oratory. A eulogy of Gregory then follows, mentioning his resemblance to some of the best pagans, principally Aristides. This admiration for the second-century sophist, most of whose work is dull and unimportant, is typically Byzantine. Other pagans whom Gregory resembles are Lysias, because he sometimes wishes to write a simple proem, Thucydides, Isocrates and Herodotus. The last name in the list is a surprise, and Psellos does not add any comment in justification. He draws an analogy between Gregory's style and the mixing of colours on an artist's palette, where the blend produces something more attractive than any of the constituents. Psellos also likens him to a lion.

Having given three pages to him Psellos devotes slightly less than one page to each of the other fathers under discussion. St. Basil earns a comparison with Demosthenes and Aristides. His brother Gregory of Nyssa is similar; while his oratory is not as good as that of Basil, his exposition of scripture is superior. On Chrysostom Psellos adds nothing to what is said in the essay devoted entirely to him. Apart from the

---

[2] Edited from Paris gr. 1182 and Oxford Auct. T. 1.11 by P. Levy, *Michaelis Pselli de Gregorii theologi charactere iudicium* (Leipzig 1912) 92-8.

assertion that pagan authors are not outclassed in all respects by the Christians the essay contains little of interest. It is too brief to permit detailed discussion and does not refer to the texts in order to justify any of its propositions.[3]

Pride of place among the essays on patristic subjects must go to a study of Gregory of Nazianzus, which had the distinction of being copied in at least nine manuscripts.[4] It has also achieved a modest fame in modern scholarly literature because of a passage cited by Eduard Norden in order to show that the unusual sensitivity of Mediterranean peoples in antiquity to the sound of language was not lost in the middle ages.[5] It is worth giving an extended résumé, because there are many references to classical authors and a good deal of the critical terminology is borrowed from Dionysius of Halicarnassus and other classical critics.

The opening paragraph is chiefly designed to make the point that Gregory is a model of all the stylistic virtues. Previous critics have had to illustrate these by citing one famous author as an instance of each. Psellos refers to various rare or lost authors as if they were still extant. Our suspicions must be aroused by mention of Aeschines Socraticus, and a few lines later there is talk of Polemon, Herodes Atticus and Lollianus. Of these representatives of the second sophistic age the last is no longer extant, and the reference to all three is most likely to derive from Philostratus' *Lives of the Sophists*. Psellos must have assumed that none of his friends and pupils could prick the bubble of his pretensions, but they make a bad start to the essay. The alternative proposition that all these authors were still available to be read by Psellos would preserve his credit but is implausible in the extreme.

There follows an obscure paragraph on the divine source of Gregory's supreme excellence. One fact is however clear beyond doubt: he did not achieve his excellence by the usual method of imitating stylistic models. Psellos expresses his admiration:

> For my part, every time I read him, and I often have occasion to do so, chiefly for his teaching but secondarily for his literary charm, I am filled with a beauty and grace that cannot be expressed. And frequently I abandon my intention, and neglecting his theological meaning I spend my time as it were among the spring flowers of his diction and am carried away by my senses. Realising that I have been carried off I then love and take delight in my captor. And if I am forced away from his words back to the meaning, I regret not being carried off once more and lament the gain as a deprivation. The beauty of his words is not of the type practised by the duller sophists, epideictic and aimed at an audience, by which one might be charmed at first and then at the second contact repelled – for those orators did not smooth the unevenness of their lips and were not afraid to rely on boldness of diction rather than skill. But his art is not of that kind, far from it; instead it has the harmony of music.

[3] Edited by Boissonade, op. cit. in n. 11 to section (iv), 124-31.
[4] Edited by A. Mayer, *BZ* 20 (1911) 27-100 (text on 48-60) and P. Levy, op. cit. in n. 2.
[5] E. Norden, *Antike Kunstprosa* (reprinted Darmstadt 1958) I 5, II 568.

The words he uses, Psellos continues, may be compared to stones with various properties. The classification which follows looks as if it is borrowed from Demetrius *On Style* 176, but once again Psellos adds a touch of specious learning. Gregory's vocabulary is 'not like that of Thucydides the son of Olorus or Nicetas of Smyrna or Scopelianus, it is that of Lysias the Athenian and Isocrates and Demosthenes, Aeschines Socraticus and Plato himself. I will not mention men like Sopater and Phoenix and all the others who achieved the status of sophists through the vulgarity of their style.' Psellos' acquaintance with Nicetas, Scopelianus and Phoenix will almost certainly have been limited to what is said about them by Philostratus, *Lives of the Sophists* 1.19 and 21, 2.22, while he may not have known either of the two extant authors called Sopater except through the mention of one of them in Eunapius' *Lives of the Sophists* 12.16, 21.2.

In the next paragraph a large number of other critics are named, beginning with Dionysius and Theophrastus, of whom Psellos could have had some indirect knowledge through a passage now missing from one of Dionysius' essays. The same type of explanation will account for a reference to Longinus, but not for one to Chrysippus the Stoic philosopher, still less for a confused passage in which orators of the second sophistic age are named as if they were critics. Psellos acknowledges that most critics lived too early to be able to read Gregory, but professes himself astonished that a pagan contemporary, Eunapius, should make no allusion to him, and that Philostorgius has nothing better to say of him than that the rhythmical movement of his prose was superior. Philostorgius was an Arian heretic who wrote a church history, and what Psellos reports of his judgment on Gregory can be traced in the surviving epitome and is confirmed in essence by Photius, *Bibliotheca* 40: 'Despite his ravings against the orthodox he did not dare to attack Gregory the theologian, but acknowledged unwillingly his educated manner.'

The central section of the essay follows the lead of Dionysius by discussing the selection and ordering of words. The task of the literary artist is compared at length to that of a jeweller working with a large number of stones. Lysias, Isocrates, Demosthenes and particularly Herodotus are successful in choosing ordinary words and blending them in such a way that they outdo their rivals. Gregory has the same gift with simple unpretentious words. 'I cannot trace the means by which his extraordinary beauty of style is regularly achieved; I merely sense them, the experience cannot be rationally explained. But when I trace his methods and establish them as the cause of his excellence, I see other sources from which grace flows into his writings.' These turn out to be features affecting whole sentences – the construction and articulation, the rhythms used, including those of the clausulae. Gregory compares favourably in this respect with the pagan writers cited a little earlier and with Plato. While the theological content of his oratory is constant, there is nothing monotonous about the rhythms employed in his clausulae.

Although he exploits rhythm to the utmost, he does not depart from prose. Whatever he said immediately took on a rhetorical character, even if he made no effort to that end, but he did not think of rhetoric and philosophy as being separated by a gulf. His work is ornamented by a display of knowledge resulting from wide reading. But when he has to explain a complicated or technical matter he is able to do so in a way which the average listener can understand. Psellos regards him as superior in this respect to Plato, who is unduly long in his exposition and disguises the significance of some of his propositions. He also states that Gregory does not employ the technique seen in Plutarch's *Lives*, where political questions are inappropriately illustrated by analogies from music and geometry.

Psellos then returns to stylistic criticism. Gregory's strength is his ability to vary style according to the occasion.

> He is at his most successful in panegyrics. Whereas Isocrates, Plato and Demosthenes could be compared with his other writings, in the panegyric he has no rival. And this genre is really much harder than the others. That is why Demosthenes and other writers, earlier and later, have shown themselves to be most versatile and productive in judicial and deliberative oratory, while in panegyric all have failed to a greater or lesser degree. Plato is a fine writer when he examines the forms in his *Parmenides* or discusses the manifold nature of the beautiful in the *Phaedrus* or philosophises about the soul in the *Phaedo*, but he is not the same when he composes his funeral oration. Demosthenes, when he indicts Stephanus for perjury and Aeschines for the false embassy, when he defends his golden crown, when he arranges his speeches on the subject of Olynthus and breathes fire against Philip, is not inferior to the triumpet of Olympia; his workmanship is rich and he organises his methods of argumentation as he wishes. But when he ventured to give a panegyric on those who had fallen in the war, he suffered a metamorphosis as great as Arceisius. Thucydides is a profound thinker, especially in his speeches, compressing his concepts together one after the other, but he too in producing a funeral oration changes style and falls far short of his usual power.

The judgments given in this paragraph are all in their different ways revealing. What is said of Plato's *Menexenus* may surprise us at first if we think of the very great admiration Psellos had for Plato. But as the present essay itself shows in the concluding paragraphs, admiration need not be uncritical to the point of allowing no reservations. Psellos did not resort to, and perhaps did not have the mental agility to formulate, the defence which has commended itself to a number of modern scholars, namely to argue that the *Menexenus* is a satirical parody. With regard to Demosthenes' *Epitaphios*, one may well ask why Psellos did not avail himself of Dionysius' judgment (*Demosthenes* 44) that it is spurious. More extraordinary and disappointing is that he should be unable to appreciate Thucydides' very different contribution to this genre. It is also typical of him to produce an allusion to an exceptionally obscure myth in which a bear was metamorphosed into a human being.[6]

Further praise of Gregory follows. Psellos appears to make only one reservation, and as there is a gap in the text here his meaning is not easy to interpret, but the point at issue is a certain lack of emotional quality. There is one further matter which puzzles Psellos: despite the great clarity of his style Gregory needs some explanation by commentators, a task to which Psellos himself contributed. Obscurity in other writers can be accounted for. Psellos does not exploit the solution he could have borrowed from Dionysius (*De Lysia* 4), who drew a contrast between stylistic and factual clarity and noted that writers of the greatest descriptive powers leave much unclear and in need of explanation.

The foregoing summary may not give a correct impression of the original. Although some passages can be translated into modern English without grave distortion or uncertainty about the meaning, there are others where florid diction or abstruse technical terms put an acceptable version beyond the reach of the translator. I have done my best to convey the enthusiasm of the medieval critic and the way he approached his favourite patristic author, which in turn throws light on his appreciation of some of the leading pagan classics.

(vi)   Response to the classics of pagan literature

The first of the essays to be discussed under this heading is a very short piece of advice to aspiring writers, in which Psellos explains the secret of his own success in a revealing passage of autobiography.[1] Although the circumstances which provoked him to write this essay are not clear, it would seem that he was asked to say why certain kinds of classical bellelettristic writing are bad models of style. The authors named are two novelists, Heliodorus and Achilles Tatius, and two Atticists of the second sophistic age, Lucian and Philostratus. All these works might seem frivolous, but it will be remembered that all were read by Photius, and as far as can be seen they continued to give pleasure to readers. Psellos admits that he had made the mistake of concentrating on these authors, but came to realise that it was like trying to run before one can walk. He turned instead to more serious literature in order to improve his style. The full text reads as follows (queries mark points where the meaning is in doubt):

> Readers of the book about Leucippe or Charicleia or any other that gives pleasure and has charm, such as the writings of Philostratus of Lemnos and all Lucian's relaxed and playful works, seem like men undertaking to build a house. But before laying the foundations, designing and setting up the walls and supports, and completing the roof, they seem to want to adorn it

---

[6] *Etymologicum Magnum* 144.22.
[1] Boissonade, op. cit. in n. 11 to section (iv), 48-52.

with paintings, mosaics and other forms of decoration. In the opinion of the majority such attempts are successful. Yet I think some have set themselves to write little books that are extravagant in language. Right from the starting point they thunder and make a powerful impact, then like the flash of lightning they are suddenly extinguished. In letters and some short addresses a style of that kind can be effective, because in such works the arrangement of the parts of the text is on a small scale, and the undemanding listener is satisfied with the obvious graces of style and the fine flowers of diction. In formal writings, however, where the argument must take many turns and make clear the ability of the author, these writers run short of the diction which as if it were springtime pours a honeyed sound into the ears. For not every style is one of grace. And just as some parts of a text must be sweetened, so others need to be made rough; just as some must be solemn, so others need to be simpler; just as some require intensity, accumulation and closely packed thought, others call for relaxation and ease. The accurate handling of style is a complex matter. It is the opposite of an initiation. There the preliminaries and sprinklers of holy water come first, after them one enters the inner sanctum, and it is necessary to carry the torch first as a worshipper in order to become a priest later. Here, if anyone wishes to become a complete master of accurate and skilful style, he should first deal with the beehive and only then go to the flowers.

I myself at first tried this method and flitted over such books as yield a dew or patina (?) or a flower that can be harvested and collected. But when my labours did not go according to plan (?), and I could not even run a short race but was out of breath just after the start, I turned to a better and more legitimate method.

So letting the Graces slip out of my hands I devoted myself to the Muses, not rejecting any of them, neither the patron of prose nor Calliope herself. Among such books Demosthenes, Isocrates, Aristides and Thucydides were specially important to me. I also included in my list Plato's dialogues, all Plutarch's works, everything of Lysias that could be found, and as a Christian author Gregory the theologian, whom I regard as the leader of all authors distinguished for serious and graceful writing.

From Demosthenes I gathered the intellectual power applied to each topic and the best arrangement of the parts of the sentence. From Isocrates natural style, the charm of mature years and ordinary vocabulary. From Aristides the pleasantness that richly suffuses his forcefulness, the accuracy of his reasoning, the very fruitful elaboration of his materials and thoughts. From Thucydides innovations in diction, tightly packed meaning, ungraceful but intellectual quality, composition (?) which is not revolutionary, variety in the formulation of his thoughts. Plutarch traversed all the graces of words, all notions expressed in periodic and vigorous form; and he charmed me by his simple narrative and the variation by which he explained an idea in an alternative manner. The arts of Lysias I used as a tool (?) for handling every composition. But in all respects the Muse, lyre, charm, trumpet and thunderous voice of the theologian satisfied me more than any other. Whenever I wanted to create obscurity and pack the meaning more tightly in what I was writing, I found sufficient guidance for this in Thucydides' speeches. In the arrangement of material and technical disposition I took the artistry of Demosthenes as a model. The style of Isocrates made it possible for me to give a natural exposition of the matter in hand, without any oddities that would have resulted in unconventional concepts. Plato was divine but difficult to imitate; what seemed to him accessible through his command of clarity (?), to me was lofty and precipitous. Those who compare him to Lysias and Thucydides and try to make him inferior to them seem to me to have read him in the wrong spirit. And if Gregory, great in virtue and in eloquence, did not stand on the other side in opposition, I should regard Plato, as far as his literary merits are concerned, as incomparable among philosophers and orators.

When I had had enough of these writers and needed some charm to add to grandeur, only then did I add to my collection of stylistic equipment the novels about Charicleia and Leucippe and all similar literature. If I am to reveal my personal opinion, I fall short of the merit and power of my various models, but my writing is decorated by all of them and their individual contributions blend into a single style. I am one, the product of many; if someone reads my books, may the one be turned into many.

It would be wrong to pretend that the comments given here are original or enlightening about the authors in question or that they match the level reached in Photius' *Bibliotheca*. On the other hand Psellos' aim was to explain how they might be exploited rather than give a full account of their merits. We may note in passing his reference to the need for obscurity, a point which arose in connection with Arethas and will recur in a controversy of the early fourteenth century. The meaning of the last sentence appears to be that he hopes for many readers who will in turn be inspired by him as a model.

Psellos makes a greater critical effort in his comparison of the two ancient novels, which enjoyed a much greater popularity in Byzantium than the other representatives of the genre, including Longus' *Daphnis and Chloe*, which has usually found more favour with modern readers.[2]

I know that many people, even some of the very well educated, argue about these two love stories, of which one concerns Charicleia, the other Leucippe, both girls of sophisticated appearance and very superior character. One group is unanimous in saying that the novel about Charicleia is better than the treatment of Leucippe's love, others on the contrary that the first is inferior to the second. I, having read both books, and studied accurately their diction and their content, do not agree with any of those who have formed a judgment of this type and abruptly declared themselves against one or the other. I have come to the view that each of the books is inferior and superior to the other in certain respects, but that the one about Charicleia is on the whole better.

For the beauty of the story about her is not entirely embellishment or pretension, nor again is it hyperattic (?) and arrogant; instead it is distinguished by its elevation. Nor is it devoid of a pleasant quality. It is decorated with dainty and beautiful words and by variation of figures, and by the novelty of the diction it is raised to a higher plane. It is finished most

[2] Text printed in Colonna's edition of Heliodorus 364-5 and Vilborg's of Achilles Tatius 166-7.

gracefully and is given life by unexpected and intense (?) ideas, and it is organised according to the precepts of Isocrates and Demosthenes. For interruptions to the narrative seem to be controlled from a distance and a conflicting element is brought back in a direct line to the main story (?).

Certainly the reader who at first finds most of the narrative too complicated will, as the story unfolds, come to admire the writer's command of the plot. And the very beginning of the book resembles the coils of a snake. Snakes hide their head inside their coils, putting the rest of their body in front; similarly this book, as if assigning the beginning of the plot to the middle into which it slips, brings the middle of the story to the beginning.

The narrative luxuriates with every flower of grace and is agreeable by virtue of the vocabulary and the eloquence of the writer. It is beautiful in its stateliness and because it seems as if most of it were composed in elevated metrical diction. It is also adorned with adventitious tales which breathe as one might say the charm of Aphrodite. The author has an elegance of expression which charms the reader's avid ears and is poetically elaborate without lapsing into vulgarity. He has solidity and as it were an epic quality diffused over his work by his eloquence.

What I know most people criticise (I mean in Charicleia), namely that the author does not make her speak like a woman or in feminine style, but her tongue rises to undue heights of sophistry contrary to the principles of art (?), this I personally cannot find words to praise adequately. The author does not introduce her as an ordinary girl but as an initiate of the Pythian god himself, so that most of her laments are oracular and she is inspired in the same way as seers by ecstasy; she is entirely the servant of Apollo's tripod and cauldron.

The author gives quite appropriate treatment to the other characters as well. As to the bizarre features of the story, which one cannot overlook, he is able to show by the good taste of his description that they are better when narrated than when performed. For instance he clears the old man Calasiris from the charge of acting as a go-between, which seems scarcely credible until our author with his manifold skills refutes the apparent guilt. What is more amazing is that in such a voluptuous and languid book he has preserved the solidity and as it were the courage of morality, and having once attracted Charicleia's character to a love of beauty he has preserved her from vulgar love, since even in defeat she does not shake off the restraints of morality.

I see that the book also touches on matters of learning, since topics of science are introduced, maxims are coined, theology is discussed, and so are some questions about the movements of the sphere ... [3] For I think, if I may use a pagan expression, that not all the figures tend to this one objective, but that the author is also close in style to the public speeches of Demosthenes, with bacchic rites and the resulting inspiration. The book also shows consideration for the reader, refreshing him with variety, newly coined words, incidents and melodramatic episodes. It contains maxims, as many as I have met in any book, and to put it briefly it is compounded of grace and charm that possess beauty mixed with sweetness. One could not find this in any other book.

---

[3] Here I omit two lines of Greek which I cannot understand.

I think that the book of Leucippe was written in polished imitation of Charicleia. But the prose, like a painter, has not transferred all the features of the original picture to its own style. It falls short in some respects, but is more sweet in its phrasing. Not giving any thought to grandeur, it is clearer because it falls short of that ideal, and is more agreeable because of the vocabulary, which is very ordinary and altogether unpretentious (?). Most readers' ears do not take delight in books because of their colloquial manner but welcome them avidly if delight in the style puts them in good humour. The author tries to elevate himself in some places, but he is like a man with arthritis; he quickly forgets the correct stylistic tone and goes back to his normal habits. For this reason he seems generally to be commonplace in his style and to fall some way short of Attic correctness.

The book is not bold in its subject matter nor does it introduce adventurous subjects; it treats events naturally, adhering to the chronological sequence. It merits the epithet pellucid, in that it makes language serve meaning and prefers the normal to the novel. When he rises to oratory his art is very open to criticism, neglecting forcefulness and the means of attaining it, but aspiring here to beauty of composition and not forgetting his usual manner.

He produces miracles and surprises together in his narrative; he causes the beautiful heroine to be cut up and buried, then he brings her back again from the halls of Hades, and he does other things of this kind elsewhere. But these things were inserted from his model Heliodorus. In the dialogue between the lovers he is negligent, and his language exposes his character. When he elaborates things which according to the rules of his craft ought to be said in a single word (?), and as it were brings into view things which one would close one's eye to if one saw them by chance, he is ignorant of the rules of his art, and because of his delight in eloquence he is prepared to make his meaning indecent. He destroys the character of the relationship between the lovers, rapidly altering the hero and then restoring him again, making only this one good observation, that time can wither even the beauty of love.

And to sum up the whole, I admire the story of Charicleia for its contents and appropriate diction, and I think it deserves praise altogether. The story of Leucippe will serve a writer in default of other resources (?), so that, if he should wish to decorate some parts of his own work with ornaments drawn from it, he can pick from a source ready to hand any embellishments that Achilles Tatius has introduced into his book. You have, my dear friend, my judgment on the books in the matters which are really important (?). I have not tackled details but given a summary account of their styles.

Most of this is self-explanatory. It may be worth adding a few notes. Psellos dates Achilles Tatius later than Heliodorus on literary grounds, which modern scholars also did until a papyrus fragment from the second century forced them to alter their view. While Psellos makes a sound if rather contorted observation about the narrative technique of Heliodorus, which modern scholars have compared with the structure of the *Odyssey*, he fails to bring out the distinguishing feature of Achilles Tatius' narrative, which is told in the first person. The comment on the miraculous element in the two novels is not justified, since there is less of it in Heliodorus than in the average Greek novel. The charge of indecency levelled at Achilles Tatius had already been made by Photius. As a whole the enthusiasm for the style of these imitative writers is of course misplaced.

The response of the Byzantines to classical drama is very hard to gauge. They suffered from the almost insuperable obstacle of not maintaining the theatre as an art form. Tragedy and comedy had no function to perform apart from serving as components of a school curriculum. It is surprising that any Byzantine should have read more widely in these genres than his teachers required of him, and the contents of the surviving manuscript copies demonstrate that the majority did not. Whether Psellos himself had the time or inclination to do so must remain in doubt. It is, however, to be noted that he unexpectedly borrows a whole line from Euripides' *Iphigeneia in Tauris* (569),[4] one of the plays forming part of the so-called alphabetic series that seems to have been almost unknown in Byzantium until it was brought to light again in the early fourteenth century. Since the line exploited by Psellos does not appear to have been well known as a quotation, there is reason to think that his acquaintance with the play may have been direct.

A different but again uncertain hint of his interest in ancient drama is given by a short anonymous treatise, preserved in a single manuscript alongside a number of other texts by Psellos or somehow connected with him.[5] It is cast in the form of a reply to a question, like many other compositions by Psellos. This may explain the selection of topics, in particular the omission of any statement about the origins of tragedy and the elements out of which it is composed. There is discussion of the structure of plots and of stage devices. Then metre, music and dancing are treated. The writer's approach is abstract and clearly depends in part on Aristotle's *Poetics*. There are some misunderstandings about metre, despite the writer's (or his source's) use of the handbook by Hephaestion. A paragraph on musical style offers some information that was not previously known about styles introduced by Agathon and the unfavourable comment they earned because of the intricate melodies. But the Byzantine reader was even less well placed than his modern counterpart to appreciate the musical element in a performance of Greek tragedy, and the whole of this paragraph has a ring of the abstract and theoretical about it. In places there seems to be unduly severe abbreviation of a source, so that the meaning is unclear. One of the few points which show a concern for tragedy as it was acted is the remark that the entry and exit of actors was understood to mark a division between acts of a play. Although an ancient authority is not named, the terminology is that used by the metricians Heliodorus and Hephaestion.

[4] Kurtz-Drexl I 228.
[5] R. Browning, 'A Byzantine treatise on tragedy', *Acta Universitatis Carolinae* (Prague 1963) 67-81, (reprinted in *Studies on Byzantine History, Literature and Education* (London 1977)).

Yet one must doubt whether the significance of the observation would have been clear to an eleventh-century reader.[6]

Having seen the limitations of this essay we can deal with Psellos' one venture into the criticism of Greek tragedy. The text is known from a single manuscript which is now unfortunately damaged, and the difficulties in deciphering and interpreting what is still left defeated not only Leone Allacci, the learned scriptor of the Vatican Library (1586-1669) but also the one modern editor who made the attempt.[7] Although the sketch that follows is based on a fresh examination of the manuscript (Barb. gr. 240), it is necessarily tentative and incomplete. The title reveals that Psellos is replying, as so often, to a question, which in this case ran 'Who wrote the better verse, Euripides or the Pisidian?' The comparison is therefore between one of Athens' three leading dramatists and a writer of verse on historical and theological subjects who flourished in the reign of Heraclius (610-41) and was the latest Byzantine author to possess a grasp of the rules of classical prosody.

'Both are graceful as far as metre and poetry are concerned, I mean Euripides of Phlius and George the Pisidian who perfected the iambic metre ... ' begins Psellos. Since they are very similar, he continues, it is difficult to see in which respects one is superior to the other, but with a knowledge of metre, an understanding of what rhythms are noteworthy, a decision is not so hard. The first point for discussion is that the metres and rhythms display innumerable differences owing to the chronological interval. At this stage, having made a correct and potentially useful observation, Psellos apparently lapses into florid verbiage, which will not be redeemed even if one day a less damaged text is recovered. When the context becomes intelligible again he seems to be saying that, since there are several parts of tragedy not only on the stage but in the whole composition and plot itself, and the metres of each part are not suitable for all, the poet must be versatile.

> Hence Sophocles and Aeschylus are more profound in their concepts and more solemn in the execution of a theme. They do not display grace or euphonious rhythm everywhere; in general they are more solemn and so to speak more decorous. Aeschylus when depicting (?) Prometheus departs a little from his usual character, and takes pleasure in pure iambics, and with words which flatter the ear he approaches his theme more elegantly. In all his other dramatic plots, especially his representation of Darius, he is usually forceful and difficult to explain (?), and one cannot know him unless one is as it were initiated into divine visions. Euripides, the author of eighty or more plays, is always statuesque and charming, not only through the charm of his words but even in the actual sufferings he portrays. Often by his sense of dramatic timing he reduced the Athenians to tears. They thought what they saw was real, when he brought Orestes on stage mad, after a suitable prologue about Tantalus and then descending to the story of his sister Electra ...

[6] O. Taplin, *The Stagecraft of Aeschylus* (Oxford 1977) 57.
[7] A. Colonna, *StudBizNeoell* 7 (1953) 16-21. Allacci's notes are in Vallicell. gr. 206-CXXX.

There follows what seems to be a confused account of the opening scene of the *Orestes*, the third play of the regular school syllabus, together with some remarks of dubious meaning about metre and style. A few lines later the meaning temporarily becomes clear. 'There are places where he falls short of what is fitting and aims more at logical force than the requirements of poetry. For instance he sets Hecuba against Odysseus, a noble hero and skilled speaker, exalting her and giving her the advantage. Odysseus' part is not unpleasingly worked out, but he is inferior to the captive queen.' The moving scene in the *Hecuba* (lines 215ff) evidently had its effect on Psellos, but the note of dissatisfaction in his judgment is more than a blemish. The remainder of the essay concerns George of Pisidia, and in so far as it can be understood in its present state appears to emphasise the wealth of detail in his descriptions. Damage in the manuscript prevents us from learning what Psellos' final judgment was. The modern reader scarcely needs to know; even if he puts aside his prejudice against the mere idea of comparing two authors so different in style and intention, the treatment of tragedy can only be described as superficial in the extreme.

(vii) The epitome of Dio Cassius

Another product of this period, which modern historians of the Roman empire are forced to avail themselves of despite its evident shortcomings, is the epitome of Dio Cassius. It was made by John Xiphilinus, who is sometimes identified with the patriarch of the years 1064-75; but one of the epitomator's own interventions tells us that he was in fact the nephew of the patriarch and wrote during the reign of the emperor Michael Ducas (1071-8). He declares his identity after reporting some details of Augustus' constitutional arrangements of 27 B.C. as described in Dio 53.21. 'I shall report each fact as far as is necessary,' he says, 'particularly from the present point onwards, because our present existence depends greatly on those times and our constitution is reminiscent of them.'

The epitome begins with book 36, and it may well be that he did not have a copy of books 1-35, whereas Photius gives us to understand that he had at least seen a complete copy. In books 36-60 he can be compared with the original. A good deal which Dio had regarded as important is omitted; at the same time there is a tendency to retain colourful episodes for their anecdotal value. This means that in books 61-9 and 72-80, where we are largely dependent on Xiphilinus, we cannot think of him as a very reliable source. His most curious intrusion is at 71.9, the account of an episode in the war of 171 against the Quadi when a hard-pressed Roman army was saved by sudden rainfall. According to Dio this was produced by the Egyptian magician Arnuphis. Xiphilinus prefers to think that it was the result of prayers offered by a legion of Christians from Melitene.[1]

---

[1] See further P.A. Brunt, *CQ* 74 (1980) 488-92.

9

From Alexius Comnenus to the Fourth Crusade

(i) The early years

The most notable event in this period is obviously the condemnation of
Italos. The atmosphere of the next few years might be clearer if the one
extant work of his successor, Theodore of Smyrna, were published. It is
found in a single copy (Vienna, theol. gr. 134). The title is 'Epitome of
ancient doctrines on physics'. Apparently it is a commentary, or more
strictly a paraphrase, since there are no lemmata, of Aristotle's *Physics*.
Pagan authors' views are given, but they are not named.[1]

Unwillingness to quote names may be a precaution, and it is found in
another context where a writer may well have decided that discretion
was advisable. Isaac Sebastocrator, who is to be identified either as the
brother or the third son of the emperor Alexius Comnenus, wrote three
essays based largely on the minor works of Proclus. He exploited his
source in such a way as to omit doctrine which could not be reconciled
with orthodoxy, converting all references to a plurality of gods into the
singular, and naming explicitly no source other than the Bible and
Dionysius the Areopagite. The three treatises by Proclus, dealing with
fundamental problems about providence, free will and the existence of
evil, do not now survive in the original Greek, but they had been
available to Psellos and a Latin translation of them was made in 1280 by
William of Moerbeke, Latin archbishop of Corinth. This translation
enables us to see that Isaac quoted a good many passages verbatim.[2]

Being a member of the imperial family he had to be as much above
suspicion as Caesar's wife. His work may nevertheless be suspected of
demonstrating a secret admiration for Neoplatonism, disguised as an
attempt to prove that unimpeachable authorities held the same views.
One wonders whether his treatises are connected in any way with the
essay by Nicholas, bishop of Methone (died *c.* 1165), aimed at refuting
Proclus' more commonly read work, *The Elements of Theology*.

That the risks inherent in Platonism did not deter devout members of
the   church   from   reading   authors   traditionally   prescribed   for
schoolchildren is shown by the example of Nicetas, nephew of a bishop of
Serrae and himself later metropolitan of Heracleia, whose main works

---

[1] W. Lackner, *Byzantinische Forschungen* 4 (1972) 168.
[2] H. Boese, *Procli Diadochi tria opuscula* (Berlin 1960).

are a series of catenae on books of the Old and New Testament. He was active *c.* 1070-1120 and before being promoted to his see held various teaching appointments, one of them at least in the patriarchal seminary. He is the author of a collection of glosses on Lycophron's notoriously obscure poem *Alexandra*. These glosses appear in the leading manuscript (Marc. gr. 476) with a note saying 'I, Nicetas, the most humble of deacons, have collected here glosses from the lexicon'. The inference has been made, rightly it would seem, that the manuscript is Nicetas' autograph.[3] The same book is also a key source for Aratus' *Phaenomena*. We see here the young cleric making his own copy of standard poetic texts of the curriculum. His teaching post was a stage on the ladder of preferment, as can be seen from the careers of other prominent churchmen such as Eustathius.

The identification of his hand allows us to go one stage further with a hypothesis; part of the book has script very similar to that found in the Venice manuscript of Aristophanes (Marc. gr. 474), which contains seven of the plays as opposed to the three that were the minimum requirement for the schoolroom. It is again one of the leading witnesses to the text and is if anything still more important for the scholia. We may suspect that it was produced at this time and probably in the same milieu as the copy of Lycophron and Aratus.

Among the other manuscripts probably written at the end of the eleventh century one may note the archetype of Epictetus (Oxford, Auct. T.4.13). But there is not much sign of scholarly activity at a high or even a competent level until the second or third decade of the twelfth century. Confidence in the value of the traditional forms of education continued, as can be seen from a report of disagreement in the imperial family on the question of the succession. Alexius Comnenus favoured his son John and had him proclaimed co-emperor, while the empress Irene did everything possible to favour her daughter Anna, the future historian, who was the oldest of the children. Irene was critical of her son and sometimes contrasted him unfavourably with Anna's fiancé Bryennius, who 'was an able speaker and no less effective as a man of action, the product of a liberal education capable of moulding character and greatly helping future heads of state to rule beneficially'.[4] Irene's ambitions for her daughter were not realised. Indeed it is extraordinary that she should have considered the possibility of her daughter succeeding when there were sons. Enthusiasm for the scheme went so far that Anna herself was involved in an unsuccessful plot to murder her brother. Her reward was to spend the rest of her life in a monastery, but she did not give up intellectual pursuits. The famous history of her father's reign, the *Alexiad*, is not the only tangible result. Modern research has extracted valuable new information from a tedious funeral oration on Anna. It

---

[3] E. Scheer, *RhMus* 34 (1879) 281-2; text in F. Ritschl, *Opuscula philologica* I (Leipzig 1866) 759.

[4] Nicetas Choniates, *History* p. 5, ed. J.A. van Dieten (Berlin 1975).

becomes reasonably certain from an ingenious construction of the available evidence that Anna encouraged Aristotelian studies and under her patronage several commentaries were produced.[5]

The striking feature of these works is that they deal mostly with treatises that had rarely if ever been the subject of commentaries. Commentators had devoted their efforts mainly to the logical works of the *Organon*. Of the two apparent exceptions to this rule the first, a paraphrase of the *Nicomachean Ethics* supposedly by Heliodorus of Prusa, is illusory. The authorship is doubtful, as the author's name occurs in a single Renaissance copy of the text written by a scribe who has a bad name as a forger, and the text itself contains nothing to prove its antiquity.[6] The other exception is more substantial, a commentary on *Nicomachean Ethics* I-IV, VII and VIII which goes under the name of Aspasius and is generally accepted as a genuine work of the second century A.D. Since Aspasius is a very shadowy figure, the matter is perhaps worth fuller investigation. For the present purpose we may accept it as a work produced in antiquity and suppose that it was either not available to Anna or did not seem satisfactory.

Under Anna's direction the study of the *Ethics* was renewed, that of some of the biological works begun for the first time, and it is quite likely that the two extant commentaries on the *Rhetoric* should be seen as part of the same collaborative enterprise. Michael of Ephesus was responsible for the zoological texts and for books V, IX and X of the *Ethics*; there are also remnants of a commentary on the *Politics*. He is reported to have complained that his eyesight suffered because he had to sit up all night in order to meet Anna's demands. The *Ethics* were divided among a small group. Eustratius, metropolitan of Nicaea, took books I and VI, the commentary on VIII is not extant and one may wonder whether it was produced, while the commentaries on II-IV and VII are anonymous. It is possible that some of them were due to Stephanus, the author of a commentary on the *Rhetoric* who says that he has also written on the *Ethics*.[7] Although Stephanus does not reveal much about himself, his remarks about contemporary hostilities between the empire and Venice are consistent with a date *c.* 1122/3 and he is perhaps to be identified with Stephanus Scylitzes, the metropolitan of Trebizond appointed in 1126 but forced to wait for some time before he could take up his appointment.[8] The writer of the second extant commentary on the *Rhetoric* mentions that his teacher was a metropolitan; the question is then whether Stephanus or Eustratius is meant.

Eustratius may be tentatively regarded as the leading figure in this group. Despite being a pupil of Italos he had had a successful career in the church until 1117, when he found himself on the wrong side in an

[5] Much of what follows is drawn from R. Browning, *PCPS* 188 (1962) 1-12 (reprinted in his *Studies on Byzantine History, Literature and Education* (London 1977)).

[6] L. Cohn, *BPhW* 9 (1889) 1419-20, on Paris gr. 1870.

[7] *CAG* 21, ed. H. Rabe (Berlin 1896) 277.28.

[8] W. Wolska-Conus, *Actes du XIV Congrès international des études byzantines* III (Bucarest 1976) 599-606.

ecclesiastical controversy involving the interpretation of St. Cyril of Alexandria and was forced to make a recantation. It is perhaps not surprising that a man who may well have been suspended from his see joined forces with a princess who was compelled to spend the rest of her life in retirement. If he was under a cloud the obscurity of his preface to the commentary on the first book of the *Ethics* is more easily explained. He says that he is writing at the request of an important person who has done him favours in the past and cannot be refused. The wording of the Greek implies that the person is a man. This was a necessary exercise of tact, but for reasons which are unknown it was no longer so important by the time he came to write a similar preface to book VI, where he addresses himself to a lady of the imperial family; but still she is not named.

The products of the circle are not on the whole of great value, except that they occasionally yield information that is not now available from any other source. The commentaries on the *Rhetoric* have been severely treated by a modern critic, who noted in particular that the anonymous one contains various misconceptions about the ancient world. These may be worth recording as an indication of an average scholar's competence. In a list of great Athenian generals he includes such non-Athenian figures as Epaminondas and Zaleucus; he has Pericles take part in a campaign against Syracuse; he confuses Aristotle's *Politics* with the lost collection of the constitutions of 158 Greek city states. In an attempt to explain the variant reading in the first sentence of Herodotus' *History*, where one branch of the tradition makes Herodotus a native of Thurii instead of Halicarnassus, he offers the opinion that Halicarnassus was a colony founded from Thurii. In fact Thurii is well known to have been a foundation under Athenian auspices in the middle of the fifth century.[9] And there is equally little sign that modern students of the *Ethics* have found anything of value in the work produced under Anna's patronage. Eustratius has been criticised for a diffuse and verbose style, for making very few useful contributions to the explanation of the text, and for being the source of a large number of errors which have traditionally marred the understanding of the work.[10] On the other hand a careful recent study of the commentary by Michael on the *De motu animalium* has shown that in several passages of this short treatise he offers the best interpretation or a useful comment.[11] And there is one difficult passage of the *Politics* where he suggests two alternative emendations of the text, each of which has found favour with modern scholars.[12]

This is the appropriate moment to mention an interesting

[9] C.A. Brandis, *Philologus* 4 (1849) 1-47, esp. 34 ff; in Rabe's edition the passages cited are at 17.2, 206.13, 46.20 and 194.12.

[10] R.A. Gauthier & J.Y. Jolif, *L'Ethique à Nicomaque* I (Louvain-Paris 1958) 70*.

[11] M.C. Nussbaum, *Aristotle's De motu animalium* (Princeton 1978) 130, 308, 325, 327, 361, 383.

[12] The notes are printed in O. Immisch's Teubner text (Leipzig 1929); see also his remarks ibid. xvi-xxi. There is a long study of Michael by K. Praechter, *GGA* 168 (1906) 861-907.

phenomenon in the textual history of the *Rhetoric*. Investigation shows that one of the lost manuscripts, which drew on both the main sources of the tradition and may well have been written in the twelfth century, offers a number of excellent readings, including four which coincide with proposals of modern scholars for the improvement of the text. Whether these readings, which presuppose intelligence and a close knowledge of Aristotelian idiom, can be the work of a Byzantine critic or are to be thought of as the only remaining evidence of a lost branch of the tradition, must remain an open question. On balance the second solution is perhaps to be preferred, and it is worth noting that in the final section of this chapter reference will be made to other Aristotelian manuscripts which are thought to be the unique representatives of another branch of tradition.[13]

Another person whose career was apparently brought to a sudden halt by the events which led to Anna Comnena being required to live in a convent was John Zonaras. He had been an important official at court, but he spent the rest of his life as a monk, exiled to a distant island. There despite the difficulty of laying hands on the necessary books he composed a chronicle of world history up to the year 1118. One of the books which did reach him has made him valuable to historians of the Roman Republic; somehow or other he found books 1-21 of Dio Cassius, which have since been lost in the original. It does not need to be assumed that the library of a remote monastery produced such a treasure for him, though that possibility cannot be excluded. But his success is one of a number of proofs that the resources of twelfth-century libraries were still notable.[14]

(ii)   Gregory of Corinth

First but by no means foremost among the other figures of twelfth-century scholarship is Gregory of Corinth, so called because he apparently followed a common career pattern by being promoted from a teaching post in the capital to the bishopric of Corinth. The reconstruction of his career is admittedly far from certain, but while there is no direct evidence of his having taught in the patriarchal seminary the character of some of the works generally ascribed to him puts his membership of the teaching profession beyond reasonable doubt. The existence of a long commentary on the rhetorical handbook of Hermogenes is sufficient to demonstrate the point.[1] His date is not easy to fix and has been the subject of controversy. His tenure of the see of Corinth falls between 1092 and 1156, years in which a bishop of another name is known to have been in office. As he refers several times to John Tzetzes, who can scarcely have made a name for himself before *c*. 1135-

---

[13] On the *Rhetoric* see R. Kassel, *Der Text der aristotelischen Rhetorik* (Berlin 1971) 70-8.

[14] On Zonaras see K. Ziegler in *RE*, s.v.

[1] On the dates of Gregory's career see R. Browning, *Byzantion* 33 (1963) 19-21.

1140 at the earliest, the latest possible date would appear to be indicated. On the other hand one of Gregory's other writings, a commentary on some hymns, exists in a copy written as early as 1126, and in the Greek-speaking area of Italy (Vat. gr. 1726). One is bound to ask how long a book would have taken to circulate to the periphery of the Byzantine world. Perhaps not long; and it may be in order to ask instead whether the references to Tzetzes are later interpolations, since investigation has revealed that the text of some of Gregory's writings is not easily established. At present it is best to assume that he was active *c.* 1120-1150.

His place in the history of scholarship, though certainly not high, is hard to assess accurately, because only one of his works has been satisfactorily edited and the authorship of some others is not beyond doubt. The editor of the short treatise on syntax has passed an unequivocally negative judgment on it. Although it evidently enjoyed popularity at times and is found in more than forty manuscript copies, its level of competence is below that of George Choeroboscus and Michael Syncellus, and from the Italian Renaissance onwards scholars have rarely if ever cited it.[2]

Two other works require a mention. One, not yet edited in its entirety, is a handbook on style. Gregory recommends models for the aspiring writer.[3] He begins with panegyric. The first three authors he names are the great Cappadocian fathers of the fourth century. After them Aristides' *Panathenaikos* and Themistius are recommended, followed by Choricius, Procopius of Gaza and Psellos. Then he turns to deliberative oratory, and here the modern reader is bound to ask whether there were still in practice any occasions in Byzantine public life when such skills could be put to use, but the question does not appear to have bothered our author. He lists St. John Chrysostom, St. Basil, Aristides, Isocrates, Demosthenes, Libanius and Choricius. Again two Christian authors head the list, but the range is wide, and he adds as a kind of after-thought Plutarch, with the reservation 'if ethical discourses belong here'. His third division of oratory is judicial, and he names Demosthenes, Lysias, Libanius and Choricius. The persistent occurrence of this last name is something of a surprise, since the number of extant copies of his works is not such as to suggest that he enjoyed a high degree of popularity, and in any case law-court speeches were not to be found among his compositions. Gregory then adds that in all branches of oratory Gregory of Nazianzus will prove to be valuable as a source of inspiration, as will Psellos, and he remarks that the four best speeches known to him are

---

[2] On the works see D. Donnet, *Bulletin de l'Institut historique belge de Rome* 37 (1966) 81-97. He has edited *On Syntax* (Brussels-Rome 1967); the essay on dialects still has to be read in the edition of G.H. Schaefer (Leipzig 1811).

[3] In what follows I depend on the excerpt given by A. Kominis, *Gregorio Pardos* (Rome-Athens 1960) 127-9. There are some uncertainties in the text. Another chapter, printed by C. Walz, *Rhetores graeci* III (Stuttgart-Tübingen 1834) 570-4, includes the advice that we may learn about the informal talk (*lalia*) and related matters from Menander Rhetor.

Demosthenes *On the Crown*, Aristides' *Panathenaikos*, and two funeral orations, Gregory of Nazianzus on St. Basil and Psellos on his mother. The blend of Christian and classical authors would probably have seemed judicious to Byzantines of all periods, and the division of oratory into three sections essentially follows the classical pattern, with the slight variation, which may not be intended to have any significance, that the wide category of epideictic or display oratory is here reduced to the field of panegyric.

The recommendations continue. 'Read Leucippe, Charicleia, Lucian, Synesius, Alciphron's *Letters*. The first (i.e. the novel by Achilles Tatius) is full of flowery grace, the second of sober grace, the third has every kind of excellence, the fourth is solemn and powerful.' Yet another appearance of novelists in episcopal reading lists is to be noted, and it may be recalled that Photius had taken a very unfavourable view of Achilles Tatius, and Gregory himself appears to have done so at another time.[4]

> The letters (of Alciphron) are very persuasive and plausible. Solemn and in all respects sublime is Philo; Josephus is best in stylistic quality in his account of the capture (of Jerusalem), and is of the same type as Charicleia. If you wish to get a good reputation nowadays you must write works that are a blend of rhetorical and philosophical notions. If you are merely rhetorical you will look like a mediocre speech writer, if you are unduly philosophical you will appear too dry and lacking in taste. So a mixture is to be commended. As an example of such a mixture take works by the great Gregory the theologian, Basil the Great, (Gregory) the bishop of Nyssa, Psellos' orations and letters, Synesius, Themistius, Plutarch and many others who to your knowledge follow their lead. On the other hand as a model of the purely rhetorical style take (John) Chrysostom or rather the moralising passages in (Symeon) Metaphrastes, Libanius, Aphthonius, Procopius of Gaza, Choricius, Himerius, Lucian, who sometimes touches on philosophical ideas as well, Demosthenes, and more particularly if you are writing for a competition (?) and with rhetorical elaboration, Lysias, Isocrates and any more recent writers who to your knowledge follow their lead. In rhetorical subjects with a narrative element follow Charicleia, Leucippe, Philostratus' *Life of Apollonius*, Xenophon, Procopius of Caesarea. The last of these in his political and deliberative oratory has a competitive and elaborate quality and is not simply a narrator. The letters of Alciphron are especially suitable for simple notions and their expression.
>
> In letters the gnomic utterances of wise men, so-called apophthegms and proverbial expressions are all useful. Often references to a myth will add sweetness or simplicity. Quotations (?) can also be helpful on occasion, for instance if you choose a line of Homer or part of a line and insert it. In letters one should avoid an oratorical or elaborate quality and aim for narrative style. For a letter is a report and conversation of one friend with another. But recent authors in our own time have not refrained from composing whole letters which resemble speeches. You too must emulate

[4] See the commentary on Hermogenes, ed. C. Walz, op. cit. in the preceding note, VII 1236.

them, but in moderation; your style will be of greater purity and entirely without ornate figures. You have as models for letters the great Gregory above all, the great Basil, the bishop of Nyssa, who is more flowery and yet ... (?), Synesius, Libanius, Psellos, and anyone else of such quality.

The advice given here has no unexpected features. The range of authors which the educated man is expected to have at his finger-tips would appear to be typical. It is perhaps worth noting that the Byzantines laid great emphasis on the art of letter-writing, and while most of the recommended models were deservedly famous, modern taste cannot help being struck by the prominence given to the fictitious letters of Alciphron, which purport to be the correspondence of fishermen, farmers, parasites and courtesans, and are among the less inviting products of the second sophistic age.

Gregory finally gives advice on the writing of iambic verses. One of his suggestions is that each line should contain a complete notion. To modern taste this seems a very bad idea, as the result is to guarantee monotony of structure. The authors who are held up as examples to be imitated are George of Pisidia, Callicles, Ptochoprodromus, and among the ancients 'Gregory of Nazianzus, Sophocles, apart from his poetic idioms, and the clearest passages of Lycophron'. Then follow the names of Homer, Oppian, (Dionysius) the periegete, Tryphiodorus and Musaeus, in a bare list without any further guidance. One may reasonably guess that Gregory thought of them as supplementary sources, useful even though they composed in hexameters rather than iambics. His suggestion about the clearest passages of Lycophron is likely to provoke a wry smile from anyone who has tried to read the *Alexandra*. The comment on Sophocles suggests that he may have had some feeling for the feature of Sophoclean style which has exercised all competent students, the elasticity of the syntax. One should not of course jump to the conclusion that Gregory was capable of appreciating Sophocles' style in the same way as the distinguished nineteenth-century editor Lewis Campbell, whose essay on the language of the poet remains fundamental to the understanding of a most difficult writer. Gregory's intellectual affinities make him closer to another figure of the Victorian era, the schoolmaster who is reported to have begun a lesson by saying: 'Boys, this term you are to have the privilege of reading the *Oedipus Coloneus* of Sophocles, a veritable treasure-house of grammatical peculiarities.'[5]

Gregory's chief claim on our attention is his book on the Greek dialects. This subject had been treated in the sixth century by John Philoponus, and there are still extant under his name excerpts which may or may not be genuine. But from the later Byzantine period Gregory is perhaps the first writer to tackle the subject and certainly the only one

---

[5] Lewis Campbell's essay is in his edition of Sophocles, vol. 1 (ed. 2, Oxford 1879) 1-107. The Victorian pedagogue has so far eluded identification.

to escape the fate of anonymity.

The work is divided into four sections, one for each of the literary dialects of the classical language, Attic, Doric, Ionic and Aeolic. Each section is composed of a series of brief observations; they have respectively 99, 177, 191 and 67 items, some of them consisting of no more than a dialect word and its Attic equivalent. Gregory says that he is offering his work to a member of the imperial family, who cannot be identified (some late manuscripts have a variant reading which makes the addressee a woman, and in view of what is known of blue-stocking princesses in the twelfth century that is by no means impossible). He then claims that while John Philoponus, Tryphon and many others have displayed an adequate knowledge of the subject, no one has yet given a full treatment of each dialect. He will take as his standard certain authors: Aristophanes, Thucydides and Demosthenes for Attic; Hippocrates and Herodotus for Ionic; Archytas of Tarentum and Theocritus for Doric; and Alcaeus for Aeolic. It turns out that quotations from other writers are given from time to time. For the first two dialects the choice of authorities was not difficult, but the small quantity of literature surviving in the other two meant that it was hard to find a large enough corpus of material. It goes without saying that Alcaeus' poems were no better known to Gregory than to us and that his information about Aeolic must be derivative except where he was able to exploit fragments quoted by well known authors. One might ask why he does not name Sappho alongside Alcaeus; the failure to do so rouses dark suspicions of ignorance. As far as Doric is concerned, it was a grave error to mention Archytas, since no book of his, genuine or otherwise, survived at the time. Gregory must have copied out the name from his source, and one is bound to wonder whether even that source was guilty of the same empty pretension. If a prose text in Doric was necessary to supplement the evidence available from Theocritus' *Idylls*, it would have been more honourable to quote instead such brief treatises as the *Dissoi Logoi*, an anonymous piece which is transmitted along with Sextus Empiricus the Sceptic philosopher, or the spurious Timaeus Locrus, a paraphrase of Plato's dialogue of the same name. Although our author behaved correctly in naming two predecessors on whose efforts he depended to a large extent, it must be said that, even when due allowance is made for the difficulties under which all medieval scholars had to work, the resulting treatise does not do anything to enhance the reputation of Gregory or either of his two named sources. Such an unflattering judgment is inevitable, unless one clings to the faint hope that a critical edition will reveal a text less marred by blemishes. The chief defect in the work as it stands is that no effort has been made to impose any structure or order on a series of disjointed remarks, which are nothing more than notes on rare or irregular constructions encountered in the course of his reading. Gregory is like the modern scholar who thinks that a satisfactory lecture or book can be made out of a card-index. He is in a way less open to criticism for the undeniable factual errors, some of

which were not easy to avoid in an age of inadequate reference books and
texts copied by hand. One can understand how he might misinterpret the
rare accusative absolute construction as an idiomatic use of the
nominative (*Attic Dialect* 7), citing Aristophanes *Lysistrata* 13 and
Thucydides 4.125, because the construction is only found in the neuter,
where the nominative and accusative case are not distinguished. But
there are more serious shortcomings. He has the besetting sin of all
scholiasts, a willingness to cite Homer as evidence of Attic usage, and at
one point he sinks even to citing a fragment of Pindar as the sole piece of
evidence for one of its orthographical rules (*Attic* 60). The assertion that
novelty of diction is a general feature of Attic (25), however appositely
illustrated by reference to Demosthenes, *Olynthiac* 3.14 'you, the people,
sit there hamstrung', is not easy to justify, and it is followed by a totally
inappropriate reference to *Iliad* 2.278 'so spoke the mass of the army',
where the syntactical point consists of a singular noun denoting the army
as a whole used with a plural verb. Gregory demonstrates an inability to
understand the common idiom whereby the subject of an indirect
question is named before the conjunction which introduces the question
and as a result becomes the object of the main verb (grammarians of
more recent times have occasionally called this the 'I know thee who thou
art' construction from its most quotable example in St. Mark 1:24) (*Attic*
62). Other oddities in the section on Attic include a failure to distinguish
the middle and passive voice (94-5) and a suggestion that one of the
forms of the third person imperative is the genitive plural of the present
participle (97). Authors unexpectedly cited include Gregory of
Nazianzus and Symeon Metaphrastes, the author of the popular series of
saints' lives. A number of points are illustrated by examples from
Thucydides book VIII. Gregory is unusual in quoting from Aristophanes'
Thesmophoriazusai, and from the scholia on that play he cites a
fragment of Euripides' *Polyidus* (*Attic* 2,3). One wonders if he had access
to the Ravenna codex, since that is the only medieval copy of the
Thesmophoriazusai to survive.

His material about Doric is just as much of a farrago. Homer is again
quoted (1, 18, 20, 116). More to the point are references to Pindar and the
dialect scenes in Aristophanes' *Acharnians*. The statement that Crete,
Rhodes, Argos and Sparta used different forms of the Doric dialect (111)
is correct, but must have been transcribed from one of his sources. The
same reliance on unchecked authority leads to the entirely false
statement that a certain Cypselas wrote in Cretan. And one must feel
some surprise on being informed that the Syracusan Sophron wrote his
mimes in Laconian. The chapters on Ionic and Aeolic do not require any
particular comment.

Opinions vary about the extent of his originality.[6] If we could be sure
that his sources were the two treatises printed by Aldus Manutius in the

---

[6] G.C. Bolognesi, *Aevum* 27 (1953) 97-120 is more favourably disposed than H. Hunger,
Die hochsprachliche profane Literatur der Byzantiner II (Munich 1978) 31 n. 8.

Thesaurus Cornucopiae et Horti Adonidis of 1496, the first attributed to 'John the grammarian' (fol. 235r-236v), the second anonymously (fol. 236v-245v), it would follow that he was adhering to them fairly closely, while adding quite a number of his own examples to illustrate various rules. These texts and others require further study before any confident verdict can be given. What we are entitled to say at present is that Gregory's contribution to the study of Greek dialects is not good enough to raise him to a position of importance in this history.

By way of appendix it should perhaps be noted that a passage of the commentary on Hermogenes which was once interpreted as preserving a fragment of Theophrastus' teaching on rhetoric cannot be treated in this way with any confidence. The name of Theophrastus indeed occurs, at least in the text as printed by Walz,[7] but the context puts it practically beyond doubt that the author or scribe has made a slip of the pen, and the reference should be to Aristotle's *Rhetoric* 1394b7-95a2.[8]

(iii)   The brothers Tzetzes

Next in chronological order and in importance come the brothers Tzetzes.[1] The elder of the two, Isaac, can be dealt with rapidly. He died young, in 1138, at Rhodes, on his way back from a military expedition to Aleppo. His surviving work, the title of which describes him as a teacher of grammar, is an essay on Pindar's metres, in fifteen-syllable 'political' verses. It appears to be entirely derivative, a paraphrase of Hephaestion's handbook and scholia, with the exception that as there were no metrical scholia on the first Olympian Ode he had to invent his own analysis.[2]

The commentary on Lycophron's *Alexandra* which all the manuscripts attribute to Isaac seems in fact to be by his brother John, who despite his limited talents and unattractive personality demands more extensive treatment. He was not cut off in his prime, but lived until shortly after 1180, reaching the age of seventy or thereabouts. Though he had an extremely fluent pen and no desire to hide his cantankerous nature behind a wall of reserve, the course of his career is not fully known. It appears that he had a post in the civil service as a young man but lost it when he was accused of having an adventure with the wife of his superior. A period of great poverty followed, and he was obliged to sell his books one by one, so that at a certain stage he possessed none except some fragmentary mathematical texts and Plutarch's *Lives*.[3] The fact is important in more than one respect. It explains and excuses errors made by John during these years in his recollections or quotations of classical

---

[7] Op. cit. in n. 3, VII 1154.23.

[8] *Pace* G. Rosenthal, *Hermes* 32 (1897) 317-20. See R. Kassel's edition of the *Rhetoric* ad loc.

[1] The best general treatment is by C. Wendel in *RE*, s.v., cols. 1959-2010, 2010-1.

[2] See further J. Irigoin, *Les scholies métriques de Pindare* (Paris 1958) 57-72.

[3] Exegesis of the *Iliad*, ed. G. Hermann (Leipzig 1812) 15 lines 13-18.

texts that he had once owned. Whether the mathematical works were retained because the copy was too poor to have any value in the second-hand book trade must remain uncertain. But the retention of Plutarch proves once more the great influence his biographies had as a source of edifying and inspiring material about the heroes of the past, and it also suggests that John Mauropous was not regarded as eccentric when he prayed for the salvation of Plutarch's soul. Tzetzes' career was spent mostly as a teacher, under the protection of members of the aristocracy and imperial family. For a time at least he received his board and lodging in the Pantocrator monastery in return for teaching. This monastery was an important recent foundation noted for its hospital, but there is no sign that Tzetzes had any special interest in medicine. The arrangement still left him short of cash, which he tried to obtain by dedicating books to patrons and charging a fee for permission to transcribe his works. These transactions were not always successful. His situation may have improved in the end, as one of his letters reports the offer of the income produced by three perfume shops, the prospect of which elicited a grateful reply.[4] It is perhaps unkind to point out that in his commentary on Hesiod's *Works and Days* 414-22 a discussion of physical theory had led him to observe that some people are naturally fragrant, including Alexander the Great and himself, 'although I do not use scents or anoint myself, or take baths either, except two or three times a year'.[5]

Tzetzes was one of the most prolific of all Byzantine scholars. He claims to have written about sixty books.[6] A great many of them result from his teaching and are devoted to Homer, whom he interpreted allegorically, and the other usual school authors. Verse predominates: Homer, Hesiod, Pindar, tragedy, Aristophanes, and the Hellenistic writers of didactic poetry Lycophron and Nicander. Prose is represented only by some notes on Thucydides and on Porphyry's *Introduction to the Organon*. The ascription to him of some notes on Philostratus' *Imagines* is not supported by any good evidence.[7] A commentary on Ptolemy's *Handy Tables* seems an untypical excursion into a technical field, and inspection of the only manuscript (Paris gr. 2162) proves that the text is in fact a work by Stephanus of Alexandria. Tzetzes was interested in some other prose authors, however. He made an epitome of Apollodorus' handbook of mythology and an adaptation of Hermogenes' handbook on rhetoric. A good deal of what he composed was in verse, the 'political' metre of fifteen syllables being his preferred type. Of his other productions the most interesting are the letters. There are 107 of them, accompanied not only by a few notes by Tzetzes but his full commentary in verse, the *Histories* or *Chiliades*, designed to explain the obscure allusions. Whatever obscurities the letters contain, they did not require

[4] Letter 83, ed. P.A.M. Leone (Leipzig 1972).

[5] Cited by M.L. West, *Hesiod: Works and Days* (Oxford 1978) 69; see also 70 for some indications of Tzetzes' faulty scholarship.

[6] Note on Aristophanes' *Frogs* 897, ed. W.J.W. Koster (Groningen-Amsterdam 1962).

[7] R. Browning, *CQ* 49 (1955) 195-200.

exegesis filling six hundred pages of a modern edition and accompanied by some brief further notes of explanation.[8]

Tzetzes was vain, loquacious and quarrelsome, and he was far from being the expert scholar whose contributions to his subject excuse personal foibles. One can sympathise with his difficulties when he says that he is forced to end a letter because his supply of paper has run out.[9] All such sympathy evaporates when one finds twice in his commentary on Aristophanes[10] the statement that he would not be writing a particular note were it not that the page was not yet fully covered with notes. But one must make allowance for other difficult circumstances. Lack of money and loss of his library was compounded by having to live in an apartment building with awkward neighbours. A letter complains that the family living in the flat above him have both children and pigs, and that a failure in the plumbing system has had disagreeable consequences.[11]

Among the least tiresome signs of his vanity is a display of a smattering of several foreign languages. Each sentence is translated into the contemporary vernacular. Although Constantinople was racially very mixed, there was no provision for learning languages and as a rule only merchants or the children of mixed marriages will have known any. Tzetzes' mother was of Georgian descent, but he does not give a specimen of that language. He makes up for it by giving a sentence in Alanic, i.e. Ossetian, and the other languages are Cuman, which belonged to the Turkic family, Seljuk Turkish, Latin, Arabic, Russian and Hebrew.[12]

His quarrelsome nature allows us to see the seamy side of literary life. One of his friends had written a funeral oration on the emperor John Comnenus (d. 1143). Someone stole this and having made some slight changes tried to pass it off as his own. Tzetzes accuses the thief of having tried in the same fraudulent way to lay claim to his commentary on Lycophron.[13] The accusation is accompanied by a boast that his authorship is known in all four corners of the globe, from Ceylon to Britain. Whereas Psellos had had some reason to be proud of his power to draw students from foreign countries, there is not a shred of evidence to support Tzetzes' outrageous boast. This case of literary theft is not the only one to emerge from his writings. Another letter complains of his commentary on an unspecified author being appropriated by a rival.[14] A note on Aristophanes reports an amusing scene at a literary gathering

---

[8] Ed. by P.A.M. Leone (Naples 1968).

[9] Letter 6.

[10] Notes on *Plutus* 677 and 833, ed. L. Massa Positano (Groningen-Amsterdam 1960). Koster's preface to the volume, pp. xlii-liii, gives a general survey of the quality of Tzetzes' work on Aristophanes.

[11] Letter 18.

[12] H. Hunger, *BZ* 46 (1953) 302-7, gives the best edition.

[13] Letter 42.

[14] Letter 56.

where Tzetzes was commenting on this author. When he came to a point where he offered his own interpretation he stated the fact, only to hear from a member of the audience that his copy too contained the same suggestion. At first Tzetzes was merely annoyed; but as the number of instances increased he began to wonder if a pupil had written down his ideas and made them available. He insisted on examining the offending volume and found that it was not an Aristophanes at all, but Euripides or Oppian, and a roar of laughter went up as he began to read from it.[15]

A prominent feature of Tzetzes' work as a commentator is his liking for allegory. He distinguished three forms: physical, which allows the Homeric gods to be taken as elements of the universe; psychological, by which the gods may be treated as emotions or intellectual powers; historical, the tradition of Euhemeros and Palaiphatos, according to which gods and heroes were originally human beings. All these forms of exegesis were exploited by the ancients in their treatment of Homer.[16]

A point that does Tzetzes some credit is his awareness of chronology. A letter to the head of the hospital in the Pantocrator monastery correctly refutes the suggestion that Galen was a contemporary of Christ.[17] He places him in the reign of Antoninus Caracalla, which is correct to the extent that Galen died in 199 and Caracalla came to the throne in 196. As evidence a quotation from a writer of the Neronian age is produced from Galen's *De antidotis*; one might have hoped for something more precise. In dealing with ancient commentators on tragedy and comedy he expresses the view that they lived less than 330 years after Euripides.[18] The exact point of this figure is not clear, but it is approximately correct to see the work of the Hellenistic scholars as being essentially complete by 100 B.C., and while it is scarcely conceivable that Tzetzes would have reckoned from a landmark that seems obvious to modern scholars, such as the outbreak of the Peloponnesian War, he might have found a source giving Euripides' floruit at about the same date. A third instance of his concern for dating is that he thinks of Homer as being more recent than David and Solomon because of the reference in *Odyssey* 5.282-3 to Solyma, which he treated as equivalent to Hierosolyma, the Greek form of Jerusalem.[19] More sensible is his effort to put right an error in the short biography of Theocritus transmitted along with the *Idylls*. According to the manuscripts Theocritus was a contemporary of king Ptolemy, son of Lagus, whereas Tzetzes knew that his son and successor Ptolemy Philadelphus was the king in question.[20]

Tzetzes was not entirely devoid of the qualities required in an editor. His notes on Aristophanes' *Plutus* include a complaint that he has no old manuscript and only two of recent date, and it seems clear that in more

[15] On *Frogs* 897, op. cit. in n. 6 above.
[16] See in general H. Hunger, *JOBG* 3 (1954) 35-54.
[17] Letter 81.
[18] On *Frogs* 889.
[19] *Allegoriae Odysseae* V, lines 157-65, ed. H. Hunger, *BZ* 49 (1956) 249-310.
[20] C. Wendel, *Abh. Göttingen* 17,2 (1920) 11.

favourable circumstances he would have consulted others.[21] Elsewhere in the notes to the same play he makes it clear that he had no more than an elementary knowledge of metre. While he understood the phenomenon of internal correption in lines 14, 44, 116, by which a long vowel may be shortened in front of another vowel, he made some serious mistakes. In line 572 he accepted without question a text which is unmetrical, and in line 505 he at first accepted a faulty variant reading, which offended against metre and syntax. Later he thought he saw how to deal with the objection to the metre, and proposed an incorrect scansion to do so. About a century later Maximus Planudes came across a manuscript recording the first view and quite rightly criticised it.[22] Any metre more complicated than iambics was almost guaranteed to defeat a Byzantine scholar, and when Tzetzes came to *Plutus* 637, which is a dochmiac dimeter, he tried to make it into an iambic trimeter.

While he thought that some of Aristophanes' plays were excellent, he was unable to enjoy the *Frogs*. He complains more than once (at lines 25 and 1144) that the poet must have been drunk when he wrote, while on 358 he remarks that the poet does little except talk nonsense in this play. The obscenity of 422 irritated him. But it does not seem to have occurred to him to leave the play out of his reading programme.

He is also critical of previous commentators. One of his prefaces begins with the assertion that 'the wise Proclus in his interpretation of this book, the *Works and Days* of Hesiod, produced nothing noble or commensurate with his wisdom or worthy of report'. Proclus should have given basic information about types of poetry, the work in question and its purpose, before passing to interpretation.[23] This criticism is really no more than a variation of the requirements posed by one of the scholiasts on the grammar of Dionysius Thrax.[24] Tzetzes continues by saying that Proclus ought to have written in a didactic manner, instead of being 'labyrinthine, unclear and in more need of explanation than the text itself'. He invites his audience to make an impartial comparison between his commentary and that of Proclus. The fact is that it would be greatly to his disadvantage, since he has nothing of any real importance to add.[25]

His best claim on our attention consists of some unusual information which he alone provides. The most striking example comes from his prolegomena to Aristophanes, part of which first became known through a derivative Latin version known as the *scholium Plautinum* because it was found in 1819 in a Renaissance copy of Plautus between the end of the *Poenulus* and the opening of the *Mostellaria*. Tzetzes' own wording

[21] On *Plutus* 137.

[22] W.J.W. Koster, *Scholia in Aristophanis Plutum et Nubes ... partim inedita* (Leiden 1927) 46-50; idem, *Autour d'un manuscrit d'Aristophane écrit par Démétrius Triclinius* (Groningen-Djakarta 1957) 72-4.

[23] T. Gaisford, *Poetae minores graeci* III (Oxford 1820) 9.

[24] Ed. A. Hilgard, *Grammatici graeci* III (Leipzig 1901) 3.27 ff, 123.25 ff.

[25] Cf. Wendel in *RE*, col. 1970 and the even harsher judgment passed by Paul Maas, *BZ* (1934) 166.

has now been recovered, in two slightly different versions.[26] The unexpected discovery of Byzantine material in a commentary on Plautus may be thought to need a word of explanation. The connecting link appears to be that a copy of Tzetzes' text (Ambr. C 222 inf.) belonged to the Italian humanist Merula, who devoted a good deal of his time to Plautus.[27]

Tzetzes begins with an account of the checking of texts of ancient drama in Hellenistic Alexandria, performed by Alexander Aetolus and Lycophron with the encouragement of Ptolemy Philadelphus. At the time Eratosthenes was librarian of the Museum and Callimachus compiled his bibliography of Greek literature. Both were then young men. The work on tragedy and comedy was matched by that of Aristarchus and Zenodotus on other poets; Tzetzes or his source should have made it clear that they concentrated on Homer. There were many later scholars, such as Didymus, Tryphon, Herodian, Apollonius, Ptolemy of Ascalon and Ptolemy of Cythera. This last name is an erroneous inclusion of a very minor epic poet; perhaps originally the reference was to Epithetes, so-called from his attacks on Aristarchus, or Ptolemy Pindarion, a pupil of Aristarchus. After these scholars come the philosophers Porphyry, Plutarch and Proclus, and this leads Tzetzes to a curious digression on Aristotle and some of the faulty information to be found in his zoological books. Further digressions follow, and then he turns to comedy. In fairness it must be emphasised that the other version of this introduction suffers less from digressions and goes some way towards correcting one mistake by stating that Zenodotus was particularly concerned with the text of Homer. It includes interesting figures about the size of the Alexandrian library; the 'external' section contained 42,800 papyrus rolls – can this have been a public lending library? – while the library in the palace had 400,000 composite books and 90,000 single books. These facts are rather ambiguously attributed to Callimachus. The plausibility of the report is perhaps lessened by the story which follows, to the effect that Ptolemy Philadelphus had ensured the collection of books in languages other than Greek, which were then translated, as for instance the Hebrew scriptures were rendered into Greek by seventy-two translators. Tzetzes then comes back to Greek poetry and reports pre-Alexandrian activity alleged to have taken place in Athens more than two hundred years earlier in the reign of Peisistratus, when a text of Homer was prepared. An interval of three hundred years would be closer to the mark. Otherwise the last piece of information is derived from the scholiasts on Dionysius Thrax, one of whom, Heliodorus, Tzetzes singles out for abuse, claiming that as a young man he had been misled by the scholiast into thinking that Zenodotus and Aristarchus were contemporaries of Pisistratus.[28]

[26] Ed. W.J.W. Koster, *Prolegomena de comoedia* (Groningen 1975) 22-48.

[27] P. Maas, op. cit. in n. 25.

[28] See further R. Pfeiffer, *History of Classical Scholarship* I (Oxford 1968) 100-102, 127-8; P.M. Fraser, *Hellenistic Alexandria* II (Oxford 1972) 463 n. 15, 474 n. 108, 488 n. 193.

At certain stages of his career Tzetzes possessed or had access to a well stocked library. His connections with the court circle, however exiguous they may have been in actual fact, invite us to speculate that he could on occasion avail himself of the riches of the imperial collection. Whatever his sources it is certain that he read texts now lost to us. He is the sole source for a number of lines from a poem of Hipponax dealing with the ritual punishment of a scapegoat in Ephesus in the middle of the sixth century B.C.; a full text might have been of great value to students of Greek religion and anthropology. He also quotes consecutively two lines of Callimachus (frr. 496 and 533) that are otherwise quoted separately.[29] Fresh examination of the manuscripts transmitting Tzetzes' own work continues to produce interesting snippets of information.[30] Among them is a genealogy of the house of Atreus, ascribed to Hesiod, which suggests that the father of Agamemnon and Menelaus was in one version of the saga Pleisthenes, who disappeared from heroic poetry because he was lame, hermaphrodite or transvestite. This adds strength to the view that the Homeric poems underwent at some stage a process of what might be called censorship, to remove elements that might be thought inconsistent with the dignity of the genre.[31]

But while it is likely enough that he read a complete copy of Hipponax and perhaps Callimachus, the number and nature of his quotations make it difficult to suppose that he drew all his learning from original sources, however rich one believes the libraries of the capital to have been. Yet even the sceptic will allow that he read some other books that the modern reader lacks. Among them was Chaeremon, the writer on Egypt mentioned already in connection with Psellos, the early books of the Roman historian Cassius Dio (some fragments are not known from elsewhere), and the collector of miscellaneous and mainly false information Ptolemy Chennos, who was known to Photius. He also refers to Ptolemy's *Geography* (*Chiliades* XI 888-9), which is generally thought not to have been known to the Byzantines until a copy came into the hands of Maximus Planudes *c*. 1300. It is not possible to say at present whether in this case Tzetzes' learning is first-hand or borrowed. In addition he knew but seems to have made little use of Euripides' *Cyclops*, a play not in the school selection; this unusual accomplishment will be discussed in more detail in the section on Eustathius.[32]

(iv) Eustathius

Of all Byzantine scholars Eustathius is perhaps the best known and at

[29] J. Irigoin,*REG* 73 (1960) 439-447.

[30] M. Papathomopoulos, *Nouveaux fragments d'auteurs grecs* (Ioannina 1980). But it is to be noted that what looked at first sight like a new fragment of Stesichorus may well have been manufactured from Aristides 45.54; see M. Davies, *ZPE* 45 (1982) 267-9.

[31] G. Murray, *The Rise of the Greek Epic* (ed. 4, Oxford 1934) 125-40.

[32] Koster, op. cit. in n. 26 above, 31 lines 155-6.

the same time the most voluminous as a writer. It has also been suggested by a leading modern authority that as a textual critic he was in a class by himself. The essential biographical facts about him can be stated briefly. He was born c. 1115, and may have held a position in the civil service at the beginning of his career. Certainly he was for a time on the staff of the patriarch's academy, and it is then that he must have produced most of his scholarly work. He was appointed to the bishopric of Myra in Lycia, but managed to delay his departure, and when the more desirable see of Thessalonica fell vacant the emperor intervened to insist that he should go there instead (c. 1174-7). In 1185 his city was besieged and captured by the Normans, and he wrote a vivid description of the appalling experience. His admirable leadership in the most trying circumstances and his attempts on other occasions to reform abuses that had grown up in the church combine to make him a sympathetic figure. The date of his death is to be placed c. 1195-9.[1]

While he lived in the capital his house was a meeting place for people with literary tastes. In the words of a funeral oration, affected by the exaggerated enthusiasm generally permitted in this genre, 'all young students of literature sought his company and his home was truly a shrine of the Muses, another Academy, Stoa and Peripatos'.[2] As a teacher of rhetoric Eustathius will have read with his pupils a number of classical texts, and if we may accept as true what he says in the preface to his commentary on the *Iliad*, he wrote that work in order to satisfy the requests of his students, and not because he had been commissioned to do so by influential members of high society. This is much the longest of his surviving works; in the Leipzig edition of 1827-30, which does not have any apparatus criticus, it fills some 1,400 pages of substantial format. There is also a long commentary on the *Odyssey*, amounting to nearly 800 pages of the same edition. As the *Odyssey* is shorter than the *Iliad*, the scale of this commentary is not so much smaller as might appear at first sight. In addition he prepared a fresh edition of the commentary on the didactic poem on geography by Dionysius Periegetes. A preface to Pindar survives, and there are traces of work on Aristophanes and Oppian.[3] Apart from all this there is a quantity of correspondence and other essays which fall almost entirely outside the scope of this book.

While it seems likely that most of his writing is to be dated to the period before his translation to Thessalonica, the chronological order of the works is not easy to establish. A number of cross-references give contradictory indications, suggesting that revisions were continually being made or even that all the main works were in preparation

[1] On Eustathius' life and career see L. Cohn in *RE*, s.v., n. 18; R. Browning, *Byzantion* 32 (1962) 186-93 (reprinted in *Studies on Byzantine History, Literature and Education* (London 1977)); P. Wirth, *Eustathiana* (Amsterdam 1980).

[2] *Euthymius Malakes*, ed. K.G. Bonis (Athens 1937) 82-3.

[3] The case for supposing that he may have composed a commentary on Oppian is put by A.R. Dyck, *CP* 77 (1982) 153-4.

concurrently.[4] A process of revision is in any case clear from the surviving manuscripts of the *Iliad* commentary, magnificent volumes of large format which despite the absence of any signature can be recognised as the author's autographs. The identification was first made by cardinal Bessarion, who owned a copy of the *Odyssey* commentary (Marc. gr. 460) and wrote on its first leaf a note stating who the scribe was but not giving any reason.[5] It is not clear what evidence he can have had, but modern scholars are convinced by a feature of a pair of volumes in Florence containing the *Iliad* commentary (Laur. 59.2 and 3). They have a large number of pieces of paper, some very tiny, pasted in, and all are written in the same script as the main text. These slips must be the author's additions, unless one wishes to adopt the remotely conceivable alternative that Eustathius had a long-serving secretary to whom he dictated not only the main text but all subsequent addenda. Such a hypothesis does not affect the status of the volumes.[6]

The Homer commentaries have not been treated sympathetically by modern scholars. It is of course admitted that his access to many texts now lost confers an adventitious value on his compilation, and a recent critic of Homer has drawn attention to Eustathius' sound instinct in describing the feelings that the poet wished to evoke in his reader.[7] But the first of these merits is not his own and the second may owe more to his sources than we are now able to detect. Taken together they cannot outweigh the fault of verbosity. Anyone who fills several pages with the exegesis of the first line of a poem must be very sure of the quality and relevance of what he has to say, and Eustathius simply does not pass the test. The preface to the *Iliad* assures us that it was written at the request of students rather than influential patrons, and Eustathius seems to entertain the idea that a student might take a copy away to read by himself. He also expresses the hope that the young will draw all kinds of benefit from reading Homer, not least when they have to write themselves.

The preface to the *Odyssey* is brief. There is no dedication and Eustathius says nothing of his intentions except that he will treat the poem in the same way as the *Iliad*, selecting from the available material and passing over many topics already treated adequately in his discussion of the *Iliad*. Otherwise the chief concern of the preface is to rebut the idea that the *Odyssey* is full of false myths. Not all the poet's stories are open to this charge. Eustathius maintains that Homer's accounts of Aeolus, the Cimmerians and Calypso have a basis in truth, to

---

[4] M. van der Valk, *Eustathii archiepiscopi Thessalonicensis commentarii ad Homeri Iliadem pertinentes* I (Leiden 1971) cxxxvii-ix. His extensive prolegomena to this and the second volume of his edition give an up-to-date survey of Eustathius' sources and methods.

[5] E. Martini, *RhMus* 62 (1907) 273-94, esp. 280-7. Marc. gr. 460 apparently derives from another autograph, Paris gr. 2702.

[6] For problems about some other alleged autographs see N.G. Wilson, *GRBS* 14 (1973) 226-8.

[7] J. Griffin, *Homer on Life and Death* (Oxford 1980), cites several passages.

which Homer has added poetic ornament, either by changing their location or magnifying their characteristics. The Cimmerians are really a race living in the north who have been wrongly located in the west so as to be near the entrance to Hades. Calypso's island has been transferred to the river Ocean. Exaggeration is exemplified by the representation of the Laestrygonians, a fierce tribe in reality, as cannibals. Aeolus, the expert in the art of sailing, is said to imprison the winds, again an exaggeration rather than a falsehood. Eustathius shows a rare trace of humour by quoting Eumaeus' words to Odysseus (14.365-6) 'Why should a person such as yourself tell lies?'

He then quotes some ancient judgments on the differences between the two Homeric poems. The story of the *Odyssey* is essentially slender, but is skilfully expanded by the poet by the addition of the journey of Telemachus, the long conversation with the Phaeacians, the brilliant deception at Eumaeus' hut and similar episodes. The main concern of the *Odyssey* is virtue: it teaches love of husbands, setting up Penelope as a model for both sexes, it invites us to avoid injustice, by showing how the suitors did not escape paying for their misdeeds. Other lessons scattered casually by the poet (all poetry has value for life) will be commented on as they occur. In this approach to the poem Eustathius follows the general principles found in the so-called 'exegetic' scholia to the *Iliad*.

In writing these and other commentaries Eustathius was able to use a number of lost books. He had for instance a copy of the geographer Strabo which did not suffer from the lacuna in book VII. He also had a wide range of lexicographical and grammatical literature to draw on. This included a work by Aristophanes of Byzantium, either complete or in a fuller version than we now have, together with a fuller version of the geographical dictionary of Stephanus Byzantinus. He knew Arrian's *Bithyniaca*. While he is generally capable of choosing good sources, one cannot give him much credit for his willingness to draw on the mass of bizarre and inaccurate information put together by Ptolemy Chennos, who had also been read by Photius and Tzetzes.

In general Eustathius repeats or paraphrases information that we already possess in the collections of scholia on Homer or in some other author whom we can still read. He does not have very much of his own to add, and he is not an acute textual critic. This last point has a bearing on a question to be discussed later.

Some matters of detail may be added here, since they show how difficult it is to answer the question whether Eustathius was regularly in touch with his contemporary Tzetzes.[8] He copies word for word short notes by Tzetzes on Lycophron 731 (607.8) and Aristophanes' *Plutus* 415 (200.46-201.7). If he had a copy of his colleague's edition of the comedies, either he did not read it thoroughly or he had only the earlier version of it. In the prolegomena to his second edition Tzetzes had managed to

---

[8] See also W.J.W. Koster & D. Holwerda, *Mnemosyne* 7 (1954) 147-52.

correct his own earlier misconception about the chronology of Pisistratus, Zenodotus and Aristarchus, but Eustathius does not succeed in avoiding this mistake (5.33-6).

Whatever reservations a modern user may have, it should be noted that Byzantine and Renaissance scholars did not regard the length of the commentaries as an insuperable obstacle. Apart from the autographs there are a number of other copies. Like the *Suda* lexicon the commentaries must have been thought to contain enough of value to justify the enormous outlay of time and writing material necessary for the production of each fresh copy. And for anyone anxious to have a full collection of ancient criticism of the greatest Greek poet, Eustathius put all that was required into a single reference book.

I turn now to consider Eustathius' treatment of other authors. His attitude to tragedy is revealed in the opening paragraphs of an essay on hypocrisy.[9] The connection of thought is not as strange as the bare statement makes it seem. The word hypocrite originally meant actor, and Eustathius cannot resist drawing a contrast between the masks and characters assumed by ancient actors and on the other hand the mask of insincerity presented by contemporary hypocrites. He sums up the purpose of drama as follows.

> It was at least possible for the men of that age to learn from such an art, and it is possible for modern man as well, to learn of the manifold changes of fortune, varieties of human character, and inexpressible diversity of life. The misfortunes of kings portrayed by the art of the actor taught, and indeed will continue to teach, that one should have no confidence in this visible existence, confidence of remaining permanently in an eminent position, but should take precautions against an upheaval. Equally the elevation of humble characters which that type of acting displayed to view showed that a man of lowly station is not wise to despair of joining God in heaven. From the same source we have learned what damage jealousy did to heroes, all of which is likely to continue in later ages. This knowledge benefits those who possess it. Nor did the ancient theatre leave friendship unnoticed or fail to give it due prominence, though it cannot bring to the safety of harbour men tossed on the sea of life ... [the meaning of the next clause is very uncertain].
>
> Why should I go into further detail about these benefits? It must be boring to readers who know already how this kind of acting accurately displayed all types of virtue and vice to the sight and hearing of the ancients, so that they could follow virtue and avoid its opposite. That advantage has come down to later generations, and so we can gather our knowledge of what is good not merely from the living but by contact with the dead through those plays, achieving a life of virtue.

A further question arises from the essay on hypocrites. Eustathius describes the behaviour of such people in social and political life. The

---

[9] Edited by T.F.L. Tafel, *Eustathii metropolitae Thessalonicensis opuscula* (Frankfurt 1832) 88-98; the passage translated here is 88.32-65.

description is reminiscent of Theophrastus' *Characters*, which Eustathius refers to once in his *Iliad* commentary (931.20). He cites as examples the brave man and the coward. The coward is the twenty-fifth in the extant book of *Characters*, but there are no praiseworthy types, and the suggestion has been made that Eustathius knew a longer text than the one we now possess.[10] The alternative explanation of the facts is that he was let down by his memory when he referred to the character of the brave man, and the characterisation of the hypocrite which he gives could perhaps be attributed to his own originality, a concept underestimated by modern scholars owing to their unshakeable faith in the power and value of source criticism. But it must be admitted that the decision in this case is difficult. If Eustathius had forgotten that Theophrastus described no good characters, he would not have found it easy to imitate the style of Theophrastus' descriptions as closely as he does, putting together a long series of traits and including allusions to Demosthenes, the Hyperborean Abaris, and customs at the Persian court. If a lost Theophrastan character is thought an unlikely source, another book by him or by a colleague in the Peripatos is a further possibility.[11]

A fact about Eustathius' knowledge of tragedy which has attracted attention is that he quotes Sophocles' *Antigone* 1165ff in full, whereas all manuscripts of the play omit line 1167. He claims (957.17, on *Iliad* 13.730) to be quoting from 'accurate copies', and if the phrase could be taken literally it would mean that he had access to a branch of tradition superior to any now surviving. But the missing line is also known from Athenaeus' *Deipnosophistae* (7.280C, 12.547C), a text which Eustathius knew well. The new edition of the *Iliad* commentary, based on close study of the autograph, reveals at one point the existence of variant readings inserted above the line, one of which coincides with the text as it is found in Athenaeus and makes it more likely that Eustathius was entirely dependent on him.[12]

Mention of Athenaeus leads naturally to consideration of another well known problem in connection with Eustathius. The *Deipnosophistae* is transmitted by one manuscript (Marc. gr. 447), now damaged at the beginning and end, and by an epitome made from an undamaged text. The epitome has superior readings in a great many passages. Eustathius, who quotes from it extensively, is believed by some authorities to be the author.[13] It is also thought to be based on the Venice manuscript because the epitomator remarks on the existence of a marginal note in his exemplar, and the note in question is found in the Venice copy (at 525C). If these two hypotheses are correct, Eustathius becomes a textual critic

[10] O. Ribbeck, *RhMus* 44 (1889) 306; O. Immisch in the preface to the Leipzig Philological Society's edition (Leipzig 1897) xl.

[11] J. Kayser, *Philologus* 69 (1910) 327-58.

[12] The details are recorded in van der Valk's apparatus criticus.

[13] P. Maas, *Kleine Schriften* (Munich 1973) 519. His view has often been accepted as correct.

of a high order, because he must be responsible for all the good features of the epitome.

The links in this chain of argument are not secure. Although other copies of the full text of Athenaeus are not attested, the possibility that there was at least one other with the scholium in question cannot be excluded, and so the epitomator might not have been working from the Venice copy. Occam's razor tells us *entia non sunt multiplicanda praeter necessitatem*. But simple solutions are not automatically correct in this kind of problem.[14] Another difficult question to decide is whether the improvements in the text credited to Eustathius as a result of the hypothesis we are discussing can plausibly be ascribed to any medieval scholar. While there is no doubt that some of them are well within the capacity of an intelligent and well-read student of the classics, others raise serious doubts. One particularly awkward case is worth citing here. The proper name Nicotheon is corrected by the epitome to Nicocreon (Machon 156 at 349E). Nicotheon is not attested as a Greek name, but it does not sound impossible in principle, since there appear to be a few names ending in -theon, of which Hemitheon seems to be the best attested.[15] That being so, what reason is there to believe that Eustathius would have been aware of the faultiness of the name offered by the Venice manuscript? It is out of the question to imagine that he was sufficiently well versed in onomastics to notice that there was anything wrong, and there is no other source which could have supplied him with the correction.[16] Whereas other alleged emendations of corrupt passages provoke varying degrees of doubt, this one is in my opinion virtually conclusive as a proof that Eustathius should not be credited with great ingenuity as a textual critic. For this reason I have thought it fair to deal with him rather more briefly than might have been expected in a survey of this kind.

We can now return to Eustathius' work on the poets. A very few traces have come to light of his study of Aristophanes. They consist of notes in late copies of the comedies (chiefly Chigi R.IV.20 and Vat. gr. 57). Most of the material coincides to all intents and purposes with notes already known from the Homer commentaries. It might even appear to be a series of excerpts from them, but the correspondence is not word for word. One does better to assume that the future archbishop lectured on comedy and used some of his notes on Homer. A few of his observations might be copied by admiring pupils and marked with his name; some marks of this kind survive in the manuscripts just cited. It is not necessary to assume that Eustathius ever went to the length of publishing his lectures.[17]

---

[14] See W.G. Arnott, *PCPS* 196 (1970) 3 n. 1, who refers to a little known dissertation by H. Papenhoff (Göttingen 1954) and to C. Collard, *RFIC* 97 (1969) 157-79.

[15] Lucian, *Adversus indoctum* 23, *Pseudologistes* 3.

[16] A.S.F. Gow, *Machon* (Cambridge 1965) 90 n. 1, was sceptical. Eduard Fraenkel also expressed to me his personal conviction that Maas could not be right.

[17] Koster & Holwerda, op. cit. in n. 8 above, 136-47, first published the evidence about Eustathius' work on comedy.

The introduction to Pindar is a mediocre performance.[18] It may be an early piece, since the title reveals that the author had not advanced beyond the rank of deacon. A good deal of it is a reworking of traditional material, such as the life of the poet. The text is verbose and florid. It does, however, have the merit of giving examples of Pindar's bold poetic usage, unconventional word order and dialect forms. Some of these examples are not drawn from the extant odes, which has led to the inference that Eustathius read more of Pindar than we now can. The inference is not quite certain, and has been doubted by at least one modern expert.[19] Perhaps the best explanation, though it cannot be more than a tentative hypothesis, is that he had a fuller text of the Isthmian Odes (cf. e.g. fr. 8 cited at 1715.63 in the Homer commentary), which in the most complete manuscript (Laur. 32.52) break off after a few lines of the ninth Ode. Eustathius is well aware of Pindar's obscurity. He does not comment on it at length, but we have already seen how this quality within certain limits could appeal to Byzantine taste. Pindaric digressions are explicitly defended by Eustathius, who admits that they can be longer than the main theme of the poem. Although they may have no obvious connection, he suggests that they may be due to the need to give an example or to confirm a maxim of general application. In most cases they serve as an encomium of the victor's ancestors, country or clan. The victor may be made to seem divine or on a level with great figures of myth and so to share in their glory.[20] The final words reveal the intention of the commentary which was to follow: 'Here our purpose is an approach in the customary manner, gathering useful knowledge to be employed by those who wish to write or in general to understand. This will not be an exegesis in the style of a commentary, but a selection from a broad field of all that is not on the beaten track or scorned by lovers of the beautiful and experts in the Muses' rewards.' What the actual result of this resolution was remains a matter for speculation. The introduction is transmitted only in a collection of essays on various subjects. References elsewhere in Eustathius' work to a Pindar commentary may be deceptive. They could conceivably be explained on the assumption that he gave classes on Pindar, for which he used a quantity of material collected in note form, but that it was never worked up into the same form as the Homer commentaries.

The commentary on Dionysius Periegetes was put together at the request of a certain John Dukas, the son of an important functionary.[21] The letter of dedication makes clear that it was a compilation, and that apart from the text itself Eustathius had an eye for material which could be of value for writers of prose (69.23-4). This motive for reading classical poetry is recurrent. The position of Dionysius in the school curriculum as

---

[18] Edited by A.B. Drachmann, *Scholia vetera in Pindari carmina* III (Leipzig 1927) 285-306.

[19] Cohn, op. cit. in n. 1 above, 1455, was sceptical.

[20] Sections 4, 5, 19.

[21] See G. Bernhardy's edition I (Leipzig 1828) 67 ff.

a text for beginners appears to be indicated (71.4-5). Eustathius says
that he will not attempt systematically to correct mistakes or fill the
gaps wrongly left by Dionysius (71.22-72.6), but he will offer answers to
some of the questions that spring to the mind of the reader. The
commentary is in fact much longer than the collection of old scholia
which must have been Eustathius' basic source.[22]

Among the rare texts read and exploited by Eustathius the so-called
alphabetic plays of Euripides, never included in the school syllabus,
should be mentioned.[23] Although it is no longer possible to maintain that
he was the only Byzantine of his time to be acquainted with them, as a
remark by Tzetzes distinctly implies a reading of the *Cyclops*, the fact is
notable, and has led to the speculation that Eustathius found a copy of
the plays which he took with him to Thessalonica. There it was
unearthed more than a century after his death by Demetrius Triclinius.
As will be seen later, the story may be more complicated, because the
manuscript written at Triclinius' request may have links with his older
contemporary Maximus Planudes. But the significance of what these
scholars did can best be expressed by quoting from a modern study of the
transmission of Euripides:

> Imagine, if you can, our world without Iphigeneia – Iphigeneia sacrificing
> herself for her nation, Iphigeneia rescuing Orestes and returning with him.
> And imagine it without that unique image of Dionysiac frenzy, the drama
> of the Theban king vainly opposing the god; and without Herakles, the
> saviour and murderer, the man in his glory, ruin and heroic resignation.
> The thought baffles the imagination. From the Italian Renaissance down
> to Gluck and Goethe, Nietzsche and Swinburne, and to our own day (not
> entirely swamped, as yet, by blithe barbarism), these great images have
> been of the essence of our lives.[24]

It was the paradoxical fate of Eustathius that while one side of his
activities may entitle him to bask in reflected glory and enjoy the
gratitude of posterity, the final judgment on his writings must be
expressed in Voltaire's words 'Le secret d'ennuyer est de tout dire.'

(v) Michael Choniates

Yet another scholarly bishop was Michael Choniates (*c.* 1138-*c.* 1222).
He occupied the archbishopric of Athens, but if this was the reward for a

---

[22] No autograph survives, but see A. Diller, *The Textual Tradition of Strabo's Geography*
(Amsterdam 1975) 181-207; on 183 he suggests that there were once two autograph copies,
as of the *Odyssey* commentary.

[23] G. Zuntz, *The Political Plays of Euripides* (Manchester 1955) 147-51; van der Valk,
op. cit. in n. 4 above, I lxxxvii ff; R. Browning, *BICS* 7 (1960) 15, reprinted in his *Studies* (cf.
n. 1 above) and in D. Harlfinger (ed.), *Griechische Kodikologie und Textüberlieferung*
(Darmstadt 1980) 259-75.

[24] G. Zuntz, *An Inquiry into the Transmission of the Plays of Euripides* (Cambridge 1965)
xix.

career as a teacher in a school under the auspices of the patriarch, it was a reward that he did not enjoy. He was appalled to discover that the Athenians barely understood his high-flown sermons, and the beauty of the undamaged Parthenon seems to have been no consolation for the loss of the educated society of the capital. He complained that after three years residence in Athens he had still scarcely learnt the local patois and felt reduced to the condition of a barbarian. In making this remark his words echo with a sardonic twist a line from Euripides (*Orestes* 485). It should perhaps be added that he was not the first person to distort what was probably a tag.[1]

Michael brought his library with him from Constantinople and made additions to it. One would like to know whether they were made exclusively through his friends in the capital. The most remarkable item in the collection, which is indeed the main reason why he figures in this history, was a copy of Callimachus'*Aitia* and short epic poem *Hekale*. Michael must have known that these were very rare texts and he took a delight in quoting from the epic in his letters. The quotations are not all easy to recognise; a few of them were noticed only recently.[2] We must be grateful for Michael's pride in his rare possession, as the book was destroyed, along with much of the rest of his collection, when the Fourth Crusade reached Athens in 1205. His later correspondence shows him trying to recover his lost property. A friend had found three volumes from his library, and Michael asks him to continue looking for his Euclid and Theophylact's commentary on the Pauline Epistles, the latter being Michael's own transcript. He offers a copy of Thucydides, if that should prove to be the only way to recover the volumes he is looking for. He gives vent to his fury against the Latins, who cannot read Greek literature in the original or even understand it with the aid of a translation. 'Sooner will asses understand the harmony of the lyre and dung-beetles enjoy perfume than the Latins appreciate the harmony and grace of prose.'[3] This is not Michael's first expression of bitter feeling on the subject; as a young man he had had occasion to complain how scarce and expensive books were, partly because booksellers were doing a great trade with Italians. These men must have been the early translators, but one may doubt whether their enthusiasm as collectors was really enough to upset the balance of supply and demand in the book trade.

A curious detail about which one would be pleased to have more information is the remark that he would like to perform dissections.[4] He alludes in this context to Galen and Aristotle, who appear to have

[1] His works were edited by S.P. Lambros (Athens 1879-80). See Letter 28, vol. 2 p. 44. The quotation had already been used in the same way by Apollonius of Tyana, Letter 34.

[2] H. Lloyd-Jones & J.R. Rea, *HSCP* 72 (1968) 134; F. Bornmann, *Maia* 25 (1973) 204-6. R. Pfeiffer, *Callimachus* II (Oxford 1953) xxxii, was uncertain whether a knowledge of these texts should be credited to Eustathius.

[3] Letters 117 and 146, ed. Lambros, vol. 2 pp. 241-2, 295-6. Letter 117 also reveals that he had lent his correspondent a copy of Nicander.

[4] Letter 102, ibid. 190.

stimulated his interest, but unfortunately he does not make clear whether he has already done any experiments, and there is no other evidence to satisfy our curiosity. Even if it were known that he had been connected with a hospital in the capital, which it is not, this would be a highly unusual interest in experimental science.[5]

(vi) A mysterious partnership

Mention must be made of an important group of manuscripts whose date and origin are still a matter for discussion. They were produced by two scribes with the occasional collaboration of others. One of the two was called Ioannikios, and he describes himself as a humble unmarried grammarian. Both he and his regular colleague had unusual handwriting: Ioannikios is extraordinarily variable and inconsistent, while his colleague shows by the general character of his hand that he had been brought up in a different tradition; he must be an Italian, as he writes quire signatures in Roman numerals. Ioannikios used to be placed in the fourteenth century, because that was the date assigned to him in the catalogue of the Laurentian Library published in 1764-70 by A.M. Bandini, who first recognised the identity of the hand in several manuscripts. Modern scholars have been slow to give independent thought to the question. It is now practically certain that the second half of the twelfth century is the correct date, although it must be noted that one well qualified modern authority is inclined to prefer the early part of the thirteenth century and to suggest that Ioannikios lived in Apulia.[1] Since his hand does not contain any obvious signs of origin in that area it is difficult to decide. I should like to put forward as a tentative hypothesis the idea that the collaboration of the two men took place, or at least began, in Constantinople, where the anonymous colleague could have lived in one of the Latin colonies. He may be supposed to have come principally in order to acquire Greek medical and philosophical texts, and it would be natural for him to form a partnership with a local scribe. The presence in one manuscript of a third hand which might be thought Italo-Greek is to be explained either by the arrival of another westerner in the capital or conceivably by Ioannikios' decision after the disaster of 1204 to seek his fortune in the west. Most Byzantines who went into exile after the arrival of the Fourth Crusade went to Asia Minor, but with his existing connections Ioannikios would have had an alternative open to him. However, the identification of an early owner of several of the manuscripts makes it unlikely that his career lasted so long.

The books written by these scribes are remarkable in more than one

[5] G. Stadtmüller, *Michael Choniates Metropolit von Athen* (*Orientalia Christiana* 33/2) (Rome 1934) 78-82, deals with Michael's literary activities during his exile.
[1] P. Canart, *Scrittura e Civiltà* 2 (1978) 151-2. G. Cavallo, ibid. 4 (1980) 214-6, favours a date *c*. 1200 and origin in Sicily. Cavallo follows J. Wiesner in P. Moraux (ed.), *Aristoteles Graecus* I (Berlin 1976) 472, in adding Paris supp. gr. 352 to the group, but this seems to me wrong.

respect. Only one contains any theological text. It is a battered copy of pseudo-Dionysius the Areopagite, which appears to be in the hand of the anonymous colleague (Barb. gr. 591). The volume also contained John Philoponus' commentary on Aristotle's *Physics*. Otherwise classical authors are the only concern of these scribes. Their main interest was in medicine. They copied many works of Galen (Laur. 74.5, 74.18, 74.25, 75.5, 75.17), Aetius of Amida (Laur. 75.5, 75.7, 75.18, 75.20), and Paul of Aegina (Laur. 74.26). More than one editor who has had occasion to collate the text offered by these volumes has noted its excellent quality.[2] Aristotle is also well represented by the *Organon* (Laur. Conv. Sopp. 192), *Metaphysics* (Paris gr. 1849), zoological works (Laur. 87.4), and *Physics*, *De caelo*, *De generatione et corruptione*, and *Meteorologica* (Laur. 87.7). Once again modern editors have been impressed, particularly by the copy of the *Physics*, which preserves a tradition of the text different from that found in all other known manuscripts.[3] The literary texts, although in a minority, are again of some significance. There is a volume containing all seven plays of Sophocles and eight by Euripides (Laur. 31.10). For Sophocles this witness is valuable, since it alone preserves the right reading in a number of places, and it is probably a descendant of the famous tenth-century Laurentian manuscript (Laur. 32.9) with a few readings incorporated from another branch of tradition.[4] It has the additional distinction of having served as the exemplar from which a knowledge of Euripides was first offered to Renaissance Italy, since it belonged to Leonzio Pilato, who translated about four hundred lines of the *Hecuba* for Boccaccio.[5] The second literary text is a copy of the *Iliad* written by Ioannikios and of no particular importance (Vat. gr. 1319). The third and most remarkable is also due to Ioannikios alone; it is the archetype of the handbook on mythology known as Apollodorus (Paris gr. 2722). This was probably a bibliographical rarity, even if Tzetzes had made an epitome of it. Certainly several of the medical texts were very uncommon. Where might Ioannikios and his associates have had access to libraries that could offer them so much? Apulia seems to me less likely than Palermo, if an Italian source is required, and if they drew on a collection in Palermo, its existence must indicate that the flow of books from Constantinople to the west had been even greater than is usually supposed. A library in the capital is perhaps a more plausible explanation. It might be thought a serious objection that several of the

---

[2] G. Helmreich, *Galeni scripta minora* II (Leipzig 1891) xi; III (Leipzig 1893) iii and v-vi; id. *Galeni De temperamentis* (Leipzig 1904) iv; A. Olivieri, *Aetius* I (Leipzig-Berlin 1935) x.

[3] W.D. Ross, *Aristotle's Physics* (Oxford 1936) 108-9. Cf. also H.H. Joachim, *Aristotle on Coming-to-be and Passing-away* (Oxford 1922) viii; P. Moraux, *Aristote Du ciel* (Paris 1965) clxxxi.

[4] N.G. Wilson, *JHS* 100 (1980) 219, reviewing R.D. Dawe, *Studies on the Text of Sophocles* III (Leiden 1978), where more information is given.

[5] A. Pertusi, *Leonzio Pilato fra Petrarca e Boccaccio* (Venice 1964) 113-17 with plates X-XI. Other literary texts annotated by the anonymous colleague are the *Odyssey* (Laur. 32.24) and Oppian (Laur. 31.39). But neither of these MSS. is a product of the partnership.

manuscripts are written on paper believed to be of Spanish manufacture, but the increasingly dominant position enjoyed by Italian traders from Pisa, Genoa and Venice in Constantinople should make us hesitate to declare that the market for paper continued to be dominated by the traditional eastern sources of supply. The riddle is not made any easier to solve by the discovery that in four of these manuscripts there are Latin notes apparently in the hand of Burgundio of Pisa (*c.* 1110-93), one of the first translators of Greek texts in the twelfth century; he is known to have acquired books in Constantinople on at least one of the occasions when he went there as an envoy from Pisa, but he could equally well have added to his library in such places as Messina, where he stayed for a while during the return journey from his embassy of 1171.[6]

One further consequence of establishing firmly the date of Ioannikios is that we can reject the widely received opinion that the manuscripts of Galen are surprisingly late, fifteenth-century copies being the rule.[7] The idea is not in itself implausible, since books used regularly by practitioners might not stand up well to the inevitable wear and tear. In fact even from a perusal of the census made early this century by Hermann Diels it is possible to see that the usual opinion is something of an exaggeration. But the transfer of more than half a dozen volumes in his list from the thirteenth or fourteenth century to the twelfth results in a substantially different picture. And in addition to volumes written by Ioannikios Burgundio owned and annotated another copy of Galen (Laur. 74.30) which has to be redated in exactly the same way.

---

[6] I owe some of the information on which this section is based to the late Alexander Turyn. A more detailed study will appear in *Scrittura e Civiltà* 7 (1983).

[7] So J. Mewaldt in *RE*, s.v. Galenos, col. 590.

10

Greek in Italy and Sicily

(i)   From late antiquity to the eleventh century

Although the object of this book is to study the history of scholarship in
Byzantium, there is one area of western Europe which cannot be left out
of the story entirely. Justinian was by no means the only emperor to take
a serious interest in Italian affairs, temporal as well as spiritual, and
throughout the period that we are concerned with parts of Italy and
Sicily continued to use the Greek language and to acknowledge the
ecclesiastical, if not always the political, authority of the eastern empire.

Justinian's conquest of Italy was short-lived. Had he had the resources
to impose his regime more permanently he might have ensured for Greek
culture a longer and more wide-spread survival than it in fact enjoyed. In
his day it seems that Ravenna, being the main point of contact between
Italy and the empire, was culturally bilingual. It has been observed that
some palimpsests in which Greek texts have been covered by Latin
script, probably at Bobbio or elsewhere in northern Italy, are evidence of
Greek book production in Ravenna or nearby. The texts in question are
Porphyry's commentary on Plato's *Parmenides* (Turin F.VI.1),
Dioscorides, Galen and medical prescriptions (Naples lat.2), Galen (Vat.
lat. 5763 & Wolfenbüttel, Weissenb. 64), and a mathematical text
attributed to Anthemius of Tralles (Ambr. L 99 sup.).[1] Even if these
books are imported rather than local products, their presence in Italy
before their reuse for Latin texts is sufficient for the present purpose.
When most of Italy ceased to be part of the Byzantine empire, the
number of people able to use them declined rapidly and it is easy to
understand why in an age of increasing poverty they were treated as a
source of writing material capable of receiving more useful texts.

Greek continued to be spoken, sometimes as a first, sometimes as a
second language, south of Rome and in many parts of Sicily, especially
the north-eastern corner of the island, which put up the longest
resistance to the Arab conquest. By the time of the Renaissance it was
almost confined to districts in the heel and toe of the peninsular and the
surroundings of Messina. In the twentieth century there are still a few
communities in Apulia and Calabria which preserve the language

---

[1] G. Cavallo in G.G. Archi (ed.), *L'imperatore Giustiniano, storia e mito* (Milan 1978)
208-10.

brought by the colonists from archaic Greece. During the middle ages the
retreat of Greek was sometimes temporarily arrested, and there is a good
deal of evidence about the literary accomplishments of the Greek
inhabitants of the region, some of it consisting of their own writings. In
addition recent advances in the study of Greek handwriting have made it
possible to identify a large number of books written in the area. It must
be said, however, that there is a tendency in recent writing on the subject
to identify as Italo-Greek many volumes about which the evidence is far
from decisive, and in what follows I shall try as far as possible to avoid
using doubtful cases to support an argument, even if the result is to
underestimate slightly the role played by this area in the transmission of
texts.[2] Certain general principles need to be emphasised. Many books
which offer no palaeographical proof of their origin in the area are known
to have passed through it at some point in their history. This movement
is due to travellers such as churchmen visiting the eastern part of the
empire or functionaries arriving from Constantinople to administer a
province, and perhaps particularly to the activity of Henricus Aristippus
and his contemporaries in the middle of the twelfth century. It should
not be regarded as a proof of a high level of culture at all times
throughout the area. But it does help to explain why the preservation of a
few texts depends largely or exclusively on an Italo-Greek copy. Another
important consideration is that although many copies of lexica look as if
they were produced by Italo-Greek scribes, the fact will cease to surprise
us if we bear in mind that Greek was increasingly becoming a second
language needing more study on the part of its speakers. Exaggerated
accounts of Italo-Greek culture can be seen in proper perspective if one
asks whether it produced any works of scholarship or fresh recensions of
classical texts and the commentaries on them. Despite the existence of
such centres as the monastery of St. Nicolas of Casole just outside
Otranto, the answer to this question is largely negative. Nor does secular
literature appear to have enjoyed greater popularity in Reggio, Messina
or Palermo.

It may be appropriate to deal here with a question which will occur to
any reader with an interest in the history of medicine in medieval
Europe. In view of the linguistic geography of Italy is it not likely that
Greek medical writings were studied at the school in Salerno in the
original language? Perhaps surprisingly this seems not to have
happened. It looks as if Latin translations were preferred. The collection of
medical and other manuscripts, produced not later than the second half of
the twelfth century by two scribes, one of whom writes an Italian rather
than a Byzantine hand, appears to have no link with Salerno.

The last flicker of scholarship in ancient Italy is associated with the

---

[2] In this respect I follow a policy opposite to that of Cavallo in his comprehensive study in
Scrittura e Civiltà 4 (1980); on this point see 160-1. The article by P. Canart, *Scrittura e
Civiltà* 2 (1978) 103-62, is also cautious in its approach; see especially 141 n. 86 for an
expression of scepticism about certain widely held opinions.

name of Cassiodorus, who established his monastery Vivarium near
Squillace in what is now the province of Catanzaro, a spot perhaps
further from the beaten track in modern times than it was in the middle
ages. The library included a section of Greek authors, in which medical
and scientific interests were prominent. The fate of the monastery and its
library are unknown. Darkness descends on the south of Italy, and the
same process of using Greek books to meet the more urgent requirement
of Latin texts can be seen here as in the north. Perhaps the best example
for our purpose is the Codex Claromontanus of the Pauline Epistles,
which was repaired in the sixth century by the addition of two leaves
from a copy of Euripides' *Phaethon* (Paris gr. 107). One is probably
justified in adding the fragments of Strabo (Vat. gr. 2061A) and an essay
on politics sometimes thought to be by Theophrastus (Vat. gr. 2306), and
it may be correct to see in the small surviving portion of Dio Cassius'
Roman History that is now preserved as Vat. gr. 1288 the remains of a
book that was discarded during the same period.[3] It is in any case clear
that the ancient libraries of southern Italy contained many treasures.

There is no trace of literary scholarship for about four centuries after
the death of Cassiodorus, by which time Sicily was mostly in the hands of
the Arabs. In the tenth century, according to a view often expressed in
recent years, classical texts began to be transcribed again. The examples
cited are not above suspicion. Diodorus Siculus' *Universal History* I-V
(Naples gr. 4*) is regularly quoted, but for no convincing reason. The
same has to be said of the rich miscellany MS. Barocci 50, which is not
the only volume to have been thought to have an Italian provenance on
account of a curious feature of its script, a ligature of the letters epsilon
and rho in the shape of the ace of spades.[4] This ligature can be seen in
books which were certainly written in other parts of the Byzantine world,
and it cannot by itself constitute proof of origin in Italy. Shortly
afterwards there are other books commonly cited in this context. Apart
from the dubious case of some Aristotelian commentaries, which are
unique or very rare but not of any great importance (Paris gr. 2064 and
fragments bound in as guard leaves with Ambr. Q 57 sup.),[5] a notable
book of indisputably western origin and probably dating from the tenth
century is MS. Pierpont Morgan 397, which until the period of the
Napoleonic wars belonged to the Greek monastery of Grottaferrata a few
miles outside Rome. While the handwriting is in some ways unusual, it is
the illumination which most clearly suggests Italian origin. The contents
are: the fables of Aesop, the novelistic text known as the *Life of Aesop*, in
a longer and more complete recension than is known from any other
source, thirty-one fables of Babrius, the Greek bestiary (*Physiologus*),
the jest-book *Philogelos*, and part of an early Greek version of the Arabic

[3] J. Irigoin, *JOB* 18 (1969) 37-55 (reprinted in D. Harlfinger (ed.), *Griechische
Kodikologie und Textüberlieferung* (Darmstadt 1980) 234-58); see his note 21.
  [4] Irigoin, ibid.; it follows that I find it difficult to accept the conclusion of his note 49.
  [5] Irigoin, ibid.; see note 63; Cavallo, op. cit. in n. 2, 167.

story of Kalila and Dimna.[6] Alongside this collection of light literature
we find the usual handbooks of rhetoric (Paris gr. 3032), which suggests
that the practices of schools in this part of the Byzantine world were the
same as in the capital and the eastern provinces. There is also an
anthology of medical texts (Paris supp. gr. 1297). A number of other
books have been attributed with varying degrees of probability to the
Italian scriptoria of this period.

It may be asked at this point why there is no mention of John the
Sicilian, who wrote commentaries on Hermogenes, exemplifying the
precepts by means of passages taken from St. Gregory of Nazianzus. The
little we know of him suggests that he did not spend his career in Sicily.
An autobiographical digression refers to an occasion when he addressed
the emperor Basil II (976-1025) in a monastery which can be located in
Constantinople, and it looks as if he may have been an exile from his
native land.[7]

(ii)   The twelfth century

When the Normans replaced the Byzantines as political masters of the
region the Greek element in the population did not go into decline as
might have been expected, and from the twelfth century there is a good
deal of evidence about the circulation of Greek texts and the importance
attached to them.[1] One part of this evidence can be exploited more fully
thanks to recent palaeographical studies. It has been demonstrated that
a hundred or more books written in a distinctive script belong to the
twelfth or in a few cases the thirteenth century and were written in this
area. A few of them have colophons explicitly stating that they were
produced near Reggio. No evidence has been found so far to cast doubt
on the attribution of all these books to the Italo-Greek area, and for
convenience the hand is called Reggio script.[2] Biblical, theological and
liturgical texts predominate, but not to the exclusion of secular authors.
The first thorough survey revealed several books written to meet
practical needs: legal texts (Marc. gr. 172), Hippocrates (Urb. gr. 64) and
Galen (Escorial T-III-7 and Marc. gr. 288). Linguistic concerns are
reflected by pseudo-Cyril's lexicon (Vat. gr. 2130). Literature is not
entirely absent: we find the novel by Achilles Tatius, together with the
formular letters and a declamation (XXVI) of the fourth-century sophist
Libanius and the fictitious letters of the Byzantine historian
Theophylact Simocatta (Vat. gr. 1349 & 1391). More striking is the
unique copy of the letters of Aristaenetus, a very late author in the
tradition of the second sophistic age who can never have enjoyed much

---

[6] B.E. Perry, *Aesopica* (Urbana 1952) xv, where further literature is cited.

[7] See H. Rabe, *RhMus* 62 (1907) 581 n. 1; S.G. Mercati, *Bessarione* 26 (1922) 214
(reprinted in *Collectanea Byzantina* II (Bari 1970) 291); F.W. Lenz, *Aristeidesstudien*
(Berlin 1964) 97-9, 113-14.

[1] P. Canart, *Scrittura e Civiltà* 2 (1978) 103-62, is the fundamental survey.

[2] The evidence is assembled by P. Canart & J. Leroy in *La paléographie grecque, Actes
du Colloque No. 559* (Paris 1977) 241-61.

popularity (Vienna, phil. gr. 310). The other text in this volume is by an author from Otranto, and so provides a hint about its place of origin and the range of authors available in the monastic library, which is thought to have provided cardinal Bessarion with a number of choice items for his collection in the middle of the fifteenth century.

Reggio script did not have a monopoly. Other styles, not all revealing their origin clearly, continued in use. One may infer on the basis of other evidence that a copy of the *Suda* lexicon dated 1205 is of Italian origin (Vat. gr. 1296).[3] In one famous case various styles are found together (Vat. gr. 300). The text is the Greek version by Constantine the African of an Arabic medical text. In its margins extracts have been written from the commentary by John of Alexandria on book VI of Hippocrates' *Epidemics*. The commentary is known from a Latin translation, but there is no other source for the Greek text. Another interesting detail about this book, worth recording even if it is not strictly relevant to the matter under discussion in this section, is a note added in the margin by a later owner. It refers to a visit of an unnamed king to the medical school at Salerno.[4]

The existence of a translation from the Arabic leads naturally to consideration of other and more famous translators. Some of them came from the north of Italy, and there is no proof that they lived in the south in order to do their work, or that any of their Greek texts were acquired in the south. Essentially such men take their place in the history of western medieval scholarship, and for the present purpose it is not necessary to give more than the briefest passing mention to James of Venice and Burgundio of Pisa. James concentrated on Aristotle, translating for the first time the *Physics*, *De anima*, *Metaphysics* and parts of the *Parva naturalia*, and making fresh versions after those by Boethius of much of the *Organon*. His activity probably belongs to the years 1130-70.[5] The work of Burgundio of Pisa (*c.* 1110-93), a prominent official who travelled as an envoy to Constantinople, is more varied. He translated patristic authors, St. John Damascene and John Chrysostom, besides Nemesius of Emesa's *De natura hominis*, the *Geoponica* and various treatises by Galen (the exact number is uncertain).[6] Meanwhile in Sicily important work was being undertaken by another man who had served on an embassy to the Byzantine emperor, Henricus Aristippus, archdeacon of the Latin church in Catania and for a short time minister at the Norman court in Palermo (d.c. 1162).[7] He himself was responsible for versions of

[3] P. Canart, op. cit. in n. 1 above, 144 n. 96.

[4] G. Mercati, *Notizie varie di antica letteratura medica e di bibliografia* (*Studi e Testi* 31) (Rome 1917) 16-17.

[5] L. Minio-Paluello, *Traditio* 8 (1952) 265-304.

[6] On him see F. Liotta in *Dizionario biografico degli Italiani* 15 (Rome 1972) 423-8, R.J. Durling, *Burgundio of Pisa's translation of Galen's Περὶ κράσεων 'De complexionibus'* (*Galenus Latinus* 1) (Berlin 1976) xxv-xxx, and Chapter 9 (vi) above.

[7] See E. Franceschini in *Dizionario biografico degli Italiani* 4 (Rome 1962) 201-6. The most important modern work is C.H. Haskins, *Studies in the History of Medieval Science* (ed. 2, Cambridge, Mass. 1927).

Plato's *Meno* and *Phaedo*, and an anonymous colleague took on the much longer and more difficult task of dealing with Ptolemy's *Almagest*. The prefaces to these three productions yield a certain amount of information. In one of them Aristippus addresses an English friend, whose identity has so far eluded the detective efforts of modern scholarship, and tries to persuade him not to return to his native land. The inducement to remain in Sicily consists of a good library and the patronage of a powerful and active king. The former is described as a *Siracusanam et Argolicam bibliothecam*, a phrase not easy to interpret precisely and perhaps meaning no more than a library of Greek literature. Some indication is given of its contents: Hero's *Mechanica* (since this survives only in Arabic, minor fragments excepted, the chances are that he is referring to the *Pneumatica*, an account of many gadgets operated by pressure),[8] Euclid's *Optics*, Aristotle's *Apodictice* (this is the *Analytica priora*), and the works of Anaxagoras, Aristotle, Themistius, Plutarch and other great philosophers. It is not at all clear what he had in mind when referring to Anaxagoras. Of the small number of surviving fragments most have come down to us in Simplicius' commentary on Aristotle's *Physics*, which would have been easily accessible, and if Aristippus means exactly what he says this is perhaps the best way of taking his words.

How many other texts did he have at his disposal? It is hard to say. His interests were obviously mainly in science and philosophy. The copy of the *Almagest* on which he depended, a gift from the emperor Manuel Comnenus to king William I, has been identified by means of its variant readings (it is Marc. gr. 313).[9] It happens to have two later marks of ownership, 'And' which is thought to be an abbreviation of 'Andegavensis', the note of possession attached to books belonging to Charles of Anjou, together with a number corresponding to its place in the medieval inventory of the papal library. The connection is logical, since Charles gave his library to the pope after the battle of Beneventum in 1266. Several other manuscripts exhibit one or both of the same marks, and it is tempting to suppose that all had passed through Aristippus' hands, especially as all the texts are mathematical or scientific.[10] On that hypothesis one would like to know whether they were all part of the emperor's gift to the Norman king. An alternative explanation of the history of these volumes would be that their presence in Sicily is due to the scientific interests of the emperor Frederick II, in which case they may not have been imported until the thirteenth century.

In his preface to the *Phaedo* Aristippus tells us that he began work

---

[8] The words 'qui tam subtiliter de inani disputat' point to the proem of the *Pneumatica* rather than fragments of the *Mechanica* preserved in book VIII of Pappus. The other view is preferred by E. Grant, *Speculum* 46 (1971) 656-69. Pseudo-Hero's *De machinis bellicis* is theoretically another possibility, but the archetype (Vat. gr. 1605) does not give the author's name.

[9] J.L. Heiberg, *Hermes* 45 (1910) 57-66, 46 (1911) 207-16.

[10] They are listed by Canart, op. cit. in n. 1 above, 149 n. 113.

while on campaign with the king at the siege of Beneventum and finished it on his return to Palermo. The anonymous colleague's preface to the *Almagest* is also informative. It appears that he had been a student of medicine at Salerno when he heard that Aristippus had acquired a copy of the *Almagest*. Braving the dangers of Scylla, Charybdis and Etna he found Aristippus observing the activity of the volcano ('prope Pergusam fontem Ethnaea miracula satis cum periculo perscrutantem'). He was not allowed to begin translating at once, as he needed an intensive course in Greek, and then as a prelude to the great enterprise he tried his hand at versions of Euclid's *Data*, *Optics* and *Catoptrics*, and Proclus' *Elementatio physica*.[11] He obtained help from a certain Eugenius, who is without much doubt the minister at court celebrated for his achievement of translating Euclid's *Optics* from the Arabic.[12] Norman court society was trilingual, and another translation made from the Arabic seems to have come into Aristippus' hands. This was of the first three books of Aristotle's *Meteorologica*, and had been made by Gerard of Cremona, presumably in Toledo. Aristippus added his own version of the fourth book, and the composite work passed into general circulation. There is no trace of the promised versions of Diogenes Laertius' *Lives of the Philosophers*[13] and of Gregory of Nazianzus, and it is likely that Aristippus never had time to begin them.

The quality and value of the translations cannot be rated very high. Although Aristippus took the trouble to revise and improve his *Phaedo*, his method had led him to retain the word order of the original as far as possible, with the result that elegance and clarity had to be sacrificed. Important later readers of his work include Petrarch and Coluccio Salutati, but it is not surprising that Leonardo Bruni made a fresh version more in keeping with the literary standards of the Renaissance. Yet the intention of making more of Plato's writings accessible in western Europe is praiseworthy and must be reckoned an important contribution to the twelfth-century Renaissance.

Modern scholars cannot expect to derive much benefit from Aristippus' work. But at *Meno* 99d he has the minor merit of preserving a Doric dialect form not found in extant manuscripts of Plato and thereby confirming a conjecture made by Casaubon.[14] This is a slender reward for the textual critic, yet not to be despised as if it were of no significance. If it is the right reading,[15] it shows that Plato added a touch of colour to his

[11] Edited by H. Boese (Berlin 1958). On p. 16 he follows a suggestion of Heiberg that the delay was due to lack of interest on the part of Aristippus. I think this unlikely, and not required by the Latin; the *mens* in question is that of the translator, not Aristippus. On Euclid see J.E. Murdoch, *HSCP* 71 (1967) 249-302.

[12] E.M. Jamison, *Admiral Eugenius of Sicily, his life and work, and the authorship of the Epistola ad Petrum and the Historia Hugonis Falcandi Siculi* (London 1957), 3-4.

[13] But the Naples codex III-B-29 is a contemporary product of the area, as can be shown from the script and the unusual composition of the quires. I have looked through it without success for traces of a Latin owner.

[14] See the edition of V. Kordeuter & C. Labowsky (*Plato Latinus* 1) (London 1940) 45.

[15] It could be an alteration made by a Greek scribe who remembered the dialect form in a similar passage in Aristotle's *Nic. Eth.* 1145 a 29.

prose by the use of dialect, as he occasionally does elsewhere.

(iii)   An essay on a Greek novel

One of the manuscripts of Heliodorus' novel (Marc. gr. 410) preserves an essay by Philip-Philagathus, a native of Cerami, a small town in Sicily between Nicosia and Troina, who became archbishop of Rossano in Calabria during the reign of Roger II (1130-54).[1] The text begins as if it were a Platonic dialogue. The author narrates how he was going down to the city gate nearest the sea in Reggio and had reached the spring of Aphrodite when he was hailed by Nicholas the royal scribe and his colleague Andrew. They told him that a large number of educated people had gathered outside the main church, and their conversation was highly critical of Charicleia, Heliodorus' heroine. Would he come to defend the novel? He agreed, despite a feeling that having entered the church he could no longer take an interest in books of this kind which he had enjoyed during his schooldays. His defence begins:

> This book, my friends, is like Circe's potion. It metamorphoses into immoral swine those who partake of it in a profane spirit, but it guides to higher secrets those who are philosophic after the manner of Odysseus. The book is didactic, teaching moral philosophy and blending the water of history with the wine of contemplation. And since human nature is divided into male and female, and the power to do good and evil is given equally to both, the book shows both together, giving evidence of good and evil in each sex. It presents good male characters in Calasiris, Theagenes and Hydaspes, and among the women Persinna and Charicleia; it shows several women and rather fewer men as notable villains, there being more evil implanted in the female sex. Piety, avoidance of one's enemies' scheming devices, the legitimate suppression of unjust force, defence against aggressors, the use of falsehood as a prescription when we have decided to help our friends or ourselves, without inflicting harm on neighbours or backing the falsehood by perjury but wisely adapting our arguments, the ability to take precautions and be winning in speech, and all other forms of wisdom – that is what Calasiris teaches you. He is graceful in his conversation, sound in planning action, resourceful in difficulties when fate tries him sharply. He gives a lesson in virtue by escaping from Rhodopis, as does Cnemon by avoiding Demaenete's improper love, and so above all do Theagenes and Charicleia. He was modest towards his beloved and did not yield to Arsace's mad passion even when flattered or beaten, while Charicleia was so modest that even in sleep and dreams she refused to speak to her lover. The couple should be a noble example of justice to us, since they refused to make themselves rich from booty, and so in particular should Hydaspes, who defeated his enemies by a combination of bravery and good fortune, and showed his justice by being content with his own property. The loving couple, who suffered continuously the trials of fate

---

[1] The text was edited by A. Colonna in his edition of Heliodorus (Rome 1938) 365-70. On the author see B. Lavagnini, *EEBS* 39-40 (1972-3) 457-63 and *Bollettino della Badia greca di Grottaferrata* 28 (1974) 3-12 (an expanded version of the preceding article).

without despair or any display of servile behaviour, are models of bravery. So the book is a model portrait of the four cardinal virtues. It shows also people who behave badly, making the proper criticisms of their wickedness and showing where that leads.

Examples follow. After this reasonably promising if rather medieval beginning Philip turns to allegorical interpretation.

> Charicleia is a symbol of the soul and the mind which orders it; for mind linked to soul is glory and grace [these two concepts are the literal meaning of the heroine's name]. This is not the only reason for her compound name; soul is combined with body, making one substance with it. You will see this more clearly if you count the units of her name, which amount to 777.

Here Philip refers to the values of the Greek letters, which served also as numerals. The values of the letters in Charicleia's name add up to the figure given.

> Since the number seven is mystical, virgin and holy, as the Italian word makes clear, her name justifiably acquires its significance through units, tens and hundreds of the seventh number, seven hundred showing its holy and perfect character, seven tens adorning the tripartite soul with four virtues, the single seven referring to the body, to which the mind is attached, keeping in the middle of the soul the five senses and matter and form, from which it is created.

We have moved within the space of a few lines from criticism of literature to number mysticism. The essay continues in the same vein. It is incomplete, owing to damage in the manuscript. Its chief importance is to show how some readers justified to themselves a taste for ancient novels. In the last resort the Byzantine approach is not so very different from the treatment of Ovid in western Europe.

11

Disaster and Recovery

(i) Nicaea

History books state that the Byzantine empire came to an end in 1453. The educated layman knows that the consolidation of Turkish power in Europe marks a turning point in political history. But if historians had been less exclusively concerned with politics they might have given equal prominence to the year 1204, when the Fourth Crusade lost sight of its objective and the Venetians with their allies captured and sacked the capital of the eastern empire. This event is significant not simply in political terms, since it marked the end for practical purposes of the empire and greatly increased the Turks' chances of successful westward expansion, but also in its intellectual and cultural consequences. Most modern visitors to Venice who admire Saint Mark's cathedral are not aware that the Greek bronze horses and many of the precious objects of the treasury, not to mention the so-called pilasters from Acre, are loot brought back from Constantinople by ruthless members of the church militant. The removal of archaeological treasures is sometimes thought to be justified by the consideration that if they had been left where they were they might have suffered a worse fate. This argument, however unpalatable it may be to nationalist feeling in some areas of the Mediterranean and elsewhere, has to be taken seriously. But whether it can be used to justify or even extenuate Venetian behaviour in 1204 is doubtful. On the one hand the physical damage sustained by Constantinople in 1453 may well have been less serious than the city's sufferings in 1204. And on the other hand the destruction of libraries by the Turks has probably been exaggerated, since there are very few indications of the loss of Greek texts in 1453, whereas it is clear that after 1204 Byzantine scholars rarely if ever show direct acquaintance with literature that we cannot read today. The libraries consulted by Photius were still being used by his intellectual successors at the end of the twelfth century and probably still contained most of the rarities listed in the *Bibliotheca*. After 1204 that was no longer true. The Fourth Crusade put an end to the survival of a quantity of literature which is difficult to estimate but certainly included two of the best works of the civilised and witty Callimachus and a much greater mass of historical literature. None of these texts can ever be recovered except by the lucky chance of finds among the papyri.

Resilience is a quality especially associated with the Jews. The years after 1204 show that the Greeks do not lack their share of it. Refugees streamed across to Asia Minor. A government in exile was established in Nicaea. Its painful and precarious existence for just over half a century was rewarded with success, and in 1261 the Greeks returned to their capital, thanks largely to the incompetence and internal divisions of the Latin rulers. Events were to prove that the success of 1261 was a pyrrhic victory from a political point of view, but it led to a period of great activity in artistic and intellectual fields. That activity drew some of its inspiration from work done in Nicaea under unpromising conditions.

The evidence about cultural life in the Nicaean empire is scanty. Few manuscripts can be attributed confidently to this milieu, and there are no outstanding scholars. But two men have left autobiographical sketches, and one of the emperors, Theodore Lascaris (1254-8), was a prolific writer and a man with a traditional Byzantine faith in the value of education. Patronage coming from such a source could not be entirely ineffectual. Theodore's correspondence includes a letter to two masters at a school which he had established in Nicaea at the church of St. Tryphon.[1] The teacher of philosophy was called Andronicus Frangopoulos, while poetry and grammar were handled by Michael Senacherim. A few notes by the latter on Homer are known (from Voss. gr. F.64 and Vienna, phil. gr. 133),[2] but they do not appear to be of any importance. Theodore and his predecessor John Ducas Vatatzes took the further step of setting up libraries. One source claims that several towns benefited in this way, and another says that by order of the founder they were to be open to the public for consultation.[3] It is not known whether this had been regular practice in Constantinople before 1204. Theodore at the very least deserves our admiration for an enlightened measure, even if he cannot be treated as the inventor of a new policy. Yet there is not much visible trace of his efforts in this direction, and it must remain doubtful how far he put his plan into effect. The most famous manuscript of a central classical author that can be followed at this stage of its history is the Paris Demosthenes (Paris gr. 2934), but the library to which it belonged was one in the monastery of Sosandra, and that was probably not one of the imperial foundations in question. Although it had been favoured by the emperor John and became the burial place of Theodore, it was in an isolated spot in the region of Mount Olympus near Bursa, and would not have been suitable as the location of a public

---

[1] Letter 217 in N. Festa, *Theodori Ducae Lascaris epistulae* (Florence 1898).

[2] The latter is rightly dated to the second half of the thirteenth century in H. Hunger, *Katalog der griechischen Handschriften der Oesterreichischen Nationalbibliothek I: Codices historici, codices philosophici et philologici* (Vienna 1961) 240, who does not mention Senacherim. It can scarcely be an autograph, although the possibility was considered by E. Maass, *Hermes* 19 (1884) 547 n. 1.

[3] F. Dölger, *Regesten der Kaiserurkunden des oströmischen Reiches* III (Munich-Berlin 1932), nos. 1826 and 1847, gives the sources.

library.[4] Perhaps little progress had been made with the new policy when
it was overtaken by the departure of the government from Nicaea.

There are, however, two books surviving from Theodore's personal
library. Some notes in a copy of Aristotle's *Physics* were identified as his
by the late Byzantine scholar John Chortasmenos. They are in a volume
which according to a note on the flyleaf was read from beginning to end
by Theodore (Ambr. M 46 sup.).[5] Exactly the same note is found on the
flyleaf of a copy of St. John Damascene's philosophical writings
(Oxford, Cromwell 13), but in this case there are few marginalia and none
that look as if they come from his pen.

Theodore's letters show him capable of appreciating the physical
remains of classical antiquity. In this respect he appears as a more
thoughtful observer than Michael Choniates, who contemplated his
surroundings in a mood of unrelieved depression. Musing over the ruins
of Pergamon he has this to say:

> The city of Pergamon, as it were floating in the air, not a dwelling place of
> spirits but a protection for mankind against demons (which these are may
> be imagined),[6] received us. It is difficult to gain a view of it, and still more
> difficult to climb up to it. It is full of impressive sights, which have aged
> and withered with time. They show as in a reflecting glass their former
> glory and the greatness of those who built them. These monuments are full
> of Hellenic ambition and are manifestations of that culture. The city
> displays them to us, reproaching us as descendants with the greatness of its
> ancestral glory. These buildings are awe-inspiring when compared with
> modern restorations, however much Aristotle may insist that all else is
> insignificant in comparison with the greatest things of the universe.[7] The
> city walls, like those of Zeus' bronze palace in heaven,[8] rise up with their
> variegated construction. A river runs through the middle of the town,
> bridged by long arches; these (I swear by the architect of the heavens) one
> could describe as natural monoliths, not composite constructions. If
> another sculptor such as Pheidias were to see them he would admire their
> equal measurements and true lines. In between the buildings are visible
> humble huts and the remains of former houses, a very painful sight. Just as
> a mouse's hole is nothing compared to the present houses, so one might say
> that the latter are nothing compared with those that have been destroyed.
> And if this same ratio can be applied to the inhabitants, how wretched are
> the living. How much inferior is the city they have inherited. On each side
> of the outer wall of the great theatre are round towers of regular stone
> construction and with friezes. These are not the work, nor the design, of the

---

[4] To my surprise I find no reference to it in R. Janin, *Les églises et les monastères des
grands centres byzantins* (Paris 1975). But its location is indicated in verses by
Blemmydes, ed. A. Heisenberg, *Nicephori Blemmydae curriculum vitae et carmina*
(Leipzig 1896) 112-14.

[5] G. Prato has recently studied this volume: *JOB* 30 (1981) 249-58, with four plates.

[6] Cf. Apocalypse 2 and 18:2 'Babylon ... has become a dwelling for demons, a haunt for
every unclean spirit, for every vile and loathsome bird.'

[7] Pseudo-Aristotle *De mundo* 391 a 18-b 3.

[8] An allusion to a recurring phrase in Homer.

present generation. Even to look at them fills one with astonishment. The towers stand on either side of the ascent and guide the visitor to the buildings beyond them. With the sight of the acropolis comes a fresh surprise. The lower part of the hill is more beautiful than its peak, the city of the dead is more beautiful than that of the living. At this sight we were half despondent, half joyful, transported into a state of happiness and pain, tears and laughter. We saw the temple of Asclepius, which one might call the home of Galen, deriving this benefit from St. Christopher, the patron of travellers.[9]

Theodore was a prolific writer, but his other works do not concern us here, except for the occasional expressions of his own ignorance, in the tradition begun by Socrates, and a remark in an encomium on the city of Nicaea. In the typically exaggerated account of its level of culture he notes the blend of pagan and Christian thought in which 'the wild olive is improved by grafting and every concept is made subservient to Christ'.[10]

It must remain uncertain how far Theodore succeeded in providing the necessary encouragement for learning and the transcription of a wide range of texts. We have already seen how one of the masters in the school he founded wrote some mediocre notes on Homer. A more important composition which belongs to the first half of the century is the so-called lexicon of Zonaras, compiled in all probability by a certain Nicephorus. The significance of this work lies in its preservation of many entries from one of the guides to Attic usage dating from late antiquity, the book by Orus aimed at refuting Phrynichus' doctrines on a series of rules about acceptable Attic vocabulary. It preserves a number of fragments of classical poetry. If the compiler was working after 1204, as seems highly probable from the way he refers to Hagia Sophia, his ability to draw directly on the text of Orus constitutes one of the very rare exceptions to the general rule propounded at the beginning of this chapter about the existence of rare texts after the fall of the capital. 'Zonaras' was much valued by several generations of scholars, if the number of surviving manuscripts is any guide to popularity; at the last count 129 were known.[11]

The most notable literary figure of the Nicaean empire was Nicephorus Blemmydes (1197-1272). He became known chiefly as the author of textbooks on logic and physics. These achieved lasting popularity in much the same way as 'Zonaras'. It has even been suggested recently that Blemmydes may be the author of the lexicon,[12] and there is nothing against the idea except that its pseudonymity is hard to explain on this

[9] Letter 80 (32 in the series addressed to George Acropolites). In a few places I have slightly paraphrased in order to make the text intelligible without further footnotes. Theodore was right in his belief that Galen practised at Pergamon.

[10] H. Hunger, *JOBG* 8 (1959) 123-55, especially 127-37, quotes from an unpublished text of wide-ranging scientific content and the encomium of Nicaea, ed. L. Bachmann (Rostock 1847).

[11] See K. Alpers, *Das attizistische Lexikon des Oros* (Berlin 1981) 11-12, and his article Zonarae Lexicon in *RE*, cols. 732-63. The earliest dated copy is Vat. gr. 10 of 1253.

[12] Alpers in *RE*, cols. 738-9.

hypothesis. Blemmydes' main interests were philosophical. His introduction to logic was written at the suggestion of the emperor. It opens with the assertion that logic is very helpful towards an understanding of scripture. Like the handbook on physics this seems to be an unoriginal compilation from Aristotle and the standard commentators. He wrote on many other subjects. His guide to geography turns out to be nothing more than a prose paraphrase of the poem by Dionysius Periegetes. A sign of the spirit in which he approached his task is that the sensuous description of Lydian women dancing in honour of Dionysus (lines 839-45) is reduced to the statement 'No one can criticise the beauty of the women of this district'.[13]

To a modern reader the only attractive book by Blemmydes is his autobiography, which contains some vivid passages and tells us a good deal about his education and intellectual development. The account of his early education reveals little that is unexpected. He speaks of four years at an elementary school mastering grammar. This was followed by a reading of Homer and other poets, whose names he does not give, then by Hermogenes and Aphthonius. At the age of sixteen he went on to Aristotle's *Organon* but could make no progress owing to the lack of a suitable teacher. His disappointment proves that by *c.* 1213 the recovery of the exiled community in Nicaea had not gone far enough to ensure the provision of much secondary education. Nicephorus spent seven years studying and practising medicine, after which he left what was then Nicaean territory in order to study mathematics with a certain Prodromus; it was necessary to cross a guarded frontier in order to reach his new teacher. He says that he was fascinated by astronomy and studied Nicomachus and Diophantus. This statement may be literally true, but it is also a way of saying that he ranged from the most elementary to the most advanced mathematics. In ordinary circumstances Nicomachus was a school text, but Diophantus with his algebraic problems was far too difficult and it was only rarely that the Byzantines attempted to read him.

The autobiography has a few other scraps of information that may be worth recording in order to give an idea of the conditions in which he worked. An unsuccessful attempt to visit Jerusalem led to his spending a winter in Rhodes in the monastery of Artamyte, in which he claims to have found a fine library. Later in his career he felt it necessary to travel in search of books not available in Nicaea or Ephesus. He made his way to Athos, Salonica, Larisa and further into Greece. It is not surprising to learn that he found many books, including some rare items, on Athos. But he does not give enough detail about his discoveries to satisfy our curiosity.

---

[13] I depend on the basic account in A. Heisenberg's edition, op. cit. in n. 4 above.

(ii) Gregory of Cyprus

It will be obvious from this account of the active but limited Blemmydes that we are not justified in passing an enthusiastic judgment on the achievements of Nicaean scholars. An impression of mediocrity is confirmed by the briefer autobiography of a younger man, Gregory of Cyprus (*c.* 1240-*c.* 1290), who became patriarch in 1283. He was not satisfied with the education offered in Cyprus, because he had to attend a school where Latin was the language of instruction and like most Greeks he never mastered it. After a long dispute with his parents he ran away and tried to make contact with Blemmydes who was then living near Ephesus. This proved impossible and he arrived in Nicaea, where he was disappointed to discover that education consisted largely of exercises in parsing and the reading of Greek tragedy. His difficulty was soon ended, since the Greeks recovered their old capital and the emperor appointed George Acropolites to a chair of philosophy. He taught 'the labyrinths of Aristotle', Euclid and Nicomachus. Gregory devoted himself to philosophy, but also read the ancient orators. For a time his own ability to write archaising prose was so slight that he was the laughing-stock of his contemporaries, but he later won their admiration, having made a determined effort to master Attic style by reading the ancient texts themselves, disregarding 'those who have corrupted all the beauties of rhetoric, its grace, solemnity, Attic and truly Hellenic quality'. It was a highly unusual independence of spirit which permitted any Byzantine to rebel against the regular textbooks.[1]

Gregory's letters offer valuable sidelights on other difficulties facing literary men. The most piquant scrap of information is his statement that a copy of Demosthenes cannot be manufactured because the population is not eating meat and it is necessary to wait until the spring for a supply of parchment. Gregory also complains of having no paper, and asks another friend whether he can spare some paper already written on one side.[2] His own literary production would have been greater if he had not been forced to spend so much time making his own copies of all the books he wanted to read.

As patriarch Gregory found himself just as uncomfortably involved in ecclesiastical debates as the other patriarch who has been described in these pages. The emperor's preoccupation with the need to obtain help from western Europe had led him to agree to a union of the Greek and Roman churches at the Council of Lyons in 1274. Gregory was on the throne at a very difficult stage of the bitter debate that ensued in Byzantium. He was forced to resign in 1289 and died soon after. He is far below Photius in intellectual capacity and historical importance, but it

---

[1] The autobiography is printed in *PG* 142. 20-29 and W. Lameere, *La tradition manuscrite de la correspondance de Grégoire de Chypre* (Brussels-Rome 1937) 177-91.

[2] These facts were brought to light by M. Treu, *Maximi monachi Planudis epistulae* (Breslau 1890) 197 and 261.

may still be worth while giving a brief account of the part of his literary output which depends for its inspiration on pagan authors.

The work which may be best known is his collection of proverbs. This proves on closer inspection not to be of any importance at all; it is nothing more than an epitome of one of the collections which circulated under the false name of Diogenian.[3] There is also a schoolbook consisting of mythological tales and paraphrases of the fables of Aesop, which contrasts oddly with the dismay that Gregory claims to have felt on discovering how limited and conventional education in Nicaea was, with its concentration on poetry and myth.[4] Equally firmly rooted in the tradition of the schools are an encomium of the sea and three declamations, two of which are conceived of as responses to similar compositions by the fourth century rhetor Libanius,[5] while the third deals with an imaginary legal case in the manner of another late rhetor, Sopater. One is a speech on behalf of the Athenians, who defend themselves against a charge of impiety, which they incurred at the beginning of the Peloponnesian war at the siege of Potidaea, when the inhabitants were driven to cannibalism. In the second the son of a rich man is supposed to have vowed a dedication worth a talent to Asclepios if his father recovers from a serious illness; this happens, and the father disinherits the son. In the third a philosopher who has persuaded a tyrant to abdicate lays claim to the reward offered for such services to the state, and the case is argued against him.

More interesting at first sight is an essay on Socrates. It is a brief encomium, and takes as its theme a statement attributed to Socrates, though not found in Plato, that reason is in command of the soul. The benefits of reason are then discussed. Gregory has no original thought to contribute. Probably the piece is no more than a fair copy offered as a model to his pupils.

A younger contemporary of Gregory must be mentioned at this point. Manuel Holobolus (b. c. 1245) was an imperial secretary and at one time a teacher in the patriarch's school. His various writings include explanations of the curious jeu d'esprit known as the pattern-poems or technopaegnia attached to the corpus of Theocritus' *Idylls*. An example of this genre in English is the Mouse's Tale in *Alice in Wonderland*. Holobolus would be important if one could be sure that the translation of some texts on logic by Boethius attributed to him in one manuscript are really his work. He would then be the first Byzantine to make the literature of the Latin west available to his fellow-countrymen. But the ascription is very far from certain, as his name has been written over an

---

[3] L. Cohn, *Philologus Supp.-B. VI* (Göttingen 1891) 236-7.

[4] Parts were printed by J. Jacobs, *De progymnasmaticorum studiis mythologicis* (Diss. Marburg 1899).

[5] One of the two was declared to be spurious by R. Förster, *Libanii opera* VII (Leipzig 1913) 110. P. Maas, *BngrJ* 1 (1920) 48-9 (= *Kleine Schriften* (Munich 1973) 486-7), denied the need to see any link between Libanius and Gregory, but that in my opinion is an excess of scepticism.

erasure, and the translator was in all probability Planudes.[6]

(iii) Other evidence

We have suggested that it would be wrong to lavish high praise on scholars of the Nicaean period and the years immediately following. Their energies were almost entirely taken up with the task of recovering what they could after the disaster of 1204 and of restoring the educational system as it had been. In this they must be reckoned successful.

There is some palaeographical evidence to fill out the picture that we have constructed. Although not many manuscripts can be dated securely to the years 1204-*c.* 1280, there are a few interesting cases. Perhaps the most striking is the Florentine codex of the Greek novelists (Laur. Conv. Sopp. 627). It contains Longus, Chariton, Xenophon of Ephesus and Achilles Tatius. For the second and third of these it is the unique source, and for the others it is very important. This tiny book, with about sixty lines of microscopic handwriting to the page, gives a hint of its origin in that it also contains some letters of Theodore Lascaris. A date before the sixties or seventies is precluded by the presence of works by Manuel Holobolus, but a date after *c.* 1280 is unlikely on palaeographical grounds. The idea that the volume was produced somewhere near Melitene on the borders of Cappadocia and Armenia rests on the false interpretation of a name occurring in a marginal note; Melitiniotes is no more than a surname of a standard geographical type.[1] Other books deserving a passing mention are a copy of Euripides (Vat. gr. 909) and a collection of poetry including Aeschylus, Pindar, Aristophanes, Hesiod, Lycophron, Oppian's *Halieutica*, Dionysius Periegetes and Theocritus (Ambr. C 222 inf.). For the text of Pindar and Theocritus this book is important as a witness, for its other contents rather less so.[2] Two copies of the usual textbooks of rhetoric can be dated (Vat. gr. 105, of 1244-54, Vat. gr. 106, of 1251), and one copy of the rather less popular book by Sopater probably belongs to this period (Vat. gr. 901). Identification of the two hands in Vat. gr. 106 with scribes found in a very large miscellany of mainly Byzantine literature enables us to say that most of the latter volume can be attributed to the same period (Barocci 131).[3] The few classical texts in it include Menander Rhetor and some of the orations of Himerios.

[6] The erasure in Vat. gr. 207 is discussed by A. Pertusi, *Annuaire de l'Institut de philologie et histoire orientale et slave* 11 (1951) 301-22. On the general question of the authorship see also S. Kugeas, *BZ* 18 (1909) 120-6 and now D.Z. Nikitas, *Eine byzantinische Übersetzung von Boethius' De hypotheticis syllogismis* (Göttingen 1982) 40ff.

[1] The erroneous view was stated by B.E. Perry, *Gnomon* 40 (1968) 416-18, and in P. Wirth (ed.), *Polychronion (Festschrift Dölger)* (Heidelberg 1966) 418-19.

[2] I am inclined to date this book rather earlier than A. Turyn, *Codices Vaticani graeci saeculis XIII et XIV scripti annorumque notis instructi* (Vatican City 1964) 106.

[3] This manuscript is described in *JOB* 27 (1978) 157-79; for the identification of the various scribal hands see N.G. Wilson, *Medieval Greek Bookhands* (Cambridge, Mass. 1973) 29.

(iv)   A second glance westwards

The Latin conquest had forced the Greeks to turn their gaze to the west
with fresh intensity. It was no longer enough to think of western Europe
as the home of a schismatic church and various small groups of
merchants who were allowed to settle in ghettoes in the capital.
Negotiations about church union had now to be conducted on rather
different assumptions by any ruler capable of a realistic assessment of
political facts. Nicephorus Blemmydes and Theodore Lascaris were
involved in such negotiations, and it is noteworthy that one of Theodore's
works is an obituary of the Hohenstaufen emperor Frederick II. Even
though Anna Comnena's history is full of the exploits of the early
crusaders, it would scarcely have crossed the mind of a writer belonging
to any previous generation to go so far in his admission of the importance
of any western ruler. Part of the reason for the change is that Theodore's
father had chosen as his second wife the daughter of Frederick.

Western influence penetrated Greece in the thirteenth century. This
was the time when a knowledge of the Arthurian legends was brought to
Greece,[1] which became a feudal country ruled by western knights from
their castles. Tangible proof of this is visible still to the traveller in the
Peloponnese. That is why Shakespeare was not indulging in a mere flight
of fancy when he included among the characters of *A Midsummer
Night's Dream* Theseus duke of Athens. But not all travellers from the
west came with aggressive intentions. Contact of a different kind is
presupposed by an anonymous pamphlet written in 1252, in which the
author explains the use of Arabic numerals and exemplifies them in the
form already current in western Europe.[2] The pamphlet seems to have
had little or no effect, since a second effort to introduce the Arabic
numerals was made about the turn of the century by Planudes. Another
visitor, the Dominican William of Moerbeke (*c.* 1215-*c.* 1286), was a
capable translator of Greek texts, and his visits to Greece and Nicaea
had important consequences. He is believed to have undertaken these
tasks at the request of Thomas Aquinas. Moerbeke had the good habit of
recording the date and his own whereabouts when he finished a
translation, and so we know that in 1260 he went to Thebes and Nicaea.
Four more texts were completed in Viterbo in 1267-8, and then we find
him in Corinth, of which he was the Latin archbishop, in 1280. For our
purposes the remarkable fact about him was not his ability as a
translator, which modern experts do not rate very highly, but that he was
able to find Greek texts which are now lost or fragmentary. In Corinth in
1280 he produced his version of three such works by the Neoplatonist
Proclus, and at a date which cannot be established exactly he laid hands
on a more complete version of Proclus' commentary on the *Parmenides* of

---

[1] K. Mitsakis, *BZ* 59 (1966) 5-7.

[2] This treatise has now been published by A. Allard, *RevHistTextes* 7 (1977) 57-107.

Plato.[3] Such finds prove that he was exceptionally clever or lucky in his search for texts.

In the meantime the Greek communities in Italy and Sicily continued in their traditional ways. Evidence is provided by some dated manuscripts. One contains the *Odyssey* and *Batrachomyomachia* (Pal. gr. 45, of 1201),[4] another philosophical texts (Paris gr. 2089, of 1223), and a third Lycophron's *Alexandra* with the commentary by Tzetzes (Escorial R-I-18, of 1255). All three may be products of the district near Otranto in the extreme south eastern corner of Apulia.[5] A fourth classical text, written for a member of the monastery of the Saviour in Messina in 1279, is Aristotle's *Eudemian Ethics* (Cambridge University Library Ii.5.44). The scribe has been identified in another copy of the same text (Vat. gr. 1342).[6] These two volumes are twins and constitute one of the two branches of the tradition. Other books of this period and apparently from the Italo-Greek region include an *Iliad* (New College Oxford 298) and Hesiod's *Works and Days* with Tzetzes' commentary (Messina, Fondo Vecchio 11).[7] The list could doubtless be extended, but whether any evidence will ever be produced to suggest a capacity for original scholarly work is another matter. The writings of the Italo-Greek authors of this period prove a certain acquaintance with the classics and a willingness to draw on them which looks just the same as the parallel phenomenon in the main part of the Byzantine world. One of the authors in question can be discovered in the act of annotating a copy of Diodorus Siculus XVI-XX (Paris gr. 1665). A certain antiquarian interest is revealed when he records having found a Latin epigram on a tomb in Acragas.[8] Yet overall the picture is disappointing, particularly in view of the brilliance of the Sicilian court during the reign of Frederick II of Hohenstaufen (d. 1250). Frederick's own interests seem to have been directed more towards the Arab world, and his willingness to question the preeminence of Aristotle as a source of all knowledge may well have led him to the conclusion that Byzantine culture, which showed at that time no sign of a similar independence of mind, had less to offer. His son and successor Manfred (1258-66) commissioned translations of Aristotle and other authors from Bartholomew of Messina, of whom nothing else is known. These were sent to the university of Paris, but their quality was no better than the average of Latin versions.[9] Soon afterwards power

---

[3] H. Boese, *Procli diadochi tria opuscula* (Berlin 1960); R. Klibansky & C. Labowsky, *Plato Latinus* III (London 1953). One of the books owned by Moerbeke has his ex-libris (Marc. gr. 258): L. Labowsky, *Medieval and Renaissance Studies* 5 (1961) 155-63.

[4] The date has been doubted, but on balance I am inclined to accept it.

[5] A. Jacob in *La paléographie grecque et byzantine, Actes du Colloque No. 559* (Paris 1977) 273, 278.

[6] D. Harlfinger, *Untersuchungen zur Eudemischen Ethik* (*Peripatoi* 1) (Berlin 1971) 6-7.

[7] On the date of this I think P. Canart, *Scrittura e Civiltà* 2 (1978) 154, is right.

[8] A. Diller, *CP* 49 (1954) 257-8; P. Canart, op. cit. 153. On these writers in general see M. Gigante, *Poeti bizantini di Terra d'Otranto nel secolo XIII* (Naples 1979).

[9] On Bartholomew see S. Impellizzeri in *Dizionario biografico degli Italiani* 6 (Rome 1964) 729-30.

passed into the hands of the Angevins and the decline of the Greek community began to be serious. By the end of the century the only important centre of Greek culture was the monastery of St. Nicholas at Casole outside Otranto.

The most famous member of this house was the abbot Nicholas-Nectarius (*c.* 1155/60-1235), who played an important part as interpreter in negotiations between the churches of Rome and Constantinople in the first third of the thirteenth century.[10] He is presumably the author of two notes on the *Iliad* attributed to Nicholas, with in one case the addition of the words 'of Otranto', in two copies of the text that reveal by their script origin in the south of Italy (New College Oxford 298 and Vienna, phil. gr. 49). The notes themselves are not important. One deals with the rocky island mentioned in *Iliad* 3.445. Ancient commentators abhorred the vacuum left by anything unidentified and suggested that the island was either Cythera or one lying off Attica. Nicholas takes up the second suggestion, specifying that it was Salamis and irrelevantly adding a citation from Lycophron, *Alexandra* 110-1. The other note concerns *Iliad* 6.488, 'I say that no man has escaped destiny', on which Nicholas observes 'We mortals often make our own destiny'. One of the manuscripts is interesting for another reason: the Vienna codex preserves a unique fragment, the allegorical commentary on Homer which is thought to be by Demo, a lady of uncertain date, and therefore offers a rare proof of an assertion sometimes made with too much confidence, that the libraries of the region preserved unique copies of ancient texts. It is a pity that this example provides us with a work that can only be described as utterly trivial.[11]

[10] J.M. Hoeck & R.J. Loenertz, *Nikolaos-Nektarios von Otranto Abt von Casole* (Ettal 1965), is the standard study. My suggestion in the text here accords well with what they have to say on p. 26 about Nicholas as a teacher.

[11] Edited by A. Ludwich in *Festschrift zum 50jährigen Doktorjubiläum L. Friedländers* (Leipzig 1896) 296-321.

12

The Palaeologan Revival

(i) Introduction

The reign of Andronicus II Palaeologus (1282-1328) has the paradoxical distinction of being the period in which the signs of incurable political and economic weakness in the empire became unmistakeable and yet the level of cultural life rose to a height as great as had ever been seen. Two men, Maximus Planudes and Demetrius Triclinius, who are known to have been in close contact for some time, are of considerable importance, while a third, Theodorus Metochites, was perhaps endowed with more of the qualities of an original thinker than a scholar, and there are a number of others who are entitled to a brief mention. Manuscripts written by or known to have belonged to all the major figures can be identified, and a great many other copies by anonymous scribes survive as a proof of the existence of an active class of intellectuals.

As an example of an important manuscript written by one such anonymous scribe the so-called Codex Crippsianus (Burney 95) may be cited. It was probably written by one of the officials of the imperial chancery in his spare time.[1] The contents make it one of the primary sources of our knowledge of the minor Attic orators Antiphon, Andocides, Isaeus, Lycurgus and Deinarchus. For the first, fourth and fifth of these writers we possess another copy, probably a twin descended from the same exemplar and certainly written at much the same time (Bodleian Library, Auct. T.2.8). The date of this second manuscript is fixed approximately by the occurrence of the same scribe's hand in a copy of the church father Theodoret produced in 1306-7 (Vat. gr. 626).[2] The minor Attic orators seem to have been very little known earlier in Byzantium, and their reappearance at this date is perhaps due to a lucky find by a scholar of the late thirteenth century.

Less valuable perhaps, but still worth a mention because of the extraordinarily diverse opinions that have been held about its date, which have ranged from the twelfth century to the fourteenth, is a copy

---

[1] N.G. Wilson, *CQ* 54 (1960) 202.

[2] Vat. gr. 626 is illustrated on plate 86 of A. Turyn, *Codices Vaticani graeci saeculis XIII et XIV scripti annorumque notis instructi* (Vatican City 1964). The identification of the hand is mine.

of several of Theophrastus' minor writings, excluding the *Characters* (Vat. gr. 1302). There is little doubt that its archaising script belongs to a fashion current in the reign of Andronicus II.[3] It appears to be the ancestor of all the later manuscripts. Curiously the text of Diogenes Laertius' *Lives of the Philosophers* which accompanies it is of no value.

(ii) Maximus Planudes

Among the first Palaeologan scholars both in chronological order and in importance comes Maximus Planudes (*c.* 1255-*c.* 1305), whose activity as a student of classical poetry can be traced as early as 1280. The width of his interests is much greater than that of most Byzantine scholars. He was concerned with scientific as well as literary texts and might well have claimed an interest in all the seven branches of the trivium and quadrivium. He had in addition one very unusual accomplishment, a working knowledge of Latin, which enabled him to translate several texts.[1]

Some of these are of theological or philosophical nature. One which he may well have regarded as his most important venture in this field, and which he perhaps undertook as a result of official encouragement, was St. Augustine's treatise on the Trinity. Certainly his version was often read and it earned the distinction of a rebuttal from cardinal Bessarion. Other philosophical works without political implications were Boethius' *Consolation of Philosophy* and Macrobius' commentary on Cicero's *Somnium Scipionis*. In the course of dealing with Boethius Planudes recognised an allusion to Juvenal's tenth Satire and translated four lines from it into Greek hexameters; it is possible that he translated more, but no other trace survives.[2]

Less exalted but very worthy motives will have lain behind versions of Donatus' *Grammar* and the *Dicta Catonis*, edifying verses which formed a regular part of the elementary school curriculum in western Europe. A more advanced text with scholastic applications was Priscian's *Syntax*, based on Apollonius Dyscolus, part of which Planudes converted back into Greek.

It is easy to understand why someone anxious to make his fellow countrymen acquainted with intellectually distinguished or otherwise valuable products of another culture should choose these authors, but one is at a loss to explain why he also rendered into Greek a large amount

---

[3] N.G. Wilson, *Gnomon* 51 (1979) 60; C. Prato, *Scrittura e Civiltà* 3 (1979) 186-7.

[1] The only comprehensive treatment of Planudes is by C. Wendel, *RE* s.v., cols. 2202-53. Despite its excellence a fair number of modifications are now needed in matters of detail. I have not bothered to specify them all in my notes, and mention here only his mistaken assertion that Planudes was instrumental in preserving Arethas' writings (cf. L.G. Westerink, *Arethae scripta minora* I (Leipzig 1968) xiv). I have omitted references to secondary literature wherever Wendel is still a sound guide.

[2] S.B. Kugeas, *Philologus* 73 (1914) 318-19. I am not convinced that there was ever a complete translation.

of Ovid. The transformation of the Roman poet's *Metamorphoses* and *Heroides* into plain prose, while conveying little or nothing of the poet's wit or grace, could perhaps give some information about classical mythology to insatiable collectors of facts. But either Planudes or a pupil went a stage further and gave the same treatment to the love poems. Here there was a temptation to bowdlerise, and the translator yielded, converting such words as *amor* and *Venus* into meaningless alternatives (see above, p. 18).[3] Censorship is in accordance with Planudes' practice elsewhere: in the *Greek Anthology* he left out many poems which he found objectionable. But it was not typical of the Byzantines to act in this way, and the only other known cases are found in some treatises by Plutarch, where Planudes' influence may again be suspected, and in Herodotus, where the account of sacred prostitution in Cyprus (1.199) is missing from one branch of the tradition, which goes back to a time before Planudes.[4]

How did Planudes come to have a knowledge of Latin? The simple answer would be that he exploited the opportunity offered by a visit to Venice on diplomatic business in 1296-7. But his appointment would rather suggest that he already knew Latin. A second explanation, not very likely, is that he learned from Manuel Holobolus. That depends on the assumption that Holobolus really was the translator of some texts on logic by Boethius, and we have already seen that the attribution is doubtful. A third possibility is worth considering. We find Planudes living in the monastery of Christ Akataleptos, now the Kalenderhane Camii. On this site archaeologists recently found a fresco of St. Francis of Assisi, and it was probably the first Franciscan house in Constantinople.[5] Although the Latins must have left in 1261, Planudes could conceivably have been stimulated by residence in what had been one of their religious houses to inquire into their culture. The difficulty in this explanation is chronological. Although it has been suggested that Planudes moved into the Akataleptos monastery in 1283 in order to take over the teaching post vacated by Gregory of Cyprus on his elevation to the patriarchate,[6] the proof of his residence dates from 1299 or 1301, and there is also evidence that Planudes lived in the Chora monastery.[7] At present we must be content to recognise that very few facts about his career can be

---

[3] Planudes' master copies of his *Metamorphoses* and *Heroides* are preserved in Reginensis gr. 132 and 133; these volumes are in part autograph, as was discovered by A. Turyn (letter to the author of March 11, 1974). The *Heroides* version has now been edited by M. Papathomopoulos (Ioannina 1976). For the amatory works see P.E. Easterling & E.J. Kenney, *Ovidiana graeca* (Supplement No. 1 to *PCPS*) (Cambridge 1965), and E.J. Kenney in *Hermes* 91 (1963) 213-27.

[4] On Plutarch see M. Pohlenz, *NGG* (1913) 338 ff, esp. 342 f, on Herodotus N.G. Wilson, *Antike und Abendland* 16 (1970) 73.

[5] W. Müller-Wiener, *Bildlexikon zur Topographie Istanbuls* (Tübingen 1977) 153-8.

[6] V. Laurent in P. Tannery, *Quadrivium de Georges Pachymère (Studi e Testi* 94) (Vatican City 1940) xix n. 5.

[7] These facts emerge from his colophon in Marc. gr. 481 and a possession note in Vat. gr. 177.

established with certainty.

While Planudes may have been able to teach any subject in the trivium and quadrivium, he was not equally interested in all of them. His concern with logic appears to be limited to the translation from Boethius. The only sign of his teaching of geometry is the existence of notes dealing with Euclid's *Elements* 6.5 and 10.32. He made his own collection of texts relating to rhetoric and music. For the former he contented himself with reducing the existing corpus of technical manuals to a more manageable size; the reduction was substantial and no doubt long overdue. As to the writings of the musical theorists, all we know is that having made a master copy of his collection Planudes was unwise enough to lend it, and it was never returned. In astronomy, arithmetic and grammar, which must be interpreted so as to include literature, his work is easier to trace and more obviously of importance.

An interest in astronomy, for a long time known through a remark by his contemporary Demetrius Triclinius, can now be documented more precisely, thanks to the discovery of an autograph copy of the two textbooks normally studied at school, Cleomedes and Aratus (Edinburgh, Advocates' Library 18.7.15).[8] The Cleomedes text has yet to be investigated to see whether Planudes made any alterations to it. But his treatment of Aratus was already notorious before the autograph became known. He deleted three passages which were factually incorrect (481-96, 501-6, 515-24) and substituted verses of his own, making use of the superior information which he found in Ptolemy's *Almagest*. Improvements to a classical author are regarded as being outside the brief of a modern scholar. Planudes' procedure appears in a better light if we think of him as revising a successful textbook, for which many a modern analogy can be cited. It is also fair to remark in his defence that he appears to be doing no more than the ancient critics Attalus and Hipparchus, who corrected Aratus in order to bring his account into line with observed facts. One of Attalus' remarks could be taken to mean that he adjusted the text accordingly. Planudes could have known about the work of these ancient critics, because one of the three copies of Hipparchus was produced in or near his circle (Vat. gr. 191).[9]

Planudes' ability to deal with arithmetic is shown by his essay on the use of Arabic numerals and his study of Diophantus. In the essay on Arabic numerals he was largely dependent on a treatise written in 1252 by an unknown author who was influenced by Italian work in this field.[10] This is doubtless the text that Planudes borrowed from a certain George Bekkos (letter 46). Planudes follows his model fairly closely but spends

---

[8] A. Turyn, *Dated Greek Manuscripts of the Thirteenth and Fourteenth Centuries in the Libraries of Great Britain* (Washington 1980) 57-9 with plates 41-2; J. Martin, *Scholia in Aratum vetera* (Stuttgart 1974) vii-viii.

[9] Hipparchus was edited by C. Manitius (Leipzig 1894); see especially pp. 20, 102, 106, 108.

[10] See above, Chapter 11 (iv).

some effort on improving the method of extracting square roots. He remarks (again in letter 46) that he was devoting a great deal of time to this problem. He uses the eastern form of the numerals instead of those found in his source, and this alteration may be the result of consulting copies of Euclid, in which they were sometimes used in the marginal scholia.[11] The autograph of his essay is preserved, but in an incomplete state (Ambr. & 157 sup.).[12] It appears to have been written *c.* 1292/3 and is part of a manuscript which contains in addition pseudo-Iamblichus, *Theologoumena Arithmeticae*, an essay of Psellos on Plato, and Diophantus, with Planudes' own commentary on books I-II.

For his work on Diophantus Planudes again depended on his ability to borrow a text: in letter 67 he is found returning one copy to a library under the control of his correspondent Theodore Muzalon, while in letter 33 he asks Manuel Bryennios to lend him another so that he can collate it against his own. It is likely that one or another of the two borrowed copies is the Madrid codex (Madrid 4678), the only surviving manuscript of earlier date.[13] A note in the margin at book II proposition 8, how to divide a given square into two other squares, reads 'Diophantus, may your soul be with Satan for having devised so many problems of such difficulty'.[14] A great mathematician of a later age, on reading this same proposition, made the following note in his copy: 'On the other hand it is impossible to separate a cube into two cubes, or a biquadrate into two biquadrates, or generally any power except a square into two powers with the same exponent. I have discovered a truly marvellous proof of this, which however the margin is not large enough to contain.' One can sympathise with the poverty that might have led a Byzantine scholar to leave his best thoughts unrecorded in this way, but it is less easy to pardon an omission which the finest mathematicians of more recent generations have been unable to make good. Planudes of course was no Fermat. But to be able to understand Diophantus at all is an achievement, and he manages to set out some of the problems in a form which is easier than that of the original and not much harder than that which they might assume in modern notation.[15] If it had not been for Planudes an interest in Diophantus might not have been kept alive and his contributions to algebra and number theory could have disappeared. At the same time one must not exaggerate his services; he may well have learned about Diophantus from George Pachymeres.

This is a convenient point to consider Planudes' work on another

---

[11] N.G. Wilson, *GRBS* 22 (1981) 400-4.

[12] A. Turyn, *Dated Greek Manuscripts of the Thirteenth and Fourteenth Centuries in the Libraries of Italy* (Urbana-Chicago-London 1972) 79. See further A. Allard, *Scriptorium* 33 (1979) 219-34.

[13] Allard, op. cit. 225-7, denied that the manuscript borrowed from Muzalon was the Madrid codex.

[14] P. Tannery, *Diophanti Alexandrini opera omnia* II (Leipzig 1895) 260.

[15] I cite Fermat's note from T.L. Heath, *Diophantus of Alexandria* (ed. 2, Cambridge 1910) 144 n. 3, and report Heath's judgment on Planudes, ibid. 48.

scientific text of importance, Ptolemy's *Geography*. Although Tzetzes may have known this text, it was clearly a rarity and Planudes complains that it had been lost for a long time and only recovered with great effort. The circumstances and the exact date of the recovery are not easy to establish. The date must be *c.* 1295/6, while the source of the find is quite unknown.[16] Planudes' own copy (Vat. gr. 177), which also records his residence in the Chora monastery, was acquired from Andronikos Oinaiotes, but nothing is known of him. Planudes was delighted by the discovery and wrote some hexameter verses to celebrate it. These reveal that the text had no maps, and so he constructed a diagram to accompany it. That may have been a single map of the world. The maps known from various other extant manuscripts are usually thought to go back to Ptolemy himself, but serious doubts have been raised.[17] It is possible to suppose that they were all constructed by Planudes from the text, the best copy of which is Vat. gr. 191, written *c.* 1296. This means that it was produced soon after Planudes' find, and although no one has ever claimed to see his handwriting in it, there are signs of his presence in the background, because it also contains Diophantus and Theodosius, an astronomical text which Planudes refers to elsewhere (letter 67). Vat. gr. 177, like Vat. gr. 191, lacks the maps, and its text represents another branch of the tradition. The question must be raised whether the excellence of its readings is in part due to Planudes' critical ability, of which there is specific evidence in his dealings with some other classical authors.

Planudes read a wide range of prose authors. Sometimes his concerns were pedagogic. He produced some grammatical notes on Philostratus' *Imagines* and *Heroikos,* Atticist works which one might not have expected to find in a school reading list. Less surprising are an edition of Aesop's fables and an anthology of excerpts from classical and patristic authors. The letter is divided into ten sections. Two are drawn from Strabo and Pausanias. For Strabo Planudes appears to have used an extant codex (Paris gr. 1393), and he made a number of corrections to the text.[18] They look like the adjustments that an intelligent man would make as he read, rather as one corrects misprints in a modern book. A third section consists of material on Roman history, most of it taken from Dio Cassius in the shortened version prepared by John Xiphilinos, the contemporary of Psellos. It may have been designed to give elementary instruction in Roman history. Of the remaining sections the only one of any note is drawn from the works of Justinian's civil servant Johannes Lydus.

[16] The apparent implication of E. Polaschek, *RE* Supp.-Band X s.v. Ptolemaios col. 745, that the find was made in Alexandria is wrong, because the patriarch of that city was not in residence; Wendel col. 2230 is right about this.

[17] A. Diller, *TAPA* 71 (1940) 62-7.

[18] A. Diller, *The Textual Tradition of Strabo's Geography* (Amsterdam 1975) 90 n. 3, gives a list, but it must be said that his information does not tally entirely with that given in the Budé edition by Aujac and Lasserre. – Diller also points out that the scribe of Paris gr. 1393 wrote two copies of Ptolemy's *Geography* with maps.

Planudes' reading of more important classical authors can be documented. He took a small part in preparing a copy of Plato (Vienna, phil. gr. 21). It offers a number of good readings, but not of a kind to suggest that Planudes was in his element when grappling with the problems presented by this type of text.[19] He also possessed a copy of Thucydides (Munich gr. 430), but here again there is no evidence that he made any substantial contribution to textual criticism.

While we are dealing with ancient prose authors it should be noted that when he re-edited the corpus of manuals of rhetoric Planudes retained among them a book which to the modern reader seems to have no place in such a collection. This was Theophrastus' *Characters*, the original purpose of which has been much disputed. The idea that they had anything to do with rhetoric is not the best explanation that can be offered.[20] Planudes, however, did not possess enough independence of spirit to depart from tradition, even though he was making a number of drastic alterations to the existing corpus. It has been suggested that he is responsible for numerous omissions which occur in the text of *Characters* 16-28 in all copies except one (Vat. gr. 110).[21] The process of abbreviation does him no credit and is not balanced by any ingenious emendations of corrupt passages.

The author who must probably be reckoned his favourite among the classics, and on whom he certainly lavished a great deal of energy, was Plutarch. In his admiration for the author of the *Lives* and *Moralia* Planudes continues a tradition that had been vigorous from at least the eleventh century onwards. His correspondence shows him at work with an enthusiasm more usually associated with the humanists of the Italian Renaissance. His devotion to Plutarch is revealed in the remark: 'I have decided to copy Plutarch's works because I greatly like the man, as you know' (letter 106). The help of friends had to be invoked to obtain parchment sheets of the right size, and it is clear that Planudes hoped for a contribution towards the expense involved. The first results are visible *c.* 1294/5, when he organised a team of scribes, doubtless the senior pupils in his school, to make a copy of the *Moralia*, treatises 1-69, and the *Lives* of the emperors Galba and Otho (Ambr. C 126 inf.). Previous readers of the *Moralia* in Byzantium had often had to content themselves with the first twenty-one of the essays. Planudes himself wrote a small amount of the text; the remainder was done by nine other hands.[22] In 1296 he had a fresh transcript of the same treatises made from this copy and added the remaining *Lives* (Paris gr. 1671). Both volumes show Planudes at work as a corrector of the text. In most passages he is

---

[19] A. Turyn, op. cit. in n. 12 above, xxiv and 214; see also E.R. Dodds, *Plato: Gorgias* (Oxford 1959) 54-6, and W.F. Hicken, *CQ* 17 (1967) 98-102.

[20] G. Pasquali, *Rassegna italiana di lingue e letterature classiche* 1 (1918) 73-9, is a fundamental treatment of the problem.

[21] P. Steinmetz (ed.), *Theophrast: Charaktere* (Munich 1960) 38-41. There is still no sign of the alleged Planudean commentary on this text, first mentioned by Gesner.

[22] A. Turyn, op. cit. in n. 12 above, 81-7.

probably doing no more than put right the errors of his scribes, but from time to time he went further. One of the corrections explicitly marked by him as his own emendation occurs in the *Consolatio ad Apollonium* 113D, where his attempt to heal a passage corrupted in the witnesses available to him is not very successful. He also noted at one point in treatise 69:[23]

> This passage is very obscure because the letters in the old copies are in many places worn away and do not yield continuous sense. I have seen an old copy in which there were many gaps, as if the scribe could not find what was missing and perhaps hoped to find it elsewhere. But here the text is written continuously because there is no longer any hope of finding the missing words. This fact must therefore be noted throughout the volume where any such obscurity occurs.

In fact, however, two later copies of the final treatises in which Planudes' influence is perhaps to be traced do exhibit frequent gaps in the text, and so it may be that Planudes came to realise the importance of preserving exactly the information given by the primary sources.

Later, but not necessarily within Planudes' own lifetime, the remaining treatises of the *Moralia* were found and added to his edition. A huge volume in Paris (Paris gr. 1672), containing the complete corpus of Plutarch's work and beautifully written on high quality parchment, is a monument to Byzantine labours on behalf of a much read author. But the usual belief that this gigantic complete text was prepared in Planudes' own scriptorium is wrong; the script points clearly to a date long after his death, and the manuscript is at best a copy of the definitive edition.[24]

An identification of Planudes' script which is likely to be correct enables us to assign to his milieu a miscellany containing pseudo-Aristotle *De mundo*, Libanius, Aristides, Philo, Josephus and some epigrams (Urb. gr. 125).[25] Planudes' reading of classical poets can be traced at the beginning and end of his career. In 1280 he was involved in the production of a corpus of hexameter poetry, from which Homer was omitted (Laur. 32.16). In 1299 (or 1301) he wrote out a fair copy of his revised version of the *Greek Anthology*. At a date which cannot be precisely determined he took a small part in the preparation of a codex containing Theocritus, Hesiod, Sophocles and Euripides (Paris gr. 2722 & Laur. 32.2).[26] He may well be responsible for another large corpus of

---

[23] M. Pohlenz in the preface to the first volume of the Paton-Wegehaupt edition of the *Moralia* (Leipzig 1974) xi n. 2.

[24] N.G. Wilson, *GRBS* 16 (1975) 95-7. See also B.P. Hillyard, *RevHistTextes* 7 (1977) 35-6.

[25] See N.G. Wilson, *GRBS* 22 (1981) 395-7. If the main hand is not that of Planudes, it must be that of a pupil. The identification by B.L. Fonkič, *VizVrem* 40 (1979) 251, is essentially right.

[26] The two halves were identified by A. Turyn, *The Byzantine Manuscript Tradition of the Tragedies of Euripides* (Urbana 1957) 233-4.

classical poetry, similar to the one produced in 1280 but with the addition of Pindar and Homer (Vat. gr. 915).[27]

The variant readings of these manuscripts and the occasional marginal notes are the evidence on which one has to base a picture of activity in Planudes' circle. In the interests of strict accuracy it may be better to speak of a circle rather the master himself, because a number of scribes took part in the production of the copies being discussed. Since it is not possible to identify the exemplars used by the scribes, there are some cases where one may doubt whether the presence of a good reading is due to the ingenuity of a scribe or the excellence of the copy at his disposal. In practice modern scholars make a rough and ready distinction between readings that seem too good to be medieval conjectures and others that could easily have been suggested by men like Planudes. As a general rule this distinction holds good, for a reason which will appear in a moment.

I now deal with the texts of classical poetry studied in the Planudean circle, taking them in approximately chronological order. To begin with Homer: the text posed relatively few problems and did not stimulate Planudes to take any special interest in it. The variant readings in the Planudean copy of the *Iliad* are reported to be trivial, while those in the *Odyssey* are barely more important.[28] In Hesiod the picture is slightly different. The two copies of the *Theogony* are not quite as close to each other as might be expected, but they share some errors and each has some good features. There are successful corrections of minor metrical faults, but where a deeper corruption challenged the reader to a more adventurous correction the result is not satisfactory.[29] If unique but erroneous readings which appear to be attempts to emend are correctly interpreted as such, it follows that several good features in these copies, which modern scholarship is inclined to accept, probably derive from the scribes' exemplars. For the *Works and Days* there are three copies to be assessed. Analysis shows that all three belong essentially to the same branch of tradition, although they are far from being identical in every detail. Their contribution is of the same type as in the *Theogony*. A mistake common to all enables us to trace back the origin of the group to Tzetzes, a fact already suggested by the presence of his commentary in several books forming part of this branch of the tradition.[30] A few small metrical and syntactical corrections are found in the text of Hesiod.[31] A handful of scholia marked with Planudes' name are little more than a paraphrase of traditional material.[32] In the pseudo-Hesiodic *Shield* and in Theognis minor corrections are again found. A few are adopted by

[27] Turyn, op. cit. in note 12 above, 33, 35. A. Garzya, *Rendiconti dell' Accademia nazionale dei Lincei* VIII 13 (1958) 216-7, thought he could detect Planudes' hand in the marginalia to Theognis.

[28] T.W. Allen, *Homeri Ilias* I (Oxford 1931) 45-6, 93-5, and *PBSR* 5 (1910) 11, 17-20.

[29] M.L. West, *CQ* 14 (1964) 175-8.

[30] M.L. West, *CQ* 24 (1974) 173.

[31] M.L. West, ibid. 169, 171, 173.

[32] Edited from Naples II F 9 by A. Pertusi, *Aevum* 25 (1951) 342-52.

modern editors.[33] It is consistent with what is known of Planudes in his dealings with the *Greek Anthology* that none of the texts of Theognis which may reflect the work of his school includes the erotic poems of book II.

The evidence for ascribing to Planudes a recension of Pindar is less secure than for other authors. The allegedly Planudean text is close to that of an important manuscript in Milan (Ambr. C 222 inf.), but it is not represented by any surviving autograph and specifically Planudean scholia have not been found. Nevertheless there is a group of manuscripts exhibiting a number of minor adjustments to the metre which seem to be consistent with the emendations of other authors carried out by Planudes, and it may not be entirely irrelevant to note that his pupil Moschopoulos prepared a fresh edition.[34]

Drama evidently did not interest Planudes much, even if the normal texts were read by his pupils. Of his study of Aristophanes there is only one trace, a correction of a metrical blunder by Tzetzes in *Plutus* 505.[35] For tragedy much the same is true, subject to a proviso that will be explained in the next paragraph. If the texts of Aeschylus and Sophocles in Laur. 32.2 reflect the activity of his circle, they do not offer a text of any particular note, and the Euripidean section of the same volume contains Triclinius' recension. A reflection of Planudes' classes is seen in some notes on Sophocles and Euripides marked with his name in one manuscript (Naples II F 9). A full publication of notes on the *Oedipus tyrannus* which may be ascribed to him shows that on this play he offers nothing of any value to modern scholars.[36]

The recent discovery of another autograph of Planudes has raised a question which cannot yet be solved. He wrote a part of a second copy of Theocritus (the first being Laur. 32.16). This copy (Paris gr. 2722) is fairly clearly a fragment of what was originally a larger book, and the ⁿtⁱₑₓ section was identified some years ago: it is the primary source of the so-called alphabetic plays of Euripides, which has numerous corrections in the hand of Demetrius Triclinius. The link between the two men is attested by a good many other pieces of evidence.[37] But the implications of the connection indicated by this manuscript are not yet clear. It used to be supposed that Triclinius found an old copy of Euripides in Thessalonica, where it might have arrived through the agency of Eustathius. That hypothesis is not ruled out by the latest discovery, if one is willing to make the further assumption that the preparation of the volume began in Planudes' circle, but was

---

[33] C.F. Russo, *Hesiodi Scutum* (Florence 1965) 40-3; D.C.C. Young, *ParPass* 10 (1955) 197-214, esp. 208 ff; M.L. West, *Studies in Greek Elegy and Iambus* (Berlin 1974) 152, 153.

[34] The existence of a Planudean recension was first argued by J. Irigoin, *Histoire du texte de Pindare* (Paris 1952) 237-69.

[35] W.J.W. Koster & D. Holwerda, *Mnemosyne* 7 (1954) 155-6.

[36] Edited by O. Longo, *Scholia Byzantina in Sophoclis Oedipum Tyrannum* (Padua 1971).

[37] N.G. Wilson, *GRBS* 19 (1978) 389-94, 22 (1981) 395-7.

discontinued, possibly owing to his death, after which Triclinius went back home with the scribe, another pupil in the school, and enlarged the volume in order to accommodate a fresh discovery. But an equally good explanation would be that Planudes found the Euripidean plays in the capital or through the researches of friends travelling elsewhere on business.

Planudes was well acquainted with Hellenistic poetry; the only obvious gap in his reading list is the absence of Callimachus' *Hymns*. His copy of Apollonius Rhodius has many distinctive readings, which could well be his own emendations, and a modest proportion of them are accepted by modern editors as correct solutions to the problems posed by the traditional text. They mostly involve minor adjustments of a metrical nature, and where a complex change has to be made Planudes' suggestions, despite a certain ingenuity, disappoint. An incidental difficulty in assessing his contribution is that some readings are shared by his copy and one or more of a group of later manuscripts associated with the Renaissance scribe Demetrius Moschus. It is not clear whether Moschus derived such readings from a Planudean copy or another source. For the present purpose they have not been taken into account, but they would probably not make much difference.[38]

In the first eighteen *Idylls* of Theocritus and the four poems current under the name of Moschus Planudes made a larger number of adjustments to the text. About forty are accepted by editors, and they consist of improvements to the metre, syntax and dialect forms. Five of these, however, are also found in a papyrus,[39] and as one of the five (at 18.2) was not very obvious the suspicion arises that Planudes was able to draw on a good source that has since disappeared. And if that is correct, he may have to lose some of the credit for the other changes. Another sign that he read Theocritus with more than usual attention is the composition of an idyll in imitation of him.[40] It consists of a dialogue between a farmer Cleodemus and his friend Thamyras. The names are not borrowed from Theocritus, nor is the diction taken exclusively from this one source. Cleodemus explains how he bought an ox for his plough from a miracle-worker, and when he got it home it turned into a mouse, which then began to do great damage. The friend's consolation includes the offer of a mousetrap. In this feeble composition Planudes shows that he knew more about the rules of the classical hexameter than most Byzantines, but his knowledge was not good enough to save him from a fair number of errors of prosody, and there are many lines in which he permits a diaeresis at the end of the third foot, creating a division in the line totally contrary to the classical rules.

Whereas Aratus had interested him keenly, he was not tempted to

---

[38] Up-to-date information is to be obtained from the Budé edition by F. Vian (Paris 1974-81).

[39] Four in Laur. 32.16 (at 2.5, 2.65, 2.146 and 18.2) and one in Paris gr. 2722 (at 15.105).

[40] C. von Holzinger, *Zeitschrift für die oesterreichischen Gymnasien* 44 (1893) 385-419.

make any special effort to improve the text of other didactic poems. His text of Nicander is one of the better representatives of the inferior class of witnesses, and editorial intervention in it is not recorded.[41] With regard to the two poems traditionally assigned to Oppian, it was not suggested by the best editor of the *Cynegetica* that the Planudean manuscript stands out by reason of its variants, while for the *Halieutica* the position is scarcely different, since the variants characteristic of Planudes' copy are either oversights or inadequate attempts to emend.[42] The extent of his intervention, if any, in the text of Tryphiodorus should become clearer when a new edition based on all the manuscript evidence is published.[43] What he did to the text of Nonnus' *Dionysiaca* is revealed by three notes explicitly recording his activity. At 42.221-3 he indicates the readings of his exemplar, while 17.73 and 48.909 are lines he invented in order to fill gaps in the text. It is tempting but perhaps unsafe to infer that he made no other changes of note.[44]

The collection of epigrams in the style of the *Palatine Anthology* shows the good and bad sides of Planudes as an editor. He did not limit himself to the contents of the Palatine codex; there are about four hundred other poems. Having made his collection he later found some more material to add to it and incorporated this as a supplement. An autograph survives, dated 1299 (or perhaps 1301) (Marc. gr. 481). He arranged five of the seven books of his collection in alphabetical order of subject, which was at least one way of helping the reader; one might have expected him to apply the same order to the authors or the opening lines of each poem. A revised version, in which the collection and the supplement were fused, has been found (Paris gr. 2744 & one leaf in Paris gr. 2722), and a few of the corrections in it can be attributed to the hand of Demetrius Triclinius.[45] Poems on homosexual themes were omitted. While many difficult passages are better preserved in Planudes' text than in the *Palatine Anthology*, presumably because of the excellence of the manuscripts he was able to exploit, other problems in the text led Planudes to offer readings which look like his own emendations, and these prove that when attempting to deal with corruptions in this type of classical poetry he was quite out of his depth.[46] Despite its drawbacks Planudes' edition enjoyed a fame greater than it may be thought to merit, since it served as the basis of the first printed version, issued at Florence in 1494, and was not replaced by the *Palatine Anthology* until

[41] A.S.F. Gow & A.F. Scholfield, *Nicander* (Cambridge 1953) 9-15.

[42] See the prolegomena to P. Boudreaux's edition of the *Cynegetica* (Paris 1908) and D. Robin, *Bollettino dei Classici* III 2 (1981) 35-6.

[43] It is promised by E. Livrea; see in the meantime his article in *SCO* 28 (1978) 49-68.

[44] The most recent discussion is in F. Vian's Budé edition of books I-II (Paris 1976) lxi-lxviii.

[45] A. Turyn, *EEBS* 39-40 (1972-3) 403-50.

[46] A.S.F. Gow & D.L. Page, *The Greek Anthology: Hellenistic Epigrams* I (Cambridge 1965) xxxviii-xl; *The Greek Anthology: the Garland of Philip and some contemporary epigrams* I (Cambridge 1968) li-liii.

the second half of the eighteenth century.

The last aspect of Planudes' work which needs to be discussed can be dealt with very briefly. His position as the head of a school led him to produce a number of works connected with the teaching of grammar and syntax. These include a lexicon (Ferrara II 155), a list of points of Attic usage, a translation of Priscian on syntax, and a dialogue between characters called Palaitimos and Neophron, which turns out to be an introduction to various topics in grammar. It does not appear that this side of his activity has any claim to be regarded as important.

Finally one may note that his enthusiasm for antiquity extended to visiting its physical remains. He accompanied a friend to the west coast of Asia Minor and saw the temple of Apollo near Miletus. He was in doubt about its identification and hazarded the guess that it might also be the Mausoleum, which is actually some fifty miles away in Halicarnassus (letter 120). On another occasion he saw the temple of Zeus built by Hadrian at Cyzicus (letter 55). It was still possible to climb up to the roof, about seventy feet high, and he records that he almost failed to do this, but had the possibility pointed out to him. He notes with annoyance that he was not told of the underground section of the building, which would also have been of interest to a tourist.

(iii) Some lesser contemporaries

George Pachymeres (1242-*c.* 1310) held various high offices in church and state. Such a career did not prevent him from writing a long series of school exercises in rhetoric in the same classical manner as Gregory of Cyprus. Pachymeres is chiefly known as the author of a long history of the years 1261-1308, in which great attention is paid to church affairs. One detail may be singled out as important for our purposes. His archaism is so deeply rooted that he even refers to the months by giving them their classical Attic names such as Elaphebolion and Gamelion.[1] But it is his other works which require a mention here. One is an introduction to the quadrivium, which appears to be entirely derivative. It does, however, have an interesting feature, in that part of the section on arithmetic derives from Diophantus, and Pachymeres may be the first Byzantine to pay any serious attention to this important and difficult author.[2] A number of copies survive, indicating the popularity of the work; one has been recognised as an autograph (Rome, Biblioteca Angelica, gr. 38).[3] Pachymeres also produced a paraphrase of Aristotle, divided into twelve sections. This enjoyed a wide circulation, and two

---

[1] II 146.1 and 249.11 in the Bonn edition. – Those who think that the same habit in Gemistus Plethon is a proof of his paganism should consider more carefully the strength of tradition.

[2] Since the date has not been established exactly we cannot tell whether he or Planudes has a claim to priority.

[3] D. Harlfinger, *Die Textgeschichte der pseudo-aristotelischen Schrift Περὶ ἀτόμων γραμμῶν* (Amsterdam 1971) 357 n. 3.

autograph copies are known (Berlin, Hamilton 512 and Paris gr. 1930, the latter containing only a few leaves in the author's hand).[4] Pachymeres has perhaps been more influential than he deserves; copies of his paraphrases were mistaken for the original Aristotelian text of *De lineis insecabilibus* when the editio princeps was prepared, and not all his phraseology was removed when editors discovered manuscripts of the original treatise.[5] Paraphrasts do not occupy an important place in the history of scholarship, but it can be recorded in Pachymeres' favour that he made a few corrections of corrupt passages,[6] and further research will no doubt reveal other instances of his capacity.

A few years younger than Pachymeres was John Pediasimos Pothos (b. c. 1250). He was a correspondent of Gregory of Cyprus, and by 1292/3 he had become professor of philosophy.[7] He is also regularly referred to as chartophylax of the bishopric of Ohrid, which was then regarded as part of Bulgaria. He may have enjoyed a great reputation in his own day, but the suggestion that he received the exceptional compliment of having a pupil of Gregory of Cyprus sent from the capital to study with him in Ohrid is mistaken.[8] Usually appointment in the provinces was tantamount to exile, and a famous bishop of Ohrid, Theophylact, had complained about two hundred years earlier that it was a filthy marsh where one had to live among the frogs and unclean barbarian slaves who smelled of sheepskin.[9] Even if Pediasimos succeeded in finding some intelligent pupils there, his literary productions do not suggest a man of more than mediocre talent. Wide interests are not matched by competence. His essay on surveying is said to derive largely from Hero's treatise on the same subject but to be vitiated by ignorance of basic rules of geometry.[10] There are also notes on Cleomedes' handbook of astronomy, on Aristotle, Hesiod and a few other authors. Analysis of his notes on Aristotle suggests that much of what he has to say is merely a reproduction of what he found in the old commentary of John Philoponus,[11] while the scholia on the pseudo-Hesiodic *Shield of Heracles* are linguistic notes of the most humdrum kind imaginable. He also wrote a brief account of the twelve labours of Heracles, which derives from Apollodorus' handbook.

---

[4] Ibid. 357-60.

[5] Ibid. 350; Harlfinger says that the same is true of the *Mechanica*.

[6] Listed ibid. 353. They may of course be the result of collation with a better copy.

[7] His notes on the *Organon* are to be found in Marc. gr. 202, which dates from that year. See in general A. Turyn, *Dated Greek Manuscripts of the Thirteenth and Fourteenth Centuries in the Libraries of Italy* (Urbana 1972) 74-8.

[8] A letter of Gregory is cited by V. Laurent, *EO* 31 (1932) 329, to prove this, but he seems to have misunderstood it.

[9] Letters in *PG* 126. 308-9 and 508, cited by D. Obolensky, *The Byzantine Commonwealth* (London 1971) 217.

[10] E. Schilbach, *Byzantinische Metrologie* (Munich 1970) 8 and 244.

[11] There is an important review of V. De Falco, *Ioannis Pediasimi in Aristotelis Analytica scholia selecta* (Naples 1926) by K. Praechter in *BZ* 27 (1927) 105-13.

This may be the right place to mention that at one time Pediasimos was thought to be identical with John Diaconos Galenos, the author of allegorical expositions of Hesiod's *Theogony* and *Iliad* 4.1-4.[12] Galenos cannot be dated precisely; the only indication is that he quotes from Eustathius.[13] His introduction to Hesiod expresses reservations about letting the young be carried away by enthusiasm for pagan authors. But his opposition to such reading matter is not absolute, and he can bring himself to applaud Plotinus and Socrates for their declared intention of directing their pupils' minds to higher things. His brief discussion of the *Iliad* passage ends by drawing a distinction between the three types of allegory, physical, ethical and theological.

George Lakapenos, a monk living in Thessaly, requires a brief mention. He testifies once again to the relentless pressure, felt in all societies which do not possess the art of printing, to abbreviate long texts. The Byzantines were compulsive letter-writers, and the largest of the many collections known to them was the correspondence of Libanius, which amounted to some 1500 items. Lakapenos presumably wished to ensure that the bulk of this collection should no longer discourage copyists or readers and he prepared a selection of 264 letters. He also devoted attention to his own correspondence with John Zarides, which dates from the years *c*. 1297-*c*. 1315,[14] to the extent of equipping it with epimerismoi or notes on parsing. This implies that he was sufficiently proud of his letters to use them as a set of models, perhaps imposing them on pupils in a schoolroom. He is also believed to be the author of a treatise on rhetorical figures in Homer and a commentary on part of Epictetus' *Enchiridion*.[15]

The last of the men to be dealt with in this section was rather younger, but his early death enabled him to receive the honour of a flattering obituary from Theodore Metochites. Joseph (*c*. 1280-*c*. 1330) is variously known as the philosopher or Rhakendytes. His family name is not recorded; Rhakendytes is in fact no more than an epithet which any monk could apply to himself. His work consists of an encyclopaedia, somewhat on the lines of the one produced by Pachymeres, who indeed appears to have been his source of information on physics, while other sections draw heavily on Nicephorus Blemmydes.[16] Essentially the book is derivative. There are a few interesting points which ought to be noted even if the credit for them does not belong to Joseph.[17] His material on

[12] The fundamental article on Pediasimos by D. Bassi, *Rendiconti del Reale Istituto Lombardo* II 31 (1898) 1399-1418, clears up the question of identity.

[13] W.J.W. Koster, *Mnemosyne* 7 (1954) 139 n. 1. It is worth noting in passing that a John Galenos is one of the scribes of Laur. 11.8, dated 1284, containing Theophylact's commentary on the Gospels; see Turyn, op. cit. in n. 7 above, 48 and plate 30.

[14] S.I. Kurusis, *Athena* 77 (1978-9) 291-386.

[15] I. Voltz, *BZ* 2 (1893) 221-34.

[16] The description of the best manuscript, Biblioteca Riccardiana gr. 31, by G. Vitelli, *SIFC* 2 (1894) 490-3, is valuable.

[17] See M. Treu, *BZ* 8 (1899) 1-64.

rhetoric included part of the handbook by Menander, but he does not appear to offer anything of real value to the editors of that treatise.[18] On the other hand it has been thought that he was original enough to recommend Byzantine authors as models of style, rather than confining himself to the usual range of classics.[19] This may be true, but the same idea is found in a text usually attributed to Gregory of Corinth, and until the attribution is proved wrong it will be better to reserve judgment.[20] Joseph's remarks on iambic metre have earned high praise from the best modern authority on the subject. He was able to state and exemplify the principle that in twelve-syllable verses the sense of each line should be complete in itself, so as to avoid enjambement. He also shows some sign of understanding the effects created by the position of the stress accent, but his doctrine on this subject is not well expressed and contains some remarks that are incoherent, at least in the form offered in the only printed edition. A properly based edition and fuller consideration of his sources are required before a favourable opinion of his capacity can be justified.[21]

(iv)   Other students of Greek poetry

Manuel Moschopoulos (b. c. 1265) was the nephew of a metropolitan of Crete. Writing to the uncle Planudes said 'Your nephew is a keen student, and still more keen as a teacher' (letter 18). The point of this remark will be understood if we recall descriptions of Byzantine schools of earlier date in which the senior boys are found acting as assistant masters. 'He gives his enthusiasm,' continued Planudes, 'and receives mine in return. He may reasonably hope to benefit from our association, since we devoutly hope by means of our best efforts to ensure our pupils' progress equally in learning and excellence of character, attending to the acquisition of other virtues as well.' The promise implicit in this report was not crowned by an entirely successful career, for in 1305-6 we find Moschopoulos writing letters from prison.[1] It is not possible to trace his biography in any more detail.

His output as a teacher and scholar was quite substantial. Apart from

---

[18] D.A. Russell & N.G. Wilson, *Menander Rhetor* (Oxford 1981) xliv; two readings are adopted from Joseph's text at 375. 21 and 26.

[19] I. Ševčenko, *JOB* 31 (1981) 305.

[20] See above, Chapter 9 (ii).

[21] P. Maas, *Kleine Schriften* (Munich 1973) 247, 252, 259, 264, is perhaps too enthusiastic in his comments on what is printed by C. Walz, *Rhetores graeci* III 559-62. It may be worth adding, although the topic strictly speaking falls outside the scope of this book, that Joseph comes close to formulating the rule governing the clausula in Byzantine prose; see W. Hörandner, *Der Prosarhythmus in der rhetorischen Literatur der Byzantiner* (Vienna 1981) 24-6 (the title of this study is misleadingly modest; it should be consulted by anyone interested in late Greek prose).

[1] I. Ševčenko, *Speculum* 27 (1952) 133-57. – I have accepted the usual approximate date for his birth, but if my interpretation of Planudes' letter is right Moschopoulos may have been about fifteen years old some time in the nineties, which entails a much lower date.

a grammar book and some linguistic exercises based on the writings of the late sophist Philostratus and some other authors, he produced versions of a number of the standard school texts. The problem of his biography has been complicated by the doubtful authorship of a grammatical text commonly attributed to him and found in use as early as 1290/1 (Barb. gr. 102). It now seems that the early dated copies do not contain his version of the work.[2] A similar problem of authorship surrounds the anthology which includes Philostratus. The most recent analysis leads to the intrinsically plausible result that part of it is due to Planudes.[3]

Moschopoulos was mainly interested in drama and other poetry. There is an unpretentious paraphrase of Hesiod's *Works and Days*; an edition of Pindar, containing only the *Olympian Odes*, and now extant in some sixty manuscripts; a selection of Theocritus, consisting of the first eight *Idylls*, again found in a great many copies. He appears to have composed a paraphrase of the first two books of the *Iliad*, omitting the Catalogue of Ships. His work on Homer included a note on metre, which has been added, probably later, to a copy of the epic transcribed in 1291/2 (Vat. gr. 29).[4] While it is clear from the selections he made from other school authors that there was a reduction in the range of reading expected of the average Byzantine schoolboy, the concentration on one and a half books of Homer casts uncomfortable doubt on the easy assumption that Byzantines of all periods knew the classical epic intimately. Moschopoulos' aim was apparently to draw up a corpus of poetry for reading in school. Although he did not include Aeschylus and seems to have devoted no more attention to Aristophanes than write a few isolated notes on the *Plutus*, these gaps should no doubt be put down to interruptions in his career. Extant manuscripts suggest that it was his intention to assemble a school anthology in which the chosen authors were accompanied by his notes (Laud gr. 54 is an example).

The quality of his scholarship is difficult to assess. The notes that go under his name are elementary, being either grammatical or simple explanations of the text. They do not imply great learning. But there are readings of interest which modern scholars have attributed to him, in some cases describing them as the products of a recension of the text. Such readings need to be analysed, in the hope of showing whether they are better regarded as the product of deliberate editorial activity or of unknown branches of the manuscript tradition. One general point of principle should be made at the outset: if Moschopoulos were given to correcting texts, one might expect him to mention and justify each of his own proposals. But his notes very rarely contain any such comment, and

---

[2] J.J. Keaney, *BZ* 64 (1971) 303-13. Moschopoulos' own contribution was to add material from Harpocration and the scholia on Aristophanes.

[3] Ibid. 313-17.

[4] Ibid. 317; A. Turyn, *Codices Vaticani graeci saeculis XIII et XIV scripti annorumque notis instructi* (Vatican City 1964) 82. On the Homer paraphrase see E. Melandri, *Prometheus* 7 (1981) 215-24, 8 (1982) 84.

this fact must raise the suspicion that he simply used the text he found as a basis for his commentary. If one wishes to see in him a critic of some ability, an assumption has to be made that he chose not to discuss these matters in a part of his work that was aimed only at his pupils, and with pupils not yet at an advanced level of understanding such a policy would have been justifiable.

From this finely balanced a priori argument one can turn to consideration of the latest results of inquiry into Moschopoulos' editions of various authors. His alleged recensions of Sophocles and Euripides have not stood up to investigation. The Sophoclean manuscripts which apparently present his version of the text have characteristic readings varying from the brilliant to the absurd, so that they cannot easily be assigned to the scholarship of one and the same man. A number of them appear in any case in earlier manuscripts; in fact they are frequent in manuscripts which seem to have been written c. 1290-1300 when Moschopoulos was still a fairly young man and probably not yet an authority capable of exercising much influence on current texts.[5] A study of Euripides' *Hecuba* as it is transmitted in Moschopoulean copies leads to a similar conclusion: the majority of readings thought to be characteristic are found in one or more earlier witnesses. A few minor emendations may remain to his credit.[6] But one of them brings his text into line with a papyrus (*Phoenissae* 1171: cf. P. Oxy. 1177), a tell-tale sign that he had an additional good source for his text which is denied to us.

In other texts where his intervention has been alleged the picture is less clear. Of several distinctive readings in Theocritus six are adopted in the best modern edition. Are they due to Moschopoulos himself? The same tell-tale sign occurs in one instance: the reading at 2.144 is also found in a papyrus. Another of the variants concerns an obscure personal name, generally given as 'Theumaridas' (2.70). Here Moschopoulos offers 'Theucharilas', which is perhaps support for Reiske's conjecture 'Theucharidas'. The mistaken lambda for delta is one of the commonest misreadings of uncial script. It suggests that Moschopoulos had access either to an uncial copy or a book deriving from it. The reading can hardly be his own conjecture; it would never have crossed his mind to remove the standard patronymic termination -*idas*.

With these examples in mind we have to consider his Pindar. Once again modern editors adopt several distinctive readings. Does he deserve the credit? The points in question are metrical. How could he have learned about metre? Either from the treatise of Isaac Tzetzes on Pindaric metre, or perhaps from Triclinius, whose presence in the

---

[5] N.G. Wilson, *JHS* 96 (1976) 172, commenting on the work of R.D. Dawe.

[6] K. Matthiessen, *Studien zur Textüberlieferung der Hekabe des Euripides* (Heidelberg 1974) 89-94. He must be held to have overtaken the results offered by G. Zuntz, *An Inquiry into the Transmission of the Plays of Euripides* (Cambridge 1965) 160-2, at least as far as the *Hecuba* is concerned, and comparable work on the other two plays of the triad has every chance of producing the same conclusions.

Planudean circle is now attested and could have had this result. The question must be left unresolved.

But on either view Moschopoulos emerges as a person of some significance, since at the very least he was able to lay hands on good copies of the texts that interested him. If his commentaries were undistinguished, he was capable of showing sound sense. At one point in the paraphrase of Hesiod's *Works and Days* his remarks are an acceptable contribution to scholarly debate.[7] Pandora's behaviour in leaving hope in the box (in fact the Greek refers to a large storage jar), while releasing evils into the world, has seemed contradictory; hope after all is one thing evidently present in the world. Ancient commentators looked for ways of explaining her action, but Moschopoulos observed that they failed to take account of verse 99, in which the will of Zeus is said to be responsible for the present state of affairs. 'So if this came about by the will of Zeus, the same problem certainly remains; for how could Zeus wish to do harm and then stop as if wishing to spare mankind? Perhaps therefore the problem is false. What is there to demonstrate that Pandora and Zeus wished to do harm to mankind to the extent of not even leaving them with some slight consolation?'

Outside the range of the school syllabus Moschopoulos' activities are harder to trace. There is reason to think that he owned a copy of Harpocration's lexicon to the ten Attic orators which became the archetype of the fuller version of the text.[8] A curiosity is an essay on magic squares, written at the insistence of an acquaintance. It is not surprising that a pupil of Planudes should have mathematical competence, and it is good to discover that there is no trace in it of numerology or other types of nonsense.[9]

Thomas Magister, who changed his name to Theodoulos on becoming a monk, was a native of Thessalonica. Very little is known of his career. The first trace of him is a copy of Aeschylus with his notes dated 1301 (Paris gr. 2884). He is spoken of respectfully by Triclinius and is last heard of in 1346, by which time he was blind.[10] His philological activity consists of a lexicon, designed to guide the writer of prose in the choice of his vocabulary, and work on Greek drama and other poetry. He wrote various essays, two of which had the unusual distinction of being accepted until quite recently as coming from the pen of Aristides. However tiresome the imitation of the Byzantines may seem, their occasional ability to fool generations of more recent scholars extorts a certain admiration. The deception was not deliberate in this case, but arose from careless editorial work by modern scholars. Close study soon reveals that the Greek could not possibly have been written in the second

---

[7] M.L. West, *Hesiod: Works and Days* (Oxford 1978) 75, 171.

[8] J.J. Keaney, *TAPA* 100 (1969) 201-7.

[9] P. Tannery, *Annuaire de l'association pour l'encouragement des études grecques dans la France* 20 (1886) 88-118.

[10] A. Turyn, *Codices Vaticani graeci saeculis XIII et XIV scripti annorumque notis instructi* (Vatican City 1964) 143.

century.[11]

The lexicon is the last notable product in a series of Atticist manuals composed over a period of more than a millennium. It has a slight additional interest in that it was one of the first texts to be edited with due attention to the relationships of the known manuscripts. Although there had already been several printed editions, in 1832 Friedrich Ritschl added to their number one which marked an important advance: its distinguishing feature was a diagram showing the links between manuscripts and early printed editions, which were traced back to four hypothetical ancestors, each symbolised by a Greek letter. It is strange that a relatively unimportant text should have been the first work of Byzantine literature to benefit from modern critical methods.[12] The index of quotations in the lexicon reveals that Thomas' tastes were quite normal. Thucydides is his favourite author, and Aristophanes is well represented. After them come the writers of the second sophistic age, Aristides, Lucian, Libanius and Synesius. The only patristic writer cited is Gregory of Nazianzus, which tends to confirm the view that he alone was deemed worthy of a place in the school curriculum.

Thomas' work on the classical poets has often been described as a recension of the texts. The use of such a term can only be the result of loose thinking. All that the evidence permits us to say is that Thomas studied the texts and made adjustments to the existing commentaries. That he searched successfully for older and better manuscripts is possible but unproven.[13] What he certainly did was to prepare his own version of the commentaries on the standard texts, and the question for us to consider is whether he did his work well or not, either for his own contemporaries or later generations. Some of his notes on Sophocles and Aeschylus were accepted as useful by Triclinius and marked with a distinctive sign. Their average level is typical of uninspired classroom practice. His version of the scholia on the first three plays of Aristophanes was taken over wholesale by Triclinius. He also prepared an edition of Pindar which included the *Olympian* and the first four *Pythian Odes*. He claims to have used a number of manuscripts, some of them old; on this last point doubts have been expressed. He made few changes if any in the text; the absence of an autograph working copy makes it hard to offer a confident opinion. He took over the existing commentary with little change, adding some notes on variant readings and points of punctuation. One amusing addition has been observed. Having to explain at *Olympians* 9.70 the story of Deucalion and Pyrrha

---

[11] F.W. Lenz, *Fünf Reden Thomas Magisters* (Leiden 1963) x-xv and 1-66.

[12] On the significance of Ritschl's 1832 Halle edition see S. Timpanaro, *La genesi del metodo di Lachmann* (ed. 3, Padua 1981) 53-4. For Thomas' treatment of two of the sources of his lexicon see K. Nickau's edition of Ammonius (Leipzig 1966) xxv-xxvi and E. Fischer's *Die Ekloge des Phrynichos* (Berlin 1974) 49-50.

[13] O.L. Smith, *GRBS* 17 (1976) 75-80, has some commendably incisive remarks on this subject. See also N.G. Wilson, *JHS* 96 (1976) 172, in support of the findings of R.D. Dawe, *Studies on the Text of Sophocles* (Leiden 1973).

he began by saying 'the Hellenes stole the idea of Noah's flood from us and give this account'.[14]

Two further points may be mentioned in connection with his work on tragedy. In dealing with Sophocles Thomas went a little beyond the school prescription and extended his coverage not only to the *Antigone* but also to the *Oedipus Coloneus*.[15] And though it is generally agreed, not without reason, that he did not concern himself with questions of metre and indeed allowed many offences against the rules of classical metre to stand uncorrected in the texts, there is one small sign that he had begun to learn the rudiments of the subject. Commenting on the *Oedipus tyrannus* (at line 350) he remarks that an alternative way of expressing the sense of the line would create an unmetrical reading. In this he is correct, because the alternative in question would have introduced a long vowel in the seventh element of the iambic trimeter.[16]

(v) Demetrius Triclinius

Triclinius lived in Thessalonica, where he presumably ran a school. There is no sign that he was a monk. He is generally believed to have been a pupil of Thomas Magister, another resident of Thessalonica whom he refers to in complimentary terms.[1] The inference may well be correct, but it is now possible to see that for a time at least he moved in the circle of Planudes. Some books from Planudes' own library came into his possession, and there are two others in which they are found collaborating.[2] Despite the advantage of being associated with a man of the widest interests Triclinius does not seem to have appreciated how remarkable Planudes was. At any rate in his career as a teacher he did not break out of the conventional mould. Nevertheless he made one very great contribution to the study of classical literature, and as a result his name figures in the apparatus criticus of editions of Greek tragedy and comedy, and he has been described as the first genuine critic produced by the middle ages, worthy to be compared with the famous humanists of the following century in Italy.

His origin and residence in Thessalonica were for a long time a matter of inference rather than proof, until clear evidence was found in a short essay on lunar theory.[3] His concern for astronomy was already known, for it was his note on the subject which first drew attention to Planudes' handling of Aratus, and in addition he wrote a brief note on the so-called

---

[14] For further details see J. Irigoin, *Histoire du texte de Pindare* (Paris 1952) 180-205.

[15] O.L. Smith, *Studies in the Scholia on Aeschylus* (Leiden 1975) 133-4.

[16] Thomas' general incompetence in metre was shown by G. Zuntz, *An Inquiry into the Transmission of the Plays of Euripides* (Cambridge 1965) 162-3. The note on Soph. *O.T.* 350 is in O. Longo, *Scholia byzantina in Sophoclis Oedipum Tyrannum* (Padua 1971).

[1] See e.g. W.J.W. Koster, *Autour d'un manuscrit d'Aristophane* (Groningen-Djakarta 1957) 16 n. 2, with the frontispiece.

[2] N.G. Wilson, *GRBS* 19 (1978) 389-94 and 22 (1981) 395-7.

[3] First published by A. Wasserstein, *JOBG* 16 (1967) 153-74.

Sphere of Empedocles, an iambic poem on astrology. Triclinius claimed to have made improvements to the metre. He also says that he found some lines unintelligible and left them out.[4]

Although there is a copy of Ptolemy's *Geography* which appears to have been corrected by Triclinius, his best energies were not devoted to scientific subjects. Whether it was lack of ability or inclination that determined the course of his studies must remain uncertain. After the death of Planudes he perhaps found it hard to make progress. It may be for the same reason that, although he owned copies of Planudes' versions of Ovid's *Metamorphoses* and *Heroides*, he failed to take his study of Latin literature any further. Another explanation, equally plausible, is that he turned his attention to Greek poetry because of a fortunate discovery. We know that he read Hephaestion's handbook on metre, and it is evident that he understood much more of it than any of his predecessors. He mastered the essentials of the simple metres of tragedy and comedy, iambic and trochaic, anapaestic and dactylic. Lyrics he failed to comprehend, as is proved by the analyses he wrote of many choral passages. But even here he has an important achievement to his credit: he knew that strophe and antistrophe should have the same metrical shape. Armed with his metrical skill he proceeded to subject the corpus of Greek drama to systematic revision. While the methods he used to restore faulty lines were not subtle, by being first in the field he assured himself of frequent mention in the apparatus criticus of modern editions. The research of the last forty years has brought to light autographs and other manuscripts which reveal more fully the extent of his operations. In his case it is right and proper to speak of recension of the texts. I will deal with each in turn.

It is convenient to take first one in which the effect of his intervention was not substantial. There is good reason to think that he made a revised version of the Planudean anthology of epigrams, incorporating the supplement in the main body, at some time after 1316. It is believed that in order to do this work he required access to manuscripts that were in the capital, and if that is so it would follow that he made a journey for the purpose. But not enough is known about his biography to exclude the alternative possibility that the books in question were lent to him for a time.[5] Secondly there is a rather uncommon text which Triclinius is now known to have revised. The only early manuscript of the fables of Babrius (British Museum Add. 22087), a tenth-century copy, is full of corrections in what is obviously Triclinius' handwriting. A full assessment of his revision may be expected in the forthcoming definitive edition.[6]

---

[4] J. Martin, *Histoire du texte des Phénomènes d'Arate* (Paris 1956) 221, and *Scholia in Aratum vetera* (Stuttgart 1974) xxix-xxxiii.

[5] A. Turyn, *EEBS* 39-40 (1972-3) 411-15.

[6] See in the meantime A. Turyn, *The Byzantine Manuscript Tradition of the Tragedies of Euripides* (Urbana 1957) 250 n. 236. P. Knöll, *Wiener Studien* 31 (1909) 202-4, gives further details.

For his text of Hesiod's *Theogony* Triclinius appears to have drawn on more than one source.[7] For the *Works and Days* he had a text equipped with Moschopoulos' commentary.[8] If he studied for a time with Planudes it is obvious that he would be likely to have known Hesiod in the edition prepared by Planudes' pupil. He made a few metrical and other adjustments to the text. His autograph copy of the two poems and the *Shield of Heracles*, the latter accompanied by Pediasimos' notes, was written partly in 1316 and partly in 1319 (Marc. gr. 464).[9]

In view of the possible link between Triclinius and Moschopoulos it might have been expected that any edition of Theocritus would have been confined to the first eight *Idylls*. This turns out not to be the case. Perhaps Triclinius wished to ensure that his pupils read more widely, perhaps he thought of himself as preparing something more like a definitive edition. His collection of twenty-seven poems of the bucolic corpus survives in a copy which was once believed to be autograph; more recent study has shown that the script has a deceptive similarity which points rather to a pupil (Paris gr. 2832).[10] In poems 1-8 Moschopoulos' commentary is marked as such, and there are only a few other notes, taken from the old scholia. For the other poems a distinction between old scholia and Triclinian notes is maintained with almost unfailing regularity. The old scholia are recast, while Triclinius' own contributions are on the whole of a factual character rather than grammatical.[11] The text of the poems follows that of Moschopoulos in 1-8.[12]

Pindar, like the dramatic texts, gave Triclinius an opportunity for the display of his superior metrical knowledge. For each of the *Odes* he wrote an introductory note on the metre. His text and commentary were based on various sources, including Thomas Magister and Moschopoulos. He added a few notes of his own and made many adjustments to the text of the poems. Occasionally he made an unsuccessful attempt to improve the meaning of a difficult passage. It has been argued that his work on Pindar resulted in two editions, one complete, the other of the *Olympian Odes* only, but this has been contested.[13]

Whereas Pindar was too difficult an author for Triclinius to make much impression on the problems of text and interpretation, with Greek drama it was another matter. Once again we find him preparing editions which go beyond the immediate needs of a school reading list. His Aristophanes included eight plays instead of the usual three, *Plutus*,

---

[7] M.L. West, *Hesiod: Theogony* (Oxford 1966) 59.

[8] Ibid. 82-3.

[9] A. Turyn, op. cit. in n. 6 above, 26 n. 43 with plates XVI, XVII.

[10] N.G. Wilson, *GRBS* 22 (1981) 395-7. This MS. has a twin, Vat. gr. 1824-5, but Triclinius' hand has not been identified so far in the Theocritus portion, even though it can be seen making notes on the text of Aeschylus.

[11] C. Wendel, *Abh. Göttingen* 17 (2) (1920), 31-7.

[12] C. Gallavotti, *RFIC* 62 (1934) 355.

[13] J. Irigoin, *Histoire du texte de Pindare* (Paris 1952) 331-64; on the editions see the reply by Turyn, op. cit. in n. 6 above, 32 n. 49.

Clouds and *Frogs*, to which the *Knights* was sometimes added. He omitted only the *Thesmophoriazusae*, *Ecclesiazusae* and *Lysistrata*, the first of which was almost unknown, while the other two were rarities. His work on the text was deservedly influential. It was available to Marcus Musurus who edited the first printed Aristophanes for the Aldine press in 1498. The numerous metrical improvements ensured a text of fairly good quality, the merits of which used to be attributed to Musurus himself, since there is other evidence to prove that he was a scholar of great learning and ability. But the discovery of a copy of the Triclinian edition of Aristophanes in a manuscript written about a century after his death and containing eight plays (Holkham gr. 88) produced a proof of what had already been suspected by some, namely that Triclinius deserved the credit for almost all the improvements to the text.[14] His edition begins with some introductory matter, of the same kind as is also found in his Pindar and his editions of the tragedians. The relative chronology of these works has not yet been established, and we do not know when he first had the idea of a standard format. The first item in the prolegomena consists of an extremely brief epitome of Hephaestion's handbook on metre. Then follow Triclinius' own notes on the same subject. These include the statement that the metrical unit (*metron*) contains two feet in all metres except the dactyl; in other words a dactylic hexameter will have six dactyls, whereas an anapaestic dimeter will have four anapaests. This is a point on which Triclinius is known to have revised his views, for in an earlier version of his Aristophanes, containing as far as we know only three plays, he had treated dactyls as identical to other metres in this respect.[15] He then goes on to explain such concepts as catalectic and hypermetric lines. The third item in the prolegomena is an essay on critical signs, which turn out not to be the same as the signs placed in the margin of ancient books to indicate various types of note in the accompanying commentaries. Triclinius is chiefly concerned with the signs marking long and short vowels. He invents notation for the dichrona, ∟ when a vowel is to be taken as short, ⅂ when it is long. He makes a good deal of a claim to be speaking only to the competent, while not caring about possible criticism from others. There follows a reference to other signs used in his texts, which he does not list in full, merely asserting that they are the result of his long labours and 'divine and mysterious inspiration'.[16] These signs are visible in the manuscript and mark changes in the metre. They derive from Triclinius' reading of the

---

[14] N.G. Wilson, *CQ* 12 (1962) 32-47. The manuscript has a twin, in which the scholia are not found, Vat. gr. 2181, described by S. Benardete, *HSCP* 66 (1962) 241-9. More detailed research into Thomas Magister's and Demetrius Triclinius' dealings with the text of one play of Aristophanes has been undertaken by C.N. Eberline, *Studies in the Manuscript Tradition of the Ranae of Aristophanes* (Meisenheim am Glan 1980).

[15] The earlier version is in Paris gr. 2821; see A. Turyn, op. cit. in n. 6 above 32 n. 49, referring back to K. Zacher, *Jahrbücher für classische Philologie*, Supp.-Bd. 16 (1888) 644-5.

[16] θεία τινι καὶ ἀπορρήτῳ ἐμπνεύσει.

ancient metrical commentary on Aristophanes by Heliodorus, which had been incorporated into the scholia. But his use of such signs as *diple*, *paragraphos*, *coronis* and *asteriskos* and of the metrical terminology in general is far from accurate. For instance, phrases by which Heliodorus referred to the indentation of a short line or the projection of a long line into the margin are taken by Triclinius to mean 'at the beginning' and 'at the end'.[17] Heliodorus was too advanced for him. The main source of his metrical knowledge has been found. It is a collection of texts annotated in his own hand (Marc. gr. 483); there are about a dozen items, of which Hephaestion's handbook is the most important, while there are also works by the brothers Tzetzes and a shadowy figure called Trichas, thought to have been their approximate contemporary.[18] One might have hoped that Triclinius would arrive at a better understanding of what Heliodorus had to say, but it is only fair to make allowances for the difficulties caused by the inadequate nature of much of the information that his sources offered him.

The Triclinian edition of Aeschylus, like his Aristophanes, does not include all the plays that we know today. But once again he did more than prepare a text of what was read in the schools. In addition to the *Prometheus*, *Seven against Thebes* and *Persians*, he knew the *Agamemnon* and *Eumenides*, the latter with some lacunae. An autograph survives (Naples II F 31). The watermarks in the paper suggest a date *c*. 1330, in other words towards the end of his career. His activity as a critic has the same merits and shortcomings as elsewhere.[19] It appears also to have been a process stretching over a period of time. There are traces of what must be regarded as a first version of his text.[20] The recognition of this fact is important to the editor of the *Agamemnon*, because for the greater part of the play the only surviving witnesses are the Triclinan autograph and one manuscript representing his earlier edition. So we owe to Triclinius the preservation of the full text of the most powerful Greek tragedy, a text which may nevertheless have been subjected to the hazards of his critical procedures. In the autograph copy scholia due to Triclinius himself are marked with the word 'ours' in many cases, though not in the plays outside the triad, while a group of notes which begin with large initials are presumably to be attributed to Thomas Magister, in accordance with a principle stated elsewhere (Vat. gr. 47) and no doubt valid here also.

[17] A full treatment is given by K. Holzinger, *SB Wien* 217 (4) (1939); see also for Heliodorus J.W. White, *The Verse of Greek Comedy* (London 1912) 384-95.

[18] The find was made by A.B. Drachmann; see further A. Turyn, op. cit. in n. 6 above, 231 n. 213. On Trichas see M. Consbruch, *Hephaestion: Enchiridion* (Leipzig 1906) xxviii-xxx, 363-99.

[19] See A. Turyn, *The Manuscript Tradition of the Tragedies of Aeschylus* (New York 1943), especially 100-16; R.D. Dawe, *The Collation and Investigation of Manuscripts of Aeschylus* (Cambridge 1964), especially 59-64; O.L. Smith, *Studies in the Scholia on Aeschylus: I The Recensions of Demetrius Triclinius* (Leiden 1975).

[20] See Turyn, op. cit. in n. 6 above, 253 n. 238, on Vat. gr. 1824, which Triclinius annotated, and *FG* (Laur. 31.8 and Marc. gr. 616), which reflect his work.

The edition of Sophocles is perhaps the least important of Triclinius' contributions to the study of tragedy. It has, however, been influential in the history of the text because it happened to be adopted as the basis of an edition by one of the most important Renaissance scholars, Adrian Turnebus (Paris 1552-3), and owing to the force of inertia which affected most editorial activity until the nineteenth century, it was not superseded until R.P.H. Brunck used better sources in his edition of 1786. No autograph copy survives, but it can be reconstructed from a pair of manuscripts (Paris gr. 2711 and Marc. gr. 470). Triclinius knew all seven plays and treated the text in his usual way.[21] For the first four plays he adapted the commentary used by his immediate predecessors, while making his own version of the earlier commentary on the other three plays. His notes on the *Oedipus tyrannus* have been edited recently and reveal something of his knowledge and technique.[22] A failure to appreciate a metrical nicety appears at line 847, where he is evidently unaware that a final short vowel can be lengthened by initial rho in the next word. As a result he proposes an unnecessary emendation. His note on line 472 records that he found a reading 'in one of the old copies', and there is no reason to doubt that this note, which is not the only one of its kind, constitutes proof of his search for ancient manuscripts which might offer him a better text. The reading in question at 472 is correct and occurs in various other witnesses, including the tenth-century Laurentian manuscript. At line 906 he claims that the line is defective, offers his own supplement, and challenges the world at large to find a better solution. On examination of his proposal one is tempted to say that Triclinius, like Molière's Monsieur Jourdan, did not realise that he was speaking prose. But it is unfair to scoff at pioneers. On the other hand it is an excess of enthusiasm to maintain that this pioneer's readings deserve to be systematically recorded in the apparatus criticus of a modern edition.

Triclinius' most notable accomplishment in his dealings with tragedy was the edition of the 'alphabetic' plays of Euripides that had remained practically unknown to previous generations of Byzantine scholars. Once again it was a modern discovery that identified his handwriting in the manuscript which is the primary authority for the text of these plays (Laur. 32.2).[23] It has already been mentioned that a still more recent find has reopened the question whether the recovery of the lost plays is due to Triclinius. But whatever the answer to that question, there is no doubt that he did the work of editing which had previously been attributed to an anonymous figure of the Renaissance. He went through the text more

[21] See A. Turyn, *Studies in the Manuscript Tradition of the Tragedies of Sophocles* (Urbana 1952) 69-79; R.D. Dawe, *Studies on the Text of Sophocles* I (Leiden 1973) 80-1.

[22] O. Longo, *Scholia byzantina in Sophoclis Oedipum Tyrannum* (Padua 1971).

[23] A. Turyn, op. cit. in n. 6 above, 224 ff. On the relation between MSS. L and P see W.S. Barrett, *Euripides: Hippolytos* (Oxford 1964) 429; on this question and all matters connected with Triclinius' work on Euripides, G. Zuntz, *An Inquiry into the Transmission of the Plays of Euripides* (Cambridge 1965), especially 193-201, his general conclusion.

than once, and his numerous interventions have been analysed. They show him using a limited range of techniques, mainly changes of word-order and the addition or deletion of particles. His level of competence has rightly been described as modest. Real ingenuity and deep understanding of the text are not in evidence. As far as the well-known plays were concerned, Triclinius produced an edition of the usual type. An early and a final version of it are known (Parma 154 and Rome, Biblioteca Angelica, gr. 14).[24] The latter is yet another autograph copy. It differs in one small respect from his other editions: the life of the poet is not by Thomas Magister but Manuel Moschopoulos. Scholia by Moschopoulos are carefully marked by a cross; Triclinius' own notes have a cross and the word 'ours'; notes by Thomas have a large initial letter projecting to the left.

Triclinius' influence can be traced in various ways. His editions were popular, and though they cannot be said to have driven all others out of circulation, they were as frequently copied as any others. His calligraphic handwriting, much superior to that of most of his contemporaries, served as a model to friends and pupils. Attention has recently been drawn to a copy of Libanius written by three scribes, one of whom is clearly modelling his hand on that of Triclinius (Moscow, Hist. Mus. 489).[25] The close study of drama in his circle had one curious by-product which is worth noting. A member of the circle, John Catraris, who is known as the copyist of several classical texts, wrote a pastiche in thirty-seven iambic verses. His offences against the rules of classical metre are numerous enough to show that he had not learned a great deal from his master. This literary jeu d'esprit would hardly be worth mentioning if it had not led to a further hypothesis.[26] Catraris is the scribe who wrote the end of the *Iphigeneia in Aulis* and the forgery *Danae* in the manuscript P of Euripides (Pal. gr. 287 and Laur. Conv. Sopp. 172). Could he also be the author of these verses? They were at one time thought to be the work of the Renaissance scholar Marcus Musurus, who was the leading figure in the circle of Aldus Manutius.[27] That view cannot now be maintained, and the ascription to Catraris is dubious. In the first place the verses of the *Iphigeneia* occur in the exemplar of P, where they are not written by Catraris, and although the exemplar was no doubt produced in the same milieu, the onus of proof must lie with those who wish to demonstrate that the verses have no previous history. Secondly, the metre, though far from perfect, points to earlier authorship, because some lines avoid the paroxytone ending, that is to say a stressed penultimate syllable, which became standard Byzantine practice. Catraris was not necessarily such an apt pupil of Triclinius as to master the fact and put it into practice. It

[24] On the Parma MS. see O.L. Smith, *Mnemosyne* 27 (1974) 414-15. On the Angelica MS. A. Turyn, op. cit. in n. 6 above, 23-42. See also K. Matthiessen, *Studien zur Textüberlieferung der Hekabe des Euripides* (Heidelberg 1974) 100-105.

[25] N.F. Kavrus, *Vjestnik drevnej istorii* (1974) 125-31.

[26] G. de Andrés-J. Irigoin-W. Hörandner, *JOB* 23 (1974) 201-14.

[27] R. Wünsch, *RhMus* 51 (1896) 138-52.

may therefore be better to assign these mediocre compositions to some grammarian of late antiquity.[28]

(vi) Theodorus Metochites

Metochites (1270-1332) was a man of great distinction both as a scholar and in public life.[1] He became the chief minister of the emperor Andronicus II Palaeologus, and when his master was dethroned he was at first exiled, then later allowed to return to the capital to end his days in the Chora monastery, now the Kariye Camii. Some years before he had been responsible for restoring its library and for the redecoration of its church with new mosaics and frescoes, which are perhaps the greatest achievement of late Byzantine art. The mosaics include a portrait of Metochites himself kneeling before the figure of Christ enthroned and offering him a model of the church whose reconstruction he had arranged. His learned pupil, the astronomer and historian Nicephorus Gregoras, gives the following description of him (*History* 7.11.2-3).

By the size of his body, the harmony of its limbs and other features, and by the brightness of his eyes he drew all eyes upon himself. In his natural ability as a speaker, his capacity for work, strength of memory and clear understanding of all branches of knowledge he achieved great heights. He was so fluent in replying to all questions, whether about antiquity or the present day, as if his tongue were a book, that his friends had little or no need of books. For he was a living library[2] and a ready store of information, far excelling all previous men of learning. The only criticism one might make of him is that he did not make it his policy to model his own style in imitation of any of the ancient writers, and he did not soften the weightiness of his thought by genial or graceful style or show a disposition to put any restraint on the productiveness of his intellect. By following his own idiosyncratic and independent path he offers the reader a style resembling a stormy sea, and as a result disturbs and irritates the ear, just as the thorn on a rose sticks into the hand as one picks it. Anyone can verify his ability from his many writings, which are full of a great variety of valuable information. The most remarkable fact about him was that, while public affairs were in such a state of confusion, with the impending storm and a whole series of responsibilities continually flooding into his mind, nothing ever prevented him from reading and writing. So skilled was he in both spheres of activity that he could work from early morning until evening in the palace, entirely devoted to the administration of public business and despatching it with great enthusiasm, as if he had no literary interests at all. Leaving the palace late he would then devote himself

---

[28] M.L. West, *BICS* 28 (1981) 73-6.

[1] The best general survey of Metochites is by I. Ševčenko in P.A. Underwood (ed.), *The Kariye Djami* IV (Princeton 1975) 19-91. See also H. Hunger, *BZ* 45 (1952) 4-19, and the stimulating monograph of H.-G. Beck, *Theodorus Metochites, die Krise des byzantinischen Weltbildes im 14. Jahrhundert* (Munich 1952).

[2] This phrase is culled from Philostratus, *Vitae sophistarum* 4.1.3, where it is used to describe the third-century rhetorician Longinus.

completely to reading, as if he were a scholar entirely detached from public life.

It is convenient to discuss Metochites by asking five questions about him. What does he preserve of ancient literature that would otherwise be lost? Does he edit or emend the texts? What commentaries did he write? In what respects is his literary criticism notable? Does he exploit the classical heritage in other ways?

On chronological grounds it is not to be expected that Metochites was able to read much classical literature that is now lost. Yet there are in his *Miscellanea* and other essays some quotations or allusions which cannot be traced to their source. A discussion of various types of constitution includes a list of Greek rulers called *aisumnetai*, in which Pittacus, Periander, Phoebias of Samos and Chaeremon of Ionian Apollonia are named. The last two are not recorded elsewhere, but as they do not look like inventions, one is driven to accept the view, admittedly not without its difficulties, that he had access to a fragment of some lost book such as the Aristotelian collection of constitutions or to an essay on ancient statecraft.[3] The same tentative explanation must be offered for a reference to military operations by Chabrias and Iphicrates, perhaps to be dated 356 B.C.[4] There are also a few snippets of Pindar which do not appear in other sources. Wilamowitz assumed that they came from some moralist, without hazarding a guess as to his name.[5] A lexicon with a rich assortment of poetical quotations would be no less plausible as a hypothetical source. Once again there is no reason to think that Metochites would have had the ability or the motive to invent the quotations. Yet that may be the right view of his apparent quotation from Sappho.[6] But the phrase was perhaps intended more as an allusion than a direct quotation. Metochites could have found the idea in Aristides. There is no need to imply any duplicity on his part.

Metochites was not an editor of texts, although his name is sometimes associated with a manuscript of Thucydides which provides a series of valuable readings (Paris gr. 1734). These readings, however, are not unique, but coincide largely with those found in an earlier witness (Vat. gr. 126).[7] Was Metochites then responsible for finding an interesting copy of Thucydides, an author whom he certainly knew well? The hypothesis has been thought to depend on an identification of his hand in the Paris

---

[3] *Miscellanea* 101 (p. 668); see U. von Wilamowitz-Moellendorff, *Aristoteles und Athen* I (Berlin 1893) 293 n. 8.

[4] I. Sevčenko, *Annals of the Ukrainian Academy of Arts and Sciences in the U.S.*, 1 (1951) 150 n. 3.

[5] U. von Wilamowitz-Moellendorff, *Hermes* 40 (1905) 129-30 (= *Kleine Schriften* IV (Berlin 1962) 183-4). The same applies to fr. 100 of Simonides (D.L. Page, *PMG* 605) and lyric adespota 103-4 (*PMG* 1021-2).

[6] Sevčenko, op. cit. in n. 1 above, 40.

[7] See the conclusion reached by A. Kleinlogel, *Geschichte des Thukydidestextes im Mittelalter* (Berlin 1965) 17.

manuscript, which is alleged to be that seen in a note in another copy (Paris supp. gr. 255), where the scribe names himself as Theodore and says that he has counted the number of folios.[8] The similarity of the script is in fact so slight that the idea must be rejected as an extravagant conjecture based purely on circumstantial evidence. The autograph of Metochites has been identified elsewhere with certainty, and as a result we may say that he perhaps had some part in the transcription of Paris gr. 1734.[9]

As a commentator he confined his attention to Aristotle. His work consists of paraphrases. In one case he has been found to copy closely his Byzantine predecessor Michael of Ephesus.[10] One can understand the importance he attached to this side of his work by noting the existence in his *Miscellanea* of an essay (no. 3) on the obscurity of Aristotle. This opens with the surprising proposition, indeed one which does not do its author much credit and may throw more light on him than his subject matter, that the obscurity in Aristotle is deliberate. The philosopher took pride in this quality, which ensured that he should not be easily accessible to all. The obscurity does not affect all his works: the books on zoology and meteorology contain much that is both clear and carries conviction. The difficulties arise in the *Physics*, *Metaphysics*, *Analytica* and *De anima*. Here Aristotle contrives not to reveal immediately how far short he falls of what he promises at the outset. On the other hand anyone who cannot appreciate the excellence of his treatment of the syllogism and related questions of logic, which cannot be improved on, is a miserable ignoramus, full of jealousy. But in book II of the *Analytica* he relapses into obscurity. The reader is wrongly tempted to blame himself for his failure to understand.[11] Similarly with the *De anima*. It begins with a very clear refutation of what previous thinkers had argued, but when he comes to the central question of whether the soul is immortal or not his discussion is such as to allow diametrically opposed interpretations. In this matter modern students of Aristotle will feel some sympathy with the perplexity of Metochites.

This chapter of the *Miscellanea* has to be read in conjunction with another (no. 5). Once again his admiration is qualified. He begins with a most enthusiastic appreciation, asserting that Aristotle has made an unrivalled contribution to the affairs of humanity. But a note of reservation follows. He is accused of making a specious display of knowledge in some fields, especially astronomy. Metochites had made himself an expert in this, but one wonders if his criticism would not have

---

[8] B. Hemmerdinger, *Essai sur l'histoire du texte de Thucydide* (Paris 1955) 43. I. Ševčenko, *Etudes sur la polémique entre Théodore Métochite et Nicéphore Choumnos* (Brussels 1962) 58 n. 5, was rightly sceptical.

[9] Ševčenko, ibid. plates 2 and 7, gives illustrations from Paris gr. 2003.

[10] H.J. Drossart Lulofs, *Aristotelis de insomniis et de divinatione per somnium* (Leiden 1947) lxxvii.

[11] This extraordinary cynicism is stated twice: C.G. Müller, *Theodori Metochitae Miscellanea philosophica et historica* (Leipzig 1821) 29 and 31.

been moderated if he had applied to Aristotle a type of historical criticism that he shows himself capable of in other contexts. It is easy to see with the benefit of hindsight that Aristotle is by no means the most expert ancient authority on astronomy, but the proper question to ask is whether he should have been able to do better in the fourth century B.C. There is a third passage which shows that Metochites allowed his frustration to undermine the soundness of his judgment: an essay on the *Metaphysics* and the handbook of Hermogenes goes so far as to assert that it would have been better if the two books had never been written.

The examination of Metochites' views on literature and other parts of the classical heritage may conveniently take its cue from the proem of the *Miscellanea*, where he harps on the difficulty of saying anything original. Metochites complains of living in the worst period of human existence, and says that he is publishing these brief notes and annotations (*Miscellanea* is a modern, if apt, title) in the hope that many readers will concur in his views. Pessimism about the state of the world was justifiable for a prime minister who saw the empire collapsing and in fact devoted some sections of the *Miscellanea* to that gloomy topic; pessimism about the possibility of saying anything new and worthwhile is an explicit admission of an attitude often loosely attributed to the medieval, or more particularly the Byzantine, world. The hold of the classical tradition had become a strait-jacket. Metochites' feelings are summed up in the following words: 'Practically every topic has been taken by others already, nothing is now left as our share at this late date; we cannot write either about matters divine, which one should expect to attend to as a first duty, or about the other subjects of secular learning.' Since he devotes one of his essays to the value of mathematics and geometry, it is natural to ask whether his general pessimism is translated into a total lack of the concept of progress in these spheres of activity. The essay is not forward-looking, but correctly asserts the value of mechanical inventions, taking as the prime example Archimedes' defensive machines which were so effective at the siege of Syracuse in 212 B.C. Here as elsewhere Metochites exploits his reading of Plutarch and fails to look forward to a future in which further inventions will be brought into use for the benefit of mankind.

Yet the concept of progress may not be entirely alien to his thought, since he also wrote on the development of mathematics. That essay includes the statement of a general principle that all branches of knowledge can be seen to start from small beginnings and proceed towards their mature form. Here the concept is teleological, and the word progress itself is not used. To a modern reader it may seem difficult to keep the two ideas apart. But presumably medieval Aristotelian thought regarded many sciences as having already reached a state of final perfection. Metochites does not go into this question. He thinks that the Greeks acquired many branches of knowledge from other cultures and improved them. In this respect his thinking is reminiscent of Michael Psellos. He accepts a tradition which recorded visits of Thales,

Pythagoras and Plato to Egypt, and repeats Iamblichus' story that Pythagoras in addition visited the Chaldeans and Indians. Astronomy came to Greece from the Chaldeans, geometry from the Egyptians. Advances were not immediate or rapid, and when one compares Euclid with Ptolemy one is inclined, says Metochites, to feel that the former is childish, until one realises that a long time elapsed between the two of them. Ptolemy has left subsequent generations nothing to discover for themselves in astronomy. As will be seen shortly, Metochites did not transmit his negative attitude in this matter to his admiring pupil Gregoras.

The same admiring pupil recorded what may seem a paradoxical opinion about his style. In the passage translated above he notes with disfavour how Metochites fails to model himself on any classical author. The criticism might have been taken as a compliment by its object. But to the modern reader Metochites is not essentially different from any other writer of Byzantine formal prose; he is merely more obscure than most. And that was one of the main points at issue when he found himself involved in controversy with his former friend Nicephorus Choumnos, another important figure in the government. Metochites defended himself against the criticism by referring to Hermogenes' standard textbook and noting that Thucydides, though one of the most difficult and stylistically unattractive of all classical authors is universally admitted to be one of the greatest.[12]

Metochites recorded his views about a number of classical authors. The most interesting and unusual of his essays on the ancients is a comparison of Demosthenes and Aristides.[13] While such a comparison between two authors does not lack parallels in earlier Byzantine criticism, the idea of comparing the genuine political oratory of an active statesman with the epideictic productions of a sophist living in vastly different circumstances half a millennium later immediately provokes the modern reader to ask whether the Byzantine critic is aware of the fundamental difficulty in the task he has set himself. A few short extracts will provide the answer.

> Since we have undertaken to give a judgment in a full and serious manner, let us now make a distinction as best we can. It appears that each of them was endowed with a capacity for speaking and power of oratory in accordance with the life span granted to him, the control imposed on him by the times, contemporary circumstances, the course of events in which they found themselves through the lottery of fate, in accordance with destiny and political movements, and in addition by their characters and

---

[12] Ševčenko, op. cit. in n. 8 above, 21-67. On the essentially mediocre Choumnos see the monograph of J. Verpeaux, *Nicéphore Choumnos, homme d'état et humaniste byzantin* (ca. 1250/1255-1327) (Paris 1959).

[13] Edited by M. Gigante, *Teodoro Metochites, Saggio critico su Demostene e Aristide* (Milan 1969), a revised version of the publication in *ParPass* 20 (1965) 51-92. My translations come from chapters 8, 34 and 35.

innate qualities. An attentive observer will see this clearly. In originality and flashes of ability when faced by each particular situation and the requirements imposed by the task in hand the two men compete with each other and simply outdo practically all other men since the beginning of time. There is no one whom one could rank above these two. Demosthenes, however, lived in a time of equal political rights and freedom, active in politics, devoted to freedom, energetic and enterprising above all others, ever ready to expose himself to any danger in the interests of his country and fellow citizens. He was aggressive and not an easy character, but slightly bitter and unrelenting in private and public quarrels. He used his oratory to give a true account of the situation, as was necessary and yet not without danger, not employing eloquence as declamation or epideictic, as he would have had to do in Aristides' day, living under the absolute monarchy of the empire, the government of the Roman Caesars which at that time ruled almost all humanity. Then he could have lived in peace, enjoying a pleasant private station in life, in very favourable circumstances, abandoning all thoughts of politics and ambition, choosing to live for himself, for the Graces of rhetoric and the audiences at his displays, absolutely without risk of loss – such a life was certainly within his reach.

Metochites can see that Demosthenes may be superior to Aristides in elevation and intensity.

But at the present time, for the situation in which we find ourselves, it is somehow more profitable that Aristides should come into the hands of literary men with an interest in oratory, and that they should try to read him constantly and measure themselves against him. In simple terms, given that he lived in conditions like ours, when oratory was really concerned mostly with epideictic, which flourished with a bountiful crop, rather than its other forms, who could be as beneficial as Aristides for the apprentice or practitioner, provided they pay careful attention to the richness of his production and his easy style, serviceable and accurate for all purposes? Demosthenes lived in a different age and aroused great admiration for his character and talent, the perfection of his command of oratory. He does not offer a spring of inspiration for those who are in Aristides' position. I know perfectly well that whichever of the two is preferred, supposing it were impossible to possess more than one of them, the effect would still be excellent and a man could derive great profit for his practical aims. Yet a great loss would result from possessing only one of them, and the necessity of making such a choice would give reasonable grounds for annoyance.

The only part of Aristides' output that commands much attention from modern scholars is the series of *Hieroi Logoi*, in which he gives a partial autobiography of a kind that has certainly no parallel in antiquity and probably none until modern times. But Metochites gives them only a passing and derogatory mention; to him Aristides' complicated psychological state is no better than old wives' tales. His admiration is reserved for epideictic productions, and here we cannot follow him, even if some historians do their best to extract from Aristides information about the state of the Roman empire under the Antonine emperors. It is, however, remarkable that he should state clearly the influence of social and political factors on classical authors. His argument will be recognised as having a certain affinity with the considerations expounded in Tacitus' *Dialogus* and pseudo-Longinus' *On the Sublime*. Metochites cannot have known Tacitus, nor is it by any means certain that he had read the Greek critic. There is a good chance that his thinking on the subject is original.

Several chapters of the *Miscellanea* deal with classical authors. Metochites does not succeed in formulating literary judgments comparable with those of Photius, and usually manages to say very little in the space of ten or more pages. But it may be worth while to give the briefest possible summary of his remarks. He particularly admired Plutarch as a general repository of wisdom with an unrivalled grasp of human history and affairs, and noted his opposition to the doctrines of the Epicureans. The only note of reservation is a regret that he does not seem to take pains over his style, and it must be admitted that Plutarch does not have the easy fluency of some other writers. Metochites' view of Xenophon is interesting. He much prefers the books about Socrates to all the other writings, because he finds in them valuable confirmation of many features in Plato's portrait of Socrates. He notes that this is a service which Xenophon has performed not only for his contemporaries but for subsequent generations down to Metochites' own time and for those who are to come after. Yet despite Xenophon's undeniable merits he does not feel that a comparison with Plato would be justifiable. Less central authors are also of interest to Metochites. An essay on Synesius, bishop of Cyrene from 410 to *c.* 413, admits that he is not quite in the front rank, while valuing him as one of the few philosophers who show a concern for style. A comparison between him and Dio Chrysostom correctly notes the admiration that Synesius felt for Dio and the extent of his borrowings from Dio's speeches on the duties of a sovereign. Metochites insists on the contrast between Dio's simple style, which depends partly on Xenophon, and that of Synesius. Other writers for whom Metochites has praise are Josephus and Philo. Without citing any passages in support of his view he states that the former is a fluent writer of simple style, while the latter is to be valued as an exponent of Platonism. But Metochites does not agree with the enthusiastic estimate implicit in the aphorism 'Philo is speaking like Plato or Plato is speaking like Philo'. Perhaps the most curious of the literary essays is one entitled 'All writers who were educated in Egypt have a harsh style'. Anyone familiar with the history of Latin literature may be reminded of the attempts to define the peculiar quality of writers who came from Africa. Metochites states his view tentatively, but nevertheless claims to have found a characteristic common to both Christian and pagan writers. The examples he offers are Philo, Ptolemy and Theon; Origen, Panaetius and Clement; Gregory Thaumaturgus and Eusebius, who were not natives of

Egypt but lived there long enough to be affected by their surroundings; St. Cyril and Synesius. The name Panaetius involves a curious mistake; there is no such author. Pantaenus must be the name intended, and perhaps the editor or a copyist is to blame. But Metochites is still at fault; not only is there no surviving work by Pantaenus, but it is known that he never wrote anything. To return to the argument: while the Egyptians are notable for their harshness, the opposite quality is found in writers from Syria and Phoenicia. Examples are Porphyry and Maximus of Tyre, Lucian and Libanius. Asiatic and Ionian writers are similar. What Metochites means by these adjectives is uncertain. No specimens of the alleged characteristics are offered in support of what is being claimed.

Literature and philosophy were not the only fields in which Metochites received a stimulus from the ancients. At the age of forty-three he took up astronomy, with the help of a tutor called Manuel Bryennius, the author of a treatise on musical theory, whom he installed in his house. Bryennius had learned from a man who had been to Persia; that may have been George Chioniades, who went there some time before 1301.[14] But it is not at all clear that any oriental learning was transmitted back to Metochites, who produced after three years of study an introduction to astronomy based in all essentials on Ptolemy. He was proud of his substantial book and of his new ability to predict eclipses. Two generations later John Chortasmenos passed a favourable judgment on him as an astronomer, noting that it was now possible to navigate across the sea of Ptolemy's thought. In his own day Metochites found a critic, no doubt motivated more by malice than scientific spirit, in Choumnos. A point on which he was vulnerable related to a difference between Ptolemy and his predecessors about the number of the spheres. Plato assumed seven revolutions, Ptolemy eight spheres. Metochites seems to have removed the discrepancy by altering the text of Plato: the number seven was converted by the addition of two letters into an adjective meaning venerable.[15] Yet whatever reservations one may have about Metochites as an astronomer, his enthusiasm for the subject was productive. His pupil Gregoras produced fresh calculations of the length of the year and made them the basis of a proposal to alter the calendar in a way which would have anticipated the Gregorian reform of 1582. The emperor was intelligent enough to see the force of Gregoras' argument but declined to accept his proposal on the ground that it would be greeted with opposition by the uneducated. There is no need to condemn his cautious response, especially as the eventual application of the same reform in the much richer and more advanced English society of 1752 led to rioting in which infuriated peasants demanded 'Give us back our eleven days'.

Another possible consequence of Metochites' work on astronomy was

[14] Ševčenko, op. cit. in n. 1 above, 28 n. 72.
[15] Ibid. 43; the Plato text is *Epinomis* 990 a 8.

the recovery of the introductory textbook of Geminus. The three early manuscripts have all been attributed to the years *c*. 1300-1330 (Istanbul, Seraglio gr. 40, Vat. gr. 381 and 318).[16]

It is best to end this account with brief mention of two chapters of the *Miscellanea* which most clearly mark the difference between Metochites and the average medieval man. One discusses the value of studying history (no. 111). Its argument is summed up in the statement:

> History broadens the mind; it raises the eyes of the intellect towards an understanding and appreciation of reality, towards knowledge of what goes on in the world.[17]

The other is a series of reflections about the richness of the written tradition about Greek history and civilisation (no. 93). Its conclusion runs as follows:

> Yet how much else of the same kind occurred among other nations? How many have lived in greater states, successfully or otherwise, and have never been thought noteworthy by their fellow countrymen, nor deserving the notice of much later generations or even their immediate successors, men who were their neighbours in time, location or place of abode? I think the reason for this may be that the Greeks quite naturally recorded in writing all their own achievements, thinking it right to give them every attention, so transmitting them to the future, that is to us, partners and successors in their race and language. There may have been similar events in other nations, contemporary with us or in previous generations. The achievements of individuals may be accorded due honour in their annals and passed on to their successors, a ready store of examples for the next generations. Just as what they did remains unknown to us because no Greek writer has chronicled it, so perhaps they are in a state of ignorance about us because their writers have not been concerned with our history.[18]

Metochites' own ability, if indeed he made any effort, to obtain information about other cultures was very slight. His essay on the Scythians lacks up-to-date information which might have been available to someone in his position; he had travelled several times as far as Serbia and might have been expected to acquire information about other foreign powers, particularly in view of the threat posed to Europe by the Turks and the Mongols. His allusion to Genoa as a state in which an extreme form of democracy had led to disaster is well wide of the mark. Yet in principle Metochites shows an awareness of other cultures all too rare in Byzantium.

---

[16] See G. Aujac's edition (Paris 1975) xci-xcvii. But examination of Vat. gr. 381 left me with the impression that it could be of the late thirteenth century.

[17] P. 743 ed. Müller.

[18] Ibid. p. 595-6.

13

The Epigoni

Epigoni is not a flattering term, but there is no injustice in using it to describe the scholars of the last hundred years of the Byzantine empire. A reflection of the low standard of their work is the validity of the general rule that manuscripts written in the second half of the fourteenth century and later are not valuable to editors. Naturally there are exceptions to the rule, but they are very few. The talents of Bessarion and Musurus were to bear fruit after the fall of the empire and in a different milieu.

The empire was diminishing rapidly in size and power, and its intellectual energies, already partly devoted to the by now perennial problem of union between the Greek and Roman churches, were further distracted by a fresh outbreak of religious controversy caused by the Hesychastic movement. In one small area the Byzantine government reasserted itself; the Latin states of the Peloponnese failed to maintain a unity of purpose and the Greeks were able to establish themselves at Mistra near Sparta. The court at Mistra did something to maintain literary studies, while in the capital schools continued their traditions. One new phenomenon can be observed: Italian scholars travel to Constantinople to learn Greek, not attempting, or not succeeding in their efforts, to learn from the Greeks of southern Italy. The instruction given in Florence for a short time by Leonzio Pilato had not been any more successful than the contact between Petrarch and the Calabrian Barlaam, which left the poet unable to read his cherished copy of Homer (Ambr. I 98 inf.).[1] So the Italians went back to the original sources. Their visits to the east had a further consequence; they returned with as many manuscripts as they could find, so laying the foundations not only of the magnificent collections still preserved in the major Italian cities but also of many others, the contents of which passed through Italian hands during the Renaissance. It may not be too cynical to suppose that the humanists' acquisitions were facilitated not so much by superior financial resources as by the inability of the Greek owners to make good use of many of the volumes in their possession.

[1] A. Pertusi, *Leonzio Pilato fra Petrarca e Boccaccio* (Venice-Rome 1964) 43-72 with plate XXXII.

Greek refugees were active in Italy for some time before the final Turkish conquest of 1453 and in a chronological sense what they did belongs to the history of Byzantine scholarship. Yet it is scholarship transplanted into a different society. Partly for this reason, partly because the little that is known of these early refugees and teachers suggests elementary instruction and the transcription of texts rather than the higher reaches of scholarly attainment, I have decided to postpone for another occasion an account of Greek studies in Renaissance Italy, beginning with the early teachers such as Chrysoloras and the first Greek copyists to establish themselves in the west. Many manuscripts can now be attributed to Peter the Cretan and Girard of Patras, who worked for the court at Mantua and presumably copied texts for the school of Vittorino da Feltre. Signs of a higher level of activity do not occur until later, when the circle of Bessarion was established and the scribe Andronicus Callistus produced texts capable of exciting the curiosity of modern editors. A better picture will result if the consumers and producers of this scholarship are studied alongside each other.

Metochites' tradition was continued by his pupil Nicephorus Gregoras (*c.* 1293-*c.* 1361), whose skill as an astronomer enabled him to make the proposal for reform of the calendar already referred to. He also composed two pamphlets on the construction of the astrolabe. He was a prolific author in many fields,[2] but most of his work does not concern us here, and in general it has to be said that he does not seem to possess the rare insight of his master. His career suffered a reverse with the fall of Metochites in the revolution of 1328, and in later years he had further difficulties arising out of the virulent religious controversies of the time, as a result of which he spent several years in prison. Among his religious writings there is one which has a certain relevance to our theme, the *Second Antirrhetika*, in which he has occasion to explain the principles of interpretation. He understands the need for presenting a complete context when discussing a passage and for knowing precisely the purpose of the text in question and the identity of the addressee. The last point arises from a recognition of the so-called 'economy' practised by the fathers of the church in some of their writings.[3] As can be seen at other stages in the history of the church, religious differences can lead to serious thought about scholarly method, and while Gregoras does not appear to be original his sound appreciation of principles does him credit.

Of his other work perhaps the most striking item is an edition of Ptolemy's treatise on musical theory. This had been used by earlier students of the quadrivium. What distinguishes Gregoras from his predecessors is his willingness not only to emend the text where it seemed

[2] On the biography of Gregoras see H.-V. Beyer, *JOB* 27 (1978) 127-55. The works are listed by J.-L. van Dieten, *Nikephoros Gregoras: Rhomäische Geschichte* I (Stuttgart 1973) 44-62.

[3] M. Paparozzi, *Rendiconti dell' Accademia dei Lincei* VIII 28 (1973) 946-7.

corrupt but also to supplement two serious gaps in it. A note by him refers to the damage caused over a period of time by inaccurate copying, but he thought that the lacuna at the end of the treatise arose from the premature death of the author. To make good the deficiency he wrote his own supplement, which attracted hostile comment from his Italian enemy Barlaam. The most recent editor of Ptolemy discounts the idea that Gregoras could have wished to pass off the supplement as part of the original text, the chief argument in support of this view being that Gregoras could have imitated the language of Ptolemy much more closely if his intention had been to deceive. As to Gregoras' ability in restoring the text elsewhere, it seems that he made a number of successful emendations, a rather larger number of suggestions which fail to hit the mark, and left some other points uncorrected. His performance, if not brilliant, must be considered respectable.

Gregoras' other dealings with antiquity can be dealt with more briefly. An autograph commonplace book attests his wide reading (Heidelberg, Pal. gr. 129). He wrote a commentary on Synesius' *Essay on Dreams*, perhaps inspired in part by his master's evident liking for this author. Gregoras cites in it the Chaldean Oracles, but he is not, as was once supposed, the sole source of any of them.[4] Some minor grammatical treatises are assigned to him; the authorship of these is perhaps not quite secure.[5] His authorship of some jejune notes on Ptolemy's *Geography* is now generally rejected.[6] There is not much significance in a declamation composed in the age-old tradition of the schools, a speech to be delivered by the envoys of Plataea before the Spartans. But some of the letters contain points of interest. One is an expression of the writer's patriotism based on historical considerations (no. 45). A summary will bring out the oddity of its construction. The Medes and Persians conquered all Asia but spared Byzantium; the Greeks of Xenophon's *Anabasis* found their first relief from adversity when they reached the city; Alexander did not conquer the city nor did any of his successors; Aeneas was summoned from Byzantium to go to the aid of the Trojans and later became the founder of Rome; ships larger than the trireme are an invention which many historians recognise as due to the inhabitants of Byzantium; the sophist Polemon was so respected that he could talk on equal terms to Roman emperors; our city has always expelled heretics. A weakness in Gregoras' scholarly equipment emerges from another letter (no. 48). It is a reply to an inquiry from a friend about the meaning of a difficult phrase in the opening paragraph of Aristides' famous encomium of Rome (II 91

---

[4] E. des Places, *Oracles chaldaïques* (Paris 1971) 119 (on fr. 219).

[5] S. Lindstam, *BZ* 29 (1929-30) 306-7.

[6] H. Hunger, *Die hochsprachliche profane Literatur der Byzantiner* I (Munich 1978) 513. I rather think Gregoras' hand is to be detected in some marginal notes in a copy of Cleomedes' introduction to astronomy and John Philoponus' treatise on the astrolabe (Oxford, Savile 52). They include chronological observations, e.g. that Posidonius lived in the period of Marius and Sulla and, less correctly, that Philoponus was a contemporary of the tyrant Phocas.

Keil). The phrase is attributed to an unnamed poet, and Gregoras is asked who the poet was and three other points of interpretation, two of them linguistic. The quotation is now believed to be from Old Comedy (cf. Aristophanes fr. 913 K and comica adespota 784 K), but Gregoras does not take this view, of which there is a hint in the context, and assures his friend that Homer is the author in question, since reference to 'a poet' can refer to Homer just as much as references to 'the poet'. That is patently false and is not a good advertisement for the state of philological studies at the time. We must hope that it is not a fair specimen of the instruction offered in the school which he ran at one time (letter 51).

Mention of Gregoras' Italian adversary Barlaam, who engaged with him in controversy about various matters, including the prediction of eclipses, turns our gaze back to the west for a moment.[7] The Greeks of southern Italy no longer enjoyed under the Angevins the same standing as they had maintained under the Normans. There is proof that they kept their culture alive, but the evidence rarely suggests that they were able to do much more. It is not to be denied that a number of classical authors were being read in the area at the time of the Palaeologan Renaissance. One can give as instances an important copy of four plays of Sophocles (Laur. Conv. Sopp. 152, dated 1282), and there are some other dated copies of school authors (Vat. gr. 2383 of Hesiod, A.D. 1287; Laur. 71.35 of Porphyry and Ammonius on the *Organon*, A.D. 1290-1; Vienna, phil. gr. 56 of the *Odyssey*, A.D. 1300). Other copies not precisely dated are interesting: the thirteenth-century text of the *Iliad*, which has been referred to already because it contains traces of the work of Nicholas of Otranto, has been bound together with a slightly later copy of some secondary works, the paraphrase of Tzetzes, pseudo-Heraclitus on allegory in Homer, and the epimerismoi of Homeric vocabulary, the last item being unique in this form (New College Oxford 298). Both parts of the present volume are likely to be products of Otranto.[8] A text of Aristotle's *Ethics* was transcribed in the nearby town of Gallipoli (Barb. gr. 75). Yet on the whole one has the impression of transcription not accompanied by advanced study; there is no scholar who can be identified, let alone mentioned in the same breath as Planudes or Metochites. Barlaam made some impression in Byzantium as a philosopher, but most Byzantines were no longer able to accept the idea that an Italian was their equal in philosophy as they had done in the time of Michael Psellos. Certainly he did not succeed in conveying anything of value to Petrarch, surely one of the most open and ardent pupils any man could wish to have.

Another Italian who went to Byzantium and cannot be dismissed as

---

[7] P.L.M. Leone, *Niceforo Gregora: Fiorenzo o intorno alla sapienza* (Naples 1975) 15-25; J. Mogenet & A. Tihon, *Barlaam de Seminara: Traités sur les éclipses de soleil de 1333 et 1337* (Louvain 1977).

[8] R.W. Hunt and others, *The Survival of Ancient Literature* (Oxford 1975), 5 with plate 1.

negligible is Simon Atumanos. He was appointed bishop of Gerace, a tiny town now known to a few connoisseurs as the source of a rare and superb wine, in 1348. His claim on our attention is that he owned the famous copy of the alphabetic plays of Euripides. But if the history of scholarship is interpreted in a wider sense than the relation of the Byzantines to the classics of pagan literature he deserves more attention, since he attempted to produce a new version of the Old Testament (Marc. gr. 7), being perhaps the only Greek in the whole of the period covered by our history to master Hebrew.[9] In 1366 he became archbishop of Thebes, where there was a large Jewish community. Few Byzantines could boast of a knowledge of Latin unless they had been brought up in the Italo-Greek region, and the concept of the 'homo trilinguis' was not destined to become a recognised ideal for another century and a half. Equally interesting and enigmatic was his older contemporary Nicholas of Reggio, active between 1308 and 1345, who translated medical texts for Robert of Anjou. Most of his energy was dedicated to Galen, and there are texts which survive in his version alone, having disappeared in the original. But it is not clear whether this surprising fact is to be put down exclusively to the excellence of the libraries in or near Reggio, because we hear that his patron received a manuscript of Galen as a gift from Andronicus III some time in the period 1332-5, and that suggests an alternative and preferable explanation.[10] It is still a proof that libraries contained a certain amount of material which remained to be destroyed in the Turkish conquest.

The career of Gregoras, hampered in his mature years by civil war and religious controversy, overlaps with that of a prolific scribe in Mistra, where the court circle provided a more peaceful atmosphere. Manuel Tzykandyles signed and dated a number of his books. We find him copying Plutarch's *Lives* at Mistra in 1362 (Canonici gr. 93 & Ambr. D 538 inf.). He was still there in 1372, but by 1374 had moved back to the old capital (Vat. gr. 674 and Zurich 170, writings of the emperor John VI Cantacuzenus). A strong interest in history among his patrons is suggested by his transcription of Arrian (Munich gr. 451, dated 1370) and Thucydides (Vat. gr. 127, dated 1372).[11] The Thucydides has an informative colophon. The author is described not as a historian but as a *rhetor*, which throws light on the spirit in which the Byzantines approached the classical texts. In addition we learn that the copy was executed at the request of Manuel Cantacuzenus, son of John VI Cantacuzenus and despot of the Morea 1348-80. A second scribe,

[9] G. Mercati, *Se la versione dall'ebraico del codice Veneto greco VII sia di Simone Atumano arcivescovo di Tebe (Studi e Testi* 30) (Vatican City 1916); A. Turyn, *The Byzantine Manuscript Tradition of the Tragedies of Euripides* (Urbana 1957) 226-7.

[10] R. Weiss, *Medieval and Humanist Greek* (Padua 1977) 117-18, gives the evidence on this point. His discussion of Nicholas also deals with the assertion that he can be described as an epigraphist, and comes to an appropriately sceptical conclusion.

[11] Apart from the usual repertoria see also R. Barbour, *Greek Literary Hands A.D. 400-1600* (Oxford 1981) 29 with plate 104.

Marcianus, took part in the copying, and it is recorded that he and a certain George Gabrielopoulos checked the text against its exemplar to the best of their ability. More practical concerns are revealed by an unusual book in which he appears in the company of at least sixteen other scribes who collaborate in the production of a copy of the medical compilation of Alexander of Tralles (Laur. 74.10; the part of the present volume which contains Galen seems originally to have been a separate codex). The names of the scribes are marked on the quires they were responsible for; one is the hegumen of a monastery, and the impression is created that every literate member of the community was pressed into service in order to prepare the book within a short space of time. But Mistra's best claim to a place of honour in the history of scholarship is that for many years it was the residence of George Gemistus Plethon, generally held to be the last original thinker in Byzantium. The extent of his unorthodoxy has probably been much exaggerated, and whatever the significance of his thought it remains uncertain whether he was educated in Mistra or elsewhere.

Although Barlaam had not made as deep an impression on Byzantine cultural chauvinism as he doubtless hoped, there are occasional signs of a realisation that western Europe had progressed to a point where it posed a real challenge. Demetrius Cydones, who continued the work of Planudes by translating Thomas Aquinas, stated his belief that the Italians were the equals of the Greeks both in theology and in secular matters.[12] In the fifteenth century, when the position was probably beyond repair, Bessarion was the author of a proposal, which may well reflect the thinking of his master Plethon, that promising young men should be sent to Italy to learn crafts in which the Byzantines had by now clearly fallen behind.[13] In scholarship too the Italians had reached the point where they were the equals of the Byzantines. Bessarion and Plethon may not have known anything of that before the Council of Florence; but later Bessarion became acquainted with Valla, the significance of whose work will not have been lost on him.

In the last half century of the empire's existence there is nothing to record, either in the capital or in Mistra, that can possibly compare with the achievements of earlier generations. Plethon's alleged attempt to restore pagan culture, which is probably no more than a figment of a deranged ecclesiastical imagination, is not accompanied by scholarship of a high order. His history of Greece from the battle of Mantinea in 362 B.C., which marked the end of the Theban supremacy, is an unpretentious recital of the facts which could be found in Plutarch and Diodorus, and it would scarcely be claimed by his admirers that a series of excerpts from Strabo is an important landmark. The same modest

[12] G. Mercati, *Notizie di Procoro e Demetrio Cidone, Manuele Caleca e Teodoro Meliteniota ed altri appunti per la storia della teologia e della letteratura bizantina del secolo XIV (Studi e Testi* 56) (Vatican City 1931), 72 n. 1.

[13] A.G. Keller, *Cambridge Historical Journal* 11 (1955) 343-8.

level of achievement is seen in John Chortasmenos (*c.* 1370-*c.* 1436), who was a patriarchal notary and became bishop of Selymbria. His best service to posterity was to preserve the beautiful illustrated herbal of Dioscorides written *c.* 512 (Vienna, med. gr. 1). Finding it in poor condition he repaired the binding so that it could still be of some use to the hospital founded in the capital by the king of Serbia. Our gratitude to him is slightly qualified by the fact that he found the uncial script difficult to read and made his own transcript of the text in blank spaces surrounding the miniatures, which spoils the appearance of the book. But evidently Dioscorides was too useful to be discarded.[14] Chortasmenos was a keen book collector, and when he found a note by Gregoras indicating Metochites' authorship of a text he remarked on the fact.[15] He also had the intelligence to identify in some notes added to a copy of Aristotle's *Physics* the handwriting of the emperor Theodore Lascaris of Nicaea (in Ambr. M 46 sup.)[16]. This is one of the rare occasions when we can see palaeographical technique being put into practice before palaeography was recognised as a field of study and a skill needed by scholars.[17] In addition Chortasmenos had the practical habit of foliating his books, numbering the leaves of each quire separately, which is not normal in Byzantine books, whereas it had not been rare in antiquity.[18] This apparently trivial detail of everyday life is a symptom of the break which occurred at the end of antiquity and of the lowering of standards which marked so many aspects of Byantium.

Detailed study of Chortasmenos has not brought to light evidence of more than average ability, and the same judgment probably has to be passed on George Chrysococces, who was a schoolmaster in the capital early in the fifteenth century. Among his pupils was the future cardinal Bessarion. Manuscripts copied by Chrysococces date from 1420-8. He had important Italian patrons, including Filelfo, Aurispa and Cristoforo Garatone. But in his case there is evidence which might be sufficient to raise him above the level of the humble copyist. It has been argued that he made important improvements to the text of the letters falsely attributed to Socrates. His copy (Wolfenbüttel, Helmstadt 806) and a Vatican codex of the thirteenth century (Vat. gr. 64) are the only witnesses of any value, and in a number of passages Chrysococces' copy offers a better text. That may be due to his own ability or a good source, and there is not yet agreement among scholars as to the correct

---

[14] For this and other details see the fundamental study of H. Hunger, *Johannes Chortasmenos (c. 1370-c. 1436/37)* (Vienna 1969). See also H. Hunger and others, *Studien zum Patriarchatsregister von Konstantinopel* (*SB Wien* 383) (Vienna 1981) 120-45, an analysis by P. Canart and G. Prato of three volumes written by Chortasmenos.

[15] I. Ševčenko, *Etudes sur la polémique entre Théodore Métochite et Nicéphore Choumnos* (Brussels 1962) 281-2 with plate V.

[16] Most recently discussed by G. Prato, *JOB* 30 (1981) 249-58.

[17] A few other cases are discussed by P.E. Easterling, *Studia codicologica* (*Texte und Untersuchungen* 124) (Berlin 1977) 179-87.

[18] E.G. Turner, *Greek Manuscripts of the Ancient World* (Oxford 1971) 18.

interpretation of the evidence.[19]

The texts produced by Chrysococces for his foreign patrons are all prose; Strabo and Xenophon for Filelfo, Aeschines, epistolographers and Dionysius of Halicarnassus' essay on Lysias for Aurispa, Diodorus Siculus and Plutarch's *Lives* for Garatone.[20] Prose is also predominant in other manuscripts attributable to him, but poetry is represented by the *Odyssey* (Vat. gr. 906) and a copy of the *Homeric Hymns* and Callimachus.[21]

A short work from the last days of the empire reinforces the impression that reading habits were maintained with tenacity even in the darkest moments of impending doom. John Eugenikos, brother of Mark, the metropolitan of Ephesus who played so important a part at the Council of Florence in opposition to the proposed union of the churches, is the author of a very short introduction to the novel of Heliodorus. It includes a hint that the novel may have been adopted for reading in school, because there is an assertion that it contains nothing dangerous for young readers. Eugenikos defends Heliodorus for the contents as much as the style, and observes that the alleged potential danger is no more real than that arising from the Song of Solomon.[22]

[19] J. Sykutris, *Philologische Wochenschrift* 48 (1928) 1284-95, was criticised by P. Maas, *BZ* 28 (1928) 430 and changed his mind, *RE Supp.-Band* 5 (1931) 981. – The MS. is described and illustrated in the exhibition catalogue of D. Harlfinger & M. Sicherl, *Griechische Handschriften und Aldinen* (Wolfenbüttel 1978) 52-4.

[20] A list is given by M. Vogel & V. Gardthausen, *Die griechischen Schreiber des Mittelalters und der Renaissance* (Leipzig 1909) 86-7.

[21] On this MS. see R. Pfeiffer, *Callimachus II: Hymni et epigrammata* (Oxford 1953) lvi and 124-5, N.G. Wilson, *RevHistTextes* 4 (1974) 139-40.

[22] H. Gärtner, *BZ* 64 (1971) 322-5.

Epilogue

When Pfeiffer wrote the history of scholarship in the ancient world, he made his narrative focus on the achievements of a series of leading characters. I have expressed elsewhere some reservation about this procedure, because it leads to neglect or inadequate appreciation of certain features of ancient scholarship, which owing to the paucity of the evidence cannot be credited with any confidence to any of the great scholars. The gaps in our knowledge of Byzantium are not so serious, and for this reason I have ventured to adopt a plan similar to the one which I found not entirely satisfactory in Pfeiffer. There is however one important difference: from time to time I am able to record anonymous scholarly activity in its proper chronological place, since it is attested by extant manuscripts and often illuminated by the identification of scribal hands. The combination of two classes of evidence offers some hope of a better picture. The real difficulty is that for the period I am dealing with we know in some ways too much. There are a number of Byzantine scholars of mediocre ability whose work survives in such large quantity that one could devote an enormous amount of time to writing monographs on each of them. Since I wished to finish my book within a reasonable time and to give a synoptic view it has generally been my practice to deal very briefly with figures of secondary importance. But I have sometimes allowed myself to spend a little longer on them, or to grant them a place which they might not be thought to deserve at all, if it seemed likely that the extra detail would help to give a clearer idea of the standards and attitudes to be expected from the average Byzantine man of letters.

The scholarship of antiquity and the Italian Renaissance has been interpreted as a creation of poets concerned with the tradition of their craft. If such an assessment is correct, it must be immediately apparent that the Byzantines had nothing in common with their colleagues of the other two periods; the only great poet of Byzantium, Romanos, is conspicuous for his hostility to the classical heritage. If instead ancient scholarship is seen as the product of a developing system of education, in which poetry originally provided the staple texts, and then had to meet the successive challenges of rhetoric and philosophy, the Byzantines appear as the inheritors of an activity that had been established for a millennium. They continued it for another millennium, during which rhetoric was studied in inverse proportion to its declining practical utility, philosophy had to work within the guidelines imposed by Christian dogma, and the literature of paganism succeeded in upholding its position against that of the new religion. The coexistence of Christian culture and its predecessor invites comparison with the thought of Erasmus, whose central aim was the revival of Christian piety through humanistic values. The methods of classical scholarship could be brought to bear on the Bible in order to restore the purity and simplicity of its message. But Erasmus' edition of the New Testament has no analogy in Byzantium. The nearest point of contact is the similarity between his assertion that even a misplaced comma is enough to cause a heresy and Photius' insistence that St. Paul's text must be punctuated correctly in order to free him from the suspicion of being thought a Manichean. But Photius' insight was never adopted by the Byzantines and made into a guiding principle.

Do the Byzantines deserve to be treated as humanists who equalled and anticipated their more famous counterparts in Renaissance Italy? The answer to that question must depend in part on the definition of the term humanism. One sense of the word, the assertion of secular values, implying a reduction or abolition of the status of religion, clearly has no application in the present context. Nor is there any sign of a rejection of Christianity in favour of paganism, unless one chooses to accept a very dubious interpretation of the ideas of Plethon. A second definition of humanism would be the belief in the value of human life such that it is a duty to help each individual to achieve his or her maximum potential. This does not necessarily imply any hostility to established religion. Whether a statement in terms as general as these can be found in any Byzantine writer must remain a matter for doubt. But a more specific version of this view, according to which the best education develops the character by acquainting pupils with the thoughts and actions of great men, is a presupposition of the Byzantine educational system, and a belief in the value of such a system is from time to time explicitly declared, as for instance in the case of Anna Comnena's fiancé. For the Byzantines it was a necessary consequence that the civilisations of Greece and Rome should be studied, and only a flash of unusually wide vision allowed Metochites to contemplate the possibility that other civilisations had a history which might be equally rewarding to study. The maintenance of such an educational programme entails the preservation of the literary texts in the best condition possible, in order that they may be properly understood and passed on to future generations. Faith in the continuing value of the ancient authors is seen in Arethas' attitude to his copy of Marcus Aurelius. The maintenance of the texts in an intelligible condition is a task to which the Byzantines applied themselves with varying success. The more active and conscientious scholars searched for additional copies of the texts in the hope of discovering the original words of the ancient authors. Humanism in these circumstances implies a mild form of bibliomania. But when all texts are equally unsatisfactory the book collector must become a critic, and at that point the Byzantines faced a test in which only a minority showed to advantage. Such a judgment does not detract from their achievement in preserving, sometimes against heavy odds, a concept of education which still appeals to civilised societies.

The modern observer may be instinctively tempted to agree with Gibbon's broadside: 'The Greeks of Constantinople ... held in their lifeless hands the riches of their fathers, without inheriting the spirit which had created and improved that sacred patrimony; they read, they praised, they compiled, but their languid souls seemed alike incapable of thought and action.' A closer look at what the Byzantines wrote and the conditions in which they worked allows a more charitable verdict.

Index

(i) Papyri

P. Ant. 72: 12
P. Berol. 5005:12
    5006: 12
    11739: 48
P. Colon. inv. 4780: 35
P. Louvre s.n.: 12
P. Oxy. 841: 68
    1177: 248
    2258: 12,34
P. Paris Archives Nationales Musée K.7
    n.17: 65
P.S.I. 1182: 35
P. Strasb. 173: 85
    621: 12
P. Vindob. 31956: 63

(ii) Manuscripts

ATHOS
Dionysiou 180: 143
Iviron 258: 64
Lavra B 64 (184): 138
    Θ 70 (932): 64
    document 31: 64
Vatopedi 747: 139
BERLIN, Deutsche Staatsbibliothek
Hamilton 512: 242
Phillips 1538: 143
BRUSSELS, Bibliothèque Royale
IV. 459: 86
CAIRO, Greek Patriarchate
296: 151
CAMBRIDGE
Emmanuel College 30: 16
Trinity College 0.3.9: 92
University Library Ii.5.44: 227
    Add. 1879.23: 139
    Add. 6678: 119
DAMASCUS, Umayyad Mosque
palimpsest fragment: 78
EDINBURGH, National Library of
Scotland

Advocates' Library 18.7.15: 232
EREVAN, Matenadaran
arm. 141: 85
ERLANGEN, Universitätsbibliothek
gr.1: 139
ESCORIAL, Real Biblioteca
R-I-18: 227
C-II-10: 136
T-III-7: 212
T-III-14: 139
FERRARA, Biblioteca Comunale Ariostea
II 155: 241
FLORENCE
Biblioteca Medicea Laurenziana
11.8: 243
28.18: 65, 86
28.27: 85
31.8: 253
31.10: 207
31.39: 207
32.2: 236, 238, 254
32.9: 137, 207
32.16: 236, 238-9
32.24: 138, 207
32.52: 203
55.4: 143-4
56.37: 76
59.2 & 3: 198
59.9: 138
59.14: 49
59.15: 148
60.3: 124
69.2: 139
69.6: 148, 151
69.13: 151
70.3: 139
70.8: 139
71.35: 268
74.5: 207
74.7: 136
74.10: 270
74.18: 207

74.25: 207
74.26: 207
74.30: 208
75.5: 207
75.7: 207
75.17: 207
75.18: 207
75.20: 207
80.9: 87
81.11: 86
87.4: 207
87.7: 207
Conventi Soppressi 152: 268
     172: 255
     192: 207
     206: 139, 151
     627: 225
Biblioteca Riccardiana
gr. 31: 243
 45: 151
HEIDELBERG, Universitätsbibliothek
Pal. gr. 23: 138
   45: 227
   129: 267
   168 & 169: 151
   252: 139
   283: 151
   356: 3
   398: 87
ISTANBUL
Metochion of the Holy Sepulchre 355: 139
Topkapı Sarayı gr. 40: 264
LEIDEN, Universiteitsbibliotheek
B.P.G. 78: 66, 86
Voss.gr.F.64: 219
LEIPZIG, Universitätsbibliothek
Tischendorf 2: 35, 85
LENINGRAD, Saltykov-Shchedrin
 Library
gr. 219: 66
LONDON, British Library
Burney 86: 166
   95: 229
Harley 5694: 124
Add. 17148: 72
Add. 22087: 250
MADRID, Biblioteca Nacional
4626: 85
4678: 233
MESSINA, Biblioteca Universitaria
gr.118: 51
Fondo Vecchio 11: 227
MILAN, Biblioteca Ambrosiana
L 93 sup.: 86
L 99 sup.: 209
M 46 sup.: 220, 271
Q 57 sup.: 211

& 157 sup.: 233
C 126 inf.: 235
C 222 inf.: 195, 225, 238
D 538 inf.: 269
I 98 inf.: 265
MONTECASSINO, Biblioteca Abbaziale
550: 23
MOSCOW, Historical Museum
gr. 231: 126
 489: 255
 501: 151
MUNICH, Bayerische Staatsbibliothek
gr.430: 235
 451: 269
 485: 138
NAPLES, Biblioteca Nazionale
II C 32: 17
II F 9: 237, 238
II F 31: 253
III B 29: 215
gr.4*: 211
supp.gr. 28: 85
lat.2: 85, 209
NEW YORK, Pierpont Morgan Library
397: 211
OXFORD
Bodleian Library
Auct.T.1.11: 168
  T.2.8: 229
  T.4.13: 127, 181
  V.1.51: 148
Barocci 3: 130
   50: 23, 73, 76, 137, 211
   131: 3, 225
   217: 114
Canonici gr.93: 269
E.D. Clarke 39: 121
Cromwell 13: 220
D'Orville 301: 25, 120
gr.class.f.114: 23
Holkham gr.88: 43, 252
Laud gr.35: 65
  54: 245
Savile 52: 267
Christ Church
Wake 5: 136
Corpus Christi College
108: 86
New College
298: 22, 227, 228, 268
PARIS, Bibliothèque Nationale
gr. 107: 211
 216: 119
 451: 125, 131
 1182: 168
 1393: 234
 1397: 139

1399: 127
1665: 227
1671: 235
1672: 236
1678: 151
1734: 257-8
1741: 139
1807: 84, 87, 129
1849: 207
1853: 139
1930: 242
1955: 151
1956: 151
1957: 151
1962: 87
2003: 258
2036: 139
2064: 211
2089: 227
2162: 191
2179: 85
2389: 86
2425: 165
2702: 198
2711: 254
2722: 207, 236, 238-40
2744: 240
2771: 140
2821: 252
2832: 251
2884: 249
2934: 136, 219
2935: 129, 138
2950: 150
2951: 124
3032: 212
supp.gr. 247: 140
          255: 258
          352: 206
          384: 138
          388: 137
          495: 143
          921: 87
          1156: 66, 86
          1297: 212
          1362: 86
Coislin   8: 66, 86
          120: 66
          123: 66, 86
          224: 119
          249: 140
          319: 151
          345: 77, 91, 127
          347: 85, 91
          387: 22
PARMA, Biblioteca Palatina
154: 255

PATMOS, Monastery of St John
109A, olim 737: 76
178: 3
RAVENNA, Biblioteca Classense
429: 137
ROME
Biblioteca Angelica gr.14: 255
                      38: 241
Biblioteca Nazionale gr.6: 85
Biblioteca Vallicelliana gr.F.10: 125
                    206-CXXX: 178
SEITENSTETTEN, Benediktinerstift
gr.1: 151
TOURS, Bibliothèque Municipale
980: 145
TURIN, Biblioteca Nazionale
F.VI.1: 209
VATICAN CITY, Biblioteca Apostolica
     Vaticana
lat.5763: 209
Barb.gr. 75: 268
          87: 139
          102: 245
          182: 151
          240: 178
          310: 120, 143
          591: 207
Chigi R.IV.20: 202
Pal.gr. 173: 139
        287: 255
Reg.gr.132 & 133: 231
Urb.gr. 35: 35, 123
         61: 137
         64: 212
         97: 139, 151
         111: 136
         124: 126
         125: 236
         130: 139
Vat.gr.   1: 84, 129, 138
          10: 221
          29: 245
          47: 253
          57: 202
          64: 271
          65: 166
          73: 97, 145
          90: 139, 141
         105: 225
         106: 225
         110: 235
         123: 16
         124: 138
         126: 257
         127: 269
         138: 151
         155: 136

177: 234
190: 86
191: 232, 234
204: 86
207: 225
218: 129, 139
300: 49, 213
318: 264
381: 264
626: 229
674: 269
676: 3, 152
901: 225
906: 272
909: 225
915: 237
1031: 84
1288: 211
1291: 86
1296: 213
1298: 97, 140
1302: 230
1319: 207
1335: 139
1342: 227
1349: 212
1391: 212
1594: 83, 85, 86, 87, 165
1605: 214
1726: 185
1809: 5
1824 & 1825: 251, 253
2061A: 211
2130: 212
2181: 252
2197: 87
2200: 63, 65
2228: 32
2249: 87
2306: 211
2369: 16
2383: 268
VENICE, Biblioteca Marciana
Marc.gr.   7: 269
          172: 212
          196: 87
          201: 138
          202: 242
          226: 87
          236: 87
          246: 87
          249: 151
          250: 151
          258: 87, 227
          269: 139
          288: 212
          313: 214

386: 151
395: 139
410: 216
416: 138
418: 138
436: 12
447: 201
451: 125
453: 34
454: 138
460: 198
464: 251
470: 254
474: 181
476: 181
479: 148
481: 17, 231, 240
483: 253
489: 70
616: 253
622: 43
app.class.4.1: 121, 139
VIENNA, Oesterreichische
     Nationalbibliothek
hist.gr.10: 140
         45: 12
         60: 151
         85: 16
med.gr.1: 35, 271
        4: 148
phil.gr. 21: 235
          49: 228
          56: 268
          67: 140
         100: 86
         123: 148
         129: 151
         133: 219
         310: 213
         314: 128
supp.gr.7: 121, 148
theol.gr.134: 180
WOLFENBUTTEL, Herzog August
     Bibliothek
Helmstadt 75a: 65
          806: 271
Weissenburg 64: 209
ZAVORDA, Library of the former
     monastery
95: 92
ZURICH, Stadtbibliothek
170: 269

(iii)   Ancient authors (up to *c*.640 A.D.)

Achilles Tatius 26, 84, 172-6, 186, 225

Aelian 134, 143
Aelius Dionysius 91, 122
Aeneas of Gaza 30
Aeneas Tacticus 143
Aenesidemus 102
Aeschines 140, 272
Aeschylus 26, 52-3, 112, 137, 152, 178, 225, 238, 247, 251, 253
Aesop 113, 211, 224, 234
Aetius 48, 57-8, 102, 143, 207
Agathias 7, 56-7
Albinus 87, 128
Alcaeus 36, 44, 188
Alciphron 186-7
Alexander of Aphrodisias 45, 87
Alexander of Tralles 58, 270
Ammonius 101, 268
Anacreon 36
Andocides 229
Andronicus 164
Anthemius of Tralles 45, 56, 139, 209
Anthology, Greek 17, 56, 82, 83, 127, 131, 138, 231, 236, 240
Antiphon 133, 229
Antoninus Liberalis 87
Antonius Diogenes 101
Aphthonius 25, 186, 222
Apollinaris 10, 53
Apollodorus 101, 191, 207, 242
Apollodorus of Carystus 113
Apollonius Dyscolus 24, 71, 77, 230
Apollonius of Perga 45, 83
Apollonius Rhodius 85, 126, 137, 239
Apollonius Sophistes 128
Appian 97, 101
Aratus 8, 25, 116, 152, 181, 232
Arcadius 77
Archilochus 150, 163
Archimedes 45-6, 83, 139, 161
Aristaenetus 212
Aristarchus (astronomer) 86
Aristides 25, 28, 75, 107, 124, 140, 168, 173, 185-6, 236, 248, 257, 260-2, 267
Aristophanes 12, 16, 22, 24, 112, 122, 126, 131, 134, 137, 138, 146, 152, 181, 188-94 passim, 202, 225, 238, 245, 248, 251-2
Aristophanes of Byzantium 143, 199
Aristotle 13, 14, 21, 22, 25, 37, 38, 41, 45, 46-8, 50, 54, 86, 95, 101, 113, 115, 123-4, 126, 131, 139, 140, 143, 154, 156, 160-1, 163, 166, 180, 182-4, 205, 207, 211, 213-14, 215, 220, 222, 223, 227, 236, 241-2, 258-9, 268, 271
Aristoxenus 25
Arrian 88, 106-7, 269
Athenaeus 114, 129, 146, 163, 201
Athenagoras 117, 125, 134

Attalus 232
Autolycus 86
Babrius 74, 146, 211, 250
Basil of Seleuceia 105
Boethius 21, 49, 213, 224, 230, 231
Brutus 88
Callimachus 12, 19, 20, 34-5, 59, 116, 122, 125, 130, 146, 164, 196, 205, 218, 272
Cassiodorus 18, 211
Chaeremon 159, 196
Chaldaean Oracles 127, 159, 163, 166, 267
Chariton 225
Chirurgici veteres 136
Choricius 31, 103, 185, 186
Chrysippus 50, 170
Cleanthes 50
Clement of Alexandria 125, 127, 262
Cleomedes 25, 232, 242, 267
Conon 96, 101
Crateuas 35
Ctesias 75, 163
pseudo-Cyrillus 43, 76, 91, 92, 212
Damascius 37, 38, 87, 103, 109
Deinarchus 148, 229
Demetrius (critic) 75, 104, 134, 170
Demetrius of Phalerum 113, 130, 150
Demo 228
pseudo-Democritus 159
Demosthenes 8, 16, 18, 24, 28, 31, 50, 72, 95, 107, 110, 129, 136, 138, 141, 168, 170-1, 173, 185-6, 188, 189, 219, 223, 260-2
Diadochus of Photice 110
Dicta Catonis 230
Dictys of Crete 130
Didymus the blind 9
Didymus the grammarian 22
Dio Cassius 139, 179, 184, 196, 211, 234
Dio Chrysostom 105, 126, 168, 262
Diodorus Siculus 88, 104, 211, 227, 270, 272
Diodorus of Tarsus 102, 103
pseudo-Diogenes the Cynic 88
Diogenes Laertius 215, 230
Diogenianos 90, 91, 122, 224
Dionysius bishop of Alexandria 53
pseudo-Dionysius the Areopagite 14, 54-5, 87, 110, 180, 207
Dionysius of Halicarnassus 104, 139, 148, 169-72, 272
Dionysius Periegetes 24, 140, 203, 223, 225
Dionysius Thrax 24, 53, 71-2, 110, 118, 194-5
Diophantus 42, 222, 232-3, 234, 241
Dioscorides 34, 85, 102, 209, 271
Donatus 230
Elias 45, 47-8
Epicharmus 113, 150
Epictetus 42, 127, 181, 243
Epiphanius 72

epistolographi graeci 88, 186-7, 271-2
Euclid 21-2, 25, 80, 83, 86, 120, 161, 164, 214-15, 223, 232
Eugenius 51-3
Eunapiua 11, 110, 144, 170
Eunomius 109
Euphorion 125
Euripides 12, 18, 20, 22, 26, 52-3, 59, 75, 115, 162, 177, 178-9, 204, 207, 211, 225, 236, 238, 246, 254-5, 269
Eusebius 55, 125, 131, 262
Eutecnius 32
Eutocius 45-6, 86
Galen 8, 35, 57, 58, 102, 105, 111, 163, 193, 205, 209, 212, 213, 219, 269
Gelasius 110
Geminus 264
Geoponica 143, 213 (see also Vindanius Anatolios)
George of Pisidia 60, 61, 75, 178-9, 187
Gorgias 140
Gregory Thaumaturgus 262
Harpocration 247
Heliodorus (metrician) 177, 253
Heliodorus (novelist) 26, 98, 172-6, 186, 216-17, 272
Heliodorus (scholiast on Dionysius Thrax) 71-2
Helladius 103, 110
Hephaestion 72-3, 177, 190, 250, 252-3
Heraclianus 104
pseudo-Heraclitus 10, 34, 268
Hermes Trismegistus 158
Hermogenes 16-17, 25, 38, 75, 104, 133-4, 190, 191, 222, 259
Hero 82, 161, 214, 242
Herodes Atticus 169
Herodian (grammarian) 35, 52, 69, 71, 75, 76, 77, 85, 140
Herodian (historian) 104
Herodotus 16, 84, 100, 125, 133, 139, 168, 170, 183, 188, 231
Hesiod 3, 19, 24, 50, 126, 131, 140, 191, 225, 227, 236-7, 242, 243, 254, 247, 251, 268
Hesychius (historian) 57
Hesychius (lexicographer) 43, 128
Hierocles 101, 128
Himerius 11, 18, 36, 95, 108, 186, 225
Hipparchus 232
Hippocrates 8, 49, 88, 102, 136, 148, 188, 212, 213
Hipponax 196
Homer 8, 10, 11, 18, 21, 22, 24, 27, 29, 31, 34, 39, 40, 44, 50, 71, 73, 78, 84, 85, 110, 111, 112, 126, 131-2, 138, 146, 148-50, 154, 156, 158, 161-2, 166, 186, 189, 191, 193, 195, 197-9, 207, 219, 221, 222, 227, 228,

237, 243, 245, 265, 268, 272
Horapollon (grammarian) 44, 51
Horapollon (author of *Hieroglyphica*) 159
Hyperides 95
Hypsicles 86
Iamblichus (novelist) 100
Iamblichus (philosopher) 162, 233, 260
Isaeus 168, 229
Isocrates 19, 50, 105, 136, 166, 168, 170-1, 173, 185, 186
John of Alexandria 49, 213
John of Antioch 144
John the Lydian 54, 58, 115, 234
Josephus 164, 186, 236, 262
Julian 10, 12, 115, 130, 132
Julius Africanus 163
Justin 117, 125
Juvenal 230
Leontius of Byzantium 15
Lesbonax 133
Libanius 11, 28-9, 36, 185, 186-7, 212, 224, 236, 248, 255
Lollianus 169
Longinus 72, 150, 163, 170
pseudo-Longinus 139, 150, 262
Longus 225
Lucian 5, 25, 103, 122, 124, 132, 139, 141, 148, 172, 186, 248, 263
Lycophron 52, 181, 187, 190-1, 225, 227, 228
Lycurgus 95, 229
Lysias 25, 52, 126, 140, 168, 170, 173
Macrobius 230
Malalas 37
Malchus 144
Manetho 85
Marcus Aurelius 126, 130, 146
Marinus 37, 38, 86, 140
Maximus (astrologer) 85
Maximus the Confessor 97
Maximus of Tyre 87, 263
Memnon 101
Menander 18-20, 31, 52, 116, 163
Menander Protector 144
Menander Rhetor 25, 139, 185, 225, 244
minor Attic orators 24, 229
Musaeus 137
Nemesius 164, 213
Nicander 140, 150, 191, 240
Nicanor 118
Nicolaus of Damascus 144
Nicomachus of Gerasa 21-2, 25, 44, 102, 222, 223
Nonnus 240
Olympiodorus 37, 46, 87, 164
Oppian 148, 197, 207, 225, 240
Oreibasius 48, 57-8, 102, 143
Origen 9, 13, 30, 53, 262

Orion 44
Orus 51, 221
Ovid 17, 231, 250
Palladius 48
Pamprepius 51
Pappus 86, 129, 139, 214
Parthenius 88
Paul of Aegina 48, 85, 102, 143, 207
Paul of Alexandria 81, 84
Pausanias (lexicographer) 91
Pausanias Periegetes 126, 127, 131, 234
Periplus of the Red Sea 87
Peter Patricius 144
Philo (engineer) 82
Philo Judaeus 111, 186, 236, 262
Philogelos 211
Philoponus 22, 44-5, 74, 87, 97, 187-8, 207, 242, 267
Philostorgius 170
Philostratus 25, 96, 100, 103, 169-70, 172, 186, 191, 234, 254, 256
Phlegon of Tralles 88, 100
Phoebammon 6
Phrynichus 5, 52, 91, 128
Physiologus 211
Pindar 24, 68, 131, 150, 189, 190, 191, 203, 225, 237, 238, 245, 248, 251, 257
Plato 8, 10, 13, 17, 19, 24, 30, 38-40, 47-8, 50, 54, 83-4, 87, 91, 95, 101, 105, 112-3, 115, 116, 121, 126-9, 131, 133, 138, 139, 148, 151, 154-4, 156, 160, 164, 168, 170-2, 173, 209, 214-15, 224, 233, 263
Plutarch 18, 103, 128, 139, 148, 151, 156, 171, 173, 186, 190-1, 214, 231, 235-6, 259, 262, 269, 270, 272
Polemon 169, 267
Pollux 5, 121, 125, 127
Polybius 138
Polychronius of Apamea 118
Porphyry 7, 13, 25, 84, 124, 133, 159, 161-2, 191, 209, 263, 268
Priscian 230
Priscus 144
Proclus 14, 21, 37-41, 44, 83, 87, 99, 121, 160, 162, 180, 194, 215, 226
Procopius of Caesarea 7, 16, 100, 186
Procopius of Gaza 31-3, 185, 186
Ptolemy 21, 25, 41, 42, 45, 47, 81, 83, 85-6, 88, 165, 191, 196, 214-15, 232, 234, 250, 262, 263, 266-7
Ptolemy Chennos 101, 196, 199
pseudo-Pythagoras 8, 128, 131
St. Athanasius 53, 55, 111, 117
St. Augustine 230
St. Basil 9, 11, 36, 69, 108-9, 111, 158, 168, 185, 186-7
St. Cyril of Alexandria 14, 43, 55, 62, 111, 183, 263
St. Gregory of Nazianzus 11, 23, 26, 36, 116, 133-4, 158, 168-72, 173, 185-7, 189, 215, 248
St. Gregory of Nyssa 11, 168, 185, 186-7
St. John Chrysostom 11, 26, 110, 111, 167-8, 185, 213
Sappho 12, 36, 163, 257
Severus 110
Sibylline Oracles 115
Simplicius 37, 38, 41, 87, 163, 214
Sopater (author of miscellany) 103
Sopater (rhetor) 124, 224, 225
Sophocles 12, 44, 52-3, 112, 137, 152, 178, 187, 201, 207, 236, 238, 246, 248-9, 254, 268
Sphere of Empedocles 250
Stephanus of Byzantium 52, 55-6, 70, 199
Stephen of Alexandria 47, 70, 136, 191
Stobaeus 96, 140
Strabo 87, 121, 133, 139, 163, 199, 211, 234, 270, 272
Suetonius 121
Synesius 140, 141, 186-7, 248, 262, 267
Tatian 45, 50, 185, 186, 214
pseudo-Themistocles 88
Theocritus 24, 188, 193, 224, 225, 236, 245, 246, 251
Theodore of Mopsuestia 15, 29-30, 105, 111
Theodoret 30, 87
Theodosius (astronomer) 86, 234
Theodosius (grammarian) 24, 42-3, 69-71
Theognis 137, 237
Theon of Alexandria 42, 83, 86, 121, 262
Theon of Smyrna 83-4
Theophrastus 86, 137, 140, 170, 190, 201, 211, 230, 235
Theophrastus (alchemist) 159
Theophylactus Simocatta 20, 59, 105, 212
Thucydides 19, 24, 50, 100, 107, 114, 125, 133, 139, 168, 171, 173, 188, 189, 191, 235, 248, 257, 267
Timotheus of Gaza 31, 44, 143
Tryphiodorus 240
Tryphon 188
Vindanius Anatolius 102-3
Xenophon 52, 107, 139, 186, 262, 272
Xenophon of Ephesus 225
Zacharias scholasticus 11, 31
Zeno 50
Zosimus of Gaza 31, 141
Zosimus of Panopolis 159